Workforce Develop

Tom Short • Roger Harris
Editors

Workforce Development

Strategies and Practices

 Springer

Editors
Tom Short
Roger Harris
Education, Equity and Work Research Group
University of South Australia
Mawson Lakes, SA, Australia

ISBN 978-981-10-1363-8   ISBN 978-981-287-068-1 (eBook)
DOI 10.1007/978-981-287-068-1
Springer Singapore Heidelberg New York Dordrecht London

Printed on acid-free paper

Springer is part of Springer Science+Business Media (www.springer.com)

Acknowledgements

The completion of this second book on Workforce Development has been made possible through the support of many people. Firstly, we would like to acknowledge and thank the executive team at the Australian Cooperative Research Centre for Rail Innovation (CRC); in particular the chief executive officer, David George; research director, Dr. Chris Gourlay, business manager, Suzanne Campbell, and adoption and commercialisation manager, Kellie Dyer. These executives, along with the editors and 29 contributing authors, have participated in a major research program conducted in the Australian rail industry between 2007 and 2014. This major research initiative was made possible through funding from the Commonwealth Government of Australia and we would like to mention with appreciation the background support received from rail organisations in Queensland, New South Wales, Victoria, South Australia and Western Australia and the Canberra-based Australasian Railway Association who participated in the CRC program. The editors and authors are grateful to the CRC for Rail Innovation for the use of project research findings, models and frameworks found in many of the chapters.

Secondly, our thanks go to colleagues from the University of South Australia and support from the university's Division of Education, Arts and Social Sciences, especially the Education, Equity and Work (EEW) Research Group members located in the School of Education who have provided an academic platform for our scholarly interest in the areas of adult education, vocational training and workforce development. During the life of this book project, the EEW research group was co-led by two of the chapter contributors, Associate Professor Michele Simons and Dr. Tom Stehlik.

The complex process of bringing together, negotiating and editing multiple submissions with national and international authors is only possible with a committed and enthusiastic team. We are particularly grateful for the skilful assistance of our sub-editor Kate Leeson for her detailed and professional editorial work on each chapter.

Finally, we would like to thank our seven guest authors from Australia, the UK, Finland, Germany and New Zealand who have added a wider and international perspective to our interest in workforce development. Each guest author is a specialist in their field and has a distinguished academic and publishing career. These include: Jill Hadley from the University of South Australia; Professor Peter Kell from Charles Darwin University; Emeritus Professor John Thompson from the University of Huddersfield Business School, UK; Dr. Jonathon M. Scott from Teesside University Business School, UK; Professor Jarna Heinonen from Turke School of Economics, Finland; Professor Thomas Deissinger and Dr. Kathrin Breuing from University of Konstanz, Germany; and Professor Brian Findsen, University of Waikato, New Zealand.

Tom Short
Roger Harris

Contents

Contributors

Dr. Tamara D. Banks is a post-doctoral fellow who researches and publishes in occupational safety and health, and organisational psychology. She leads a research program in occupational concerns in the mining sector and has extensive research interests in road safety. Dr. Banks is a member of the Centre for Accident Research and Road safety Qld (CARRS-Q), a research centre of the School of Psychology and Counselling at the Queensland University of Technology.

Professor Herbert C. Biggs is a Principal Research Fellow with research and teaching experience in rehabilitation counselling and industrial/organisational psychology. His current research includes safety culture developments in organisations in the construction, heavy transport and rail sectors. Dr. Biggs is a member of the Centre for Accident Research and Road safety Qld (CARRS-Q), a research centre of the School of Psychology and Counselling at the Queensland University of Technology.

Dr. Kathrin Breuing studied Business and Economics Education and Economics at the University of Konstanz. She became Assistant Lecturer in 2007 and received her Ph.D. in 2013. Her major research interests include user choice in the VET system and further training issues.

Dr. Roslyn Cameron is a Research Fellow with the School of Management, Curtin Business School, Curtin University, Australia. Ros's research interest include: workforce development; coaching; skilled migration; workforce planning and skills recognition. She is a Fellow of the Australian Human Resources Institute (FAHRI), Co-Convenor of the Mixed Methods Special Interest Group of the Australian and New Zealand Academy of Management (ANZAM) and a foundational board member of the Prior Learning International Research Centre (PLIRC) based at Thompson Rivers University, BC, Canada. She has been part of research teams awarded four major workforce development projects for the Australian rail industry including: Coaching and Mentoring; Skills Recognition; Skilled Migration and: Attraction and Image.

Dr. Lisa Davies is a Lecturer in the School of Education, University of South Australia. Her research interests are centred in adult learning, workplace learning, organisational cultures, sociology of work and learning, educational psychology and theories of learning. Prior to joining the University, Lisa had been employed in a variety of related roles, as a management consultant, human resources manager for a software company and an adult educator teaching management and organisational behaviour. Within the CRC for Rail Innovation, Lisa has been the project manager of a project on the use of skills recognition in the Australian rail industry. Research outcomes have included co-authored conference publications: *Skills Recognition in Australian Rail: Emerging Opportunities in a Safety Critical Industry* (2012) and *Skills Recognition in the Australian Rail Industry: Opportunities and Challenges* (2012). Two manuals for HR practitioners, *SR Strategies for Human Resource Practitioners* (2012) and *Skills Recognition Best Practice* (2011), have also been released, as well as a handbook and website for SR assessors and applicants, and the final report on the project. Lisa is a member of Adult learning Australia and is on the editorial board of the *Australian Journal of Adult Learning*.

Dr. Thomas Deissinger is Professor of Business and Economics Education at the University of Konstanz, Germany. He completed his Ph.D. at the University of Mannheim on the history of vocational education in England, and has been Professor in Konstanz since 1998. His research interests include the Dual System, comparative VET research, history of VET and VET policy. National and European research projects have focused on school-based VET, informal learning and hybrid qualifications.

Nathan Dovan is a Research Associate who has research experience in rail incident investigation, road worker safety and program evaluation in community safety. Together they were the research team for a 2-year CRC Rail Innovation funded project in rail incident investigation. Dovan is a member of the Centre for Accident Research and Road safety Qld (CARRS-Q), a research centre of the School of Psychology and Counselling at the Queensland University of Technology.

Professor Brian Findsen has worked in the field of adult and continuing education for over 30 years, primarily in his home country of New Zealand but also in Glasgow, Scotland, from 2004 to 2008. He completed his doctorate in adult education at North Carolina State University in the USA. He is currently a professor of (adult) education in the Faculty of Education, University of Waikato, New Zealand. His main research interests include older adults' learning, sociology of adult education, social equity issues and international adult education. He has co-edited *The Fourth Sector: Adult and Community Education in Aotearoa New Zealand* (1996), individually wrote *Learning Later* (2005) and co-authored *Lifelong Learning in Later Life: A Handbook of Older Adult Learning* (2011).

Jill Hadley is a part-time professional doctorate in education candidate at the University of South Australia and has worked extensively over the last 30 years in the Vocational Education and Training environment within public, enterprise and private training organisations as a lecturer, education manager, faculty manager and project manager. She has written a wide range of commercial learning resource materials for both human services and business services training provision. From various positions held in education institutions over many years, and as a consultant to private and public Registered Training Organisations, Jill has been instrumental in leading change in the VET arena. Currently, Jill is working at the University of South Australia as a part-time lecturer in project management, teaching research methods to master's degree students.

Dr. Roger Harris is a Professor in the School of Education, University of South Australia. He has had extensive experience in VET research, with a focus on national training reform, workforce development and adult learning. He has presented at national and international conferences and published widely, including books on competency-based education (Macmillan 1995), on- and off-job training (NCVER 1998) and rethinking work and learning (Springer 2009), as well co-writing 18 research monographs (NCVER). Recently, Roger was Director of the 3-year Australian research consortium, *Supporting VET providers in building capability for the future*. He has been a member of the South Australian Training and Skills Commission, and a Research Fellow for 3 months at the Institute for Adult Learning in the Singapore Workforce Development Agency. Currently he serves on the Academic Boards of two private higher education providers, and as Program Leader of the Workforce Development Program within the CRC for Rail Innovation. He has been Editor of the *Australian Journal of Adult Learning*, and is now Co-Editor of the *International Journal of Training Research*.

Dr. Jarna Heinonen is Professor in Entrepreneurship, a teacher of entrepreneurship studies at Turku School of Economics (TSE) and the Director of TSE Entre – the entrepreneurship research group. Jarna's lecturing includes entrepreneurship, particularly entrepreneurial behaviour, as well as developing and promoting entrepreneurship in different contexts. She supervises theses at master's and doctoral levels, as well as within TSE's eMBA program, of which she is the Academic Director. She has acted as a governmental advisor and expert in a number of national and multinational expert assignments in the field of entrepreneurship and SMEs. Jarna is interested in multi-disciplinary entrepreneurship research and has directed, supervised and conducted more than a hundred national and international research projects in the field of entrepreneurship since 1992. She was a Leverhulme Visiting Research Fellow at Kingston University, UK, in 2006.

Dr. Kieren Jamieson has a Ph.D. in the study of decision making in the adoption and selection of information systems. His research focuses on the elements of technology adoption and use that are subject to social and organisational influences. Kieren has an industry background with experience in a rage of technical, operational and managerial roles in large information systems implementations. His synthesis of research and industry experience underpins his interest in understanding the antecedents of positive and negative organisational outcomes from technology implementations. He is a Senior Lecturer at Central Queensland University, Australia.

Dr. Lesley Jolly is an anthropologist whose initial research field was gender in Aboriginal Australia. In 1995 she started working on a gender project with the Engineering faculty at the University of Queensland and went on from there to help found the Catalyst Centre for Research in Society and Technology and work on projects as diverse as the development of career paths for construction managers, the learning of maths in pre-tertiary school and community settings and many aspects of engineering education. In 1997 she left the University of Queensland to set up her own consultancy, called *Strategic Partnerships*, which supplies research, evaluation and project management services. She was the first chair (2008–2012) of the Educational Research Methods group of the Australasian Association for Engineering Education. She is a member of the Australian Evaluation Society and is on the committee organising the 2013 conference in Brisbane. Current projects include an Actor Network Theory analysis of the role of conferences in creating the field of Engineering Education (with colleagues from University of Technology, Sydney) and an investigation of the way positivist epistemologies impact on the teaching and learning of engineering (with colleagues from University of Southern Queensland).

Associate Professor Lydia Kavanagh is a chemical engineer who returned from industry to academia over a decade ago. She is currently employed by The University of Queensland as the Director for First Year Engineering and as such has oversight of 1,200 students each year. Lydia's research focuses on engineering education and includes issues such as work integrated learning, graduate competencies, successful student teamwork, online learning and strategies for transition to first year. Currently she is involved in an international project concerning 'flipping the classroom' and establishing learning partnerships. Lydia won a national teaching award for excellence in 2012 for her work with students, curriculum and teaching scholarship. She is an Associate Editor of the *Australian Journal for Engineering Education*.

Professor Peter Kell is the Head of School of Education, Charles Darwin University, Australia. His research interests include literacy and language, the internationalisation of education, vocational education and the mobility of students and workers in the Asia Pacific. He has recently published two major books entitled, *International Students in the Asia Pacific: Mobility Risks and Global Optimism* (with Gillian Vogl) and *Literacy and Language in East Asia: Shifting Meanings, Values and Approaches* (with Marilyn Kell). Peter has worked in Asia at the Hong Kong Institute of Education (2009–2011) and has been Visiting Professor at the Universiti of Sains Malaysia. He has extensive experience in transnational programs, some of which have involved the International Associations of Universities, the World Bank, the Asia Pacific Future Research Network and the Centre for Excellence in Asia Pacific

Professor Ian Lings is currently Head of School at Queensland University of Technology Business School Ian (Advertising, Marketing and Public Relations). Ian obtained his first degree in chemistry from Nottingham Trent University in the UK, and after several years with Shell UK, he obtained first an MBA and later a Ph.D. from Aston University, UK. His research is centred in two theoretical domains.

Firstly, social and organisational psychology, applied to internal marketing, service relationships and service quality. His research in this area is applied to exploring the firm-employee-customer triad. Secondly, strategic management theory in which his research is applied to the management of the firm-market relationships as a strategic resource. Ian's teaching interests include services marketing, marketing research and marketing strategy. He is also QUT Business School's Higher Degree Research Coordinator. Ian has been published in a range of journals including the *Journal of Service Research*, the *Journal of Business Research*, *Long Range Planning* and the *Journal of Services Marketing*. Ian co-authored the research student focussed *Doing Business Research: A Guide to Theory and Practice* published by Sage (2008), and is the Associate Editor of the *European Journal of Marketing* and sits on the international advisory board of the *Journal of Service Management*.

Katie Maher is a Ph.D. student and research assistant with the David Unaipon College of Indigenous Education and Research at the University of South Australia. Her Ph.D. research concerns the involvement of Indigenous and culturally diverse peoples in the Australian railways. Katie also works on an Australian Research Council Discovery grant on Indigenous knowledge pertaining to environmental protection. Katie also speaks and reads Mandarin and has a keen interest in China.

Dr. Cameron Newton is an Associate Professor in the School of Management at the Queensland University of Technology in Brisbane, Australia. He teaches quantitative research methods and organizational psychology to undergraduate and postgraduate students. His research interests include organizational culture, occupational stress, biofeedback using heart-rate variability and stress interventions.

Dr. Liza O'Moore is a Civil Engineer who graduated from the University of Queensland in 1987. She returned to UQ in 2001 to take up an academic position in the School of Civil Engineering. She is a Senior Lecturer and teaches primarily into the first and second years of the BE degree programs. Liza has research interests in engineering education in the areas of transition and preparedness for first year, graduate competencies and large class teaching. She has been the recipient of School of Engineering (2005, 2006) and Faculty (2007, 2012) Teaching Excellence Awards. In 2011 Liza was awarded an Australian Learning and Teaching Council (ALTC) Citation for Outstanding Contribution to Student learning. On behalf of the QLD Office of Higher Education (OHE), Liza has also been committee member advising on the accreditation of Associate Degrees in Engineering in the VET sector.

Dr. Janene Piip is a researcher and tutor at the School of Education, University of South Australia, Australia, and facilitator of business, community and social development. Janene's research interests include leadership, management and productivity in organisations, performance management of teams and career development of individuals in organisations. She has worked on CRC for Rail Innovation projects such as developing a leadership and management capability framework and coaching and mentoring. Janene has recently completed her doctorate at the University of South Australia and researching leadership talent practices in Australian rail organisations.

Dr. Sukanlaya Sawang is a Senior Lecturer at QUT Business School, Australia. Her research primarily focuses on two main areas within the field of organisational effectiveness: psychological wellbeing and innovation adoption. Sukanlaya has developed considerable research and impact within both of these spheres. She received a number of awards – including the 'Emerald Management Reviews Citation of Excellence'; the 'Best Paper Awards' from the Academy of Management (AOM); and the 'AGSE International Entrepreneurship Research Exchange' award. Her research has been published in various journals, such as *Technovation, Journal of Small Business Management* and *Applied Psychology: International*.

Dr. Jonathan M. Scott is Head of the Centre for Strategy & Leadership and a Reader in Entrepreneurship at Teesside University Business School, having completed a Ph.D. (University of Ulster 2003). He is a Director of Enterprise Educators UK (2011–2014). His collaborative research focuses on access to finance for small and medium-sized enterprises (SMEs) and he has a particular interest in strategy, as the co-author (with Thompson and Martin) of the forthcoming textbook *Strategic Management: Awareness and Change*, 7th Edition (Cengage 2014). He was a Visiting Research Fellow at TSE Entre in 2009, 2010 and 2012 and will be conducting collaborative research on differences in entrepreneurship between developed and developing countries as a Visiting Research Fellow at Waikato Management School, New Zealand, between January and April 2014.

Neroli Sheldon has a Master of Human Resources and Organisational Development degree and has worked over the past 20 years in the private and public sectors in management and training and development roles. She has extensive experience on vocational educations in the forestry and timber industry sector and is currently working as a researcher at the Southern Cross University Business School. Neroli has taught recruitment and performance management units at graduate level and is the secretary of the Human Research Ethics Sub-committee at Southern Cross University. Neroli's current research interests include precarious employment, contemporary career paths and attraction and image of certain industries and careers. She is also interested in the use of therapy dogs in supporting literacy development in school children. Neroli has co-authored *Managing Performance Improvement* published by Pearson Education (2010) and contributed to a number of journal articles and conference proceedings in attraction and image of rail careers, career paths and business research ethics. Outside of her university work, Neroli sits on the management committee of Story Dogs Inc., a reading support program where selected children read to an accredited therapy dog and its owner.

Dr. Tom Short is a Research Fellow and Lecturer at the University of South Australia. His research activities include leading workforce development projects within the CRC for Rail Innovation, an Australian Government Initiative (2008–2014). His academic and work experiences are drawn from senior management, consulting, education and research roles spanning areas such as human resource management, workforce development, leadership and adult education. He has published widely on these topics in books, journals, national and international conference proceedings, professional publications and currently serves on the editorial board of three international journals. Tom is a Chartered Fellow of the Chartered Institute of Personnel and Development, a Fellow of the Australian Human Resources Institute and formerly Director of the Performance Improvement Centre, a consulting and training business situated within the University of Auckland, Faculty of Education, specialising in the professional development of workplace educators, trainers, assessors and teachers of adults.

Dr. Michele Simons is Professor and Dean of Education at the University of Western Sydney. She brings more than 20 years of experience as an educator and researcher in policy, context and issues associated with vocational education and training and workforce development. Michele has published widely in a range of areas including workplace learning, the role of workplace trainers and vocational education teachers, career development for vocational education trainers and teachers, and national reform in the vocational education and training sector in Australia.

Dr. Tom Stehlik is a Senior Lecturer, School of Education, University of South Australia, and has over 20 years of experience in collaborative educational research with industry partners including SAPOL, TAFE SA, DECD, NCVER and BHP Billiton. Dr. Stehlik was seconded to the South Australian Social Inclusion Unit during 2005–2006 to participate in the evaluation of the state government School Retention Action Plan, and has recently co-edited a book entitled *Changing the Paradigm: Education as the Key to a Socially Inclusive Future* (2011, Post Pressed). His research practice has included significant experience in qualitative research methodologies working closely with schools, communities and workplaces using ethical and appropriate approaches

Dr. John Thompson is Emeritus Professor of Entrepreneurship at the University of Huddersfield and, part-time Professor of Social Entrepreneurship at Anglia Ruskin University. He has had visiting links with Universities in Australia, Finland and New Zealand. He is a Board Member of The Case Centre (formerly the European Case Clearing House) and he has served on the Boards of the Institute for Small Business and Entrepreneurship, Enterprise Educators UK and UK Business Incubation. He has written over a dozen texts on entrepreneurship and strategy as well as several chapters and journal articles, and he is an active researcher and case writer. His main interests are identifying people with the potential to be entrepreneurs and social entrepreneurs. In 2009 John received the Queen's Award for Enterprise Promotion.

Dr. Gregory Tibbits is an Engineering Education expert at University of Queensland where he evaluated the effectiveness of train driver simulators, specifically seeking to understand why the simulators are used the way they are. Greg situated his thesis in terms of the diffusion of innovations and approaching the problem using the theory of practice as developed by Pierre Boudieu. He has a Bachelor of Science (Hons IIA) from the Australian National University and a Graduate Certificate in Economics from the University of Queensland.

Associate Professor Michelle Wallace is an Associate Professor of Human Resources in the Southern Cross University Business School. Michelle's Ph.D. related to power in organisations and workplace HRD. Michelle has supervised many workplace research projects, Masters, DBA and PhD theses in the area of human resource management and has researched human resource practices in numerous organisations. Michelle has previously held the role of Director of the Master of Human Resources and Organisational Development and is currently Director of the DBA at Southern Cross University. Michelle's current research interests include attraction and retention of workers, women in middle-management, international/transnational teaching and learning, ethics, DBA training and supervision, workplace learning and casualisation of the workforce. Her recent publications include works on HRM, power and identity in organisations, organisational change and career development. Michelle has co-authored a number of books including *Teaching and Learning in Transnational Higher Education: Enhancing Learning for Offshore International Students* (2008) and *Transnational Doctoral Education and Research: An Asian Focus* (2012). Michelle is on the editorial boards and is a reviewer for several journals. She is a Chartered Member of the Australian Human Resources Institute (AHRI) and a member of the British Academy of Management and the Australia New Zealand Academy of Management (ANZAM).

Abbreviations

ABS	Australian Bureau of Statistics
AFAC	Australian Fires Authority Council
AHRI	Australian Human Resources Institute
ANZSCO	Australia and New Zealand Standard Classification of Occupations
ANET	Australia National Engineering Taskforce
APS	Australian Public Service
APSC	Australian Public Services Commission
AQF	Australian Qualifications Framework
ARA	Australasian Railway Association
ASQA	Australian Skills Quality Authority
AWPA	Australian Workforce and Productivity Agency
CA	Competence assurance
CALD	Culturally and linguistically diverse
CEO	Chief executive officer
CEDA	Committee for the Economic Development of Australia
CIPD	Chartered Institute of Personnel and Development
CMS	Critical Management Studies
COAG	Council of Australian Governments
CRA	Craft Regulation Act
CRC	Cooperative Research Centre
CHRD	Critical Human Resource Development
DEEWR	Department of Education, Employment and Workplace Relations
DQR	German Qualifications Framework
ESOL	English for Speakers of Other Languages
FMI	Frontline Management Initiative
GDP	Gross domestic product
GFC	Global financial crisis
HR	Human resources
HRD	Human resource development
HRM	Human resource management

ILO	International Labour Organization
IQ	Intergenerational Qualification
LLN	Language, Literacy and Numeracy
MBA	Master of Business Administration
OD	Organisational development
OECD	Organisation for Economic Co-operation and Development
RCC	Recognition of Current Competency
RPL	Recognition of prior learning
ROI	Return on investment
RTO	Registered Training Organisation
SR	Skills recognition
STEM	Science, Technology, Engineering and Maths
TAFE	Technical and Further Education
TNA	Training Needs Analysis
UNESCO	United Nations Educational, Scientific and Cultural Organization
VET	Vocational Education and Training
VTA	Vocational Training Act

Chapter 1
Workforce Development: Moving from Perspectives to Practices

Tom Short and Roger Harris

Abstract Workforce development is an overarching term used to describe a wide range of education, training and professional development activities carried out in the workplace. In this series of two books, we have endeavoured to follow the emergence of workforce development from initial concept to final application. In our first book, *Workforce development: Perspective and issues*, we brought together a compilation of education and training topics and asked our authors to firstly, draw on their expertise in human resource development and adult education and secondly, reflect on their recent experiences of researching in the Australian rail industry We aimed to show that workforce development is an amalgam of ideas and developments that are currently shaping the organisational landscape in a period of rapid change and uncertainty. In this second volume we have extended our discussion to consider how these perspective and issues have translated into workable strategies and practices used by organisations. In this chapter, we describe the background to our book and examine further what the collective term workforce development means by analysing each part separately.

Background

The 20 chapters in this second volume build on a range of perspectives and issues that were presented in *Workforce development: Perspectives and issues*, and they draw on research findings to amalgamate many of these ideas as workable strategies and human resource development (HRD) practices. It is our hope that leaders in organisations will consider these insights when they deal with the ever-present challenges of growing and surviving in today's volatile business environment.

T. Short (✉) • R. Harris
School of Education, University of South Australia, Mawson Lakes, SA, Australia
e-mail: tom.short@unisa.edu.au; roger.harris@unisa.edu.au

T. Short and R. Harris (eds.), *Workforce Development: Strategies and Practices*,
DOI 10.1007/978-981-287-068-1_1, © Springer Science+Business Media Singapore 2014

Global frameworks on business improvement, such as the UK Investor in People Award (which was launched in 1991 and is now used in over 70 countries), recognise the positive connection between a solid workforce development strategy and resulting business success. These international standards contribute substantially to the widespread uptake of workforce development practices and address the key issues affecting people in an ever-changing workplace.

In this book we discover how a selection of Australian organisations has dealt with a number of workforce development challenges following the global financial crisis (GFC). Some reports suggest that the Australian economy has out-performed many other developed countries since 2008, and unemployment has remained lower than elsewhere (CEDA 2013). However, as a consequence of the GFC, negative returns on superannuation funds coupled with an ageing population has delayed the planned retirement of older employees. Simultaneously, a steady infusion of Generation Y employees into the workplace means that many organisations now have up to four generations working together. This occurrence brings an array of new challenges and possibilities for HRD practitioners who lead workforce development projects, because each of these generational cohorts (described as Veterans, Baby boomers, Generation X and Generation Y) has a unique perspective on society, employment, lifestyle and how they interact with people in the workplace (Hammill 2005).

Aside from these obvious challenges, there are further conundrums in traditional industry sectors, because the imminent loss of longer serving skilled workers will coincide with a shortage of younger people who are not interested in pursuing an industrial career. Therefore, attracting and retaining younger engineers and then transferring knowledge from one generation to the next will become a pressing need and may impose a new organisational landscape where these intergeneration cohorts will need to build increased levels of cooperation to save their industry from a catastrophic loss of tacit knowledge. Arguably, this type of intergenerational cooperation could soon become the key component of a truly sustainable organisation development strategy and is recognised in major industry reports (PWC 2006; ARA 2008). Therefore, how leaders make optimal use of the human potential existent within four generations could become the key ingredient – a notion labelled loosely as '*generational competence*, which describes the behaviour organisations must engage in to meet the needs of four generations' (Jimenez 2009, p. 50).

Workforce Development Strategy

The phrase *workforce development strategy* is used throughout this book and in the literature so it is appropriate to begin by asking the question: 'what is a workforce development strategy and what does it mean for HRD practitioners in organisations?' In our first book we explored this question by delving into the discourse used by educationists, policy makers, scholars and practitioners to reveal an assorted range of interpretations that draw from the areas of vocational training, human resource management and professional practice. Those who study workforce development draw inspiration from these diverse influences, but above all believe that the term has come about in response to the workplace challenges created by influences such as globalisation, workforce mobility, the individualisation of work and a 'shift from individual competence to organisational capability' (Mitchell and Fetter 2003; Harris and Short 2014, p. 5).

Nonetheless, we have delved into this question further by separating the phrase and examining each word to clarify our interpretation, understand the influence on management decisions and assess the implications for workplace education and training practice. To begin, *workforce* is a singular term used to define a collective pool of labour supply available for an organisation. In other explanations it can be referred to as the totality of human resources within an organisation or industry who are available for labour deployment. Irrespective of the terminology used, managers and leaders long for the ideal workforce which can include but is not limited to having sufficient numbers of competent people at the right time to deal with a diverse range of challenges. To senior executives, the ideal workforce would be perceived as highly productive, working in a harmonious way, embracing change, cultivating innovation, working efficiently and not incurring waste of any kind. Given these high expectations it is not surprising that the ideal workforce is an elusive concept and perhaps more of a management desire than reality, mainly because an organisation's workforce is exposed to external and internal influences which can distract individuals from achieving many of these goals. The research findings in our chapters indicate that classifying the workforce in the twenty-first century is becoming an open-ended activity, because it is less predictable, ever-changing and able to accommodate different types of employment. For example, technology has dispersed workforces into virtual workplaces, where team productivity, positive working relationships and collective approaches to developing people are much harder to achieve. Nowadays, a workforce can be segmented into core or peripheral workers, full time or casual employees, or people employed in other organisations that are part of the wider supply chain. Moreover, a modern workforce can include individuals from diverse cultures, with uneven standards of literacy, language and numeracy skills. For HR managers, this increasing workforce diversity can lead to inevitable variations in work performance, employee engagement and employment tenure.

Secondly, the word *development* has grown in popular HR discourse to mean a range of things and is associated with learning processes beyond, but not excluding, education and training. Development implies not only learning new knowledge and skills, but also acquiring the meta-competencies to reflect critically, transfer learning to multiple contexts and engage in the process of continuous improvement. The notion of meta-competency has been around for some time and is a term used to distinguish higher order abilities which are connected with being able to learn, adapt, anticipate and create (Burgoyne 1989, in Brown 1993).

As an organisational activity, *development* is aimed at improving the performance of individuals and work groups, but in recent years these goals have extended to include the betterment of individual lifestyles and the wider society. Organisational *development*, which has obvious connections with the *workforce*, is a collection of learning activities that assists an organisation to 'deal appropriately with changes in its internal and external environments by making best use of the individual and collective capacities of its members' (Cooke 1992, p. 41). In the early 1990s, organisational development became an essential business activity and has remained popular, especially as private and/or public sector organisations have become subsumed with managing change, restructuring, dealing with conflict and/or performative, objective-based goal setting activities.

Thirdly, *strategy* and *strategic* have become popular words in contemporary business communication but may have become misused, or sometimes overused. Both of these terms borrow practical meaning from military discourse and have varying interpretations, but the word *strategy* derives from the Greek word *strategos* which translates to the art of the general (Nickols 2012). In simple terms, *strategy* defines a process or series of decisions that can determine how leaders in an organisation plan and deploy their resources to maximise the achievement of *strategic* or longer-term goals, while at the same time protecting valuable resources and assets from harmful opponents or competitors. Strategy can be planned and positioned at different levels, or at multiple levels, so a workforce development strategy would contribute normally to a higher order organisational strategy. Purcell (1989, p. 72) refers to 'first, second and third' levels of strategy, which can be translated loosely into corporate, competitive and functional. In this interpretation, functional strategy relates closely with day-to-day performance activities of a tactical nature and helps to ensure compliance and the implementation of plans. Therefore, and interpreting Purcell's findings further, it is possible that workforce development activities are more closely related to the implementation stage of a strategic plan and therefore become more tactical in definition. This deduction may come as a surprise to some readers, but in the course of editing these books, our researchers have become more engaged with the growing area of critical management studies and a background debate about the strategic contribution of workforce development activities. At the end of this book and its previous companion edition, it is likely that many of our readers will weigh-up the key findings and arguments from 40 chapters and their own experiences to make up their own minds.

Strategy is also affected by an organisation's health and has resource implications, so struggling enterprises may choose to focus their entire strategy on survival during difficult times, while another more established business might focus on becoming more sustainable and use innovation to stay ahead of competitors (Johnson and Scholes 1993). The determining factors that shape strategy and what it means to be strategic are likely to come from the environments in which organisations operate, the way in which these influences are diagnosed and how the internal environments are subsequently arranged to deal with challenges from an increasing range of external events. In recent years it has become much more difficult for organisational leaders to be strategic, or to define a fixed and/or concrete longer-term strategy, because of rapid changes and episodic aftermaths thrown up by global economic conditions, international conflicts and unexpected weather events. Highly detailed strategic planning activities, most prolific in the 1980s and 1990s, were arguably unsuccessful in some settings and have given way to less onerous, but equally demanding discussions that focus on strategic choices, business adaptation and organisational culture (Ward 2012).

In summary, and to clarify in our readers' minds what the collective term *workforce development strategy* means, we suggest the term is captured appropriately in one report by the Australian Workforce and Productivity Agency (AWPA 2013, p. 10). The report comments on the volatile nature of globalisation and connects workforce development strategy with the need to position Australia as a growing knowledge economy that is able to improve productivity, meet current and future labour needs and also promote social inclusion. Contained within this broad strategy are plans and goals to improve language, literacy and numeracy and actions to ensure that the tertiary education sector is strengthened to deal with these challenges. Later in this book many of the individual chapters will address various dimensions of this agenda and be expressed in an industrial context.

Workforce Development Practice

The second theme embodied in the sub-title of this book builds on *strategy* and highlights the area of *practice* as something uniquely different. In this context we regard *practice* as the specific activities, tactical actions or business processes that organisations put in place to achieve their strategies. In the area of workforce development, *strategy* tends to focus on 'the why/what', while *practices* are more concerned with 'the how/when', and they utilise processes, techniques or frameworks to complete activities that contribute to achieving the overall strategy. In many of our chapters, it will be possible for readers to see the interrelationship between strategy and practice and how the implementation of one workforce development activity impacts on another. Examples of practice include: how organisations choose to source their learning and development materials from internal or external services; how workforce development is organised through a centralised function or delegated to line managers; different ways of developing individuals, the use of group or individual learning activities and how technology can be integrated to deliver workplace education and training in the most effective ways.

Why This Book?

The genesis for this book has been the research undertaken by most, though not all, of the chapter authors who contributed to the Workforce Development Theme of the Australian Cooperative Research Centre for Rail Innovation (hereafter CRC). Their chapters are 'spin-offs' from this research, extended and reframed to make the chapters more generic to workplaces in general. Naturally, however, in some of the chapters data included or case studies presented necessarily relate to the Australian rail industry. These have been incorporated merely to furnish recent examples that may help to clarify workplace development strategies and practices for readers situated in other industries and countries. This CRC is a consortium of 19 Core Participants (including seven universities), 14 Supporting Participants and 8 Other Participants, collaborating in a 7-year program of research (CRC 2013). The total program has been worth over $100 million (cash and in-kind), with funds coming from the Australian Government, participating rail companies and participating universities, and in-kind from rail companies and especially the universities. It is the single biggest research program in the history of Australian railways. The editors of this volume are the Deputy Leader and Program Leader respectively of the Workforce Development Theme in this CRC, while 16 of the 20 chapters have been written by university researchers engaged in research projects for the CRC.

That explanation of the beginning then leads to the question of why this second book. There are two main reasons, relating to breadth and depth. Much of the work in this volume is underpinned by applied research carried out by the contributors on their particular topics for the CRC. The ideas in this book have evolved from these various research projects, where many of the writers have elaborated and reshaped their contribution in the first volume – progressing their earlier work on perspective and issues into strategies and practices. They have, of course, submitted their respective research reports and useable products to the CRC as a requirement of their funding. These, however, were developed with the Australian rail industry firmly in mind and for its use. As university researchers, the contributors have presented at numerous conferences and workshops on their specialist research topics, but these speeches run the risk of being heard only by attending audiences. They have also published journal articles in their own areas of expertise, but again, these articles are more likely to be accessed by a narrow audience in the specialist fields of research. We, the editors, desired to have this contemporary research aggregated into *one* volume that could be accessed readily by a far wider readership through the medium of a book – and using a distinguished publisher with a capacity to providing word-wide reach. This was our first and more pragmatic reason for this endeavour.

The second reason is more fundamental. The editors, with backgrounds in adult education and human resource management, had become increasingly intrigued with the emergence of the term, 'workforce development'. We puzzled over whether this was merely another marketing fad or buzz-word, or whether it was a genuine attempt to encapsulate the need for reconceptualising organisational policies and practices in a post global financial crisis world? We desired to collate the ideas from all of the hitherto discrete components in our research program into one volume in order to explore and interrogate more deeply this notion not only for the educational enlightenment of ourselves and our chapter writers, but also for considered and no doubt critical analysis by a wider audience who may well be wrestling with similar issues and concerns. In the end, the amount of information was so substantial that we agreed to break the topic into *two* volumes and hence, this second volume builds on the first volume, subtitled as perspectives and issues, to become focused on strategies and practices.

Who Is the Book For?

The book is intended to have wide appeal and will be of value to executives and senior human resource practitioners who engage in professional development. Additionally academics, students, human resource practitioners and adult educators who work across multiple disciplines such as business, psychology, education and the social sciences will find value in this collection of strategies and practices. We believe the knowledge and learning in each book chapter will transfer across many boundaries and borders – not only inside an organisation, but at the same time recognising the similarities, differences and relevance for a range of external contexts.

What Is the Structure of This Book?

For the sake of clarity and transferability between each companion volume we have retained many of the parts' headings to reflect key themes in Book 1. We believe this format will enable readers to flip between volumes and make connections between the theoretical perspectives and industry practices. Chapters 1 and 20 introduce and close this volume. In between, the other 18 chapters are clustered in four parts that the editors and contributors considered were prime overarching facets in workforce development. Part I: 'Sustainability, Growth and Diversity' examines a range of issues and developments in the external environment that affect workforce participation and considers strategies to build longer-term sustainability, securing growth and diversity. Part II: 'Building Capability and Capacity' looks within organisational settings to consider a range of workforce development themes and reports on a range of activities used to build human capability and capacity. Part III: 'Developing Leadership Talent and Innovation' concentrates on leadership, the development of leadership talent, techniques used to develop leaders and also delves into the value of intrapreneurship as a process for leading change and innovation. Finally, Part IV: Harmonizing Across Boundaries and Borders: Case Studies draws on industry examples and considers how workforce development strategies and practices can be transferred across boundaries and borders.

Another way to interpret the 20 chapters is to consider each parts as a segment in a holistic strategy on workforce development as shown in Fig. 1.1. In this concept model, Part I chapters can be thought of as one strategy to resource employees and focus on how an organisation can attract and make full use of a wider labour supply. In Part II, we have assembled a collection of chapters to emphasise a range of outlooks,

Fig. 1.1 A concept model of workforce development strategy and practice

workplace systems and technologies that help to maximise the utilisation of human resources. Part III deals with building culture – not only among leaders and managers, but everyone in the organisation, especially when improvement, innovation and workforce performance are critical to success. Finally, Part IV brings together a range of chapters that report on structured and competence-based approaches to workforce development. These approaches provide an opportunity for harmonisation across boundaries and borders.

Part I, 'Sustainability, Growth and Diversity', comprises six chapters. Peter Kell in Chap. 2 provides an overview of the global shifts in migration policy, global mobility and uses international case studies to illustrate the complexities around policy formulation in skilled migration. The chapter discusses the impact of global mobility and includes an assessment of the implications for human resource managers, especially in the corporate sector, and the need to look beyond traditional forms of labour supply. The chapter concludes with advice to corporations and business on how to negotiate a global market, suggesting that an informed and holistic approach to interpreting globalisation and settlement is essential in sourcing global talent.

From the sourcing of global talent we move on in Chap. 3 to consider strategies and practices that attract talented people to less glamorous industries. Michelle Wallace, Neroli Sheldon, Roslyn Cameron and Ian Lings examine what young graduate Australian engineers want from a twenty-first century workplace. The authors draw our attention to the growing shortage of talented engineers in traditional sectors and highlight how many organisations struggle to attract quality candidates, especially when the image of the wider industry is not high. They further suggest that gaining knowledge of young engineers' preferences for career benefit and progression can inform branding and communication strategies.

The related issue of enhancing career pathways is the third perspective, provided by Neroli Sheldon and Michelle Wallace in Chap. 4. The idea of providing explicit career pathways has long been recognised as an important workforce development strategy for attracting and retaining employees, but with blurring organisational boundaries and altering employment relationships, the notion of career path has changed markedly in recent years and become ambiguous. Using a five stage analytical framework (situation, problem, implication, need and solution), the authors explore the strategic and operational importance of career paths to industries, organisations and individuals. The chapter considers the demand for engineers and skilled technicians in the Australian rail industry and illustrates how a new Rail Career website is being used to promote the industry and generate greater interest. However, this concept has broader utility.

Brian Findsen, in Chap. 5, addresses the diversity element of this section by drawing attention to the place of older adults in an aging workforce. Following the global financial crisis in 2008, many older workers who were contemplating retirement have been forced to participate in longer employment, including workplace training. Therefore, as organisations experience the onset of a three or four generational workplace, this widening gap in generational diversity has implications for workplace education and training. Importantly, it opens up the debate about how adults learn, relearn or unlearn effectively when coping with workforce development requirements and reignites discussion on the value of training older adults. The author discusses a learning organisational framework and win-win scenario that includes, engages and enhances learning opportunities for workers of all ages.

The final chapter in Part I focuses on issues of equity and diversity in the workplace. Katie Maher explores the extent to which Diversity Management approaches, which are based on a business rationale of diversity as a productive asset, are inclusive of historically underrepresented ethnic groups and Aboriginal peoples. Chapter 6 proposes that equity and diversity work is not just about ethnic minority groups, but also about the dominant, white culture. Drawing on interviews with employees in human resource, learning and development, training and assessment, operational and service roles in a range of Australian rail companies, the author identifies some problems with achieving equity and diversity in the workplace with particular attention given to challenges in recognising the knowledge and skills of a culturally diverse workforce.

Part II, 'Building Capability and Capacity', moves from these broad-ranging, organisational perspectives on sustainability, growth and diversity in the first part to consider strategies and practices that organisations can use to build capability and capacity. This section includes four chapters and begins with Chap. 7 by Tom Short which looks at formal workplace mentoring as a strategy for employee engagement. This chapter explores the emergence of formal workplace mentoring as one human resource development strategy for dealing with the transfer of knowledge and comments on the motivational benefits of using mentoring programs in situations where other forms of learning might be less effective. With the overarching goal of building capacity through the engagement of people, Australian rail organisations supported the formation of an industry mentoring framework to assist workforce development strategy and guide harmonised practice across the nation.

Technologies such as online tools, simulations and remote labs are often used in learning and training environments, both academic and vocational, to deliver content in an accessible manner. They promise efficiencies of scale, flexibility of delivery and face validity for a generation brought up on electronic devices. In Chap. 8, Greg Tibbits, Lesley Jolly, Lydia Kavanagh and Liza O'Moore remind us that learning outcomes are not the same in all circumstances and contextual and cultural factors can lead to the failure of technology which has been successful elsewhere. Chapter 8 draws on their studies of the use of simulators and simulations within the vocational environment of the Australian rail industry to consider how the broader context of the training/educational curriculum affects what works for whom under what circumstances. The chapter concludes with a curriculum model that draws attention to the root cause of attitudes that can impact on simulator effectiveness.

In Chap. 9, Tom Short and Roger Harris deal with the emerging topic of *generational competence* – a term used loosely to describe how organisations deal with the education and training needs of a multi- generation workforce. In traditional industries it is estimated that organisations could soon have up to four generations working under the same roof. The literature indicates that this new condition is created by a range of factors, including societal changes in retirement living, returning workers and skills shortages in less popular vocations. The chapter describes how the transfer of tacit knowledge from experienced workers to new starters is becoming a major issue in traditional industries and is not helped by age-related variations in the acceptance of technology, attitudes to authority, decision making, organisation of work and approaches to learning. Taking care not to overemphasize the characteristics of one age group over another, the authors draw examples from the literature and a range of industry research findings where generation-related issues have emerged as a potential challenge for workforce developers.

There are many current and emergent issues in the area of how to conduct skills recognition processes and in Chap. 10 Lisa Davies explores the challenges of recognising abstract skills in managers such as the holistic or softer skills associated with leading people. In vocational settings skills recognition assessments, including Recognition of Prior Learning (RPL), are a well-established part of formal training programs, yet tacit skills and soft skills are less likely to be recognised in competency based frameworks. In this chapter the author discusses issues concerning the contextualisation of abstract skill and suggests a range of strategies for identifying and or capturing tacit knowledge in difficult work scenarios. Moreover, the author suggests that informal skills recognition processes can be of equal value during wider or non-technical skills development activities. The author then details ways in which the learning of abstract skills can be facilitated in the workplace.

Technology has become such an important part of organisational life and in Chap. 11 Kieran Jamieson, Sukanlaya Sawang and Cameron Newton examine lessons learnt from a study of the use of e-learning within the Australian rail sector. By examining the social, organisational and technical influences on the way employees perceive and use e-learning, the authors were able to explore factors that inhibited or advanced its organisational effectiveness and discovered a range of twelve factors beyond the systems themselves. From the research findings, the authors then were able to make a number of practical recommendations that organisations should consider before implementing e-learning. These recommendations have been grouped into four themes: Policy and Planning, Design, Technology and Education. The chapter concludes with an important message for managers and HR practitioners that e-learning projects should be treated like any other organisational change and include substantial communication to employees on the reasons for implementation and anticipated benefits.

Part III, 'Developing Talent, Innovation and Leadership', comprises five chapters that consider interesting ways in which organisations can building leadership capability through the use of competence frameworks and individualised learning techniques to build talent and encourage innovation. In Chap. 12, Tom Short, Tom Stehlik and Janene Piip detail research findings from a 2 year project aimed at developing an industry-wide leadership capability framework. Drawing on major studies and practical experiences in an industrial setting, the chapter discusses why leadership is so important to organisations in a globally competitive world and details a range of tools and techniques that can be used to build a strong leadership culture. Key elements include the need to secure sustained commitment from senior executives, the argument for developing leaders at the front line as a priority, the duality of developing hard and soft skills in an industrial setting and the need for leaders to become more self-aware. The authors present a conceptual diagram to guide organisations through these key elements.

Ros Cameron in Chap. 13 reports on workplace coaching as an emerging intervention in an era when attracting, developing and retaining quality employees is a major issue for organisations. Coaching draws upon an array of theoretical foundations and approaches, which means the practice is not straightforward. In this chapter the author looks at the development and deployment of workplace coaching in an industrial setting where performance, learning and improvement are ever-present. The chapter outlines research findings and suggests that coaching can be used effectively not only to shape very precise changes in behaviour but also to stimulate change and align human resource development interventions with strategic goals. To conclude, the chapter offers some insights into how the effectiveness of coaching activities can be evaluated.

In Chap. 14, Janene Piip and Roger Harris remind us that leaving the identification of leadership talent to chance has enduring consequences for organisations. Drawing on industry research from frontline, middle and senior managers, the chapter states that spotting and developing leadership talent is more important in knowledge based economies because talented leaders are important sources of competitive advantage. However, the authors found that the calibre of talent is a direct result of a number of factors relating to what organisations and individuals do to identify and develop talent. The chapter highlights three areas of talent: task or technical skills, human relationship skills, and change and conceptual skills. These three skills sets lead to six capabilities of talented leaders and are described as a chapter summary.

Chapter 15, by Jill Hadley, considers the influences of workplace context on training programs and how nationally accredited courses leading to qualifications can demand learning outcomes that may not align with an organisation's need. In this chapter the author recounts an example in the Australian public sector where a high level of satisfaction expressed by learners and trainers following successful implementation of in-course workplace projects as part of an internal leadership development program were contrasted with external assessment reports from national auditors that indicated further attention to attain the national competency standard. The author questions whether the option of providing a nationally accredited course is the best choice in an environment where contextual competence is critical.

Chapter 16 invites us to expand our view of topics routinely included in the workforce development portfolio to incorporate innovation and what the author's term the 'intrapreneurial mindset'. John Thompson, Jarna Heinonen and Jonathan M. Scott examine the contribution of people to workplace innovation and change and offer a framework for identifying potential intrapreneurs in an organisation. Today, most of us are familiar with the use of *entrepreneur* through the media's coverage of successful leaders such as Sir Richard Branson and Bill Gates, but intrapreneurs are thought to establish and foster entrepreneurial activity within large organisations. The authors suggest that intrapreneurial people are required to drive the change agenda, but it is debatable just how seriously organisations seek to identify those people with intrapreneurial attributes and encourage them to identify and seize new opportunities.

Part IV, 'Harmonising across Boundaries and Borders: Case Studies', includes three chapters that consider the challenges of implementing education, training and workforce development strategies across organisational or industry boundaries and national or international borders. These challenges are not mutually exclusive to the many issues presented in other parts of this book and are influenced by policy decisions, often way beyond the reach of organisational leaders.

Chapter 17 offers insight into the German vocational education and training system and its coexistence with personnel development. Thomas Deissinger and Kathrin Breuing focus on two aspects they consider to be relevant for a discussion of workforce development: (i) the links between continuing training and personnel development in and for company workplaces with initial training, especially the apprenticeship system, and (ii) the issue of how companies try to cope with changes in their environment – with demographic change at the forefront – to maintain the quality or their workforce in the future. The chapter comments on workforce development activities in the face of democratic change and in particular, the issue of accomplishing effective knowledge transfer within intergenerational groups.

One of the challenges facing industry in Australia relates to the ways in which it is able to harness the opportunities offered by the national Vocational Education and Training (VET) system. The VET system with its network of registered training organisations, and infrastructure of Training Packages and the Australian Quality Training Framework, offers the potential to assist organisations to develop approaches to training which are truly national in scope and focus. However, significant barriers to realising this goal exist. In Chap. 18, Michele Simons and Roger Harris outline the architecture of the VET system, and then analyse the unique needs and issues that industry faces in its efforts to work with the national training system, and strategies and practices that the industry can use in dealing with them to meet workforce development needs.

In Chap. 19, Tamara Banks, Herbert Biggs and Nathan Dovan report on a distinctive research project that aimed to create a common and harmonised approach to one aspect of safety management through structured training and development within an industry sector. Using their work in the Australian rail industry as a recent case study, the chapter reports on the significance of training needs analysis activities as part of program development; in this case, the development of a common capability framework for rail incident investigators. The authors report that for training strategies to be effective, they must appropriately address deficiencies in workforce knowledge or skills.

In Chap. 20, the editors conclude the book by reflecting on workforce development as an emerging field of practice. They distil five messages that emerge from previous chapters, eight challenges in implementing workforce development and summarise the main strategies and practices that have been suggested by chapter writers. The chapter concludes by reasserting two earlier points – firstly, that workforce development is 'more than the sum of its parts' and secondly, that how these component parts are configured and aligned in particular organisational contexts may be the deciding factor evaluating the longer-term value of workforce development initiatives to an organisation's strategic intent and sustained success.

References

ARA (Australasian Railway Association). (2008). *A rail revolution.* Canberra: Australasian Railway Association.

AWPA (Australian Workforce and Productivity Agency). (2013). *Future focus: 2013 National Workforce Development Strategy.* Canberra: Commonwealth of Australia. http://www.awpa.gov.au/our-work/national-workforce-development-strategy/Pages/default.aspx. Accessed 28 Oct 2013.

Brown, R. B. (1993). Meta-competence: A receipt for reframing the competence debate. *Personnel Review, 22*(6), 25–36.

CEDA (Committee for Economic Development of Australia). (2013). *Economic and political overview 2013.* Melbourne: Committee for Economic Development of Australia.

Cooke, R. (1992). Human resource strategies for business success. In M. Armstrong (Ed.), *Strategies for human resource management: A total business solution.* London: Kogan Page.

Hammill, G. (2005). Mixing and managing four generations of employees. *MDU Magazine,* Winter/Spring. Fairleigh Dickinson University, Teaneck. http://www.fdu.edu/newspubs/magazine/05ws/generations.htm. Accessed 30 Oct 2013.

Harris, R., & Short, T. (2014). Exploring the notion of workforce development. In R. Harris & T. Short (Eds.), *Workforce development: Perspectives and issues* (pp. 1–16). Singapore: Springer.

Jimenez, L. (2009, June). Management implications of the multi-generational workforce. *Profiles in Diversity Journalism, 11*(3), 50.

Johnson, G., & Scholes, K. (1993). *Exploring corporate strategy* (3rd ed.). Hemel Hempstead: Prentice Hall.

Mitchell, R., & Fetter, J. (2003). Human resource management and individualisation of Australian labour law. *The Journal of Industrial Relations, 45*(3), 292–325.

Nickols, F. (2012). *Strategy: Definitions and meaning.* Mt Vernon: Nickols Website. http://www.nickols.us/strategy_definition.htm. Accessed 19 Nov 2013.

Purcell, J. (1989). The impact of corporate strategy on human resource management. In J. Storey (Ed.), *New perspectives in human resource management* (pp. 67–91). London: Routledge.

PWC (PricewaterhouseCoopers). (2006). *The changing face of rail.* Canberra: Australasian Railway Association.

Ward, B. (2012). *The end of strategic planning and what that means for you.* Edmonton: Affinity Consulting and Training Site. http://www.affinitymc.com/end-strategic-planning/. Accessed 19 Nov 2013.

Part I
Sustainability, Growth and Diversity

Chapter 2
Global Shifts in Migration Policy and Their Implications for Skills Formation, Nations, Communities and Corporations

Peter Kell

Abstract This chapter provides an overview of policy and trends that have shaped the nature and character of migration and more particularly skilled migration and its place in the dynamics of global mobility. I explore some of the theoretical underpinnings of the framing of skilled migration as well as some of the counter tendencies that have produced a backlash against the movement of foreign workers globally. I use some international case studies to illustrate the complexities of the role of the state in policy formation relating to skilled migration. I identify a contradiction between the state's role in mediating and brokering an influx of migrants and skilled workers and its role in sustaining a discourse of national unity. I also discuss the implications for corporations the new paradigm of skilled migration and its associated politics. I conclude with advice to corporations on how to negotiate a global market, suggesting that an informed and holistic approach to interpreting globalisation and settlement is essential in sourcing global talent.

The New Paradigm for Migration

Global mobility and migration is an ever-present feature of contemporary society and amongst the most contentious policy issues for the state to resolve. The International Organization for Migration has stated that there were 214 million migrants globally and predicts that this number will rise to 405 million in 2050 (Kukacs 2011).

An important feature of this global mobility is the large number of workers relocating either permanently or on a temporary basis to undertake employment in another country. Many developed nations such as Australia are aggressively competing for a share of this large pool of workers and have established new visas

P. Kell (✉)
School of Education, Charles Darwin University, Darwin, NT, Australia
e-mail: Peter.Kell@cdu.edu.au

T. Short and R. Harris (eds.), *Workforce Development: Strategies and Practices*,
DOI 10.1007/978-981-287-068-1_2, © Springer Science+Business Media Singapore 2014

and regulations for the recruitment of migrant workers in both the permanent migration category and temporary worker visa categories. Of the 190,000 permanent migration places available in 2013 a total of 129,250 places were assigned for migrant workers (Philips and Spinks 2012, p. 2).

According to Castles (2000) in the second half of the twentieth century international migration emerged as one of the main factors in the social transformation and development of all regions in the world. This trend towards global mobility is set to continue as a characteristic of the continued globalisation of the world economy, which promotes the seamless movement of capital, goods, services and people. This chapter documents some of the policy developments and the tensions and dilemmas that emerge from this in terms of the integrity of the nation-state project.

Migration is interpreted as the result of economic and social development and migration can contribute to further development and improved economic and social conditions. Yet Castles (2000) argued it can also result in inequality and stagnation and this is often dependent on the type of migration, its social and economic context, the stakeholders and the policy framework in which migration is undertaken. Castles identified several different forms of migration, which he explored in his book. They included:

- temporary labour migration, which involves men and women in limited employment for a contractual period. The period may vary from months to years;
- highly skilled business migration involving migrants with qualifications as professionals and managers with technical skills who are able to work with global corporations. Many of these workers enter countries under skilled or business 'programs'.

These two categories represent a 'new paradigm' of migration, which departs from earlier migration programs that were based on building population through mass settlement as a means of economic and national development. The 'new paradigm' of migration emphasises the economic need of national economies within the paradigm of globalisation (Armitage 2012). In this context there is also a reversal from what is termed the 'supply' side where migration policy is framed around the characteristics and needs of migrants to one where immigration policy is reframed around the needs of the economy and those skills identified as needed by governments and industry to sustain economic growth. Phillips and Spinks summed up this shift in policy orientation to skilled migration:

> The resulting changes to the skilled migration stream were designed to shift the balance of the program away from independent skilled migrants, without prearranged employment in Australia, towards sponsored skilled migrants with employment arranged prior to their arrival. (2012, p. 4)

This new paradigm has also seen a shift in migration policy to recruitment of short-term and temporary migration to fill identified shortages. Countries that have been 'classical' destinations for migration like Australia, the United States and Canada are shifting to adopt so-called German 'guest-worker' programs where people reside for a limited period of time, performing some form of employment as a condition of entry. This change from the old paradigm is evident in Australia where skilled migrant arrivals in 2007–2008 totalled 110,570 people, surpassing the 108,500 permanent arrivals (Armitage 2012). This is also evident in the shift away from family reunions as a category for entry in Australia with these entries plunging from 50 % in 1996–1997 to 32 % in 2012–2013 (Phillips and Spinks 2012, p. 3).

The contemporary role of government and the state since the 1980s has shifted towards a reliance on the unfettered power of market forces and a trend towards deregulation. Immigration policy within the new paradigm represents a reversal of this trend as governments have been simultaneously intervening to promote and facilitate migration and also erecting barriers and restrictions to migration. Governments have been enlisted to produce policies and programs that compensate for market failures in the supply and demand of labour and have been utilised by capital and industry to mediate the cyclic tendencies of scarcity and surplus that typifies the global labour markets of contemporary global capitalism. The state is also forced to adopt contradictory roles, which include facilitating, promoting and managing the mobility of labour to ensure that there is not a critical shortage of labour. The reproduction of a workforce that is capable of enabling nations to compete effectively in a global economy is now part of the political legitimacy around claims by governments about capable economic management. The metaphors of competition also frame the role of the state in positioning nations in a favourable position in what the OECD terms 'a looming war for skills' (Armitage 2012, p. 1).

Metaphors about national survival dominate the discourse of skilled migration. Governments are continuously under pressure, particularly from peak industry groups, to provide incentives for potential entrants and to provide the systems that would enable business to access imported labour under favourable conditions.

At the same time as the state is under pressure to source foreign workers, the state is also seen as having a role in preserving the social and cultural integrity of the nation-state in the face of an influx of foreign workers. The dilemmas around sustaining and affirming national unity and identity are key policy issues in contemporary social policy and politics and a global flashpoint in domestic politics. As mobility increases there has been a growth of anti-immigration sentiment within formal political institutions and also a growth of ultra-nationalist parties on the fringes of these institutions that are hostile to foreigners. This includes the emergence of ultra-nationalist parties such as the British Nationalist Party, the National Front in France and Finnish First in Finland, amongst others, who stridently promote reliance on a 'home-grown' workforce and urge the repatriation of foreign workers. There is a view promoted by many anti-immigration advocates, which is shared by some blue-collar workers in developing nations, that skilled migrants will take away jobs from local workers and undermine their wages and employment conditions. These right-wing groups have skilfully exploited these anxieties and created the impression that these sentiments are a concern of a majority of the population, even though as political organisations they hold minority positions. Their institutional power has been amplified beyond their numbers as they have held the balance of power in some parliaments.

Even the most benign and affluent nations that historically welcomed foreign labour like Singapore and Australia have experienced this backlash against migration. This has led to increasingly restrictive policies and qualifications on the entry of foreign workers and their dependents to placate the backlash. A consequence of this has been a conflation of categories of foreign entrants such as international students, temporary workers, skilled migrants and refugees. Recently skilled migrants and temporary workers have been confused with asylum seekers and those who also have legal claims as they have been placed in the same risk profiles as illegal immigrants and visa over-stayers. In some countries such as the UK this has led to restrictive policy settings where international students are included in the total quantum for all forms of migration and this has displaced legitimate skilled migrants from the limited positions available.

The pressures on skilled migration are a consequence of several interrelated factors. These include a growing global demographic pattern of a falling birth rate and an increasing ageing of the populations of the developed world. At the same time there is a growing population in the developing nations of the world. In the absence of employment opportunities migration becomes one of the few options for economic and social advancement. This is evident in the fact that all OECD members saw a drop in their population of young people between 1960 and 2010. This trend is evident in South Korea (−26.1 %), Poland (−19.1 %), Canada (−17.24 %) and Japan (−17.2 %) and among the G21 countries like China who recorded a decline of 20.2 %. This shrinkage is in sharp contrast to Africa where 60 % of the population are estimated to be under the age of 25 and this is projected to increase to 75 % in 2015 (OECD 2012, p. 19).

Other factors that create the conditions for skills shortages include underinvestment in domestic training and vocational education in any sector experiencing growth. Countries such as Australia have experienced a situation where the overall number of students in training has increased and private expenditure in training has also increased but there are also gaps in aligning the graduates of the training system to unfilled vacancies and shortages. In short people are not training for jobs where there are vacancies and shortages. Other factors include reluctance on the part of the domestic labour force to undertake jobs that are considered low status, dangerous or low skilled and have poor pay. These factors also include remoteness and lack of incentives to undertake employment in rural and remote settings even though policies aim to promote regional employment. Restrictive policies by professional associations and professional registering authorities, and industrial relations structures that marginalise foreign entrants have all contributed to skills shortages and restrictions on the mobility of foreign workers. Overall the reasons for skills shortages are complex, multifaceted and involve interrelated factors. In Australia's case skills shortages can be partly attributed to restrictions on the mobility of workers from the Asia-Pacific region where there is a large potential workforce in a range of skilled and unskilled occupations. A key question for future Australian governments is why Australia is not capitalising on its proximity to the fastest growing region to obtain a workforce that can enhance connections with the region.

The OECD has outlined several policy lessons for skills development that incorporate encouragements for people to learn throughout their lives to acquire the skills needed for fulfilling lives but also meeting the demands of the economy. These factors are diverse and provide the environment where people are able to acquire and utilise skills in a productive way through their lives. The policy lessons include gathering information about the changing skills demands to guide action and planning and then engaging social partners in learning and skills development, as well as designing and delivering curricula and education programs to enable the development of both 'soft' and 'hard' skills. The OECD emphasises the importance of ensuring there are high quality training programs that promote access and equity by ensuring access to, and success in, quality education for all. This includes the need for governments to ensure that costs are shared, that the tax system does not discourage investment in learning and skills formation, and that the private sector is encouraged to invest in education and training (OECD 2012, p. 18). One other lesson is the need to maintain a long-term perspective that overcomes the challenges of cyclic economic conditions.

These internal policy lessons are juxtaposed with the need to foster international mobility of skilled people to fill gaps as they arise. The OECD identifies a need to facilitate the entry of skilled migrants and a need for efficient ways to enable entry and implement border control and workplace enforcement. Another approach is to design policies that encourage international students to remain after their studies. The advantage is they have qualifications that can be easily evaluated and they are familiar with the host country and its job market. Receiving countries should also make it easier for skilled migrants to return to their country of origin as a recognition of the need to build capacity in sending countries. According to the OECD, this can be done through assistance to municipalities to provide housing to returning migrants and also tax concessions particularly for higher level skilled migrants (OECD 2012, p. 19).

Part of the new environment for skilled migration is also the promotion of cross-border skills policies where developed nations are encouraged to invest in skills abroad and also in higher education with the objective of sourcing a wider talent pool in other countries. This has the advantage of providing well-trained workers for host countries and international companies based in other countries as well as reducing emigration (OECD 2012, p. 19). There is a now a series of complex policy factors that influence the nature and character of immigration and more particularly skilled migration.

Analysing the factors that contribute to immigration is important in understanding how skilled migration might be optimised and also an explanation for some of the historic patterns that typify global mobility. Migration systems theory is an important theoretical tool to explain some of the influences that contribute to exchanges of population between two or more nations. Cultural ties influence decisions about migration destinations and these have also been stimulated by historic colonial legacies. Castles (2000) cited the examples of Caribbean migration, where residents of Jamaica have departed to Britain, residents of Martinique have departed to France, and those from Surinam go to the Netherlands. These initial movements have established what

Stahl (1993, cited in Castles 2000) called 'beaten pathways' where established networks with facilitators and institutional ensembles support migrants through these pathways (Jessop 1990). These links persist over several generations and ensure that these migratory chains are perpetuated in various forms. Migration systems theory provides some explanation for the narrow spectrum for sourcing skilled migration that typifies inbound migration in many countries and is also an explanation of the difficulties in expanding skilled migration recruitment in what are often seen as 'non-traditional sources'. In the case of Australia the dependence on English-speaking European sources such as the UK and Ireland in high-skilled professions has seen a diminished pool of applicants but there are difficulties in sourcing from alternative locations owing to an absence of connections and institutional ensembles that might create migration pathways with non-traditional sources in Latin America, China and Africa. The institutional ensembles that facilitate the recognition of qualifications from some countries such as the UK and Ireland might not be favourable to recognising qualifications and experience from other non–English speaking countries such as China and this acts as a brake on expanding the scope of recruitment.

The benefits of migration are generally assumed to flow to the destination where there is seen to be a transfer of wealth. The dominant interpretation is that skilled migration siphons off skilled labour and capable people from poorer countries. This view of migration has been incorporated in what has been termed the 'brain drain' effect in removing younger and more energetic people and reducing pressure for social change in poorer countries. Theories of development in the post-war era have assumed that temporary visitors and workers such as students returning to less developed countries would benefit those countries by contributing personal wealth and investment capacity when they return. However these assumptions are challenged by the globalisation of work and finance that allows the repatriation of funds to the developing world. The volume of overseas remittances from migrant workers has grown from $US 2 billion in 1970 to $70 billion by 1985. The World Bank (2013) has estimated that remittances to developing countries reached $372 billion in 2011.

The assumption that temporary migrants and students will benefit their homelands on return fails to recognise the lack of sophisticated infrastructure and the failure of industrialisation in many parts of the developing world. In contrast to a short-term view of immigration as providing a temporary front-end stimulus to the development of a more advanced economy, some nations such as the Philippines have recognised the futility of trying to provide domestic jobs. This means that some nations that are unable to develop an industrial infrastructure become a net exporter of workers to the developed world. Developing nations such as Bangladesh, the Philippines and several Pacific Island nations have configured their activities in education, skills formation and languages towards supplying the developed world with workers at various levels in the occupational spectrum. This new view of mobility provides a benefit to the sending country as workers repatriate funds to their families and this is now recognised as a major source of foreign exchange and investment funds for economic development. In the Philippines the Overseas Workers Welfare Administration (OWWA) provides a range of services to assist workers to go overseas.

However the abuse and exploitation of temporary workers is an ever-present theme in contemporary migration. An estimated 2.5 million people are illegally trafficked with an estimated 1.4 million in the Asia-Pacific, which comprises 56 % of global trafficking. Trafficking is a global phenomenon involving people from 127 countries going into 137 destinations. It is estimated that 95 % of trafficked workers experience physical or sexual abuse and that 43 % of women and girls experience some form of sexual abuse (ILO 2007). Trafficking and exploitation are a spectre over legitimate programs sponsored by governments. Many legitimate recruitment schemes are subject to abuse by exploitative employers as well as organised crime.

Most recently in Australia the operations of the 457 temporary business visa subclass have been in the spotlight, attracting the criticism of the Australian union movement as well as former Australian Prime Minister Julia Gillard. This visa offers employers the opportunity to recruit foreign workers on a temporary basis when local labour is not available. This visa has attracted criticism that holders are exploited and not offered assistance with their employment rights. Trade unions have also criticised this visa, expressing concerns that employers have used it to undercut local wages and undermine working conditions (Phillips and Spinks 2012, pp. 10–11). In response to these criticisms the Australian government has reviewed this visa category and introduced new guidelines on the required level of English proficiency and the integration of market-based wage requirements to ensure award wages are not undermined. Many of the new measures are designed to protect the interests of local workers, with employers and applicants being required to undertake a skills assessment to prevent fraud. Employers who intend to use the 457 visa also have to make undertakings about local training requirements and a commitment to source local labour. Despite these reforms concerns about 457 visas persist even though Australian businesses must be accredited to use this visa. The controversies here highlight the tensions and risks that skilled migration creates for workers, business and government because these types of schemes, regardless of their viability and function, have been subject to the general backlash against immigration in contemporary times.

Consequent harsh and uncompromising restrictions and regulation of skilled migrants has also created a climate of instability and considerable uncertainty for potential skilled migrants and sponsoring employers. It is unlikely that entry requirements will be relaxed in this political climate as the discourse about immigration goes to the heart of the discussions about preserving jobs for 'locals', and maintaining a sense of national unity and is a hot political issue.

The next section illustrates some of the contemporary debates associated with skilled migration and global mobility. The key feature of these international case studies is that political tensions are emerging from the global financial crisis as local economies are characterised by unemployment and job shrinkage and there is a simultaneous need for an inflow of workers aligned to the needs of the global economy. At the same time there is a domestic backlash politics where questions of entitlement, national unity and identity confront global mobility.

Confronting Global Mobility with Local Politics:
The Case of Singapore

The tensions around skilled migration are well illustrated in the case of Singapore where until the global financial crisis skilled migrants were encouraged. As a developed and rich nation emerging from the postwar Asian economic miracle, Singapore has experienced a dropping birth-rate and has identified a need for a pipeline of migrant and temporary workers to meet critical labour shortages.

Population and immigration are now seen as the most volatile political issues in Singapore in the wake of the global financial crisis. The population of Singapore is predicted to grow from 5 million to 6 million in 2020 and to 6.5 million by 2030. Singaporeans are having fewer children and the rate of population increase from births is moderate (Banyan 2013). Already almost half of Singapore's population is born overseas and the predicted population growth is modest.

The Singapore government has adopted a strategy of innovation, entrepreneurial endeavour and migration to position itself within a global market framework. In education the Singapore government positioned itself under the notion of the 'global schoolhouse' where international higher education providers, international students and research will be combined to provide the impetus for innovation and economic growth (Kell and Kell 2013; Kell and Vogl 2012). Citizenship with short periods of qualification was used as an incentive to attract and retain migrant workers and their skills in industries such as finance, banking and international trade, which are vital for Singapore's future economic survival.

As a consequence of the tight economic conditions these relatively benevolent and generous entry requirements have been changed. The Singapore government has been under pressure from a growing tide of opposition to immigration, which coincides with shrinking support for the government. The government has tightened up entry requirements for migrant workers and expressed sympathy for Singaporeans who perceive that they are under threat from immigrants. The response from the Singapore government has been a concern to preserve the interests of 'core' Singaporeans, risking the consensus around multiculturalism and the importance of global connections for Singapore (Banyan 2013).

In many respects Singapore reflects a classic policy response to skilled migration where the erosion of political support for skilled migration has resulted in a reversal of policies designed to promote mobility. The Singapore government was formerly committed to cosmopolitan notions of nationalism but has been forced to revert to narrow notions of nationalism in order to placate perceptions that migrant workers are a threat to the interests of Singaporeans. Although the opposition have less than 10 % of seats in parliament, the potential for migration to trigger a political problem for the government indicates that, even in the most benign settings, recruiting for a global workforce is a sensitive political issue (Banyan 2013).

Border Protection Versus Free Enterprise: The Case of the United States of America

Immigration is also a key political issue in the United States and featured as a major source of differentiation between the Republicans and Democrats in the 2012 presidential election. Barack Obama was able to capitalise on this issue and appeal to many diverse groups, including Hispanic voting organisations and other groups, in forging a coalition for reform of US immigration laws. The United States, like Australia, has been a historic destination for migrants but the emergence of right-wing patriot and conservative groups linked to the extremist Tea Party have been a powerful force in calls to restrict immigration. While some conservative forces oppose immigration, others linked to industries such as agriculture in the southern states that share borders with Mexico are pressing for change to liberalise entry of foreign workers. These industries have been dependent on legal, as well as illegal, workers to provide a workforce in these labour-intensive industries. While these industries are seeking unskilled labour, other industries such as information technology are also seeking skilled workers. These proposals for change to immigration confront significant opposition to immigration that includes formidable barriers such as the security that protects the southern borders of the United States. This includes official border patrols mounted by the US immigration service supplemented by right-wing vigilante groups, promoted as patriotic organisations, who also patrol the border informally. These organisations stridently promote the view that immigration is 'out of control' and bad for the economy.

US business proposes that an in-flow of some 200,000 workers annually will be required to meet the country's labour and production needs. In response to this the US is attempting to regulate this illegal inflow and also provide protections for the workers, many of whom are long-term residents in the US but are unable to access many of the services that citizens and permanent residents are eligible for. Recent attempts to reform US immigration law have, like in Australia, sought to boost the number of available visas for skilled workers, particularly IT workers and students who have completed their studies in the US. In addition the visa regulations for seasonal agriculture workers are being re-written and this involves negotiations between the peak union body the American Federation of Labour Council of Industrial Organizations (AFL-CIO), the United Farm Workers Union (AFW) and peak industry bodies (Economist 2013).

Some of the criticisms are that illegal workers are 'underground', evading tax and the responsibilities of citizenship. The new legislation proposes the payment of outstanding taxes and passing other background checks and a compulsory civics test. This is meant to be the start of the journey towards full citizenship but many illegal workers find obtaining official and formal records of employment difficult and the bonds and charges required by government are too high for many unskilled and low-paid workers.

As the American economy has slowly recovered the pressure for reform has increased and the need for more flexible visa conditions has been urged as other countries such as those in Latin America compete for highly skilled workers. Many employer groups are arguing for increased visa options as well as opportunities to promote the benefits of temporary workers in the face of growing anti–foreign worker sentiments. In support of broader reforms, Steve Case, the founder of American Online and an advocate for entrepreneurial and business initiatives, points to the proportion of start-up companies founded by foreigners in Silicon Valley, which has dropped from 50 % 10 years ago to 42 % today, as evidence of the impact on business of restrictions on skilled migrants. Rather than siphoning off activity, and creating competition for local jobs, Case and others argue that many high-skilled temporary workers stimulate the economy through creating new businesses. The need for skilled workers in economic recovery is also evident in the need for the US to rebuild its eroded infrastructure including roads, bridges, ports, railways and utilities. The American Society of Civil Engineers has estimated that the US needs to invest in over $3.6 trillion of infrastructure and capital works. The scarcity of both capital and qualified labour continues to be an impediment to economic recovery in the US (Economist 2013).

The costs and delays of processing visas are identified as impediments for employers, yet the demand for the American business-sponsored H1BS visa exceeds the limited 65,000 visas that are available. In 2013 the applications for H1BS visas exceeded the allocated number in less than 5 days. At the same time as this debate rages in the US, Canada has announced a new business 'start-up visa' that costs $US 74,000 for foreigners to create new businesses in Canada (Economist 2013).

Reversing the Pathways of Global Migration: The Case of Latin America

These tensions in policy in some countries such as the US and Australia coincide with several global changes in mobility where countries that were previously the source of migrant workers are now destinations for workers. Latin America, traditionally a source of skilled workers, has seen spectacular economic growth in the last decade and is experiencing shortages of skilled workers. As many European and North American nations stagnate economically there are shifts in growth and opportunities in Latin America for potential migrants.

Even though there is a great frenzy over immigration from Mexico to the US, net migration has actually fallen to zero. The global movement is now from European nations such as Portugal and Spain to Latin American countries such as Brazil and Argentina. The net movement of capital from remittances is an indicator of this shift. For example remittances from Argentina to Spain total $1 billion, which is four times the movement of capital the other way (Schumpeter 2013).

Foreign corporations and global firms such as Volkswagen and L'Oreal are relocating production plants and service centres to generate a presence in Latin America. Brazil's growing economy has created over 12.5 million new jobs and recruitment companies are reporting that 71 % of Brazilian employers are experiencing difficulty in sourcing employees (Schumpeter 2013).

While Latin America is opening up to migrant workers, the opportunities for permanent settlement are limited by restrictions on property and citizenship. In contrast to countries like Australia and the United States, where a high level of the population was born overseas, Mexico has 1 % and Brazil has less than 0.3 % who were born overseas. At present these countries lack policy expertise around migration and have yet to respond effectively to the changing global balance after the global financial crisis (Schumpeter 2013).

The Clash Between Training, Migration and Local Jobs: The Case of Australia

In developed nations there is a collision between the need to maintain a sustainable and viable training infrastructure and a skilled migration program. When there are perceptions that this balance is unequally weighted this has the potential to trigger the political crises that are described in this chapter. I have previously described the political consensus developed at the turn of the twentieth century in Australia as:

> A consensus between Australian labour and capital that the establishment of the training system would remove the need to import cheap labour if the state paid for training. Using training as a protection for Australian workers was one of the foundations of the White Australia Policy and has remained intact in public policy even in the face of Australia's commendable record as a destination for migrants. But this training and migration nexus has been an uncomfortable consensus that has now shifted because of progressive cuts and underinvestment in the training sector. (Kell 2012)

The shift in the balance has changed as the state has underinvested in training and this has created a position where the training systems cannot meet the demand for skilled workers in industry. Shortages are compounded by other deficiencies in the training system where there is wastage of training effort on cheap low-level courses that give quick profits to providers and do little to meet skills shortages. This is also at the expense of general education programs that are important for giving students and workers pathways to higher-level qualifications.

At the same time high-level qualifications that are useful in a more complex post-industrial economy based on knowledge and high-tech manufacturing are in the minority. As I have mentioned,

> Too much of the training effort in the past few years have been directed to the 'jobs of the past' and those that are subject to technological change or economic and seasonal cycles such as retail, tourism, hospitality and low-income jobs. (Kell 2012)

Training providers, in both vocational education and training and higher education, have indulged in a race to the bottom of the skills profile, seeking to reduce costs of training and improve turnover. This means that high-cost courses in areas such as engineering have been assigned a 'niche' course status and this has meant that the supply of workers and professionals in these areas is dwindling. Policies based on a concept of a training market have operated in Australia without sufficient consideration for the labour market and long-term labour workforce planning.

As the training sector has failed to provide a supply of workers, the state has been forced to mediate over this market failure and facilitate skilled migration. In Australia this has major political implications as it triggers a backlash from those in the community who feel threatened by foreign workers who, even though there are shortages, might be seen to take their jobs away. The former Australian Prime Minister Julia Gillard drew attention to what has been called 'rorts' or abuses by employers of the short-term 457 visas, demonstrating this political sensitivity. Gillard singled out employers in the IT industry in particular for special criticism for being deficient in their use of these visas, saying that in one state 1 in 20 imported workers were workers in information technology. In a spectacular display of local politics, Gillard claimed that employers had used these visas and had not sought to recruit local Australian workers.

Matt Barrie, the Chief Executive Officer of Freelancer.com who is an advocate for the IT industry, defended the role of skilled worker visas, saying that: 'There wouldn't be an IT industry in Australia if it wasn't for the fact that we could draw from overseas labour. The bigger problem is the government has under-funded and ignored the technology industry and education in particular' (Moses 2013). Barrie and others accused the former Australian Prime Minister of blatant vote mongering and of attempting to placate the trade union movement. This dispute illustrates the bitter political tensions and dilemmas that have arisen as a consequence of the increased global mobility of workers. This situation has greater symbolic value in Australia owing to the former historic consensus involving a nexus between training and migration in Australian society, but is not unique as this is a global trend as a consequence of the new paradigm of immigration.

What Are the Implications for Human Resources Management in the Corporate Sector?

The environment that human resources operate within is now shaped by the global competition for professional workers across the spectrum of occupational profiles. A global outlook is now the new default position for all corporations and they need to reorient their outlook from a limited national and regional perspective to an expansive global perspective. In the earlier sections of this chapter I have identified the inability of national skills formation policies to fulfil labour requirements and the limitations that developed from short-term policy combined with the consequence of an ageing demographic. This is unlikely to change as governments, in the face of austerity, reduce the funding to skills training and the demographics of developed nations become entrenched. The rhetoric of the importance of skills training has not been supported by an expansion of the Australian training system and future growth is most likely to come from private expenditure and fees.

In adopting a global outlook management needs to look beyond traditional sources of labour and outside the 'beaten pathways' and tap into developments in growth regions across the globe. This means that traditional source nations such as the UK and Ireland might need to be complemented with programs that capture labour in places experiencing booms but patchy employment opportunities such as China, Brazil and other parts of Latin America, and others experiencing political uncertainty and turmoil such as in the Middle East. It is worth noting that graduate unemployment is very high in China even though the economy is experiencing growth.

Business and corporations are in a political struggle with opponents of migration and the growing ultranationalist movements in many host countries. The latter have dominated the policy debates virtually unchallenged and shaped the regulatory environment of skilled migration of escalating restrictions and disincentives. There is an important role for corporations to advocate for the recognition of global mobility as a policy norm. This means corporate representation and advocacy need to move away from divisive claims that the minimum wage in Australia is too high for Australia to be globally competitive and that lower wages are an attraction for skilled migrants. This is counterproductive to the broad interests of enterprise and business. It is also not a position that will generate a consensus between organised labour, government and the community to support skilled migration.

Corporations need to be advocates for the normalisation of global mobility and be prepared to advocate for skilled migration and migrants themselves. Business and those charged with promoting skilled migration also need to reconceptualise skilled migration away from narrow instrumental goals associated with work and build a more holistic vision of migration and settlement, like those captured in earlier migration programs. These themes may revisit some of the ambitions of the past that are associated with a desire for a better and more secure life, opportunities that promote a sense of affiliation with and most importantly a sense of creating a new way of life. These sentiments, often centred on emotions, have far more drawing power than instrumental aspects of careers and jobs.

To do this effectively corporations, and more particularly the human resources sections of these organisations, need to have specialist advice on skilled migration that appreciates the instrumental aspects of employment as well as the social and emotional aspects of resettlement. This advice also needs to have a high level of skills in interpreting and implementing national policies on skilled migration and the nature of the global skills market. Whether this will be an in-house or contracted service will depend on the importance assigned to this task. It will however need to adopt a holistic view of the needs of potential migrants to incorporate the needs of inbound professional workers that includes assistance, advice and support in areas such as housing, schooling, acculturation and financial assistance for set-up costs in a new homeland. This has become very important as skilled migration is becoming increasingly feminised. Customised and multifaceted services are needed that are not just front-ended for pre-departure and arrival but are also framed within a longer-term period of several years to ensure retention.

The most numerous, and in most cases underutilised, source of skilled migrants is international students. They are a prime source of potential skilled labour that has the advantage to corporations of having already self-funded the front-end costs of their arrival and experienced a new cultural context. Corporations need to develop closer relationships with international higher education providers in a strategic and systematic way to source this rich vein of potential talent in the overseas student population.

No corporation that claims a global status can ignore the importance of adopting strategies that actively source high-level labour across the globe and the need to configure its human resources section to capture and source talent in this context. Corporations need to work in partnership with government, unions and the community to overcome the tide of anti-migration hysteria and to avoid industrial relations and labour policies that spawn this backlash politics.

Conclusion

Global mobility will increase as the differentiated impact of globalisation exacerbates the divisions between rich and poor nations and fuels migration. This differentiation happens within and across societies in the developing world. In the developed world the combination of underinvestment in training and vocational education, an ageing demographic and sustained economic growth, even in tough times, provide pull factors that will continue to influence mobility. While globalisation promotes the transfer of services and goods including capital and creative resources across borders with minimum regulation, this does not apply to the mobility of workers. In developed western nations the state occupies a contradictory position of simultaneously promoting skilled migration and mobility to maintain a supply of workers to industry while also having to maintain the perception that an inflow of foreign workers will not compromise working and living standards of locals and the integrity and unity of the nation. The state has to mediate and broker skills formation on behalf of industry and also manage the cultural politics of national identity. This means that policy associated with skilled migration cannot be separated from other public policy issues in areas such as industry policy, regulation, citizenship, regional development and population. In preserving its legitimacy the state has used administrative and legislative functions to escalate the regulation and monitoring of the activities associated with migration and the influx of foreigners but also the politics of national identity and entitlement. How these contradictions and tensions are managed by the state in developed nations will shape the future of skilled migration.

References

Armitage, C. (2012, April 9). *Australia a world leader in skilled migration, Australian*. http://www.smh.com.au/opinion/political-news/australia-a-world-leader-in-skilled-migration-20120408-1wjm0.html. Accessed 23 Apr 2013.

Banyan. (2013, April 6). Grave concerns: Can Singapore both value the past and plan for the future? *Economist, 407*(8830), 32.

Castles, S. (2000). *International migration at the beginning of the twentieth century: Global trends and issues*. Oxford: Blackwell.

Economist. (2013, April 6). Immigration reform: Getting there. *Economist*, 37–38.

International Labour Organization. (2007). *Forced labour statistics factsheet*. http://www.ilo.org/sapfl/Informationresources/ILOPublications/WCMS_181953/lan--n/index.htm. Accessed 25 Apr 2013.

Jessop, B. (1990). *State theory: Putting the states in their place*. Cambridge: Polity.

Kell, P. (2012, December 10). Rich and poor: A training divide. *Campus Review*. http://www.campusreview.com.au/blog/2012/12/rich-poor-a-training-divide/. Accessed 12 Apr 2013.

Kell, M., & Kell, P. (2013). *Literacy and language in East Asia: Shifting meanings, values, approaches*. Dordrecht: Springer.

Kell, P., & Vogl, G. (2012). *International students in the Asia Pacific: Mobility, risk and opportunity*. Dordrecht: Springer.

Kukacs, K. (2011, November 28). *The latest developments in skilled migration policy*. Paper presented at the Australian Industry Groups National Personnel and Industrial Relations conference, Canberra.

Moses, A. (2013, March 14). Gillard accused of desperate 'vote mongering'. *Sydney Morning Herald*. http://www.smh.com.au/it-pro/government-it/gillard-accused-of-desperate-votemongering-20130314-2g2pa.html. Accessed 13 May 2013.

OECD. (2012). *Better skills, better jobs, better lives: A strategic approach to skills policies*. OECD Publishing. doi:10.1787/9789264177338-en. Accessed 28 May 2013.

Phillips, J., & Spinks, H. (2012). *Skilled migration: Temporary and permanent flows to Australia*. Canberra: Parliament of Australia.

Schumpeter. (2013, April 6). The new world: Long the exporter of talent, Latin America is now importing it. *Economist*, 68.

World Bank. (2013). *Topics in development*. http://www.worldbank.org/WBSITE/EXTERNAL/TOPICS/0,contentMDK:21924020~pagePK:5105988~piPK:360975~theSitePK:214971,00.html. Accessed 25 Apr 2013.

Chapter 3
What Do Young Australian Engineers Want? Strategies to Attract This Talent to Less Glamorous Industries

Michelle Wallace, Neroli Sheldon, Roslyn Cameron, and Ian Lings

Abstract Chapters in Book 1 of this two-volume set explored literature pertaining to the shortage of engineers in Australia, the ageing engineering workforce, issues of skilled migration, and career development and pathways. The companion chapter to this one in Book 1 explored attraction and image issues of certain industries that required a pipeline of engineers. This chapter will reflect on our research with final-year engineering students in Australian universities and TAFE colleges regarding their career aspirations, industries and/or organisations that they identify as attractive employers, and their perceptions of a low-profile industry, namely the Australian rail industry. This chapter will also discuss specific, evidence-based strategies and activities to enhance the image and attraction of low-profile industries.

Introduction

Concern has been expressed that Australian universities are not graduating sufficient engineers to meet growing demands. From the mid-1990s to 2004 there was a decline in the number of domestic engineering students in Australia (Birrell et al. 2005). Since 2005 there has been a turnaround in the number of students undertaking engineering tertiary education. Between 2001 and 2008 domestic enrolments

M. Wallace (✉) • N. Sheldon
Southern Cross University Business School, Gold Coast, QLD, Australia
e-mail: michelle.wallace@scu.edu.au; neroli.sheldon@scu.edu.au

R. Cameron
School of Management, Curtin Business School, Curtin University, Bentley, WA, Australia
e-mail: r.cameron@cqu.edu.au

I. Lings
QUT Business School, Queensland University of Technology in Brisbane,
Brisbane, QLD, Australia
e-mail: ian.lings@qut.edu.au

T. Short and R. Harris (eds.), *Workforce Development: Strategies and Practices*,
DOI 10.1007/978-981-287-068-1_3, © Springer Science+Business Media Singapore 2014

increased by 9.2 % and international enrolments by 90.4 % (Engineers Australia 2010). For several years Engineers Australia have been warning that this slight increase only makes up for the previous decline in numbers and does not supply a large enough pipeline for Australia's infrastructure needs (Engineers Australia 2010; Kaspura 2012). In addition, there has been a decline in the number of women undertaking university engineering courses; the numbers peaked in 2000–2001 and have since fallen to below 15 % (13.5 % of domestic students), yet women make up 54.7 % of all university students (King 2008; Mills et al. 2007, 2011).

Against the backdrop of rail expansion in Australia, this relatively flat rate of graduating engineers has increased competition for engineering skills. Many enterprises and industries vie for the skills of these engineering graduates and some, such as the rail industry, are concerned that their image prevents them attracting or retaining the best talent. There is a perception that 'glamour' industries such as mining attract the best and brightest of our engineering graduates.

A Brief Look at Engineers' Preferences

LinkedIn's In Demand Employer rankings for 2013 (HC Online 2013) offer an interesting list of the top ten employers preferred by the Australian workforce. These are:

- Rio Tinto – mining, iron ore, minerals
- Leighton Contractors – earthworks, road, mining
- Google – distribution systems, Python, Google awards
- John Holland – rail, earthworks, project control
- Origin Energy – gas, upstream, oil/gas
- Microsoft – cloud computing, partner management, enterprise software
- Worley Parsons – FEED, EPC, refinery
- NBN Co Ltd – stakeholder management, project delivery, transmission
- Qantas – airlines, aviation, airports
- Accenture – business transformation, business process design, management consulting.

It is interesting to note that mining, construction, utilities, transportation, information systems and business processes figure prominently in the Australian list. Arguably, nine out of the ten Australian-based organisations employ engineers across a range of industries. (The global list has more companies involved in technology such as Apple and Amazon, and packaged consumer goods such as Unilever, Proctor and Gamble, and PepsiCo.)

Clearly, these particular Australian-based companies have an industry image that is highly attractive to potential employees. As Wallace et al. (2014) showed, the elements of an employer's or industry's image relate to benefits that potential employees look for. These are:

- **Interest benefits.** Interest value is the extent to which the employer provides an exciting work environment, novel work practices and makes use of its employees' creativity to produce high-quality, innovative products and services.

- **Social benefits.** Social value is based on perceptions that an employer provides a working environment that is fun, happy, and provides good collegial relationships and a team atmosphere.
- **Economic benefits.** Economic value is the extent to which recruits think that an employer provides above-average salaries, compensation packages, job security and promotional opportunities.
- **Development benefits.** Development value is based on potential recruits' perceptions that an employer provides recognition, self-worth and confidence, career-enhancing experiences and a springboard to future employment.
- **Application benefits.** Application value is based on a recruit's perception that the employer provides opportunities for employees to apply what they have learned and to teach others in an environment that is both customer oriented and humanitarian.
- **Travel benefits.** Travel benefits relate to the opportunities that the employer offers to travel for work.
- **Culture benefits.** Culture benefits accrue from a work environment that includes an open and supportive management structure.
- **Prestige benefits.** Prestige benefits arise from wider perceptions that working for the employer is highly regarded.
- (Adapted from Ambler and Barrow 1996; Lievens and Highhouse 2003; Slaughter et al. 2004; Berton et al. 2005; Lievens et al. 2005, 2007.)

What factors attract graduating engineers to work for a particular employer or industry? Our research was specifically aimed at finding out what young engineers value in an employment relationship and what they perceive that a less 'glamorous' industry, in this case rail, offers or does not offer them in terms of employment benefits. While the rail industry was the case focus in this research, our findings can be extrapolated to other industries with low brand profiles.

Our Research Methods

We developed a mixed methods research design. In 2009–2010 we undertook interviews with engineering academics, Technical and Further Education (TAFE) teachers, careers advisors, commercial recruitment consultants and rail industry staff across Australia. At this time we also ran focus groups with university and TAFE engineering students, current rail engineering graduates and rail apprentices.

We then developed a survey instrument to measure dimensions of employer image based on the perceived employer benefits outlined above. These questions appeared first in the survey to measure how important they were overall to potential employees. We then repeated the questions with a specific reference to rail as the employer that respondents needed to consider. This survey could be replicated for other industries/organisations by substituting the name of the industry or organisation.

In addition, we included certain items to compare the perceptions of rail relative to competitors. The benchmark competitors chosen were private construction and engineering consultancies, public utilities (gas/water/electricity), local or state government (e.g. councils), mining (oil/gas/coal) and the defence forces as these had been identified by engineering students in the focus groups as attractive employing industries. In addition, we undertook a series of regression analyses on subsets of the data to see if different demographic segments of the market were attracted to different perceived benefits. We looked at gender and age.

Finally, we surveyed HR professionals from rail organisations. We included two sets of questions. The first measured HR professionals' views of which benefits they consider to be the most important to engineering graduates. The second set asked HR professionals to benchmark rail as an employer against the five competing industries mentioned above.

Our Findings

pre covid

In the focus groups the employment characteristic preferences that graduating university and TAFE engineers mentioned most often were remuneration, continuing career development, security, diversity of experience and flexible work conditions. The importance of ongoing career development opportunities is supported in the literature (for example, Clarke 2013; De Vos and Dries 2013; Crawshaw and Brodbeck 2010). Almost all the TAFE students interviewed for this research expressed the desire to articulate from TAFE to university through a work-sponsored engineering degree. This strongly suggests that university pathways are an important consideration in the early stages of an engineer's career, which, in turn, has implications for employers competing to attract graduates.

The research highlighted the problem of low brand awareness for rail as an employer. Students in focus groups were largely unaware of the breadth of employment opportunities in rail enterprises. Most students had not had rail brought to their attention through their studies or been exposed to rail organisations through campus activities such as careers fairs or work placements. The literature (for example DEEWR 2008; Kargar and Qasemi 2008) confirms that work experience, in particular, is a very powerful means of transmitting useful career information to students.

We concluded that rail had a low or fuzzy brand profile with students; they simply did not know what rail stood for or what it might offer them as an employer. While low brand image may be seen as a liability in attracting talent, the message here is that rail or other low brand profile industries or organisations have good scope to raise that profile through targeted strategies.

We were surprised that university careers advisors appeared to have little or no knowledge of current opportunities within the rail sector. However, detailed knowledge of industry careers is not the focus of a careers counsellor and efforts to encourage careers advisors to take a greater interest in the opportunities in the rail sector will need to be initiated and maintained by the rail industry.

The knowledge of commercial recruitment consultants varied depending on their level of engagement with rail organisations. However many described a lack of willingness on the part of rail organisations to view the recruitment consultant

Table 3.1 Aspects considered important by students

Important benefit	Important factors of the benefit
Development	Gaining experience to support their career progression
	Working in an organisation that enhances their career flexibility in the future
	Recognition and appreciation for their work achievements
	Support from their organisation for their continued learning
Economic	An attractive employment package (superannuation, travel, allowances, etc.)
	A competitive salary
	Good promotion opportunities in the organisation
	Job security in the organisation
	Working in an industry that has a secure future
	Flexible working conditions
	Promotion based on merit rather than length of service
Interest	The opportunity to work on interesting projects
	The opportunity to design and innovate
	The opportunity to work on a variety of projects
	The opportunity to use cutting edge technology
Social	Having a good relationship with the team
	Supportive and encouraging team
	Having a good relationship with the management

Table 3.2 Aspects considered unimportant by students

Unimportant benefit	Unimportant aspects of the benefit
Application	Working for an employer that is environmentally responsible
	Working as part of a diverse workforce
	Working for an organisation that makes an important contribution to our nation
	Working for an organisation that is customer focused
Prestige	Working for an organisation that has high status
	Working in an industry where the workload is not too heavy
	Working for an organisation that wins big contracts
	Working in an industry that is easy to get into
	Working for a multinational organisation
	Working for an organisation that is positively reported in the media
Economic	Working for an organisation that has a streamlined, simple recruitment process
	The opportunity to rotate jobs within the organisation
Interest	The opportunity to work for a high profile organisation
Travel	The opportunity to work interstate
Culture	Working for an organisation that makes quick decisions
	Working in a high pressure environment

as a 'partner'. The above table lists specific factors within the eight benefits that students consider most important when considering a potential employer (Table 3.1).

It is also insightful to understand which factors of these benefits students considered to be unimportant. Those ranked as least important by students correspond primarily to application and prestige benefits. The above table lists these aspects (Table 3.2).

From the above survey results it appears most engineering students are seeking economic, development, social and interest benefits from their jobs. In particular the economic benefits that potential employees deem important include salary, promotion opportunities, job security and flexibility. The other benefits that employees consider important are working on a variety of interesting, innovative projects in which they will be using cutting edge technology and having a good relationship with their team and managers.

When respondents were asked to report their perceptions of how well a career in rail would provide these benefits, it became apparent that most respondents did not have a clear view of whether a career in rail would or could offer the benefits that they deemed most important. However, when provided with rail careers brochures students reflected a high level of interest. This led us to conclude that rail has a weak brand image as an employer.

Although there was a low sample size of women in the survey, it appears that women were seeking different employment benefits to men. Women appeared to consider prestige, culture and social benefits when evaluating the attractiveness of an employer, and men considered economic and interest benefits, and to a lesser extent the opportunity to travel. There was also a significant difference between younger and older respondents. Younger respondents appeared to consider interest benefits the dominant factor in evaluating the attractiveness of rail as an employer, whereas older respondents (22 years and over) appeared to value economic and prestige benefits, and the opportunity to travel. It appears that jobs in the rail industry are generally thought to be less attractive than those in mining, consultancies and defence force jobs and generally comparable with government jobs. It also appears that a career in rail is seen as providing benefits that potential recruits do not consider important and not providing the benefits that they consider to be important.

Survey results for the HR professionals can be compared to students' results. The following bar chart shows the opinion of rail HR professionals and students' views of what is important in terms of the following job characteristic preferences: developmental benefits, social benefits, interest benefits, economic benefits and application benefits (Fig. 3.1).

These results suggest that HR professionals and engineering students are fairly well in agreement about what is important in engineering jobs. However, HR professionals overemphasise the importance of development benefits and underemphasise the importance of social benefits compared to engineering students. Rail HR professionals also have a different view of how rail compares to other industries than do engineering students. They vastly underestimate students' perceptions of the status of working for consultancies and overestimate students' perceptions of the status of working in mining. These may have an impact on how careers in rail are positioned in the minds of potential recruits or give rise to communications that do not position rail against its competitors in a favourable light. The message is that HR professionals may need to tune in more comprehensively to the needs and perceptions of younger members of the workforce.

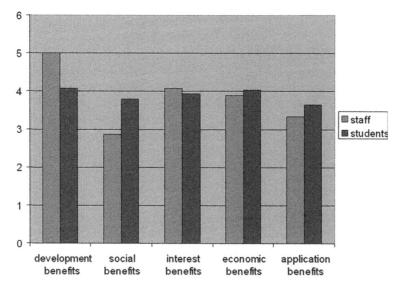

Fig. 3.1 Importance of job characteristic preferences

In summary:

- Rail was identified to have a low brand profile with potential recruits; however, there is great potential to raise that brand profile.
- Potential recruits value quite specific career benefits and industries/organisations need to craft their brand message (and organisational cultures) towards these values.
- There is a great deal that rail or other low brand profile industries/organisations can do to raise student awareness of careers in their industry/organisation.
- There are segments within the potential labour market (e.g. mature age, skilled migrants) and attraction messages can be tailored to these groups.

The issues raised in this paper and the lessons learned from this research are eminently applicable to other industries with low brand profiles wishing to attract and retain talent. The following strategies are evidence-based in that they come from our reading of the literature and our research findings. These strategies are applicable to a wide range of industries and organisations.

Strategies for Attracting Engineers to Lower Profile Industries/Enterprises

The engineering pipeline starts in the school education system well before graduates start to consider career, organisation and industry choice. Therefore, the first strategies listed suggest ways in which low brand industries can proactively reach out to school students and start to build their brand image at an early age.

Building Relationships with Parents and Peers

The influence of parents and peers on a young person's career choices needs to be more strategically managed by those organisations with lower brand image. By presenting at school/parent forums, organisations can influence pre-engineering high school students. Online resources targeting primary and high school students such as the Engineers Australia's EngQuest program are available and may be good sources of information for parents and peers. While Engineers Australia already has some resources in this vein, low profile firms that need to attract engineers could make much better use of online materials.

Working with Schools

Industries with an interest in encouraging young people to study engineering can work with primary and high school teachers to deliver STEM (science, technology, engineering and mathematics) subjects in a direct, fun, informative and inclusive manner. This will better ensure that students including young women develop the skills, interest and motivation to consider engineering as a career. Organisations need to actively engage with schools to 'normalise' engineering as a career choice for young women and promote their industry/organisation through activities such as:

- school excursions to meet with engineers and see them at work
- visits by engineers, including practising female engineers, to classrooms
- working with groups such as Boy Scouts and Girl Guides
- providing classroom materials and case studies involving the work of engineering
- sponsoring STEM prizes
- sponsoring professional development for teachers in STEM.

Participating in Tertiary Education Activities

Low brand industries/organisations need to view universities as a significant source of talent, and therefore increase engagement and financial support to them. They should drive activities on campuses such as careers days, engineering competitions, work experience placements and in-class and online presentations that are engaging and demonstrate that their industry/organisation offers what the younger workforce requires in a job. Their engineering pathways need to be advertised widely and understood by academics. Industries/organisations need to be proactive and make every effort to:

- use case studies and course content
- raise their profile through sponsorship of prizes, scholarships, equipment and so on
- participate in co-teaching opportunities
- promote graduate careers
- organise internships.

Working with Careers Advisors

Careers advisors at secondary and tertiary institutions are ideally placed to promote engineering careers. The rail industry needs to initiate and maintain a relationship with careers counsellors, sharing information and participating at fairs and events organised by career advisors. A further strategy would be to develop an engineering careers resource for counsellors, including an interactive online one for students.

Improving Relationships with Professional Recruitment Consultants

Organisations can improve relationships with recruitment agencies by taking a more strategic approach to the role of professional recruiters in building an industry or organisational brand. Other suggestions include:

- providing comprehensive information that can be given to potential employees
- participating in joint presentations
- providing opportunities for recruiters to understand your industry/organisation.

Ensuring Recruitment Processes Make It Easy for People to Apply for Your Jobs

In a nutshell, your organisation needs to ensure the recruitment process is professional and user-friendly. This may be a potential employee's first interaction with the organisation. Other suggestions include creative workforce planning strategies such as:

- up-skilling entry-level engineering graduates (vocational to professional)
- relaxing the rules for employing skilled migrants and foreign students
- seeking recruits from industries that are in decline, for example, manufacturing
- recruiting early retirees from the Australian Defence Force and other organisations.

Websites and Social Networking

Websites and social media can be managed to attract engineers. Make sure they are fun and interactive, and appeal to high school students who have an interest in the STEM subjects and engineering students. Other strategies include:

- providing an online training section for teachers and counsellors
- promoting career paths through a website. See Rail Career Pathways (www.railcareerpathways.net.au), which provides employees, job seekers, students and parents, school career advisors, rail HR personnel and others with career path information for jobs in engineering and other rail careers

Encouraging Young Women to Your Industry/Organisation

Strategies organisations can adopt to create an environment attractive to female engineers include:

- career management policies that are more responsive to gender issues
- a workplace culture that explicitly supports work–life balance and workplace flexibility
- increasing the visibility of female engineers as role models and leaders
- promoting gender-neutral networking
- parity in remuneration and making career development opportunities more explicit
- better harnessing of existing qualified female migrants
- flexible work arrangements, including part-time work.

Publicity and Advertising

Improved media and public relations are critical to countering negative media and rail commuter experiences which foster an unfavourable image of rail careers to potential employees including engineers. Targeted publicity and advertising should promote the industry as an absorbing and, sustainable career of choice. See Portfolio of Best Practice Attraction and Image Strategies (www.ara.net.au/best_practice/) for practical, best practice, branding and attraction strategies that can be adopted by the rail industry.

Other strategies include:

- multiple employment value propositions that take into account the varied job characteristic preferences of different segments of the labour market
- recruitment campaigns with materials that are realistic and match the employee brand
- advertising through multiple media including recruitment advertisements, websites, educational materials and word-of-mouth endorsements
- greater engagement with commercial recruitment consultants, educators and students to promote information on rail career opportunities
- publicity, such as the CEO being quoted in newspapers and news stories about the organisation
- advertisements to signal a recruitment campaign is imminent.

Conclusion

Our research revealed that engineering graduates should not be viewed as a homogenous group. There are both gender and age differences in the perceived benefits of working for a particular industry. We have offered a number of strategies that raise an industry or organisation's brand profile. However, these need to be targeted at particular segments of the potential labour market. In addition, a number of strategies need to be used together to achieve maximum impact.

At the time of writing this chapter, the economic outlook for Australia appears less rosy. Engineering graduates have clearly expressed that remuneration is one of the benefits they value. However, job security, development opportunities and diversity of experiences and flexible work conditions are also very important. Low-profile industries, as well as adopting the strategies outlined above, would be well served if they emphasised these benefits in the employment propositions they offer potential employees.

References

Ambler, T., & Barrow, S. (1996). The employer brand. *Journal of Brand Management, 4*(3), 185–206.

Berton, P., Ewing, M., & Hah, L. (2005). Captivating company: Dimensions of attractiveness in employer branding. *International Journal of Advertising, 24*(2), 151–172.

Birrell, B., Sheridan, J., & Rapson, V. (2005). Why no action on engineering training? *People and Place, 13*(4), 34–47.

Clarke, M. (2013). The organizational career: Not dead but in need of redefinition. *International Journal of Human Resource Management, 24*(4), 684–703.

Crawshaw, J., & Brodbeck, F. (2010). Justice and trust as antecedents of careerist orientation. *Personnel Review, 40*(1), 106–125.

De Vos, A., & Dries, N. (2013). Applying a talent management lens to career management: The role of human capital composition and continuity. *International Journal of Human Resource Management, 24*(9), 1816–1831.

Department of Education, Employment and Workplace Relations (DEEWR). (2008). *Views of engineering students: Report of a survey of final year university engineering students.* Canberra: Commonwealth of Australia.

Engineers Australia. (2010). *The engineering profession: A statistical overview 2010* (7th ed.). Barton: Engineers Australia.

HC Online. (2013). *Most in-demand Australian companies revealed.* http://www.hcmag.com/hr-news/most-indemand-australian-companies. Accessed 30 Oct 2013.

Kargar, J., & Qasemi, F. (2008, January/February). Recruiting young engineers. *IEEE Industry Applications Magazine, 14*, 50–55.

Kaspura, A. (2012). *The engineering profession: a statistical overview* (9th ed.). Barton: Engineers Australia. http://www.engineersaustralia.org.au/sites/default/files/shado/Representation/Stats/statistical_overview_2012.pdf. Accessed 20 Mar 2013.

King, R. (2008). *Addressing the supply and quality of engineering graduates for the new century.* Sydney: Garrick Institute.

Lievens, F., & Highhouse, S. (2003). The relation of industrial and symbolic attributions and a company's attractiveness as an employer. *Personal Psychology, 56*(1), 75–102.

Lievens, F., Van Hoye, G., & Schreurs, B. (2005). Examining the relationship between employer knowledge dimensions and organizational attractiveness: An application in a military context. *Journal of Occupational and Organizational Psychology, 78*, 553–573.

Lievens, F., Van Hoye, G., & Anseel, F. (2007). Organizational identity and employer image: Towards a unifying framework. *British Journal of Management, 18*(s1), S45.

Mills, J., Mehrtens, V., et al. (2007). *CREW revisited in 2007 the year of women in engineering: An update on women's progress in the Australian engineering workforce.* Sydney: Engineers Australia.

Mills, J. E., Gill, J., et al. (2011). Getting it together: Feminist interdisciplinary research on women and engineering. *Women's Studies International Forum, 34*, 13–19.

Slaughter, J., Zickar, M., et al. (2004). Personality trait inferences about organizations: Development of a measure and assessment of construct validity. *Journal of Applied Psychology, 89*(5), 85–103.

Wallace, M., Lings, I., et al. (2014). Attracting and retaining staff: The role of branding and industry image. In R. Harris & T. Short (Eds.), *Workforce development: Perspectives and issues* (pp. 19–36). Singapore: Springer.

Chapter 4
Enhancing Career Pathways

Neroli Sheldon and Michelle Wallace

Abstract Providing explicit career pathways has long been recognised as an important strategy for attracting and retaining employees. In this chapter we consider the strategic and practical implications of research conducted for the Australasian rail industry in developing explicit career pathways for current and potential employees. The chapter will use the experience of the Australasian rail industry to provide a contextual case. However the strategies and practices for enhancing career pathways are applicable to other industries and organisations, particularly those with a relatively low brand image.

Introduction

This research into career pathways in the Australasian rail industry was conducted against a backdrop of broader socioeconomic changes characterised by growing individualisation of employment arrangements. Employee demands for greater flexibility and changing psychological contracts have seen the employee rather than the employer taking prime responsibility for career development. This has led many academics and organisations to conclude that the career path is dead. However, research exploring contemporary career development confirms the role organisations continue to play in the development of their employees and the benefits of continuing this tradition for both employer and employee.

The need for a career pathways guide for the Australasian rail industry became clear from the findings of research conducted by the Cooperative Research Centre for Rail Innovation, a partnership between the Australasian rail industry and universities. Their 2011 scoping project concluded that the absence of explicit career paths

N. Sheldon (✉) • M. Wallace
Southern Cross University Business School, Gold Coast, QLD, Australia
e-mail: neroli.sheldon@scu.edu.au; michelle.wallace@scu.edu.au

in the rail industry and inconsistent terminology, entrance requirements, and training and development requirements were restricting the understanding of career paths available in the rail industry both of internal recruits and more broadly in the external labour market. Earlier research into the attraction and image of rail careers confirmed that the provision of reliable and explicit career path information acted as an attraction and retention factor and enhanced the image of an industry or organisation as an attractive employment option (Wallace et al. 2011).

Methodology

The researchers chose an action research methodology because the research addressed a real-life work problem, that of documenting career paths, and because the action research design enabled partners from the rail industry to be involved as co-researchers and active partners. Research participants included academics, an expert panel of rail operational, HR and workforce planning personnel, seconded rail staff, the Project Steering Committee (PSC) and the end users. As co-researchers, the PSC members participated in interviews and focus groups, which were part of the information gathering; this was both explicit (in documentation) and tacit (in key informants' corporate knowledge). They provided feedback throughout each stage/cycle of the research and made decisions about careers to be documented, the content of each career path and the design of the website.

Action research is also flexible and able to respond to the changing needs of the research. In this research, the design emphasised the collection, analysis and presentation of career path information on an ongoing, cyclical basis where improvements to the career pathways model could be accommodated. The early cycles for this project were used to help the research team decide how to conduct the later cycles. Finally, action research provided the participants with a model that could be used to document future career paths after the formal research concluded.

Action research tends to be cyclic, where similar steps recur in a similar sequence. The model used in this research is the well-known model of plan, act, observe, reflect and then, in light of this, plan for the next cycle (Atweh et al. 2002). Whilst the research reported on in this chapter principally relates only to the development of engineering career pathways, the methodology was successfully replicated for the development of career pathways in the following functional areas of the rail industry: trades, operations and corporate support areas.

Research methods included desk research to gather, document and analyse relevant career paths information from across Australasia including position descriptions and training plans, teleconferences, focus groups, one-on-one meetings/interviews, secondments and a rail expert panel who were called upon to review drafted career paths. The cycles were conducted between February 2011 and August 2013 and involved over 10 rail organisations in Australasia and over 150 participants.

There was extensive industry consultation throughout the project including final approval of the content and design of the website. The risk of incorrect or incomplete information being disseminated was ameliorated by a number of checks and balances including triangulation between data from the seconded rail employees, panel of rail experts, PSC and end user trials.

Contemporary Careers: An Overview

In past decades a career was seen as the responsibility of the employer. However, increasingly career responsibility has shifted to the employee (Baruch 2001) with organisations performing a more supportive as opposed to the traditionally directive role in enabling employees' career success. The demands of a dynamic global market have resulted in organisations adopting work arrangements that facilitate flexible patterns of work. It is generally accepted that flexible work arrangements such as part-time, fixed-term contracts and casual work benefit employers and those employees wanting better work–life balance or needing to balance work with family responsibilities. However, the growth in flexible work arrangements poses a number of challenges for organisations in relation to talent management and for employees in terms of career development.

A career is now often described broadly as 'the unfolding sequence of an individual's work experience over time' (Hoekstra 2011, p. 159) or 'the sequence of employment-related positions, roles, activities and experiences encountered by a person' (Arnold 1997, cited in Gunz et al. 2011, p. 1616). Sometimes the term 'boundaryless' is used to describe careers that take place across multiple organisations and/or industries over an individual's working life.

While many practitioners and employees may agree with the literature that reports the demise of the traditional career path, other research suggests many individuals are still seeking traditional career paths (Sammarra et al. 2013; Clarke 2013). Recent research also found that some employers expressed a preference for promoting traditional organisational careers for their key employees (De Vos and Dries 2013) and that, especially for professionals and managers, continuing a career in one organisation over a long number of years was not uncommon (Clarke 2013).

Other academics (for example, De Vos and Dries 2013; Preece et al. 2011) have highlighted the relevance of career management and the continuing existence of traditional career paths in certain organisations or industries. Indeed, as we will see later in this chapter, for those industries dependent on skills in high demand, such as engineers, considerable investment is made to attract and retain employees through offering competitive rewards and continuous development of transferable skills in exchange for an employee's high performance and flexibility (Crawshaw et al. 2012).

Clarke (2013) also found that, regardless of the assumption that younger employees are comfortable moving from organisation to organisation and between industries, university graduates still considered developing a career within a single organisation highly desirable. It is often generalised that different generations have contrasting expectations of career development; however research indicates that professional development and career opportunities are desired by employees regardless of age

(Clarke 2013). In fact, according to Deloitte (2013) young employees facing the prospect of being in employment for the next 50 or 60 years expect their employers to provide career development opportunities.

To some extent, employers are able to measure the success of their internal career path policies and procedures through performance measures such as successful project completions and recruitment and retention metrics, including exit interviews and performance reviews, but how do contemporary employees measure career satisfaction? Career satisfaction refers to the extent to which individuals believe their career progress is consistent with their own goals, values and preferences (Barnett and Bradley 2007).

Traditionally, career success has been associated with vertical, incremental rises generally through a small number of organisations with related increases in responsibility and remuneration. Whilst it is likely that many employees today define their career success more broadly than simply upward advancement, research indicates that when the economy is uncertain and career predictability unreliable employees continue to seek traditional hierarchical advancement within an organisation (Dries 2011; Clarke 2013; Sammarra et al. 2013). While there are numerous models that describe the components of a career path, we consider that Jenkins and Spence's (2006) model remains relevant. Their model describes five fundamental components of a career path:

- movement (vertical or horizontal moves within or across organisations)
- mobility (the degree to which a path naturally promotes job or position change)
- formality (the degree to which career paths are made explicit)
- expertise (the degree to which socialised expertise is needed)
- connectivity (the degree to which a career path intersects with closely related paths or occupations).

The Continuing Relevance of Career Pathways: The Australasian Rail Industry

As we noted in the companion chapter in *Workforce development: Perspectives and issues* (Harris and Short 2014), engineering expertise is critical to the economic innovation and productivity of nations, as well as driving sustainable social and economic development. In this section we will explore the enduring strategic and operational importance of career paths to industries, organisations and individuals. We consider how the observations and lessons learned in the Australasian rail industry can be applied to other industries and organisations, especially those with low brand awareness. The model shown in Fig. 4.1 will frame the conversation.

Fig. 4.1 Situation, problem, implication, need, solution

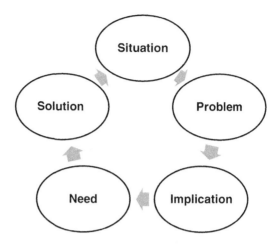

Table 4.1 Examples of current large rail projects by global region

Projects by region	Jul 2013	Nov 2013	Category	Jul 2013	Nov 2013
Africa	15	16	Heavy rail	82	83
Asia	107	114	High-speed rail	77	82
Australasia	32	34	Light rail systems	158	163
Central America	5	5	Metros	137	139
Europe	229	250	Railway stations	46	48
North America	16	85	Future contracts	17	30
South America	14	15			

Source: www.railway-technology.com/projects/ (accessed 26 July 2013 and 29 November 2013)

Situation: The Global Growth in Demand for Rail Services and Infrastructure

The Australian passenger rail industry has experienced a resurgence in popularity over the past decade, driven by factors including strong economic growth and employment in capital cities, environmental concerns, lower train fares, rising fuel prices and costs associated with passenger vehicles, such as parking. Industry revenue is expected to grow at 3.8 % to 2014 (IBISWorld 2013). Likewise, the Australian freight transport industry has experienced growth over the past 5 years, primarily through the resources boom and growth in the non-bulk or intermodal market segments. IBISWorld (2013) reported that rail freight transport revenue is expected to increase at a rate of 4.6 % through 2013–2014. These trends are reflected elsewhere in the world, as can be seen in Table 4.1, which shows growth in global rail projects between July 2013 and November 2013.

The statistics show all regions recorded growth in the 5 months between July and November 2013, with the largest growth in Europe and North America.

Problem: Demand for Engineers and Skilled Technicians and Subsequent Shortages

The growth in global rail infrastructure has contributed to the demand for and subsequent shortages of engineers. In Australia, engineering and related technical disciplines are one of the occupational groups in highest demand and in 2013 over 18 engineering and engineering technologist positions were listed by the Department of Immigration and Border Protection (2013) as 'in demand'. According to Engineers Australia, the combined number of domestic engineering graduates and engineers entering Australia through the skilled migration program will not satisfy Australia's demand for such workers (Kaspura 2011). This trend will continue to exert pressure on the rail industry's capacity and is compounded by projections that top growth sectors by 2020 are expected to include engineering, and specialised trades related to resources development and construction (Wilson 2010).

Engineering shortages are not restricted to Australia, as UNESCO (2010) reported a growing worldwide scarcity in almost all engineering fields. As Table 4.1 illustrates, the number of projects underway or coming on-stream represents continuing significant investment in rail transport and infrastructure. Australia is competing in a global employment market for mobile engineering expertise and thus attraction and retention of engineers and other key talent becomes a pressing human resource management problem.

In addition, the ageing of the workforce in the rail industry is more pronounced than in the Australian workforce as a whole. In 2011 the average age of the Australian worker was reported at 38.6, whereas the average age for a rail worker was estimated at 41.3 (Wallace et al. 2011). There is risk of the loss of tacit knowledge in rail organisations as the older age groups reach retirement and a gap in the 26–39-year age group emerges. This latter group is where supervisory and managerial skills are built and contribute to organisational capability.

Implications: Skills Shortages Impact on Meeting Rail Infrastructure Commitments

The implications of engineering and technical/trades skills shortages for the Australian rail industry are well documented (for example, Australian National Engineering Taskforce 2010; Wise et al. 2011). While the complexities of estimating supply or demand make it hard for the industry to make definitive estimates of the shortfall of rail engineers in Australia, Wise et al. (2011) reported that demand for rail engineers in Australia will continue to significantly outnumber the estimated number of engineers expected to be employed on rail infrastructure projects. It is estimated that rail organisations will need to access over 300 engineers, 700 operations staff and 700 tradespersons every year to 2015 to meet demand and cover age retirement (ANET 2010). An internet search on 29 November 2013 indicated 30 additional future contracts in large rail projects.

These trends have long been of concern to the Australasian rail industry, and several projects funded by the Cooperative Research Centre for Rail Innovation attempt to address engineering skills shortages including improving the attraction and image of rail careers through making explicit career paths open to engineers in the rail industry.

Australia competes in the global market place for engineers, with large rail construction projects in Asia and Europe draining Australian capacity. The consequences of these skills shortages range from minor or moderate financial concerns or delays to major concerns such as those reported by Engineers Australia (2010), where a significant proportion of projects in the reported period did not proceed due to the shortages.

Need: Attract More Engineers to Rail Careers

The need to attract more engineers into rail careers starts with creating the conditions for young people to engage with science, technology, engineering and mathematics (STEM) subjects in primary and high school, which are needed to study engineering. The next step is encouraging these individuals to study engineering and seek careers in the profession. In particular, the low levels of girls participating in the STEM subjects and the gender disparity in engineering courses as well as the leaky pipeline of qualified women in the engineering profession need further action. Chapter 7 in *Workforce development: Perspectives and issues* (Harris and Short 2014) described a range of initiatives that attempt to address the issues that have resulted in skills wastage and engineering skills shortages in most countries.

The career development literature suggests that making visible career pathways and the qualifications, competencies and experience needed to progress through such pathways is an effective strategy for communicating the value of working in an organisation or industry to potential recruits (Carter et al. 2009). The objective of the career pathways for the Australasian rail industry project was to map career pathways for rail occupations in an online format with downloadable components accessible to both current and potential employees, including those contemplating skilled migration and to the broader public including high school and university students and their advisers and influencers. Table 4.2 summarises the stages and principal activities involved in documenting rail career paths and designing the rail career pathways guide for the Australasian rail industry. The model could be replicated by other industries.

The research team viewed industry-based career path initiatives in Australia and overseas in order to identify a model for the Australasian rail industry. Australian career path models reviewed included 'Starting Out' developed by the Manufacturing Industry Skills Council and 'MakeIt' by the Transport and Logistics Industry Skills Council. The researchers also reviewed initiatives in other countries including the 'Get Moving Public Transportation Occupational Guidebook' prepared by the John J. Heldrich Center for Workforce Development at Rutgers, the State University of New Jersey. In addition, we also reviewed engineering professional standards

Table 4.2 Stages and principal actions in documenting rail career paths

Stage	Action
Stage 1 Identify model	Examine career path initiatives by other industries and organisations where possible. Decide on information fields, format and medium (i.e. paper-based, website, etc.) for providing information to the public
Stage 2 Gather information	Gather information such as position descriptions, career maps, workforce planning documents, training plans, etc. that can be used to inform career paths
	Create database or catalogue of job families grouped by main functional/divisional area (in the rail industry this equated to engineering, trades, operations, corporate support)
Stage 3 Analyse information	Analyse existing information and identify gaps in information
	Identify Australian and New Zealand Standard Classification of Occupations (ANZSCO) codes, and academic and professional requirements
Stage 4 Draft career paths	This may need the input of experienced employees with knowledge of possible career moves rather than HR generalists
Stage 5 Review career paths	By a range of stakeholders including technical experts, line managers and HR practitioners
Stage 6 Design website	Aim for simple design and software to facilitate ongoing maintenance of website as jobs change and new jobs emerge
Stage 7 Conduct user testing	Include end users (current employees, line managers, potential employees, recruiters, students, teachers, parents) and focus on navigation, readability, usefulness
	Include IT/website specialists to test IT design and functionality
Stage 8 Promote and launch	Promote through industry and educational networks including careers advisors and recruitment consultants
Stage 9 Conduct analytics	Conduct analytics to use in promotional activities and for future improvement
Stage 10 Update website	Update content as needed

documented by Engineers Australia and industrial awards. Most career pathways documentation available in Australia was aimed at the vocational sector and targeted school students. In addition, it did not provide the information current and potential employees needed to make informed career choices.

The team also evaluated the use of flowcharts and agreed that graphical representation was helpful to viewers but should be kept simple and avoid:

- trying to attempt to convey both vertical and horizontal career paths;
- multiple entry/exit points through university or vocational training; and
- aligning with vocational awards and organisational pay scales.

User testing was an essential component of the research and included end users from the rail industry and from the broader recruitment market and website/information technology students from Southern Cross University who reviewed the website from a web developer's perspective. Analytics conducted by the CRC for Rail Innovation in the 2 months after the site was launched in October 2013 have indicated over

1,000 visitors with the majority of visitors from Australia. User testing and visitor numbers confirm that the content and format of the career paths website is meaningful, the appearance and style of the site is attractive, and the useability is acceptable.

Results and Final Products

Unlike many industries some of the rail industry's key employers are large public organisations that still foster formal and explicit career paths. While some job families such as cleaning have been replaced through outsourcing, there remain over 60 job families for which career paths are established and supported within the rail industry. Many of these, including engineering, accounting and human resources, reflect traditional linear careers where all entrants begin at the bottom as graduates and work their way up through a series of well-defined jobs undertaken in strict order. This trend was also observed in non-professional job families including trades, technicians and train drivers.

The research found that rail career paths were largely un-documented. While related information including position descriptions, job families, competencies and training requirements existed in the rail industry, the information was dispersed, inconsistent and primarily used for administrative purposes, rather than to assist current and potential employees make career decisions.

The researchers agreed that the career pathways guide template should include the following fields:

* ANZSCO code and occupation title
* alternative job titles
* rail safety worker status
* brief description of the occupation
* knowledge, skills and attributes
* working conditions
* entrance requirements and ongoing training and development
* value of the career (link to data on salary ranges and employment prospects)
* where to go for more information
* related jobs (which may form part of a career path gained through lateral moves)
* flowchart.

Throughout the research many hundreds of jobs were considered. To better ensure the ongoing maintenance of the website, the PSC rationalised the number of job families based on their strategic and operational importance to the organisations. Other job families were described briefly in the 'A–Z of rail jobs' which is found on the website. Table 4.3 summarises the job families documented.

Information such as qualification structures or competency standards is likely to change over time. To ensure the accuracy and currency of information, including qualification structures and competencies, the website provides links to relevant sources of information including Australian training bodies, relevant industry skills councils, universities offering rail-specific degrees and professional associations. The following screenshots of the Rail Career Pathways website briefly describe

Table 4.3 Summary of the career pathways guide for the Australasian rail industry

Rail sector	Job family/career path	Related jobs
Engineering	12 engineering disciplines	Over 25 related occupations
Trades/technicians	12 trades and technical job families	Over 25 related occupations
Operations	14 job families including customer service, on-board services, timetabling, fare compliance, signalling, train driving	Over 25 related occupations
Corporate support	24 job families including finance, payroll, administration, HR, marketing, law, workplace relations, training and development, health and safety, IT	Over 50 occupations

some of the content and features of the home page, a sample of a career path, and the 'A–Z of rail jobs' function.

The Rail Career Pathways website can be viewed at www.railcareerpathways.net.au.

The Rail Career Pathways Homepage: By selecting a menu item (for example 'Engineers'), the viewer is provided with information on the importance of engineering to the rail industry and links to examples of current infrastructure projects.

Example of Career Path – Civil Engineer: By selecting a specific job family (for example, civil engineer) the viewer is provided with information on the ANZSCO code and occupation title, alternative job titles, safety status, brief description, required knowledge, skills and attributes, working conditions, entrance requirements and ongoing training and development, related jobs and likely career pathways (in a flowchart). This page also provides links to other websites including relevant educational providers and professional associations.

A–Z of Rail Jobs: This provides a brief description of over 200 jobs and their entry requirements.

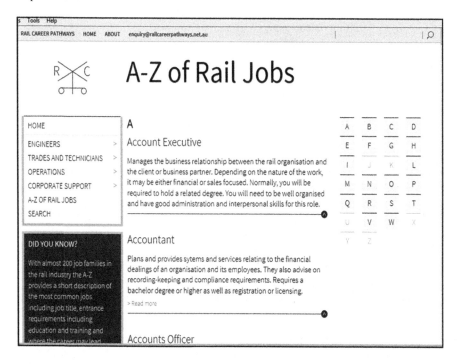

Practical Strategies for Using the Career Pathways Guide

The career pathways guide for the Australasian rail industry is intended first and foremost to provide career information to current and potential employees. However there are other ways rail organisations can use the website. It can provide an industry-validated source of reliable career information for careers advisors and recruitment specialists, skilled migration agents, lecturers, teachers and other influencers of career decision making including parents and family members. This can be done by:

- links to the website from industry association websites
- links to the website from corporate websites
- links to the website from industry-specific recruitment agencies
- links to the website from relevant school or university websites.

In particular, we see additional benefits to rail employees such as line managers, HR specialists, training and development teams, talent managers and workforce planners where a one-stop shop of comprehensive career path information will save time and resources searching multiple databases or documentation such as position descriptions, competency maps and progression frameworks based on awards. The information can be used to:

- focus performance management conversations between an employee and supervisor
- provide context for exit interviews
- inform recruitment activities including the development of selection criteria, interview scenarios or behavioural interviews questions
- assist with training needs analysis or audits
- assist with workforce planning
- assist with PR and promotional activities in schools and universities.

Applicability to Other Industries

Rail Career Pathways is a one-stop website providing comprehensive information on career opportunities in the rail industry. It provides a validated approach for gathering, developing, reviewing and disseminating career path information that could be readily adopted by other industries. Attempting to document career paths across an industry is a complex task and it is hoped that the research model applied in this project is equally as useful as the actual design of the career pathways guide and website.

The action research model is designed to solve real problems and thus is applicable at both organisational and industry-wide levels. The following questions may assist in determining whether the model and templates presented in this chapter are appropriate to a particular industry.

- Do the skills/knowledge needed take many years to develop?
- Does the industry/organisation struggle to find staff in the general employment market?

- Does the industry/organisation believe that explicit career paths are positively correlated to attraction, engagement and retention of employees?
- Does the industry/organisation employ staff mainly on a permanent basis?
- Does the industry/organisation support structured career progression e.g. internships and graduate programs?
- Does the industry/organisation have a tradition of documenting job information such as position descriptions, training plans or competency maps?
- Is the industry/organisation willing to adopt a research action model where participants are co-researchers and the researchers facilitate the process rather than perform the role of expert consultants?
- Is the industry/organisation willing to share information?
- Is the industry/organisation willing to allow their staff time to scope and review drafts?
- Is the industry/organisation willing to host and maintain the website?

This last point is important because career paths change over time. Some roles will disappear and others emerge through developments in technology and further changes to the way organisations structure work. For such a product to retain relevance in the employment market and for current employees it must be perceived as accurate and up-to-date.

Conclusion

Organisations continue to invest in employee careers because of the value those careers represent for the organisation and because they enable the organisation to retain critical skills and knowledge. Making career paths explicit, as well as the qualifications, competencies, training and development needed to move through a career path, supports individual careers and organisational human capital management. Whilst the focus of this chapter is the Australasian rail industry, the research model and lessons are applicable to other industries seeking to make their career paths more explicit as an attractor and retainer of key occupational skills. Similarly, the templates for documenting career paths and the website design and architecture could easily be replicated for other industries.

References

Atweh, B., Kemmis, S., & Weeks, P. (2002). *Action research in practice*. London: Taylor and Francis e-Library.

Australian National Engineering Taskforce (ANET). (2010). *Scoping our future: Australia's engineering skills shortage*. Canberra: ANET.

Barnett, B., & Bradley, L. (2007). The impact of organisational support for career development on career satisfaction. *Career Development International, 12*(7), 617–636.

Baruch, Y. (2001). Employability: A substitute for loyalty? *Human Resource Development International, 4*(4), 543–566.

Carter, G. W., Cook, K. W., & Dorsey, D. (2009). *Career paths*. Chichester: Wiley Blackwell.

Clarke, M. (2013). The organizational career: Not dead but in need of redefinition. *International Journal of Human Resource Management, 24*(4), 684–703.

Crawshaw, J., van Dick, R., & Brodbeck, F. (2012). Opportunity, fair process and relationship value: Career development as a driver of proactive work behaviour. *Human Resource Management, 22*(1), 4–20.

De Vos, A., & Dries, N. (2013). Applying a talent management lens to career management: The role of human capital composition and continuity. *International Journal of Human Resource Management, 24*(9), 1816–1831.

Deloitte. (2013). *Resetting horizons: Human capital trends 2013 Australian edition*. UK. https://www. deloitte.com/view/en_GX/global/services/consulting/human- capital/e8b2b2df0720e310VgnVC-M1000003256f70aRCRD.htm?id=gx:th:GHCT13. Accessed 26 Aug 2013.

Department of Immigration and Border Protection. (2013). *Skilled occupation list – 1 July 2012*. Canberra: Commonwealth of Australia. https://www.immi.gov.au/skilled/general-skilled-migration/pdf/sol.pdf. Accessed 12 Dec 2013.

Dries, N. (2011). The meaning of career success: Avoiding reification through a closer inspection of historical, cultural and ideological contexts. *Career Development International, 16*(4), 364–384.

Engineers Australia. (2010). *The engineering profession: A statistical overview 2010* (7th ed.). Canberra: Engineers Australia.

Gunz, H., Mayrhofer, W., & Tolbert, P. (2011). Career as a social and political phenomena in the globalised economy. *Organization Studies, 32*(2), 1613–1620.

Harris, R., & Short, T. (Eds.). (2014). *Workforce development: Perspectives and issues*. Singapore: Springer.

Hoekstra, H. (2011). A career roles model of career development. *Journal of Vocational Behavior, 78*, 159–173.

IBISWorld (2013). *Rail passenger transport in Australia: Market research report*. Melbourne. http://www.ibisworld.com.au/industry/default.aspx?indid=1889. Accessed 12 Dec 2013.

Jenkins, D., & Spence, C. (2006). *The career pathways how–to guide*. New York: Workforce Strategy Center.

Kaspura, A. (2011). *The engineering profession statistical overview* (8th ed.). Canberra: Institute of Engineers.

Preece, D., Iles, P., & Chuai, X. (2011). Talent management and management fashion in Chinese enterprises: Exploring case studies in Beijing. *International Journal of Human Resource Management, 22*(16), 3413–3428.

Sammarra, A., Profili, S., & Innocenti, L. (2013). Do external careers pay off for both managers and professionals? The effect of inter-organisational mobility on objective career success. *International Journal of Human Resource Management, 24*(13), 2490–2511.

United Nations Educational, Scientific and Cultural Organization (UNESCO). (2010). *Engineering: Issues, challenges and opportunities for development*. Paris: UNESCO.

Wallace, M., Sheldon, N., et al. (2011). *Rail attraction and image final report*. Brisbane: CRC for Rail Innovation.

Wilson, P. (2010). *People@work 2010*. Melbourne: Australian Human Resources Institute.

Wise, S., Schutz, H., et al. (2011). *Engineering skills capacity in the road and rail industries*. Canberra: Australian National Engineering Taskforce.

Chapter 5
Developing a 'Win-Win' Scenario: Understanding How Older Workers' Learning Can Be Enhanced Within Organisations

Brian Findsen

Abstract Employee turnover in traditional industries is starting to hurt organisations as global mobility of people grows and long-serving and experienced Baby Boomers retire to make way for younger generations. Simultaneously, as the population in most countries continues to age, many older adults are faced with dilemmas concerning their future engagement with ongoing employment. For organisations there are manifold challenges with respect to recruiting, retaining and retraining older workers as they endeavour to be competitive in an ever-changing economic environment. This chapter investigates the perspectives of employers and older employees on learning and development within an organisational framework. Learning prospects for workers are necessarily related to this over-arching environment in which organisations are responding to wider societal attitudes and practices towards older workforce membership. Such a framework is nestled within a dynamic global economy in which neo-liberalism has taken hold in many countries. The final section of this chapter discusses learning strategies for individual workers and their employers that are more likely to result in mutually positive outcomes.

Introduction   + *pandemic*

The global financial crisis has produced special, usually detrimental, conditions for older people who may be forced out of the labour market prematurely or voluntarily choose to reduce or surrender full-time paid employment (Beatty and Visser 2005; Davey 2006). For organisations there are manifold challenges with respect to recruiting, retaining and retraining older workers as they endeavour to be competitive in an ever-changing economic environment. However, such organisations seldom

B. Findsen (✉)
Faculty of Education, University of Waikato, Hamilton, New Zealand
e-mail: bfindsen@waikato.ac.nz

T. Short and R. Harris (eds.), *Workforce Development: Strategies and Practices*,
DOI 10.1007/978-981-287-068-1_5, © Springer Science+Business Media Singapore 2014

operate without considering national/regional governmental priorities, particularly policies that may inhibit or enhance agencies' likelihood of supporting employability of older workers and associated training and development opportunities.

In this chapter I investigate the perspectives of employers and older employees on learning and development within an organisational framework. Such a framework is nestled within a dynamic global economy in which neo-liberalism has taken hold in many countries. Learning prospects for workers are necessarily related to this over-arching environment in which organisations are responding to wider societal attitudes and practices towards older workforce membership. I will analyse current issues pertaining to older workforce participation. This includes how myths can actively dissuade older workers from active engagement in workplaces, and what constitutes knowledge for workers and the extent to which they can control its acquisition. I argue that both employers and workers need to acknowledge and go beyond prevailing assumptions about older adult learning and appreciate the diverse potential purposes of workplace learning within a lifelong learning agenda. In addition, I outline the broader possibilities for learning in accord with adult learning perspectives and effective principles.

A Changing World, a Changing Workplace

The dynamics of a particular workplace and workers within it need to be contextualised from the perspective of globalisation and its multiple impacts at varying levels of organisations. Barnett pointed to the problematic connections between learning and work, primarily related to 'conditions of supercomplexity' (1999, p. 29) in which the pace of change renders understanding partial at best. A global economy demands flexible labour markets, and sophisticated technological modes of communication involving networked systems and infrastructures wherein patterns of work and of consumption are forever on the move. Globalisation has immediate effects on organisations, both private and public, in regard to producing a workforce that can be responsive and efficient; in this sense, the market is a primary determinant in the development of information/knowledge in a 'learning economy' (Field 2002). Yet large corporations do not usually function entirely independently of the state. Governments have a responsibility to weigh up the relative influence of open markets on citizens and to monitor the effects of neo-liberalism in a democracy (such as heightened accountability, quality assurance, minimal government spending). Governments often intervene in the market to minimise the negative impact of market forces. The rise of the 'evaluative state' (Barnett 1999) is no accident. There is an imperative to measure the effectiveness of public spending in manifold types of organisations such as in education, health and social welfare; in the private sector similar fine-tuning of expenditure is the rule rather than the exception. In short, many organisations may interpret learning and development as a luxury rather than as a necessity for workers in hard economic times (Beatty and Visser 2005).

So, what does this have to do with older workers? Regardless of the precise kind of industry – agriculture, business, health, tourism, manufacturing, trade, personal services – older adults occupy places of employment, either full-time or part-time, where these macro forces influence the decision making of investors, managers and other stakeholders. Older workers, defined arbitrarily as 65 years old and beyond (though some studies describe people beyond 45 in this same category: see the study by Lundberg and Marshallsay 2007), constitute an important element in sustaining industries and organisations in this rapidly changing world of work. While the attitudes of significant numbers of employers are ageist, older people continue to increase numerically in most countries and cannot be ignored as important human capital, especially in the future when younger workers will be fewer proportionately than older (Centre for Research into the Older Workforce 2005). For a variety of reasons such as decreased fertility, longer life expectancy and better health services, the population structures in most countries will age to the extent that the dependency ratio will precipitate economic crises unless governments, employers and individuals respond imaginatively. State provision of pensions and superannuation schemes may be under special scrutiny to limit public spending; thus, this forces individuals to account for their own financial security in a more expanded lifespan (Encel 1997). This ideology of individualism is consistent with a neo-liberal agenda: it is the responsibility of individuals to look after themselves in a 'risk society' (Beck 1992).

In most countries, there is an arrangement of training and development involving individual workers, employers and the state. If the organisation is directly state-funded then the government may have an immediate stake in worker education and professional development. In private organisations the state may only have a role from the viewpoint of policy (regulations and legal requirements) and the main protagonists become the employer and the individual worker. In some instances, trade unions will have significant input into a worker's learning portfolio.

In many societies the traditional pattern of the life course involving education, work and leisure has been thoroughly disrupted (Riley and Riley 1994). The assumption that we are educated first, get a job/career and then retire to leisure no longer holds. Further, life transitions seldom occur in an orderly manner. There is a need for a person to engage in lifelong learning (Wain 2004) and not think of schooling or tertiary education as a finishing post; to thrive rather than survive in a postmodern world we need to engage in ongoing learning across numerous sites (e.g. workplace, family, religious institutions). While formal education may prepare people for work, this is not necessarily the case. Education is not always wedded to employment though this may be a principal purpose in many governments' and students' minds; education also has diverse purposes beyond the acquisition of work (Findsen and Formosa 2011). The notion of 'retirement' needs to be retired itself. The super-complex world necessitates a divergent range of options for people entering their third age (Laslett 1989) where continuing full-time or part-time work is a possibility, not a certainty. As an Australian-based study (Lundberg and Marshallsay 2007) identified, many current older workers want to carry on working beyond 'retirement age' (usually associated with the provision of superannuation) for a multitude of reasons.

Older People and Prevailing Myths

Many myths have been perpetrated within most societies that limit the way in which people in later life conduct their lives. These myths can be of a more general nature and/or can be extended to older workers and to learning environments, including workplaces. At a more general level I have previously (Findsen 2005) described the following myths:

- *Homogeneity*: older adults are not a uniform group and consist of considerable diversity according to gender, socioeconomic status, ethnicity, (dis)ability and so on. There is no generic 'older adult' without qualification of the term. Yet, paradoxically, older adults may wish to be labelled in a collective fashion to effect political influence.
- *Decrepitude*: A powerful image derived from a medical perspective is that older people are frail, in declining health and suffer cognitive and physiological decline. This is based on a deficit notion of older adulthood. The reality is that the majority of older people are in good health, are mentally alert and wish to contribute to the society of which they are part.
- *Dependence*: older people are often depicted as dependent on the younger generations, especially family, for their daily needs. While the reality of some decline in physical functioning cannot be ignored, most older adults wish to retain their independence. However, the notion of interdependence is perhaps more accurate to describe older people's relationships inside and outside the family environment, including places of work.
- *Consumerism*: while older adults may be portrayed as 'takers' from the rest of society, particularly in terms of social provision, many older people contribute significantly to local communities and in the workplace. Older adults engage in volunteering to a large degree, helping to prop up community agencies and social services. Many older people want to contribute positively to their communities and offer considerable life experience and wisdom in the process.

In terms of learning contexts (inclusive of workplaces), Withnall et al. (2004) identified myths of a cognitive character (e.g. 'older people are too slow to learn anything new' and 'older people forget things'), physical (e.g. 'older people have mobility problems' and 'older people are deaf'), dispositional (e.g. 'older people live in the past and don't change') and attitudes towards learning (e.g. 'older people are not interested in learning', 'older people are not interested in information and communications technology' and 'older people only want to learn with other older people'). As with any myth, there are usually elements of truth – hence, their persistence when objective evidence points to other interpretations. Finally, Rothwell et al. (2008) have identified myths about older workers. Given the importance of these mistaken beliefs to the central argument of this chapter, I will reproduce them here with brief critical comments.

1. *You can't teach an old dog new tricks.*
   Comment: The decline in cognitive functioning of older people up until around age 70 is negligible. Older people can learn new things although it may take a fraction longer than for youngsters.

2. *Training older workers is a lost investment because they will not stay on the job for long.*

   Comment: In comparison with young workers, they provide greater stability and arguably are less likely to leave the workplace, given employment uncertainty.

3. *Older workers are not as productive as younger workers.*

   Comment: Productivity does not decline as a function of age. In fact, older people can offer greater dependability and a capacity to make more informed decisions than younger groups.

4. *Older workers are less flexible and adaptable.*

   Comment: Older workers are just as adaptable as younger. They may more readily question why change needs to occur.

5. *Older workers are not as creative or innovative.*

   Comment: General intelligence levels are comparable to younger workers. New production ideas are more frequent from workers over the age of 40.

6. *Older workers cost more than hiring younger workers.*

   Comment: Regardless of age, workers with tenure tend to cost more. The reality is that many older people are on the periphery of the workforce and, once outside of it, find it difficult to re-enter.

7. *Benefit and accident costs are higher for older workers.*

   Comment: Older workers tend to take fewer sick days. While some costs such as workers' health insurance may be higher, older workers have fewer dependents. They statistically have lower accident rates than other age groups.

This discussion around myths emphasises that in many locations the capacities of older people are under question. It is unfortunate that numerous beliefs about what work older people can undertake and what learning they can do are erroneous and based on ageist assumptions. These assumptions are not easy to eradicate and persist in many work situations (McGregor and Gray 2002). While education for general society is required to help alleviate the detrimental effects of such beliefs, in workplaces they are arguably even more urgent. While some managers operate from an ageist perspective, even older workers themselves can believe that they do not deserve their paid work and/or they are taking the place of a younger worker. Sooner or later, the reality of changing age structures and ongoing human capital demands due to globalisation will require managers and workers alike to rethink their positions, as there will be fewer younger people eligible for work and more seniors around with considerable wisdom that employers can take advantage of.

Lifelong Learning and Older Workers

While the concept of lifelong learning has proven quite elusive, it has nevertheless been adopted enthusiastically at multiple levels of international organisations (e.g. UNESCO, ILO), governments, institutions and individuals. It has often been coupled with allied concepts such as 'the learning economy', 'the learning society' and 'the learning organisation' and has been recognised by corporations and companies as expressing ideals of engaging workers in ongoing enquiry, usually, but not exclusively, related to their work tasks. Pedler, Burgoyne and Boydell have defined the learning organisation as one that 'facilitates the learning of all its members and continuously transforms itself in order to meet its strategic goals' (1991, p. 1). This learning may be determined by the employer or, perhaps less often, negotiated by employees with managers to meet perceived and real needs in the work context. While learning itself may take many different forms according to varying purposes, it is usually related to one or more approaches: cognitive, social or emotional (Illeris 2004). It may be competency-based (Gonczi 2004) or self-directed (Knowles 1984) or according to some other philosophical orientation. Depending on one's position within an organisation, unless it is organised along the lines of a flat, democratic structure, the social stratification of the workplace may impede the capacity and/or autonomy of that person to meet learning needs. More typically, managers have greater discretion about and access to funding for professional development; in comparison, workers tend to have little autonomy in what constitutes really useful knowledge for them and for the employer. Further, as older workers tend to be more marginalised in part-time, casual or seasonal jobs, their likelihood of securing training and development is severely diminished (Rothwell et al. 2008). In the wider perspective of lifelong learning (Findsen and Formosa 2011), four major themes pertaining to the work environment are frequently emphasised in the literature:

1. *The learning economy*: Workers, including older adults, need to respond to global market forces which pressure organisations into a competitive mode and expect workers to be flexible, knowledgeable and adaptable. Given the uncertainty attached to retaining one's paid job or the need to change occupations later in life, many older people are rethinking retirement plans and may seek further qualifications in a formal education context. If their early education achievement was not high, then a return to education is normally beyond the bounds of possibility (and compounded by the fact that few governments have proactive policies to support such initiatives). At the other end of the financial scale, those older adults with solid education careers and extensive social capital (Field 2003) may more readily return to study, including for more recreational purposes (Findsen and McCullough 2008).

2. *Personal fulfilment*: Consistent with the liberal tradition in adult education, the need for personal advancement and human development has always been strong. This aspect of lifelong learning relates to an individualistic stance as opposed to a collectivist approach. Learning in a work environment may lead to personal growth, depending on the nature of the task or knowledge construction, but for most workers their endeavours are restricted by employers to more utilitarian purposes. Yet within this discourse, Beck's (1992) notion of the reflexive individual is consistent with a postmodern agenda. While we may live in 'the risk society', from a government perspective it is incumbent upon us as individuals to reduce uncertainty through our self-directed learning.

3. *Active citizenship*: This third theme emphasises the social responsibility of citizens to develop themselves for their own betterment but more especially for the maintenance of a democratic society. Active citizenship requires a person to

participate in civil affairs, to go beyond the 'economic citizen'. Older people can enhance their prospects of contributing to society through active ageing strategies. In the world of work, the potential to consolidate social capital is enhanced, as social relationships in the work environment can positively support personal and community development. In short, being a worker does not negate the role of engagement as an active citizen.

4. *Social inclusion*: Given that historically there have been subordinate groups who have not prospered in mainstream educational provision and for whom neo-liberalism has been problematic, many governments have initiated social equity schemes (those providing additional resources to marginalised groups) to mini-mise the detrimental effects of market forces. In particular, indigenous sub-populations (e.g. Māori in New Zealand) and new immigrants have exemplified this theme in action. Some older people may also be seen from this perspective to deserve additional social services to counter-balance poverty or poor adjustment to older age. The underlying idea is one of social justice, to minimise social exclusion. Arguably, when older adults engage in paid work they are more likely to avoid social exclusion; access to education either in the workplace or elsewhere may also help to alleviate potential social isolation.

In the work context these themes still have considerable relevance. Understandably, from an employer's perspective, the paramount objective is to develop the efficient worker to contribute positively to the organisation's primary outputs (and profit, if a private company). In effect, this is an emphasis on the first theme. Yet the other themes should not be lightly dismissed. The 'economic citizen' should also be a 'critical citizen', one with a critical intelligence (Mayo and Thompson 1995), one who connects work with the rest of his/her life and thinks expansively about global/national issues. Self-growth and fulfilment may not be a direct objective of training and development but this should also be encouraged. In addition, social inclusion is directly applicable to work contexts for older workers in how they are valued (see McGregor and Gray 2002 for a critique of the treatment of older workers in New Zealand).

What Kind of Learning/Education?

At a fundamental level it is useful to distinguish between 'learning' and 'education'. Learning is commonly believed to occur in a wide variety of contexts and may be formal, non-formal or informal. Jarvis (1985) explained these terms as follows:

- *informal learning*: the process whereby every person acquires knowledge, skills, attitudes and aptitude from daily living
- *non-formal learning*: any systematic, organised, educational activity carried on outside the formal system to provide selected types of learning to particular subgroups of the population
- *formal learning*: the institutionalised, chronologically graded and hierarchical educational system.

The significance of these distinctions in types of learning should not be lost because older adults have traditionally been involved in non-formal and informal learning rather than formal. This relates to their frequent membership of various clubs and community organisations in which they may have responsibilities (Golding 2011) and the realisation that we continue to learn on a daily basis from more incidental happenings in our lives. Having noted this point, there is still considerable potential for older adults, perhaps supported by an enlightened employer or government policy, to participate in formal learning for a variety of purposes such as job enhancement, changing one's career in later life or for self-fulfilment (see research by Findsen and McCullough 2008 on the engagement of older adults in formal learning in Greater Glasgow). These forms of learning are complementary and not mutually exclusive.

The distinction between 'learning' and 'education' can be significant too. This point is well explained by Withnall (2010) in her investigation of 'learning' in the UK. Older people in her survey held a myriad of perspectives on what might constitute learning (e.g. acquiring knowledge; changing one's understanding; it's about living) but were more conversant with education (as an extension of schooling). Learning tends to be individualistic and concerned with processes associated with cognitive, social and emotional growth. On the other hand, education relates to organised, often hierarchical learning and is commonly graded and credentialised. In the context of older workers, they are more likely to undertake on-the-job learning on a daily basis; however, their desire for and/or access to training/education may be less plentiful and usually associated with improved performance at work.

Prospects for Learning for Older Workers

To be explicit, in the workplace learning can be of a varied nature ranging from informal to formal. For many workers, learning will be in the form of training wherein they are expected to grasp specific skills and knowledge to perform their tasks more efficiently; they may have little option but to be involved and there could be coercion to participate. On the other hand, particularly aligned to self-directed activities, learning may be self-determined, discretionary and not necessarily tied to measureable outcomes. Hence, the motivation to be involved may be multi-faceted and ever-changing; it may be intrinsic or extrinsic. Ideally, intrinsic motivation is more desirable as it tends to be longer-lasting and not based on external rewards (Knowles 1984). However, employers may offer a combination of incentives for workers to get involved in further learning.

Rothwell et al. (2008) identified the 'Protean career' pattern, which is directed primarily by the worker rather than the employing organisation. In this sense, workers contract themselves to employers and tend to be more mobile. From this approach there tends to be greater flexibility for workers, though they will still be subject to prevailing labour force dynamics. Alternatives in these careers include finding a new career; building on skills in an existing job; changing the location of work to another organisation; phasing work and learning to retirement; and joining the contingent workforce. This career pattern is more indicative of professionals whose expertise is more likely to be in demand but may apply to self-employed workers.

Perspectives on Learning and Older Workers

The field of adult education more generally is replete with learning principles from a variety of philosophical perspectives (see Merriam et al. 2007 coverage of many of these approaches). While most of these are readily transferable to a work context, a key dimension is the extent to which workers have control of what to learn. Gonczi (2004) has stressed how organisations and employers have accepted the learning paradigm of competence, based on behaviouristic notions of learning, too readily and unthinkingly. In this scenario, learning in the workplace is usually reduced to workers performing prescribed behaviours to maximise outputs in the most efficient available means. Learning outcomes are predetermined by employers; workers become little more than cogs in a machine in a factory-type environment. Gonczi argued that if organisations accept the concept of competence as problematic then managers/human resource personnel at least can argue for a more holistic approach that incorporates humanistic elements. He did not dismiss a competency-based paradigm but stressed that such an approach needs to be counter-balanced by learning that enables (older) workers to be thinking, imaginative beings. He recommended the integration of propositional knowledge (knowing *that*) with instrumental and pragmatic (knowing *how*). As a consequence, the restrictive dichotomies of mind–body and thinking–doing are dissolved.

A relatively new emphasis in adult learning has been the concept of 'situated learning', which has conceptual links back to the work of Lave and Wenger (1991). From this perspective, knowledge is created through group participation involving novices (new recruits) and experienced workers. Collectively they engage in work tasks in a community of learning. The idea of 'learning to do' is inextricably connected to 'learning to become'. Learners/workers are engaged in a continual process of co-constructing knowledge, exemplified in some apprenticeship situations. Through a variety of means (scaffolding, modelling, mentoring and coaching), workers build their own knowledge that should lead to better understanding of the overall context of work. In this way a community of learning is developed, sustained and improved. In this context, it is not assumed that an older worker is necessarily the source of wisdom (a mentor); even if the older worker is very experienced, he/she is able to continue learning in this on-the-job situation.

Another way of conceiving of the work environment, applicable to older workers, is from the Canadian author Daniel Pratt (1998). He explained the rationale for five different perspectives on teaching and learning. In its broadest sense, teaching may be described as the art and science of helping adults to learn (Knowles 1984). Such a definition opens the door to manifold roles for both teachers and learners, from more traditional, passive renditions of learners to more proactive ideas of learners engaged in active learning, consistent with Gonczi's more integrated view of learning. Pratt explained that learning cannot be understood in isolation from other factors in the teaching-learning environment, namely, the teacher, learners as a group, content (curriculum), context (as in a training and development site in an organisation) and the ideals of the teacher that influence the direction of learning. He referred to five approaches to teaching-learning:

1. *A transmission perspective*: delivering content. This is a longstanding and traditional mode of teaching, commonly used in higher education but also in training contexts; it is teacher-centred and content heavy. Learners are usually relatively passive, as portrayed critically in Freire's (1984) banking education methodology.
2. *An apprenticeship model*: modelling ways of being. In this perspective learning is usually enacted outside the classroom in real-life situations. The purpose is to enculturate learners into a learning community. The content and teacher take centre stage but the learner develops competence over time.
3. *A developmental perspective*: cultivating ways of thinking. This approach is related to developing intellectual capabilities among learners wherein they develop cognitive maps of content. It tends to be learner-centred as the development of intellectual ability is valued highly.
4. *A nurturing perspective*: facilitating personal agency. In this approach, it is the skill and knowledge of the teacher that is crucial in facilitating learning. Learning is most influenced by a learner's self-concept and self-efficacy. A high degree of reciprocal respect from teacher to learner is a key component in the success of this approach. Ultimately, the learner should become self-reliant and self-sufficient.
5. *A social reform perspective*: seeking a better society. From this perspective the objective of learning is to change the world for the better through the articulation and implementation of a social vision. The teacher adopts an explicitly ideological position of effecting social change. In this approach, the ideals of the teacher (and then the learner) become a key driving force. The focus is upon the collective rather than individual learner aspirations.

Obviously, none of these perspectives is mutually exclusive; most teaching-learning environments, including those of older workers, include a hybrid approach. In an organisational context, the traditional transmission model, once dominant and reinforcing of social hierarchies in organisations, has largely given way to more learner-centred approaches that seek to develop, nurture and cognitively stimulate workers. The challenge for older workers as learners is to actively engage in whatever opportunities emerge and dissociate themselves from a dependent relationship often associated with more formal learning contexts.

Given the new dominance of electronic communication and social media in many workplaces, the emphases for training and development have to change to keep agencies competitive. There is latent high risk here for older workers whose knowledge and competence in new technology is doubtful, at least for the current generation of older workers. Employers need to be patient and understand that many older adults did not have access to this kind of technology until well into their careers. Organisations such as Seniornet provide some opportunities outside the workplace for older people to upgrade their capabilities in new technologies but similar experiences need to be provided inside work environments. It is quite commonplace for older people to experience considerable anxiety around new technologies; once this attitudinal barrier is overcome then progress can be quite rapid (Findsen 2005).

Barriers to and Challenges for Older Workers' Learning

In the adult education literature, barriers to learning are commonly classified as personal/dispositional, institutional, situational and informational (e.g. Darkenwald and Merriam 1982). Applied to older workers, these can be presented as:

- *Dispositional*: the tendency to believe that one is not capable of learning. I have already discussed this myth, but it is difficult to overcome. The notion of workers learning in a community can help to break down this self-doubt as group support may be more available.
- *Institutional*: In this case, an organisation can unintentionally erect barriers to exclude groups/individuals. An agency may convey the message that older adults in the workforce are less worthy of training. The organisation may have structured learning contexts that work against the interest/abilities of older workers (e.g. based primarily on e-learning). Equally, work teams may be set up that render older workers marginal to the enterprise. Policies and practices may inadvertently favour younger workers (e.g. provision of childcare facilities; gymnasium has equipment unsuited to older adults). The relative advantage of this set of barriers is that, providing there is an anti-ageist attitude among employers, these barriers are relatively easy to dismantle.
- *Situational*: These barriers are related to hindrances often outside the control of the company but still a nuisance for the older worker. For instance, this may include transport that is not conducive to getting workers to the job readily; or there may be a complex family arrangement or crisis that may lessen the commitment of a worker to work tasks. These can be remedied should an employer become cognisant of the impediment but this relies on an open communication system.
- *Informational*: These barriers relate to how organisations organise their communication systems, including marketing. To what extent are workers on the shop floor included in company messages? How much leeway do workers have to participate in organised company training and development? In a democratic work context these issues are less problematic but if the organisation is large and/or bureaucratic this kind of barrier may persist.

When these barriers act in tandem, the overall context for workers can be quite negative and the motivational level can be affected accordingly. Sensitive employers will know their workers and life circumstances to minimise the effects of learning barriers.

Strategies for Employers to Engage Older
Workers in Learning

It is a taken-for-granted assumption in adult learning/education literature that the needs, interests and aspirations of learners (including older workers) should be negotiated in terms of design for learning (e.g. Freire 1984; Knowles 1984; Merriam et al. 2007). In the workplace such considerations are significant in terms of 'buy-in' from workers, control of the learning and the quality of eventual outcomes. No employer/trainer who wants to gain commitment from workers would operate differently. In line with this approach, Rothwell et al. (2008, pp. 116–117) identified specific 'learner characteristics' of older adults that should be taken into account in planning and implementing learning opportunities for older workers. They presented ten 'key foundational principles' as follows:

1. Adults are problem-centred in how they regard learning experiences.
2. Adults are motivated by consideration of personal growth or gain. They wish to know 'what's in it for them'.
3. Trainers can plan ways to increase learners' motivation to learn.
4. Gauging expectations before a learning event is critical.
5. Trainers should plan to provide feedback and recognition to learners.
6. Individual differences in learning style should be considered when learning activities are planned.
7. Planned learning experiences should take into account adult lifespan development, needs and values.
8. Learning experiences should take into account ways to encourage on-the-job transfer.
9. Mature workers need a psychological supportive climate in which to learn.
10. Hands-on activity promotes learning.

It is important to acknowledge that each of these principles is not necessarily unique to older adults as workers. Items 7 and 9 are closer to being more directly applicable to older workers but, as I previously argued, heterogeneity is a hallmark of older people. From a critical standpoint, the characteristics of the (older) adult learners framework is problematic in the sense that it may be more accurate to refer to the life circumstances and material conditions in which older workers conduct their lives (Phillipson 1998) which, in turn, influence their propensities and access to learning opportunities, both within and outside work environments.

From an organisation's perspective, it is imperative to demonstrate at least equality of treatment of older workers in comparison with younger. A sound knowledge of the circumstances of older workers both as individuals and as a collective is a fruitful starting point for devising relevant learning events with and for older workers. While the notion of 'career' may be problematic (given that in our neo-liberal economic/political context people may need to change employment often), an employer's awareness of longer-term learning goals for workers is recommended. Elements that are supportive of older workers in the workplace include flexibility of work/learning patterns, rewards systems that appeal to older people (quite often intrinsic rather than extrinsic), challenging tasks, job sharing and opportunities to enlarge job projects (Rothwell et al. 2008).

Concluding Remarks

Older workers' need for learning and development should be understood from a variety of perspectives. At a macro level, the neo-liberal environment, related to dynamics of globalisation, has created a workplace context where organisations operate competitively and learning outcomes associated with work tasks often take precedence. Accordingly, a competency-based learning paradigm has assumed prominence because behaviours of (older) workers can more readily be monitored and assessed. Counter-arguments for different, more open conceptions of learning need to be continually asserted to avoid the reduction of training and development to only those events that are measureable and 'official' skills and knowledge.

Myths abound concerning the nature of older adulthood, including older people's learning capabilities. The vast majority of these stereotypes and ageist assumptions have little credibility, especially as ageing Baby Boomers are smashing such preconceptions. However, within the workplace such false assumptions are not easily replaced by more positive views of older people as workers/learners. Among employers particularly there needs to be a spirited attack on ageist views and age discrimination. Yet older workers themselves are not exempt from labelling themselves in similar ways, suggesting that social change in wider society and in workplaces will be evolutionary rather than revolutionary.

The ideas of what constitutes effective teaching and learning in workplaces also need attention. As the perspectives presented by Pratt (1998) demonstrate, there are several legitimate ways of viewing learning, all of which potentially can be operationalised in specific work contexts. While barriers to learning for older workers continue to hamper some people's engagement in learning, there should be ongoing dialogue between management and workers as to what is most effective in that context. It is dangerous to be overly prescriptive, even when attempting to identify those principles of adult learning that best suit mature workers.

While the viewpoints of management, trainers and workers on what constitute suitable learning opportunities are likely to continue to differ, an integrated and holistic stance towards learning and development is likely to reap better outcomes. The co-construction of learning plans in individual and team contexts is a useful way of gaining input and commitment from workers for more formal learning. In addition, it is important to recognise that non-formal and informal learning can also be very positive elements of a worker's overall experience. Hence, encouraging workers to engage in learning in a variety of contexts, in terms of formality and hierarchy, should enhance their learning and development to create a win-win scenario for employers and workers.

References

Barnett, R. (1999). Learning to work and working to learn. In D. Boud & J. Garrick (Eds.), *Understanding learning at work* (pp. 29–44). London: Routledge.

Beatty, P. T., & Visser, R. M. S. (Eds.). (2005). *Thriving on an aging workforce: Strategies for organizational and systematic change*. Malabar: Krieger.

Beck, U. (1992). *Risk society: Towards a new modernity*. London: Sage.

Centre for Research into the Older Workforce. (2005). *Do employers need older workers?* (Briefing Paper No. 5). Surrey: South East England Development Agency.

Darkenwald, G. G., & Merriam, S. B. (1982). *Adult education: Foundations of practice*. New York: Harper Row.

Davey, J. A. (2006). The labour market. In J. Boston & J. A. Davey (Eds.), *Implications of population ageing: Opportunities and risks* (pp. 189–220). Wellington: Institute of Policy Studies, Victoria University of Wellington.

Encel, S. (1997). Work in later life. In A. Borowski, S. Encel, & E. Ozanne (Eds.), *Ageing and social policy in Australia* (pp. 137–156). Melbourne: Cambridge University Press.

Field, J. (2002). *Lifelong learning and the new educational order*. Stoke on Trent: Trentham Books.

Field, J. (2003). *Social capital*. London: Routledge.

Findsen, B. (2005). *Learning later*. Malabar: Krieger.

Findsen, B., & Formosa, M. (2011). *Lifelong learning in later life: A handbook on older adult learning*. Rotterdam: Sense.

Findsen, B., & McCullough, S. (2008). *Older adults' engagement with further and higher education in the west of Scotland: Tracking educational journeys. Final report*. Glasgow: Department of Adult & Continuing Education and the West of Scotland Wider Access Forum.

Freire, P. (1984). *Pedagogy of the oppressed*. New York: Continuum.

Golding, B. (2011). Older men's learning through age-related community organisations in Australia. *International Journal of Education and Ageing, 1*(3), 237–252.

Gonczi, A. (2004). The new professional and vocational education. In G. Foley (Ed.), *Dimensions of adult learning* (pp. 19–34). Crow's Nest: Allen & Unwin.

Illeris, K. (2004). *The three dimensions of learning*. Denmark: Roskilde University Press.

Jarvis, P. (1985). *Sociological perspectives on lifelong education and lifelong learning*. Athens: Department of Adult Education, University of Georgia.

Knowles, M. S. (1984). *Andragogy in action*. San Francisco: Jossey-Bass.

Laslett, P. (1989). *A fresh map of life: The emergence of the third age*. London: Weidenfeld & Nicholson.

Lave, J., & Wenger, E. (1991). *Situated learning: Legitimate peripheral participation*. New York: Cambridge University Press.

Lundberg, D., & Marshallsay, Z. (2007). *Older workers' perspectives on training and retention of older workers*. Adelaide: National Centre for Vocational Education Research.

Mayo, M., & Thompson, J. (Eds.). (1995). *Adult learning, critical intelligence and social change*. Leicester: NIACE.

McGregor, J., & Gray, G. (2002). Stereotypes and older workers: The New Zealand experience. *Social Policy Journal of New Zealand, 18*, 163–177.

Merriam, S. B., Caffarella, R. S., & Baumgartner, L. M. (2007). *Learning in adulthood: A comprehensive guide* (3rd ed.). San Francisco: Jossey-Bass.

Pedler, M., Burgoyne, J., & Boydell, T. (1991). *The learning company*. London: McGraw Hill.

Phillipson, C. (1998). *Reconstructing old age: New agendas in social theory and practice*. London: Sage.

Pratt, D. D. (1998). *Five perspectives on teaching in adult and higher education*. Malabar: Krieger.

Riley, M., & Riley, M. (1994). Structural lag: Past and future. In M. Riley, R. Kahn, & A. Foner (Eds.), *Age and structural lag* (pp. 15–36). New York: Wiley.

Rothwell, W. J., Sterns, H. L., Spokus, D., & Reaser, J. M. (2008). *Working longer: New strategies for managing, training, and retaining older employees*. New York: American Management Association.

Wain, K. (2004). *The learning society in a postmodern world*. New York: Peter Lang.

Withnall, A. (2010). *Improving learning in later life*. London: Routledge.

Withnall, A., McGivney, V., & Soulsby, J. (2004). *Older people learning: Myths and realities*. Leicester: NIACE.

Chapter 6
Workplace Equity and Diversity: Towards Recognising a Plurality of Knowledge and Skills

Katie Maher

Abstract This chapter focuses on issues of equity and diversity in the workplace. It explores the extent to which diversity management approaches, which are based on a business rationale that diversity is a productive asset, are inclusive of historically under-represented ethnic groups and Aboriginal peoples. It proposes that equity and diversity work is not just about ethnic minority groups, but also about the dominant, white culture. The chapter proposes that current workplace standards and practices tend to be based on western norms that can privilege the majority white culture with 'unearned assets'. Drawing on interviews with employees in human resource, learning and development, training and assessment, operational and service roles in a range of Australian rail companies, it identifies some problems with achieving equity and diversity in the workplace, with particular attention to challenges in recognising the knowledge and skills of a culturally diverse workforce.

Introduction

Since the 1990s many Australian organisations have come to use the term 'diverse' to describe their workforce. Increasingly, government organisations and private corporations have promoted diversity management plans and policies. These developments have followed reports that, with changing population demographics and growing migration, the labour force is increasingly comprised of racial groups other than white people, and that it is in the business interest of organisations to address this diversity (Zanoni et al. 2010). According to Zanoni et al. (2010) the concept of diversity has 'revolutionized the understanding of differences in organizations, as it portrayed them for the first time in the history of management as strategic assets,

K. Maher (✉)
School of Education, University of South Australia, Adelaide, SA, Australia
e-mail: katie.maher@mymail.unisa.edu.au

T. Short and R. Harris (eds.), *Workforce Development: Strategies and Practices*,
DOI 10.1007/978-981-287-068-1_6, © Springer Science+Business Media Singapore 2014

which, if well managed, could provide a competitive advantage' (2010, p. 12). Australia has largely adopted this corporate rhetoric. This 'business rationale at the core of diversity has often been used to explain the popularity of this notion within the US business world (Edelman et al. 2001) and, later, its diffusion to other western countries (Boxenbaum 2006; Jones et al. 2000; Süss and Kleiner 2008; Zanoni and Janssens 2008)' (Zanoni et al. 2010, p. 12).

There is no fixed definition of diversity. It is often used to include and refer to a heterogeneous population group including, for example, people of different ages, genders, dis/abilities and sexual orientations as well as people of various racial, ethnic and religious origins. Here I will refer predominantly to issues of ethnicity and race, with consideration given to Aboriginal peoples and other historically under-represented (non-white) ethnic groups, as well as to dominant white cultures. I particularly focus on attempts to manage diversity in the workplace, which has become known as 'diversity management', and which might be described as a suite of human resource strategies that have become popular in corporate culture in western countries including the US, Canada, the UK and Australia since the 1990s. Diversity management has typically included such practices as diversity awareness training for managers, targeted training and recruiting of Aboriginal and migrant employees and setting employment targets for historically under-represented 'equity' groups. While in some ways similar to equal employment opportunity and other approaches to access and inclusion of historically under-represented cultural groups, diversity management has particular ways of conceptualising and 'managing' diversity.

Diversity management is based on the logic that 'diversity is conducive to corporate productivity, and that as a result, there are market incentives for firms to diversify their workforces' (Mills 2011, p. 47). According to this business rationale for diversity management,

> Companies properly managing diversity would attract and retain skilled workers in an increasingly diverse labour market, better service increasingly diverse markets by matching diverse customers with a more diverse workforce, improve organizational learning and creativity through employees' exposure to a wider range of perspectives, and increase organizational flexibility in increasingly turbulent contexts (Amason 1996; Cox and Blake 1991; Ely and Thomas 2001; Kochan et al. 2003). (Zanoni et al. 2010, p. 12)

In this chapter I attempt to critique diversity management 'as an approach to better include marginalized groups in the workplace' (Mills 2011, p. 46). Drawing on data gathered from interviews with employees and employers in various Australian companies with links to the rail sector, I consider the extent to which current approaches to diversity management are equitable, particular in terms of their capacity to recognise the knowledge and skills of a diverse workforce.

Recent Diversity Developments in the Australian Rail Sector

I take the rail industry as the focus of this study on workplace equity and diversity. The rail industry is a particularly useful sector in which to study diversity management, given its historically important place in industrial and corporate development in

Australia, its geographic spread, its position across public and private sectors, and its links with transport, construction, communications and other industries. The rail industry also has a long history of cultural plurality in the workplace (Fitch 2006; Hicks and Hill 1993), although formal diversity policies are relatively new to the sector.

Diversity management in the rail sector has developed in the context of a declining and increasingly privatised rail industry, the downsizing of the permanent rail workforce, transforming technologies, growing competition from faster, more fashionable and more convenient forms of transport, and growing links with the resource sector. Whereas large state owned and run railway workshops and related public rail services were the heart of the rail industry of decades past, most of the sector has since merged into a conglomeration of corporations – many of these multinational – involved in construction, operations and maintenance, engineering and infrastructure, transport and communication, and 'asset management' services. A growing proportion of Australian railway association member companies – those engaged in constructing, maintaining and/or servicing rail transport – are also engaged in the exploration, mining and processing of minerals.

The integration of diversity into business goals picked up pace in the mid-2000s. With increasing pressure to remain a competitive transport provider, Australian rail has, over the past decade, attempted to 'change its face', as indicated in key Australasian Railway Association (ARA) strategic reports such as *The changing face of rail: A journey to the employer of choice* (2006) and *A rail revolution: Future capability identification and skills development for the Australasian rail industry* (2008). These reports promote the need for the Australian rail industry to embrace a diversity of cultures and social groups in its workforce. The diversity push was backed by concerns over the need to replace an ageing workforce and by the knowledge of increasing population mobility. As part of this change of face, rail corporations were advised to capitalise on an increasingly diverse population demographic. In these reports, the ARA targeted a number of employee groups including Aboriginal people and migrants with the intention of increasing the recruitment, retention and skills development of these groups to meet skills shortages and fill human resource needs in the current and future rail industry. *A rail revolution* noted 'limited access to skilled migrants' as a workforce risk to the rail industry (ARA 2008, p. 14). *The changing face of rail* noted that 'the Aboriginal population was significantly under-represented in the industry and that this group could satisfy a substantial number of positions required from the industry' (ARA 2006, p. 60). In the following Section I discuss some attempts by rail companies to develop a culturally diverse workforce.

A Study of Equity and Diversity in Rail

This research draws on interview data from a national study on recognition of skills and prior learning in the rail industry, funded by the Cooperative Research Centre for Rail Innovation. Semi-structured interviews were held with human resource, operations and learning and development managers, trainers and assessors, equity and diversity representatives and employees in various roles including drivers, guards and customer service officers from a range of Australian rail organisations. Fifteen organisations participated in the study, including: passenger and freight rail services, rail construction and infrastructural development and rail training and development companies; small, medium and large companies; government, quasi-government and privatised companies; local, national and international corporations. Fifty-nine interviews were conducted at the workplace or by telephone during working hours. They lasted approximately 1 h and were recorded and transcribed. The interviews were conducted by one male and five female ethnic majority researchers (including myself) who were part of the larger research project team. While this was a semi-structured interview process and questions varied, we generally asked interviewees for their views on:

- What barriers might prevent particular equity groups, such as Aboriginal or migrant employees, from having their skills and knowledge recognised?
- Do Aboriginal people, migrants or other equity groups face any particular difficulties in the workplace, particularly with regard to having their skills and learning recognised?
- Who benefits from having their skills and knowledge recognised (in recruitment, training, assessment and performance development) processes and who misses out?

In the interviews we aimed to explore organisational practices that impacted upon recognition of skills and learning, and upon equity and diversity work more broadly, including, for example, recruitment practices and training programs. They were designed to facilitate conversation around many aspects of recognition of skills and learning, and to invite people in the workplace to reflect on the kinds of work their organisations have done and could do. We drew further data from equity and diversity management plans and policy documents collected from Australian rail corporations.

The interview protocol was drafted and discussed with a research team of vocational education scholars. Interviewers were instructed to engage in dialogue with interviewees and to attempt to understand their views rather than mechanically reading through the interview questions. Ethics approval for the study was given by the University of South Australia Human Research Ethics Committee. As the intention of this study was to locate and address equity and diversity problems, rather than point a finger at particular corporations, and due to ethical requirements for the study, the names of the companies studied and the company representatives interviewed have not been disclosed.

Data analysis was assisted by the use of NVivo software, and the research team worked together to identify and report on themes. As my research focus was on equity and diversity, I took a prominent role in identifying and analysing equity and diversity themes. My analysis was informed by recent scholarship in critical diversity and equity studies (Ahmed 2007a; Janssens and Zanoni 2014; Bunda et al. 2012; Mills 2011). I considered how employers and employees in Australian rail corporations, and Australian workplaces more generally, understand 'equity and diversity', and how they view diversity within their organisations. While offering no quick fix 'how to' guide to equity and diversity in the workplace, I attempted to locate some problems with the way diversity was constructed and practised and to point towards more equitable ways of valuing cultural plurality in the workplace.

Findings

A number of pertinent findings around 'managing diversity' emerged from interviews with rail employees. Interviewees described various ways in which diversity has been viewed and managed in Australian rail companies in recent times, and what some of the implications are for race equality. The research team identified a number of key issues from the research data, as outlined in the following discussion.

It's Pretty Well Equitable Across the Board

At all companies consulted, and across roles within those companies, the majority of interviewees we spoke with indicated that they felt all employees in their organisations were treated fairly. Most trainers, human resource managers, learning and development managers, infrastructure managers, train drivers, guards and customer service officers we spoke with – the large majority of whom were white men or white women – said they did not regard equity as a problem for Aboriginal or migrant employees. Some interviewees suggested that equity and diversity were not a concern in their organisation as they employed few or no (non–English speaking background or visibly different) migrants or Aboriginal people. The equity and diversity implications of employing few or no non-white employees was rarely questioned or raised.

We asked human resource managers, learning and development managers, and trainers/assessors whether they felt some groups were more likely to have their skills and learning recognised than others. The majority responded that they felt workplace processes were equitable. A trainer/assessor from a large public state passenger rail company said: 'I'd say it's pretty well equitable across the board.'

One human resources manager from a large public state passenger rail service said:

> In terms of the type of work that my team did, I think that you could safely say that we don't differentiate on the basis of someone's background in any way whatsoever, because we're only really looking at their history, their training history particularly, and what was in that training, and then applying that, so it's actually quite objective in that regard.

A learning and development manager from a large public passenger rail service, when asked whether there were any barriers that might prevent equity groups from having their skills recognised, responded: 'Not that I'm aware of.' Many interviewees were not aware of equity groups such as Aboriginal or non–English speaking background migrants facing difficulties in accessing and benefitting from skills recognition. One human resources manager from a large public state passenger rail company informed us: 'No, there's no issues re equity groups and access to training and equal employment opportunity that come up.'

Despite this perception of being 'pretty well equitable', white employees continue to be over-represented in rail companies, particularly in higher level and better paid roles. The capabilities of Aboriginal and historically under-represented racial groups continue to be undervalued, not only in economic terms but in social and cultural terms.

Tilbury and Colic-Peisker in their Perth case study of skilled refugees, employment and social inclusion also found that, while inequity continues to exist, there is a general presumption of non-discrimination:

> Employers we interviewed almost universally denied the existence of discrimination in the Australian workplace. A general presumption was that outright racial discrimination no longer occurs within the context of a modern multicultural nation. American and European research shows, however, that developed Western societies moved from 'blatant' prejudice and discrimination towards 'subtle' prejudice and discrimination which 'slips in under the norm, unrecognized as prejudice' (Pettigrew 1998, p. 84). (Tilbury and Colic-Peisker 2007, p. 114)

Research into whiteness has critiqued the way white people, as the dominant racial group, acquire economic, cultural and social advantage. Peggy McIntosh (1989) has brought attention to the 'invisible package of unearned assets' that white people can 'count on'. As Janssens and Zanoni have explained: 'These advantages derive from existing inequality structures and thus remain invisible to white people, but are obvious to non-whites' (2014, p. 4).

Equity and diversity work continues to be obstructed by these subtle cultural norms which afford unearned advantage and dominance to white people (Zanoni and Janssens 2014; McIntosh 1989). Scholars such as Zanoni et al. (2010), Bunda et al. (2012), Ahmed (2007a, b) and McIntosh (1989) have brought attention to how critiques of white ways of being, knowing and doing might assist in addressing continuing inequalities in the workplace.

I Treat Everybody the Same

There was a perception among many interviewees (the large majority of whom were white) that all employees should be treated 'the same' and an assumption that if people were, or appeared to be, treated the same then this was fair. An operations manager from a medium-sized state passenger rail service explained: 'I treat everybody the same. I don't care who you are or what you are, what gender you are, you're the same to me. If you want to do this job, you do it the same as them.'

An interviewee from a multinational infrastructure contractor, when asked whether everyone had the same opportunity to undergo skills recognition, commented:

> Yes, because I'm giving the same information to everybody, so it's got nothing to do ... if you're employed by us, because we have these standards, practice and procedures that we go through ... You are going to come into our system and you are going to go across these hurdles, and it doesn't matter who you are.

The assumption that standard practice and procedures that were 'the same for everyone' somehow ensured equity for all was shared by interviewees in various roles. This suggested a lack of acknowledgement of 'unspoken cultural norms' (p. 4) (Janssens and Zanoni 2014) and how wider structural inequalities can disadvantage equity groups. Few questioned the possibility that current practices and processes were based on white, western ways of doing and knowing. One learning and development coordinator from a state passenger rail service noted that no particular issues had come up with Indigenous or ethnic minority employees at her company. When asked whether the language used might be problematic for some employees she replied:

Interviewee: It possibly could be but I've not come across it yet ... Because we work on the rail language here.
Interviewer: A language unto its own!
Interviewee: And we have our own language, so yes.

Like many other learning and development managers, and trainer/assessors in rail, this interviewee indicated a perception that the 'rail language' was neutral and fair. The work of Light et al. (2011) have revealed something of the ways in which 'often-neutral organizational policies are used to discriminate, legitimate discrimination, or both' (p. 41). They have pointed out how employers are more likely to believe structures are equitable when formal procedures are in place:

(E)vidence abounds about racial stereotypes affecting formal performance evaluations (McKay and McDaniel 2006; Roth et al. 2003) and merit-based personnel decisions (Castilla 2008; Elvira and Town 2001; Roth 2006). The idea of meritocracy is thus more than a matter of individual attitudes. Formal meritocratic procedures and rhetoric can become an institutionalized cloak for ongoing ascriptive bias – a legitimating discourse, where managers, employers, and judges exchange symbols of meritocracy for equality ... When formal procedures are in place, managers (and judges) are more apt to believe the structure is unbiased and that unequal outcomes therefore reflect differences in merit. (Light et al. 2011, p. 43)

A number of interviewees presented the view that, as workplace processes were designed to be equitable, then they must be equitable. We also saw evidence of interviewees equating 'competence' with fairness, and assuming that if employees are expected to achieve the same standard of 'competence' then the same process must be used to achieve this. One learning and development manager from a public registered training organisation informed us that their organisation had trained a group of thirty Aboriginal trainees. When asked, 'Did that process work any differently to how it generally does?' they responded: 'No, it can't. They have to be competent, it doesn't matter what background or race or gender or any of that, and it's purely competent or not competent.'

A train driver trainer/assessor from the same company, when asked if there might be some employees, such as Indigenous or migrant employees, who experienced difficulties having their skills recognised, replied: 'Not within the area that I work within the company, it's very dry, very black and white'. Light et al. have observed that 'Whites ... remain reticent to acknowledge potential structural and historical impediments that minority groups face. Consequently, meritocracy remains a key cultural justification for inequality (see Lamont 2000), while the effects of continued racial bias often go unacknowledged' (2011, pp. 42–43).

I'm Not Aware of Any Policy

While some companies did have equity and diversity policies, employers and employees were not necessarily aware of these policies. As one operational manager from a medium-sized state public passenger rail service commented: 'I'm not aware of any specific policy we have for those groups who may be disadvantaged, or having the skills recognised in a different manner.'

Findings from the research interviews and literature suggest that equity and diversity are not, overall, greatly prioritised and valued within rail. Most employees, other than those such as equity and diversity officers with specific duties around equity and diversity, did not necessarily regard diversity work as part of their duties.

One of the misconceptions about diversity policies and programs is that they exist 'for' non-white others who lack required skills and knowledge, rather than recognising all (including white) Australians as part of cultural diversity. Nirmal Puwar has pointed out how, 'In policy terms, diversity has overwhelmingly come to mean the inclusion of different bodies' (2004, p. 1). Rather than seeing diversity as something non-white others bring to the white employer, diversity might be seen as ways of being, doing and knowing in which plurality is valued. And indeed white Australians have at least as much to learn from cultural diversity as Aboriginal Australians and ethnic minority groups. Diversity policies do not get done if white employers detach themselves from the 'problem' of diversity.

One common example of this in Australia can be seen in the rationalising of the need for Aboriginal employment policies and designated Aboriginal engagement roles. An employee from one company expressed her view that a designated Aboriginal engagement or employment officer/manager was required to improve the conditions for employing Aboriginal people in the company she worked for, but that senior management would not agree to appoint an Aboriginal employment or engagement officer (or manager) as the company had too few Aboriginal employees. The company neglected to recognise the value of Aboriginal engagement for employees across the company.

A number of companies consulted as part of this study suggested that Aboriginal employment was not a concern for them, as they had few Aboriginal employees. It could be argued however that Aboriginal (and white) engagement was more of a problem in these companies as they were failing to include Aboriginal peoples within the workforce. Likewise, equity and diversity policies are just as important in those companies with a majority of white employees.

Some Particular Fits That You Would Want

A number of interviewees commented on the requirement for employees from under-represented cultural groups to be able to 'fit in' or 'blend in'. Such views tended to be based on perceptions that 'different' cultures did not fit in, and that those who are different ought to be the ones making the adjustments, rather than the workplace becoming more inclusive. One learning and development manager from a passenger rail service commented:

> So we found with one of our newer sites there's a big, I suppose, requirement for a lot of people to make sure that they definitely fit in, and they did a lot of that type of testing with them when they actually came on. ... The L & D [learning and development] component [of the human resource strategy] for the business that we need to start rolling out, part of that will be us building basically a capability competency framework where we'll actually look at that in a lot more detail, and start to set, I suppose, from the top, what are those type of soft skills, so not on the technical side but those type of skills that we want in our workforce, and culture that we're going to bring in, and then that will have a lot of things in.

The comments from this interviewee suggest a need for caution around potential cultural bias in the assessment of 'soft skills'. The interviewee also indicated that the industry was looking for 'particular fits' for 'diverse roles across the business':

> We've got many diverse roles right across the business, but at the same time I suppose there is a commonality in a lot of the skills that are required in those roles, so from that soft skill side and maybe not so much from the technical side because they are very specialised, but from that soft skill there is, I suppose, for our type of industry, a particular, you know, some particular fits for areas that you would want.

One learning and development manager from a small freight company explained the problems that one of the company's few women employees faced with 'fitting in' at work:

> We did have one lady, and she came through – she went through the system. But it didn't really work very well. I mean, it's still very male-dominated out there, you know. And she's not bashful in coming forward, so there was always some altercation out there occurring because someone restricted her rights, or she had to take the call from the kids, or she had to go back home, because the kids were sick. So there was a lot of issues, and I must say that [our company] did everything that they could to kind of bend, and to accommodate her, whatever, but she was, she's just one of those people that, nothing's ever good enough, and to a certain degree, you've got to blend in with the workplace, I mean you've got to try and work in with people.

This response suggests that the company was not accustomed to accommodating requests to take leave to attend to family needs, and speaking out about restrictions of one's rights could be regarded as an 'altercation'. While non-majority employees are expected to 'blend in', and competency standards and assessment practices are seen to be fair and equitable, historically under-represented groups continue to miss out. Tilbury and Colic-Peisker, in their study of refugees and employment, pointed to how employers can discriminate against under-represented racial/ethnic groups:

> Some suggested that the visibly and culturally different simply did not have job-relevant characteristics including communication abilities, or 'cultural knowledge', or that they would not 'fit in' with other staff (what Constable et al. 2004 call the 'tea-room mentality'). This was often stated in general terms, as a 'soft skill' related to 'Australian-ness'.... 'Ability to fit in' with the existing team of workers or work environment was identified both by employers and by the refugees as a significant, yet invisible, barrier to appropriate employment. (2007, p. 115)

One key marker of race equality, according to Janssens and Zanoni, is an argument for 'pluralism through the majority and the minority's mutual acculturation' (2014, p. 3):

> All employees should be allowed to bring their entire set of identities to work rather than be required to assimilate into the dominant culture based on the majority's identity. The underlying idea is that power inequality originates in organizational settings which are infused with cultural norms reflecting historically dominant (ethnic) identities, foreclosing the expression of others. Many organizations remain 'monocultural' and require (ethnic) minorities to assimilate to such norms. Yet such expectation is not only unethical, it is also unrealistic. (Janssens and Zanoni 2014, p. 3)

We Are Almost Happy to Teach Them

Some rail representatives also presented themselves and their companies as taking a benevolent approach to 'allowing' non-white employees in to the company and in 'helping' them to 'blend in'. Consider the following comments from a training and assessment manager:

> Where you might have people of different cultures and what we've been used to here in Australia, then we are almost happy to teach them how to blend in from a societal point of view ... [For] workers coming from overseas to blend into Australia, society and industry, I think they need a little bit of assistance with not just blending into that trade, but also blending into the workforce in that trade ... Especially, um, women, and I don't mean that in a derogatory sense, I just mean that a lot of our trades aren't, um, focused on encouraging female workers into our trades and that is something we've got to look at as well.

It is 'workers coming from overseas' who are seen to 'need a little bit of assistance' to 'blend in', rather than the view that the organisation might play a more active role in cultural change towards a more inclusive workplace.

When viewed, managed and practised from the perspective of a dominant, white employer, diversity tends to position non-white groups as marginal (Zanoni et al. 2010; Ahmed 2007a) and often as deficit, particularly in the case of Aboriginal groups (Bunda et al. 2012; Norris 2010; Mills 2011). Employees from historically under-represented groups tend to be positioned as lacking required skills and knowledge and their capabilities are undervalued. Janssens and Zanoni noted how formalised human resource management procedures 'continue to be culturally biased, valuing the skills and the qualities of the ethnic majority (Acker 1990; Bond and Pyle 1998)' (2014, p. 2).

Other interviews indicated some of the ways 'cultural differences' were viewed as external to organisational productivity, to be tolerated rather than valued. One train driver from a medium-sized state public passenger rail company gave the following example:

> When you talk about the cultural differences we had an incident where at [place named] a railcar was involved in a fatality, and a Maori chap wanted to bless the train afterwards. We've had Aboriginal people from their side, Aboriginal railcar drivers, where railcars had

been involved in fatalities, and they've wanted to do something that's suited them. Now if it's something that is for the individual, doesn't affect anyone else, and it satisfies their cultural needs, we've never objected to any of that. We've allowed them to do that.

Here 'their cultural needs' are seen as superfluous to the organisation and will be tolerated provided 'it's something that is for the individual, doesn't affect anyone else'. This implies however that where cultural needs are considered to affect others, they will not be tolerated. If attending to cultural needs requires an employee to take time off work, for example, which will require changes to the work roster and affect his/her line manager and co-workers, then the company is less happy to accommodate.

The white interviewee in the quotation above positioned himself as a representative of the firm, 'we', and in a position of power relative to the non-white other: 'We've allowed them to do that.' The relationship between the company and Aboriginal people was presented as one where the company 'makes allowances', intimating an unequal relationship that is less mutually beneficial than diversity management promotional material would suggest. Furthermore, 'Since the corporation was presented as racially neutral, any changes to policy or practice were understood as helping Aboriginal peoples' (Mills 2011, p. 69).

Other interviewees also suggested that their companies were acting to 'help', provide opportunities to or make allowances for non-white applicants and employees. Some comments suggested that, despite great efforts on the part of white employers, those who were not part of the dominant culture lacked required skills and knowledge. One compliance/competency officer from a national quasi-public infrastructure company commented on difficulties with accommodating skilled migrants:

> We've gone through a process, probably a couple of years ago, we went to the overseas market to try and obtain some signal electricians. That process did and didn't work. It worked across probably 30 per cent … The issue that we had with the other 70 per cent was the amount of recognition that needed to happen … Two that I had an experience with came from Singapore. What they were called and recognised as in signals in Singapore with their qualifications, how they were recognised there didn't match across to our requirements … They had to go through the full process of providing evidence and providing, getting workplace observations done, and doing scenarios at the [training organisation]. This went on for, I think around about 6–12 months, so we just tried and tried and tried, but at the end of the day we ended up having to send these two gentlemen back to Singapore.

Mills, in her research on diversity management in the Canadian context, noted how on the face of evidence that non-white others 'were not being successfully incorporated into the workforce' employees and employers 'needed to construct alternate explanations that did not disrupt their understandings of their own positions as representatives of the company' (2011, p. 70). Employees and employers in Australian rail companies may respond similarly when diversity initiatives do not succeed; it is 'the other' and not the company who is constructed as lacking. While it may be true that the skills and knowledge required of signal electricians in Singapore differs from Australia, the interviewee did not mention other factors contributing to the employment situation apparently not working for the majority of skilled employees recruited from overseas.

Andersson and Guo noted that 'the knowledge possessed by immigrants is not acceptable, transferable, or recognizable because their experiences and credentials are deemed different, deficient and, hence, inferior' (2009, p. 435). Shah and Long suggested that shortfalls in recognising the prior knowledge and skills of migrants are a barrier to effectively embedding migrants in Australian workplaces, indicating that 'some part of the human capital can be left behind political borders because it is not recognised' (2004, p. 29). A responsive recognition process needs to account for the language and communication needs of many culturally and linguistically diverse workers and 'to develop a grounded and useful "working language"' (Kell and Vogl 2009, p. 89).

So They Just Put Them Back to the Training Again

'Cultural awareness' training was one of the most common initiatives undertaken in organisations to promote diversity. As one interviewee put it, 'The organisation often sees training as a solution to everything'. Training was often taken as the answer to addressing diversity requirements, with employees trapped in a 'training for training's sake' approach. Training can be acted out as a 'tick box' solution, the target being to train a certain number of people in a given topic (recently branded 'cultural fitness' in some organisations). As Ahmed has pointed out, when the workplace becomes 'one that focuses on measurable and marketable consumer satisfaction' (Blackmore and Sachs 2003, p. 141) by way of tick boxes, "good practice" toolkits and training then 'Diversity and equality become "things" that can be measured, along with other performance outcomes' (Ahmed 2007b, p. 596). But equity and diversity work requires more than ticking the 'diversity training completed' box.

One learning and development manager informed us of how the company she worked with had tended to respond to incidences of cultural misconduct through repeated ineffective sessions of cultural awareness training. Despite repeated training, bullying remained a problem in her organisation:

> [Training] doesn't solve the problem. It just ticks boxes for, like, management so they can say well they've got no excuse now and they can put the onus back on the individual … its quite difficult sometimes like you'll have to convince managers that training isn't the solution … Because there has been a couple of incidents, like we're currently training 600 [track] workers in just culture and dignity and respect so it's about you know how not to bully or bait a worker in the workplace because it's a really significant problem and … its actually the third time people have been through this training. And they're still, and they're still … And it's still happening so they do the training again. I mean how ridiculous is that? And expensive!

According to Taksa and Groutsis' research into diversity in the NSW railways, 'The implementation of policies and strategies designed to prevent diversity-related problems, including anti-harassment and bullying training provided to 800 managers and 3300 employees up to 31 August 2008, has not stopped claims of harassment, bullying and discrimination related to gender and ethnicity' (2010, p. 176).

Janssens and Zanoni argued that popular approaches to diversity management are not effective as they tend to limit their focus to individual cognition rather than addressing 'the structural dimension of privilege, domination, disadvantage and deprivation' (2014, p. 3). They also noted that diversity training in its various guises has tended to have limited impact, and may even exacerbate race inequality:

> Based on the social psychological insight that information may reduce bias (Fiske 1998), training modules familiarize employees with anti-discrimination law, suggest behavioural changes, and increase cultural awareness and cross-cultural communication (Pendry et al. 2007). However, some studies indicate that information about out-group members' culture actually reinforces group stereotypes and prejudices (Ellis and Sonnenfeld 1994; Rynes and Rosen 1995), does not change attitudes toward particular groups (Kulik and Roberson 2008), and does not necessarily result in behavioural change (Hite and McDonald 2006). (Janssens and Zanoni 2014, pp. 2–3).

The work of Janssens and Zanoni offers some insight into 'organizational practices that foster the valuing of multiple competencies and the ability to express multiple identities' (2014, p. 1). Their analysis indicated that race equality is 'fostered by practices that broaden dominant norms on competencies and cultural identities, and avoid reducing ethnic minority employees to mere representatives of a stigmatized social group.' (Janssens and Zanoni 2014, p. 1). Janssens and Zanoni endeavoured to imagine alternative approaches to doing diversity that are better placed to support race equality:

> Diversity Management practices that broaden norms and offer multiple understandings of competence and multiple identity positionings are effective in fostering ethnic equality because they subvert Western perceptions of 'otherness' in terms of, ethnicities, 'races', cultures, religions etc. Specifically, they destabilize the dominant hierarchical system of binaries which values the ethnic majority over the ethnic minority in work settings: e.g. skilled/unskilled, productive/unproductive, and thus valuable/valueless ... The pervasive structural inequality sustained by these collectively shared linguistic categories cannot be corrected at the level of individuals' cognition – for instance through training – as individuals rely on them to make sense of social reality and act upon it. Inequality rather needs to be addressed by changing the discursive structures through organizational practices and processes at the core of the organization. (Janssens and Zanoni 2014, p. 12)

Some of Them Had a Hard Time Proving to Me

Comments from a number of interviews indicated that managers, trainers and assessors were aware that their companies were not recognising the skills and knowledge of non-white others as well as they could. An external trainer and assessor from a quasi-public national infrastructure company noted that he found it difficult to fairly assess the competencies of some culturally and linguistically different employees:

> Some of them had a hard time proving to me that they had [skills and experience], both migrant and Indigenous ... Could be cultural differences, maybe I missed some of their subtle movements that I didn't pick up, but yeah I did have a hard time trying to get it out of some of them.

A number of other interviewees, including human resource managers, operations managers, learning and development managers, and trainers and assessors indicated a lack of expertise in engaging with jobseekers and employees who were from different cultural backgrounds. A learning quality and accreditation manager from a large state passenger rail and infrastructure company observed that one risk with recognising the skills and knowledge of culturally and linguistic diverse peoples is that

> We might not have the people in-house that have that background knowledge and under-standing to recognise those skills in others or we might employ people to do that who have that background knowledge, for instance an external provider. I would see that as a risk, that there might be some misalignment between the worker's skills they are demonstrating and the perception of what those skills are.

Interviewees noted difficulties with matching skills and experience across languages and locations. Our findings suggested that it could be more difficult for employees from historically under-represented ethnic groups to voice concerns. Consider the following exchange with a human resources manager from a large public state passenger rail organisation:

> If somebody's particularly vocal ... we would certainly be prepared to have a conversation around what they're asking ... Having said that then I think, for example, somebody from a culturally and linguistically diverse background may be less likely to be vocal simply because they don't have the capacity to communicate.

Australian literature on workplace experiences of (non-white) migrant employees indicates that 'migrants are not being employed in occupations that match their skills' (Kell and Vogl 2009, p. 88). Many skilled migrants and refugees are not familiar with the local employment context and unaccustomed to the language used. They may not 'describe or "translate" their skills, abilities and experiences in ways that make them more apparent to employers' (Constable et al. 2004, p. 11). Billett discussed how lack of proficiency in English is not just a matter of language incompetence but brings with it 'personal dimensions of the capacity to be competent' (2009, p. 50). Not speaking the dominant language well can undermine workers in many ways and lead to under-recognition of skills and knowledge in a range of areas. As Hull (1997) has noted, 'not being able to speak English means not being able to defend yourself in the workplace ... even when you do your current job very well' (1997, xiv cited in Billett 2009, p. 50). Reflection on such results 'broadens the concept of required skills, which might extend to managing working relations with others, which can occur on unequal bases' (Billett 2009, p. 50).

The findings of this study indicated that many rail companies could advance their work in valuing multiple forms of knowledge and skills. Janssens and Zanoni have explained that:

> Organisations have traditionally valued the competencies and skills of the social groups in historical positions of power, downplaying the value of those of less privileged groups (Acker 1990; Cockburn 1991; Steinberg 1990). What is competence and, conversely, who is competent is consequently not an ethnicity-neutral (nor gender-neutral) decision. 'Competence' involves judgment and ethnicity (and gender) affect assumptions about skill, resulting in decisions that (white) males are the more competent, more suited to the job than are others (Acker 2006), particularly in the US–European context. Ethnic inequality at work

has therefore a structural component as the dominant groups in society have historically decided on the value of particular competences and skills and organizational practices (such as recruitment, wage setting) create hierarchy in which ethnic (and gender) inequalities are maintained in organizations (Acker 2006). (Janssens and Zanoni 2014, p. 3)

That Sort of Thing Would Strike Me as Discrimination

One learning and development manager from a medium-sized public state passenger rail company, when asked if there might be any equity issues in relation to who is able to get skills recognition and who might miss out, replied: 'I would have to say that sort of thing would strike me as discrimination. I don't think we'd suffer from that type of thing in here.'

This is an example of how organisations, through a fear of being accused of discrimination, refuse to acknowledge race inequality within their organisations. An equity and diversity worker from the same company had stressed how current recruitment procedures, with their requirements for lengthy and complex written applications and psychometric testing, deterred and disadvantaged Indigenous and non–English speaking background cultural groups. Here is another interesting comment regarding the 'delicacy' of acknowledging discrimination in an organisation that 'commits' to equity.

Interviewer: Do you perceive that everyone in your workforce has equal access to skills recognition, or will have equal access to skills recognition?

Interviewee: Yeah, look I honestly don't see that as an issue. [Company named] is pretty big, they have a number of initiatives that are aimed at equity in access, and I wouldn't consider that to be a problem. I think if we as a training department made it a problem, we'd be up for a please explain.

Interviewer: So that's sort of embedded in the whole [company named] culture, is it, that they try and make sure that you're getting the best out of people by giving them all a fair go?

Interviewee: Absolutely, and very big on Indigenous and female diversity.

Interviewer: What, they have initiatives that encourage Indigenous people and women to come into the rail industry?

Interviewee: Absolutely, yeah, rail processing, mining, you name it, we have specific departments that is all they do.

Note how this company, which is both a mining and rail company, claims to be putting considerable attention into developing a number of equity and diversity initiatives. The most resource-rich corporations are often the best placed to promote slick and glossy diversity policies and initiatives. But in many cases discriminatory practices, including gaining unequal benefits from the exploitation of Indigenous and Third World resources, underlies the promotion of these exemplary policies and strategies.

Companies wishing to mine resources (and build railways to transport those resources) on Aboriginal land and in 'Third World' nations have economic incentives to invest in the employment of historically under-represented ethnic groups. Whether these companies bring long-term benefits (economic, social and ecological) to Aboriginal and other ethnic minority communities is however open to contestation. Given the unfair advantage that such organisations continue to hold in terms of resource richness, and the fact that auditing and reporting practices tend to be based on white standards, then those companies that privilege whiteness may also be best placed to produce the best equity and diversity policies and documents. As Ahmed put it:

> If resource privileged organizations are more likely to be racially privileged, then there may even be an indirect correlation between being 'good at race equality' and institutional forms of whiteness. Race equality becomes a form of capital that measures existing forms of capital, which are unevenly distributed across the sector. (2007b, p. 598)

Equity Groups … That's Pretty Much Been Addressed Now

Responses indicated that some rail industry representatives believed that their organisation had already addressed equity and diversity by developing equity and diversity policies and initiatives. The implication was the job is now complete, and there is nothing more to do. Consider the following exchange with a human resources manager from a large public state passenger rail service:

Interviewer: What about in terms of making sure that training or your recruitment practices are as accessible to equity groups …?

Interviewee: Yes, we've done a lot of work in that regard, and there's been a lot of good initiatives implemented to make sure that our recruitment practices and facilities, etc., are accessible to different equity groups, so whilst there may have been some issues, I understand that basically, in terms of recruitment and training, that's pretty much been addressed now.

When equity and diversity policies are set up, this can give the misleading impression that diversity has been addressed, overlooking the fact that equity and diversity need to be continually worked at. This company, like other rail companies, had not solved the problem of race inequality. By promoting various initiatives, however, the company presented itself as addressing diversity, and the ongoing inequality experienced by historically under-represented groups was overlooked. The writing up of an equity and diversity management plan can be regarded as a job completed. A written document, and previous programs, can be used as an excuse not to do further work. This works against the realisation of race equality, which requires continual work. As Ahmed has observed:

> To be seen as 'being diverse' leads to the failure to commit to 'doing diversity', as the organization says it 'is it', or even that it already 'does it', which means that it sees there is nothing left to do. (2007a, p. 244)

Towards Race Equality

Janssens and Zanoni stated that:

> Despite two decades of research documenting and theorizing power inequality between the majority and historically underrepresented groups in organizations (Linnehan and Konrad 1999; Prasad et al. 2006), our current knowledge on how organizations can actually achieve power equality remains poor. (2014, p. 1)

Conceptualising and managing diversity as a strategic business asset has important implications for equality among a culturally diverse workforce. The term 'diversity' has to some extent replaced 'outdated' terms such as 'equal opportunity'. Yet inequalities continue to exist in the workplace. From one perspective, organisations in general do not wish to bring attention to that inequality – it is concealed by images of happy smiling faces, a many coloured workforce working together. It does not fit or adhere to the current business model and subsequently people – at least those who do not feel the inequality – do not take it on.

From another perspective, there is the argument that people are more likely to support 'equity and diversity' work if it is framed positively rather than negatively. But this opens the question, when the negatives are concealed, how does that enable and obstruct equity and diversity work? What does it mean for those people in the workforce (and those excluded from the workforce) who experience this inequality?

When diversity is constructed in such a way, it becomes cut off from 'systemic disadvantage that produce[s] persistent unequal outcomes' (Mills 2011, p. 49). Ahmed (2007a, pp. 235–236) have further explained, '(w)hat is problematic about diversity, by implication, is that it can be "cut off" from the programs that seek to challenge inequalities within organizations, and might even take the place of such programs in defining the social mission' of the organisation.

By failing to give due attention to the history and structure of power relations, the current, popular business rationale for diversity tends to work to the benefit of white employers and employees. Diversity policies tend to neglect 'the greater context of historically determined, structurally unequal access to and distribution of resources between socio-demographic groups (Ely 1995; Kanter 1977; Prasad et al. 2006; Siebers 2009; Thomas and Alderfer 1989)' (Zanoni et al. 2010, p. 14).

The question might be asked, if diversity management professes to value diversity, then what is it doing to address the inequitable structures shaping the employment experiences of historically under-represented groups?

There is no quick-fix 'how to' guide to 'doing diversity' in the workplace. Diversity work is never done, or finished, but it is possible to move towards valuing cultural plurality in the workplace. As I have attempted to show, there are ways of more equitably recognising the knowledge and skills of a culturally diverse workforce.

Critiquing the way workplace standards and practices privilege white norms shows some of the ways in which the skills, knowledge and experiences of non-white others are undervalued. It shows how diversity concerns everyone and how treating everyone 'the same' does not equate with treating all people equally. It reveals that often when companies claim to be helping others it is the dominant culture that benefits most. It indicates that, when diversity management is framed chiefly within a business rationale, it fails to adequately include historically under-represented peoples and points to the importance of organisations considering not only economic rationales but also cultural and social values in diversity. It enables equity to be viewed as more a problem of whiteness and less the problem of Aboriginal people or non-white others. This questioning of standards and practices enables a valuing of the plurality of knowledges, skills and cultures in the workplace.

References

Acker, J. R. (2006). Inequality regimes: Gender, class, and race in organizations. *Gender and Society, 20*, 441–464.

Ahmed, S. (2007a). The language of diversity. *Ethnic and Racial Studies, 30*(2), 235–256.

Ahmed, S. (2007b). 'You end up doing the document rather than doing the doing': Diversity, race equality and the politics of documentation. *Ethnic and Racial Studies, 30*(4), 590–609.

Andersson, P., & Guo, S. (2009). Governing through non/recognition: The missing 'R' in the PLAR for immigrant professionals in Canada and Sweden. *International Journal of Lifelong Education, 28*(4), 423–437.

Australasian Railway Association (ARA). (2006). *The changing face of rail: A journey to the employer of choice.* Canberra: Australasian Railway Association.

Australasian Railway Association. (2008). *A rail revolution: Future capability identification and skills development for the Australasian rail industry.* Canberra: Australasian Railway Association.

Billett, S. (2009). Workplace competence: Integrating social and personal perspectives. In C. R. Velde (Ed.), *International perspectives on competence in the workplace: Implications for research, policy and practice* (pp. 33–54). Dordrecht: Springer.

Blackmore, J., & Sachs, J. (2003). Managing equity work in the performative university. *Australian Feminist Studies, 18*(41), 141–162.

Bunda, T., Zipin, L., & Brennan, M. (2012). Negotiating university 'equity' from Indigenous standpoints: A shaky bridge. *International Journal of Inclusive Education, 16*(9), 941–957.

Constable, J., Wagner, R., Childs, M., & Natoli, A. (2004). *Doctors become taxi drivers: Recognising skills – Not as easy as it sounds.* Sydney: Office of Employment, Equity and Diversity, NSW.

Fitch, R. (2006). *Australian railwayman: From cadet engineer to railways commissioner.* Sydney: Rosenberg.

Hicks, P., & Hill, A. (1993). *Ripping up the tracks: Stories of courage, loyalty and betrayal in the railways industry.* Adelaide: Multicultural Artworkers' Committee.

Hull, G. (1997). *Changing work, changing workers: Critical perspectives on language, literacy and skills.* New York: State University of New York Press.

Janssens, M., & Zanoni, P. (2014). Alternative diversity management: Organizational practices fostering ethnic equality at work. *Scandinavian Journal of Management*, http://dx.doi.org/10.1016/j.scaman.2013.12.006

Kell, P., & Vogl, G. (2009). Global immigration, the labour market and vocational education and training in Australia. In A. Heikkinen & K. Kraus (Eds.), *Reworking vocational education: Policies, practices and concepts* (pp. 77–96). New York: Peter Lang.

Light, R., Roscigno, V. J., & Kalev, A. (2011). Racial discrimination, interpretation, and legitimation at work. *Annals of the American Academy of Political and Social Science, 634*, 39–59.

McIntosh, P. (1989). *White privilege: Unpacking the invisible backpack.* Michigan: Institute for Social Research, University of Michigan. http://www.isr.umich.edu/home/diversity/resources/white-privilege.pdf. Accessed 4 Mar 2014.

Mills, S. (2011). The difficulty with diversity: White and Aboriginal women workers' representations of diversity management in forest processing mills. *Labour/Le Travail, 67*, 45–76.

Norris, R. (2010). *The more things change: The origins and impact of Australian Indigenous economic exclusion*. Queensland: Post Pressed.

Puwar, N. (2004). *Space invaders: Race, gender and bodies out of place*. Oxford: Berg.

Shah, C., & Long, M. (2004). *Global labour mobility and mutual recognition of skills and qualifications: European Union and Australia/New Zealand perspectives* (Working Paper No. 56). Melbourne: Centre for the Economics of Education and Training (CEET).

Taksa, L., & Groutsis, D. (2010). Managing cultural diversity: Problems and prospects for ethnicity and gender a work. In G. Strachan, E. French, & J. Burgess (Eds.), *Managing diversity in Australia: Theory and practice* (pp. 169–187). Sydney: McGraw Hill.

Tilbury, F., & Colic-Peisker, V. (2007). Skilled refugees, employment and social inclusion: A Perth case study of three communities. In V. Colic-Peisker & F. Tilbury (Eds.), *Settling in Australia: The social inclusion of refugees* (pp. 108–128). Perth: Centre for Social and Community Research, Murdoch University.

Zanoni, P., Janssens, M., Benschop, Y., & Nkomo, S. (2010). Unpacking diversity, grasping inequality: Rethinking difference through critical perspectives. *Organisation, 17*(1), 9–29.

Part II
Building Capability and Capacity

Chapter 7
Formal Workplace Mentoring: A Strategy for Engagement

Tom Short

Abstract Leaders in traditional industries, such as rail, are becoming distressed as more Baby Boomers move into retirement and employee turnover increases. Moreover, these same organisations are contemplating how they can manage the transfer of substantial and highly valued tacit knowledge from their departing experts to younger or less experienced colleagues. The challenges are complex, not least because of the many variables existent within industry contexts. For leaders the key questions are how to recognise, engage and motivate longer-serving employees while developing the next generation in a business environment where structured and traditional forms of training are costly and less effective in meeting these development needs. In times of economic hardship, when training budgets are generally under scrutiny, managers look for more effective ways to train and develop their people.

This chapter explores the emergence of formal workplace mentoring as one human resource development strategy for dealing with the transfer of knowledge, and comments on the motivational benefits of using mentoring programs in situations where other forms of learning might be less effective. In particular, the chapter describes how research conducted in six Australian rail organisations during 2011–2013 identified a nine-step mentoring framework and industry Code of Mentoring Practice for rail organisations to use. However, the study highlighted a series of hidden dangers within mentoring concepts that can reverse employee engagement and warns managers to avoid dysfunctional mentoring arrangements.

T. Short (✉)
School of Education, University of South Australia, Mawson Lakes, SA, Australia
e-mail: tom.short@unisa.edu.au

T. Short and R. Harris (eds.), *Workforce Development: Strategies and Practices*,
DOI 10.1007/978-981-287-068-1_7, © Springer Science+Business Media Singapore 2014

Background

Education and training initiatives are developing constantly to meet the challenges of a fast-changing and dynamic workplace. In Australia, the imminent loss of longer-serving experienced workers and concurrent shortage of younger people, who are not attracted to pursuing a career in industry (Wallace et al. 2011), foreshadows a potential breakdown in how organisations disseminate tacit knowledge and experience from departing Baby Boomers to the remaining work groups. This dilemma puts the succession of an organisation's intellectual capital and core competence at risk. Quite apart from the obvious cost disadvantage of engaging in wasteful remedial learning, a failure to capture tacit knowledge from highly committed Baby Boomers can leave departing employees with a feeling of 'uncompleted obligation', at the same time frustrating and disengaging those employees who remain and have to learn afresh. In writing about the ageing workforce and an era of lost knowledge, DeLong reminded us that 'career development processes [such as those contained within mentoring] are needed to retain and build long-term workforce capability' (2004, p. 49). Needless to say, structured education and training programs can help overcome some of these knowledge and skill gaps, but there is widespread recognition of the limitations of formal classroom-based training (Klasen 2002), and studies show that most learning occurs in the development phase where 90 % of all learning comes from on-job experience (70 %) and working around good practice (20 %) (Lombardo and Eichinger 2000).

In these environments, the learning is more likely to be less formal, spontaneous, just-in-time and provided by a significant other person who has the trust and respect of colleagues. This paradigm is thought to capture the time, space and place where people truly learn how to deal with work-related issues, overcome occupational challenges, discover work engagement and build new opportunities. To meet these needs, organisations are increasingly adopting formal mentoring and coaching techniques as a way of delivering professional development, building employee capacity and passing on much-needed tacit knowledge. One seminal author, Kram (1983), focuses on the flexibility of mentoring and how it creates confidence to deal with not only work-related issues and career advancement but also relationship-building processes and psycho-social support.

Once subordinate to more popular training methods, workplace mentoring is starting to 'outshine its allies in many other Australian workplaces' (Barker 2012, p. 24). In this chapter I consider a range of findings that show the value to be gained from integrating workplace mentoring into a workforce development strategy; review research outputs which include a comprehensive framework for implementing formal workplace mentoring; and offer guidance on how to organise the all-important matching process between mentor and mentee. Mentoring is thought to be beneficial for both the organisation and employee; but at the same time, I have exposed a number of hidden dangers that can arise from poorly executed mentoring programs and the downstream damage created by a negative experience.

Literature

The literature on business excellence suggests that when employees are satisfied and engaged in their work the resulting positive mood contributes to an overall improvement in customer satisfaction and these results help to enhance business performance (Oakland 2004). Therefore, it makes sense to consider which human resource development (HRD) or workforce development strategies have the greatest impact on employee engagement. Mentoring is rising up the list of high-engagement activities because it puts individuals at the centre of their own learning, especially in larger or complex organisations where the needs of individuals can be easily overlooked. These favourable outcomes have positive implications for the individual and organisation. In times of increased workplace change and uncertainty mentoring can help to build morale, promote job satisfaction and improve levels of retention (Lo and Ramayah 2011; Herrington et al. 2006). Importantly for skilled vocational settings, mentoring allows organisations to utilise the skills of experienced staff by encouraging the transfer of tacit knowledge to mentees who may be new to the organisation (Koc-Menard 2009).

What Is Mentoring?

Before going further, it is helpful to reflect briefly on the history of mentoring and how the topic has risen to prominence in a modern workplace setting. Firstly, mentoring is not a new education and training concept, or HRD fad, but has historical connections with Greek mythology. More recently mentoring became popular in sixteenth-century Europe, when younger people were indentured as apprentices to older craftsmen who passed on knowledge and skill to develop their apprentices' competencies. Kram and Isabella (1985) suggested that the essence of mentoring is an intensive long-term relationship between a senior, more experienced individual (the mentor) and a more junior, less experienced individual (the mentee, sometimes called protégé).

Secondly, studies on mentoring are increasing. Books and articles on mentoring began appearing in scholarly and practitioner publications in the late 1970s and early 1980s, but this interest has gained momentum. Information taken from one academic search engine located on the internet shows that publications since 1980 have increased to over 400 articles per year, with a clear bias towards the disciplines of social sciences, business and management, and psychology. Therefore mentoring is an activity that traverses easily across traditional academic disciples in much the same way as other HRD activities such as coaching and leadership. In 2012 a survey report issued by the Australian Human Resources Institute (AHRI) showed that 64 % of 111 responding organisations were participating in formal workplace mentoring schemes and over half of these organisations had senior executives overseeing the programs.

Table 7.1 Formal and informal mentoring programs

Formal mentoring	Informal mentoring
Initiated without support from organisation	Usually initiated by the organisation
People are driven by similarity and attraction	People are driven by a work-related need or agenda
Mentor and mentee self-select	Mentor and mentee usually matched by a third party
Initial emotions are positive	Initial emotions can be apprehensive or awkward
Often has low organisational visibility	Often has high organisational visibility
Unstructured meetings, as needed	Meetings structured by program facilitator
May have no explicit goals	Explicit organisational goals

Thirdly, mentoring has grown to become part of HRD language and is contained within the activities of workforce development (Harrison and Weiss 1998). Industry studies relating to leadership development (Short et al. 2011) and career planning (Baugh and Sullivan 2009) show that the emerging non-technical skills of leadership and management, such as being caring, inclusive and authentic, are woven into the fabric of good mentoring practice. This is because mentoring has strong connections with role modelling, capacity building and leadership behaviours. Other supporting literature details the benefits that accrue for those involved in formal mentoring processes:

- stabilising and reinforcing company values (Bamford 2011)
- increasing the levels of organisational engagement and loyalty (Ragins and Kram 2007)
- promoting professional development for both mentor and mentee (MacGregor 2000)
- improving communications across organisational levels and silos (Bamford 2011).

Formal or Informal

Finally, the literature and empirical evidence suggests that, while formal and informal mentoring share similar characteristics, there are clear distinctions between the two approaches. Informal mentoring occurs spontaneously in many workplaces as a result of good communication and collaboration between like-minded colleagues. Informal mentoring is highly satisfying for both the mentor and mentee because it is natural, often unnoticed, is longer-lasting and occurs as a result of a pre-existing good relationship. On the other hand, formal mentoring is planned and programmed by the organisation, is highly visible, has a pre-determined timespan and is usually attached to an end goal. A selection of the key differences is illustrated in Table 7.1.

It is common for members of an informal mentoring dyad to choose each other, but in formal arrangements great care is taken to ensure the mentor and mentee are properly matched – a process often assigned to the HR function, but not always done very well. Opinions vary on which method of matching is the most effective, but all techniques are bound by ethical considerations associated with the vested interests of those involved such as the need for confidentiality and awareness of power differentials within the mentoring dyad. Therefore, organisations planning to embark on formal mentoring programs are advised to develop effective strategies for dealing with ethical issues (McDonald and Hite 2005) and implement processes to limit the chances of someone having a negative mentoring experience (Eby and McManus 2004). Later in this chapter, I outline a selection of strategies for dealing with matching and ethical topics.

Approach to Research

In this chapter I use findings from a wider research program undertaken by the Cooperative Research Centre (CRC) for Rail Innovation, an Australian government–funded initiative conducted between 2007 and 2014. The study on formal workplace mentoring and coaching (P4.119) was located within the theme of 'workforce development' and focused on the benefits of using formal mentoring programs and frameworks in the rail industry. The researchers [we] used a multi-method research design to draw on a wide range of qualitative and quantitative information. According to Lincoln and Guba (1985), mixed methods in qualitative research programs achieve high levels of dependability and trustworthiness by incorporating multiple sources of evidence into the research design. Our study included a structured review of academic literature and practitioner reports to identify a range of emerging themes within formal mentoring arrangements. Later, we compared this information with the experiences of mentors, mentees, human resource professionals and executives in six organisations using interpretive and thematic techniques of analysis. We used case studies and semi-structured interviews to establish the value of mentoring and ascertain the level of support needed from senior managers to develop a sustainable mentoring culture. Finally, we used our research findings to develop readily-available materials and specific training programs to form hardcopy and web-based resources for use by the industry.

Findings and Discussion

Uptake of Workplace Mentoring and Need for Leadership Support

There can be no doubt that mentoring is becoming popular in workplace. Moreover, survey findings from the AHRI found that two-thirds of Australian organisation (including rail) had started formal mentoring programs. Of the one-third remaining, 67 % of these organisations said they were planning to start mentoring in the next 12 months (AHRI 2012).

In a similar way to other HRD projects, the research evidence also overwhelmingly supported the need for executive commitment and encouragement. Our research found that when senior managers volunteered to become mentors, they were seen as positive role models and they were frequently overwhelmed with requests from mentees who wanted to link up with them to learn from their vast knowledge and experience. In the AHRI survey, 57 % of organisations reported the appointment of a director or senior manager to oversee the mentoring program.

Where Mentoring Is Directed in Organisations

This study showed that mentoring programs are effective in a wide range of disciplines. One organisation used mentoring to assist new graduates to settle in to their workplaces. Graduates reported the value of mentoring in helping them to build new networks and spot career opportunities early in their employment, thereby saving wasted time on false starts. In complex workplaces, experienced leaders such as trusted mentors can provide a guiding hand or help in the navigation of people, places and relationships by introducing new starters to previously unknown situations and career possibilities (Piip 2013). Another organisation used mentoring to help trainees handle the challenges and pressures of an 18-month intensive driver training program. Train drivers in the rail industry deal with a complex blend of technical knowledge, safety-related awareness and detailed information about routes and environmental conditions. In these settings, the preferred mentors were not on-job trainers or direct supervisors, but seasoned drivers with substantial experience and a genuine interest in helping fellow colleagues to cope. A third organisation used mentoring to help managers build new internal networks and improve workplace relationships. Mentoring across organisational silos helped mentees to understand supply-chain processes and the challenges faced by other colleagues, especially when the internal supply chain breaks down. These findings confirmed the contribution of mentoring as a relationship-driven process for developing careers, providing psychological support and learning from experienced colleagues (Ragins 1997). However, in spite of these reported benefits, responding organisations were reluctant to implement mentoring programs more widely, instead choosing to experiment or target key areas of pressing need. The occupational groups that were targeted included graduates, drivers, senior managers, new apprentices and engineers.

These mentoring programs were established for specific purposes; the top six of these are indicated in Table 7.2. Perhaps the most obvious feature in Table 7.2 is the correlation between the purposes and the rail industry's need for improved leadership, retention of tacit knowledge and a realisation that mentoring is one learning process that can address many of these workforce development needs simultaneously. These organisational shortfalls in leadership were first identified in a major industry report (ARA 2008), but the problem is not exclusive to rail.

Table 7.2 Reasons for supporting mentoring programs

Purpose	Org 1	Org 2	Org 3	Org 4	Org 5	Org 6
Enhancing leadership	✓	✓			✓	✓
Transferring tacit knowledge	✓	✓	✓	✓		✓
Role modelling		✓	✓	✓	✓	✓
Providing access to experience	✓	✓	✓		✓	✓
Improving communications	✓		✓	✓	✓	
Retaining and engaging employees	✓		✓	✓		

The wider literature indicates that the need for effective leadership and management development are ever-present topics of discussion in fast-changing organisations and a priority for the future (Mutte 2006). These priorities are a reality made more challenging in Australia by a 2012 UK report showing that Australian organisations had the lowest level of leadership talent in the developed world, despite investing more on leadership development than other major economies (CIPD 2011). Moreover, the characteristics expected of a talented leader have also changed to accommodate a different kind of workplace where command-control techniques of leading work teams are no longer appropriate. New models of leadership focus on individual development, especially in remote or online relationships. It is thought that successful leaders consider leadership a shared task, and in doing so set out to look after people. They often learn these relationship skills from more experienced leaders and mentors who have learnt how to manage people over many years in industry communities such as rail (Piip 2013).

Mentoring Framework

The aim of the study was to consider how a common framework could be used to harmonise formal mentoring in the Australian rail context. In recent years other similar frameworks have been integrated into HRM practices and/or organisational development projects to improve a range of business objectives; so, as a consequence, rail organisations were familiar with using frameworks to guide policy and practice.

However, the growing diversity of specialised industry sectors, such as rail, made it highly unlikely that any one prescriptive solution would be able to take full account of the situational variables. For this reason, we created a broad framework of key actions to accommodate the contextual requirements of rail settings. To meet these research objectives we developed a nine-step mentoring framework as shown in Fig. 7.1. Each of these nine steps signifies a key stage in implementing formal workplace mentoring and is supported with checklists and guidelines to aid implementation. The framework in Fig. 7.1 is segmented into three key sections. Section 1 relates to executive leadership, vision and support for the adoption of a formal workplace mentoring program; Section 2 focuses on planning and organisation considerations; and Section 3 deals with implementation and evaluation.

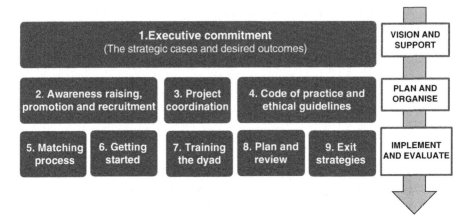

Fig. 7.1 The nine-step rail mentoring framework™ (Included with permission from the CRC for Rail Innovation)

We found that mentoring shared similarities with other HRD strategies in that it succeeded and survived only when members of the executive team propelled the initiative and became involved. Therefore, Step 1 of the mentoring framework requires senior leaders to identify and value the contribution of mentoring from the outset, by first aligning mentoring with other HRD activities in such a way that greater numbers of stakeholders can benefit from taking part. Alignment is an over-used and sometimes misunderstood term in HR language (Short 2008), but in relation to mentoring it means ensuring that the organisation's managers, work team leaders and individual mentees are all in agreement on the purpose and value of workplace mentoring. Part of this step includes making important decisions on how extensively the mentoring will be applied. While it may seem intrinsically unfair to restrict the number of people who are allowed to partake in mentoring, it is highly unlikely that organisations would be able to support mentoring for everyone, especially at the early stages of program deployment. In the companion volume to this book, readers will recall how similar dyadic meetings, such as performance appraisal, had swept through organisations in the 1980s and beyond, only to fall into disarray some time later because the system required an unsustainable workload for the participants – especially when the system was perceived to have little benefit.

Following Step 1, the intermediate three steps (2, 3 and 4) are contained within the planning and organisation section and require organisations to promote the value of mentoring, raise awareness of what is involved and identify a pool of willing advocates. Studies show that when people have received a positive mentoring experience elsewhere they are more likely to volunteer and promote another program. In this study, informal workshops were aimed at raising awareness, offering advice and recruiting a pool of volunteer mentors. Later these volunteers became involved in facilitated training programs and matching processes to form mentor–mentee dyads. Step 3 is arguably the most important feature of a formal workplace mentoring program and can make all the difference between success and failure.

Mentoring is no different to many other structured workplace communication processes, such as team briefing (Garnett 1981) and quality circles (Oakland 2004) in that they all require a dedicated coordinator to plan and organise the programs. Typically, an in-house project coordinator sets up a steering group to oversee the project, establish resources, develop meeting schedules, conduct matching processes, develop training courses and lead review meetings on a regular basis. For participants, the mentoring coordinator might be the single point of contact and often a reliable trouble-shooter in resolving problems. Depending on the size of the host organisation and numbers taking part in the mentoring program, the coordinator role can be a full-time or part-time position – normally, but not always, located within the HR department.

Step 4 is the final activity in the planning section and involves the use of a code of mentoring practice. One key finding in this study was a realisation that mentoring involves highly ethical processes requiring trust and confidentiality among participants, including coordinators in the host organisations. We found that, in addition to offering substantial benefits such as increased engagement, better morale and improved retention, workplace mentoring could be undermined by unethical practices and negative mentoring experiences. Negative mentor behaviours can include taking credit for the mentee's accomplishments, politicking and sabotage, abuse of power, mentee neglect, poor attitude and inappropriate delegation (Eby and McManus 2004). Likewise, mentors reported their share of problematic mentees. Negative mentee behaviours include the exploitation of mentors, deception, over-dependence, sabotage and an unwillingness to learn (Eby and Allen 2002). The organisations studied found that participants engaged in mentoring at a deep and psychological level, where the mentor and mentee were each putting their reputation on the line. Therefore, bad practices or unwanted ethical behaviours might create consequences beyond the mentoring activity. For these reasons and to help build ethical practice such as encouraging behaviour to meet professional standards, a Rail Mentoring Code of Practice was created:

Rail Mentoring Code of Practice (included with permission from the CRC for Rail Innovation)

1. Confidentiality and personal safety
2. A mentee-driven agenda
3. Voluntary participation
4. Open and transparent processes
5. Training support for participants
6. Supervision for mentors
7. Early termination with no blame
8. Planning and goal-setting agreements
9. Ethical conduct
10. Independence from other HR programs

The third and final section of the mentoring framework includes steps 5–9 and deals with the implementation and evaluation of programs. Step 5 focuses on the process of selecting and matching mentors with mentees. The literature reminds us

Table 7.3 Benefits for mentors and mentees

For the mentor	For the mentee
Developing interpersonal skills	Introduction to new ideas
Learning the art of reflective dialogue	Increased confidence and self-awareness
Nurturing new networks	Increased motivation and creativity
Helping someone to learn and develop	Achieving professional aspirations

that if personality types and/or work styles are significantly different there may be a problem initiating and maintaining a productive mentoring relationship, largely because there should be a sense of accomplishment for both the mentor and mentee. Our findings show that individuals are drawn to mentoring for a variety of reasons and at the beginning mentees will be concerned about whether their new mentors have the knowledge, skills and experience that align with their perceived needs. This study found three types of matching criteria: mentor endowments; preferred ways of communicating; and value of the networking opportunities provided by the mentor.

- *Endowments:* depth of knowledge, skill or experience offered to the mentee and level of support.
- *Preferences:* agreement about the most effective way of communicating and method of learning.
- *Content:* the substance of the social exchange and potential to build new networks.

Above all, mentees will ask to what extent their mentor is able to provide psychological support, assist in career development, provide external networking opportunities, be a positive role model and help overcome unwanted organisational forces or politics. Our research indicated that when the members of a mentoring dyad were matched well, the overall benefits were of great value to the host organisation and mentee, as shown in Table 7.3.

We found that matching processes varied among organisations. They included HR selection; using questionnaires and profiling tools; facilitated self-selection; and total self-selection by the mentees. The success of matching correlated with the participants' choices, but in most cases facilitated self-selection was the most successful. In this arrangement, HR staff organised awareness-raising sessions, invited interested mentors/mentees and used a range of selection processes to bring like-minded people together. Mentoring dyads that shared similar backgrounds and were previously known to each other had a quicker start, while strangers needed time to build trust and develop their mentoring relationship.

The four-quadrant diagram in Fig. 7.2 indicates the speed at which positive mentoring relationships can be established and is based on the similarities between members of the mentoring dyad and the extent to which they knew each other before the program. In this study, similarities included, but were not limited to, occupational interests and backgrounds, approaches to dealing with problems, personality types, family circumstances or simply approaches to work.

Fig. 7.2 Mentoring relationships (Included with permission from the CRC for Rail Innovation)

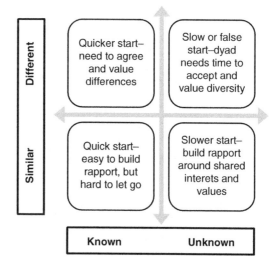

- When the mentor and mentee were known to each other and shared similar matching criteria, the relationship was cosy and developed quickly. Motivation was shared by the dyad, but this energy prolonged the mentoring meetings and distracted the dyad from achieving their goals or made meetings less productive.
- When the mentor and mentee were known to each other, but shared different perceptions or desires within the matching criteria, the relationship started easily but soon became strained unless members of the dyad agreed to value or put aside any differences. Sometimes mentees deliberately sought unlikely mentors as a personal challenge and opportunity to grow, but these relationships needed careful monitoring by the program coordinator.
- When the mentor and mentee were unknown to each other, but shared similar preferences in the matching criteria, the new relationship was based on early mutuality, but members typically held back until the relationship was more established and seemingly beneficial. This process was time-consuming and not always tolerated by the host organisation.
- When the mentor and mentee were unknown to each other and shared different views from the outset, a mutual relationship took a long time to develop, or even incurred a false start. The exception was a development dyad where the mentee was deliberately looking for challenge in the relationship, but this difference was acceptable to the mentor.

Step 6, entitled 'getting started', is another notable part of the implementation section and involves bringing mentors and mentees together to explain the roles and expectations – not only briefing each participant on the program goals, but also identifying the need for further training. During this step, program commencement dates are negotiated, training plans are established and a reliable system for monitoring progress is agreed with the mentoring coordinator. Getting started requires participants to make a commitment to uphold the principles and

Table 7.4 Getting a mentoring program started

Clarity of purpose	Identify outcomes and benefits early in the mentoring program
	Ensure outcomes are transferred into viable and well-understood objectives for the mentee
Training and briefing	Ensure mentee understands the concept of mentoring
	Ensure skills gaps are minimised
	Provide learning support for the mentee
Selection and matching	Take part in matching processes and be prepared to have an influence on how the matching is achieved
Process review and measurement	Be prepared to resolve problems within the relationship
	Be prepared to make adjustments to the program
Standards of ethical and pastoral care	Use an agreed code of practice
	Maintain high standards of ethical behaviour
Supporting participants	Support mentees throughout the program
	Manage the program in a professional manner

Included with permission from the CRC for Rail Innovation

standards detailed in the policy documents or mentoring code of practice. Table 7.4 summarises Step 6.

In this study the literature and practitioner reports placed a great emphasis on the importance of training participants, yet the findings indicated that a mixture of training or development is undertaken. Organisations utilised a mixture of internal and external resources to prepare employees for mentoring, based on learning needs and prior experience. Therefore, Step 7 reminds organisations to prepare and deliver effective training for mentors and mentees because studies reveal that training is not always undertaken beyond the awareness-raising activities in Step 2. In the same way that managers learn how to conduct effective selection interviews or facilitate performance management meetings, so must workplace mentors learn how to conduct and lead mentoring sessions. Typically learning programs would include how to:

- develop high quality learning content and resources
- identify options on the various ways of running a mentoring session
- gain input from subject matter experts
- develop processes to help coordinators assess the readiness of candidates
- plan, run and review mentoring meetings
- blend mentoring with other training programs, but retain independence
- create healthy mentoring relationships
- define criteria on which programs can be evaluated at a later stage.

Step 7 also involves making decisions about mentors' access to professional supervision. Supervision is a formal arrangement with someone who is experienced in professional development and can provide regular peer group support. This role can be undertaken by the mentoring coordinator or another trusted person who is valued by the mentor. The supervisor's role is to work with the mentor to develop the mentor–mentee relationship and often involves sophisticated learning techniques such

Fig. 7.3 A successful
mentoring meeting (Included
with permission from the
CRC for Rail Innovation)

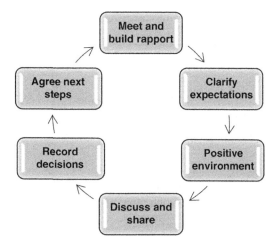

as critical reflection and rethinking practice based on positive or negative experiences. Supervisors may be able to help the mentor with legal concerns, ethical decisions, any breaches of confidentiality, dealing with complaints and how to manage professional boundaries.

Planning and progress reviews between mentors and mentees vary greatly, but, unlike informal arrangements where the mentoring process is more spontaneous, formal programs operate within other work-related systems and timescales. The study found that in busy work environments it is all too easy to adopt a random approach to planning and reviewing mentoring goals, and mentees can be left feeling stranded, so Step 8 was built in to encourage members of the dyad to plan meetings in an organised way by using structured templates, agreements and guidelines. Mentoring plans ensure that expectations are documented, review meeting are scheduled, feedback is discussed in a positive way and progress is communicated to other stakeholders. One approach to conducting a successful mentoring meeting captures many of these elements and is outlined in Fig. 7.3.

To conclude this section, the nine-step mentoring framework recognises that some mentoring relationships may become dysfunctional or break down. Step 9 deals with strategies and practices to manage a termination process by allowing either member of the dyad to exit the relationship without fear of blame. Unlike informal mentoring arrangements, it is not always easy to walk away from workplace mentoring arrangements without other colleagues noticing and this can add unwanted levels of anxiety to an already fraught situation. The study found that relationships can break down for many reasons such as poor matching or when the need for mentoring has expired, but the literature reminds us that maturation is a normal phase of the mentoring cycle (Kram 1983). In formal mentoring programs, exit strategies can be aided by:

- ensuring the participants know how long the mentoring program will last
- using planning processes to agree on objectives and success criteria
- allowing people to terminate the mentoring without blame
- recognising and celebrating success

Table 7.5 Evaluation of mentoring programs

For the individual	For the organisation
Mentor satisfaction	Noticeable improvements in staff retention
Tangible return on expectation	Increased work satisfaction
Willingness to take part again	Positive engagement
Willingness to become a mentor	Effective transfer of tacit knowledge
Changes in behaviour attributed to mentoring	Improved leadership behaviour
Resolution of challenging issues or situations	Improved communications between functions

- discussing and planning the exit strategy in advance
- maintaining momentum to prevent fade.

Evaluation of Mentoring

Mentoring programs differ from coaching and training in so far as they do not deliberately set out to define measurable performance outcomes or business goals. Mentoring is more holistic; it wraps around other types of workplace development to build relationships, bridge organisational solos, or simply help people to cope with work demands and pressures. In some ways, mentoring is an antidote to more formalised systems such as performance management, but this comparative softness makes mentoring programs more challenging to evaluate in a traditional way. The evaluation of mentoring therefore eludes HRD professionals in much the same way as other forms of learning and development and makes it vulnerable in difficult times. In mentoring dyads, each mentee sets their own agenda and forms a personal view on whether the program produced a satisfactory outcome.

Moreover, because mentoring takes place at different times and in different places, the initial outlay for training and matching participants is variable, and the up-front cost of appointing a mentoring coordinator can take time to become established and demonstrate a quantifiable return on investment. In this study, I found that the challenge of realising the much sought-after financial benefit from mentoring prevented organisations from investing in a program coordinator and this affected the sustainability of their mentoring initiative. In one organisation, an otherwise excellent mentoring program soon fell into disarray after 2 years when the mentoring coordinator was withdrawn because of cost considerations. Mentoring requires executives to rethink their approach to evaluation.

A CIPD report in the United Kingdom on coaching (McGurk 2010, p. 2) talked about the current obsession with quantitative evaluation techniques and the crudeness of using 'return on investment' language because it failed to capture the 'richness of learning interactions' (2010, p. 9), which have obvious, but less definable, links to business outcomes. In this study the benefits of workplace mentoring were attributed by respondents to a range of individual and organisational considerations. Programs were evaluated using diverse, but oddly connected, criteria, as shown in Table 7.5.

Mentoring and Workforce Engagement

In the title of this chapter, I have attempted to make an important connection between workplace mentoring and employee engagement. In an era where group training is becoming, or has become, less affordable due to the specialisation of careers or inability to take people off the job en masse, mentoring offers a convenient and less disruptive approach to workforce development. The literature indicates that mentoring increases job satisfaction and encourages individuals to take ownership of their own development, drawing guidance from respected role models to inform decision making and help modify peoples' behaviours. In this study, we found that mentoring engages individuals at a deep psychological level and helps mentees to cope with changing or unexpected work situations. However, this research also came across the destructive presence of toxic mentoring behaviours when people are attracted to mentoring for the wrong reasons. I conclude this chapter with a range of findings that draw attention to what has become known as 'negative mentoring experiences' (Eby et al. 2000, p. 5) which can undermine mentoring programs by contributing to heightened levels of disengagement.

Inappropriate Matching

Mentoring can become negative when conflicting values, work styles and personalities exist between the mentor and mentee and the relationship becomes dysfunctional. This scenario can happen when the mentor fails to accommodate or value differing perspectives put forward by the mentee and has difficulty getting beyond their own narrow-minded ideas. In this situation there is a philosophical and psychological clash between the mentor and mentee, preventing each side from compromising on what is needed to achieve a satisfactory outcome. To overcome this situation, organisations can use psychological tools, such as Myers Briggs Type Indicator® to identify personality traits and characteristics.

Distancing Behaviour

When either member of the mentoring dyad becomes disengaged, they respond by neglecting important deadlines and meetings, they put distance between themselves and avoid contact. When a mentor is mentoring more than one mentee, as can happen in smaller organisations, the mentor may inadvertently (or deliberately) play favourites or make deals with other mentees behind closed doors. This distancing behaviour can be minimised by working with the mentoring coordinator to monitor and document review meetings and progress reports.

Manipulating Behaviour and Politicking

Sometimes a mentor can be drawn to mentoring because it enables them to use their positional power to influence the mentees, put other people down or use overt intimidation to get their own way. Studies have shown that manipulative and/or narcissistic mentors have little regard for the wellbeing of their mentees and delegate their own work freely, but take credit for any positive outcomes. However, when things go wrong, these same mentors blame the mentees for mistakes, often to other people, and avoid taking responsibility for the errors.

Lack of Mentor Expertise

When a mentor is wrongly selected or trained and they have a lower level of self-awareness of what it means to be a mentor, the mentor may be insensitive to the mentee's needs or simply difficult to communicate with. Mentors can sometimes project personal anxieties into their mentoring relationship, such as bringing problems from home, becoming overly critical of others and showing insensitivity to the needs of the mentee. People who volunteer and later become competent mentees take pride in the range of roles they fulfil, such as advisor, developer, broker, challenger or affirmer. Training and awareness-raising sessions are obvious ways of improving technical competency and developing the range of interpersonal skills needed, but a bad attitude or personal problems can add toxicity to the relationship and get in the way of someone becoming a professional mentor.

Conclusions

I have outlined a range of key strategies and practices in the emerging area of formal workplace mentoring within a sample of Australian rail organisations. The systematic review of global literature revealed that mentoring is fast becoming a popular method of workforce development in an era when traditional training courses may be too expensive or generic for individual needs. In the course of our research, we discovered that mentoring is part of the HRD function, but can be derailed when there is no support from the top, no budget to pay for training and a low level of interest within the host organisation. Awareness-raising sessions can be used to offset any negativity and restore a belief in the value of mentoring. The research found many benefits within formal programs, but warned against the use of bad practices or inadvertently tolerating negative mentoring experiences. To assist, we used the research findings to develop a Rail Code of Mentoring Practice and nine-step implementation program to help rail organisations follow the right pathway. This guidance stressed the need for careful matching between mentors and mentees, and part of the matching process can involve a range of logistical considerations when arranging mentoring meetings. This issue is particularly important in Australian rail where people can be dispersed across large geographical borders and organisational boundaries. Respondents indicated the need for careful planning, timeliness of meetings, a tolerance of shift patterns and an opportunity to pull out of mentoring if the relationship was not working.

The findings showed that mentoring complements other forms of HRD in a holistic way, but is better placed outside the cluster of performative techniques such as on-job training, coaching and performance management. Mentoring programs may not always provide a neat and tidy solution to business issues and this makes quantitative evaluation strategies elusive. However, this study indicated how mentoring can change the mood of those involved and make them more amenable to engage in ways that have quantifiable outcomes such as high levels of presenteeism, greater discretionary participation and employment longevity. This benefit was highly relevant in the case of vulnerable groups such as apprentices and graduates who have a low level of retention when the employment relationship fails to meet their needs.

Finally, the findings in this study suggest that many mentoring programs are still in their infancy and may never become widely available to all employees. The effort of coordinating and training scores of mentoring dyads may be perceived as too messy and simply overwhelm HRD professionals. I foresee that organisations are more likely to engage in trial programs for targeted groups of employees first and later extend them on the basis of need. Trial programs will allow organisations to review and make adjustments based on survey feedback from each participant.

References

Australasian Railway Association. (2008). *A rail revolution: Future capability identification and skill development for the Australian rail industry.* Kingston: Australasian Railway Association.

Australian Human Resources Institute (AHRI). (2012). *Coaching and mentoring.* Melbourne: Australian Human Resources Institute.

Bamford, C. (2011). Mentoring in the twenty-first century. *Leadership in Health Services, 24*(2), 150–163.

Barker, R. (2012, May). Performing acts. *HR Monthly,* pp. 24–25. Melbourne: Australian Human Resources Institute.

Baugh, S., & Sullivan, S. (2009). Developmental relationships and the new workplace realities: A life span perspective on career development through mentoring. In S. Baugh & S. Sullivan (Eds.), *Maintaining focus, energy and options over the career* (pp. 27–50). Charlotte: Information Age Publishing.

CIPD. (2011, May). Training trends are still a mixed picture. *Infographics feature in People Management,* Chartered Institute of Personnel and Development, 40–41.

DeLong, D. (2004). *Lost knowledge: Confronting the threat of an aging workforce.* Oxford: Oxford University Press.

Eby, L. T., & Allen, T. D. (2002). Further investigation of protégés' negative mentoring experiences. *Group and Organization Management, 27*(4), 456–479.

Eby, L. T., & McManus, S. E. (2004). The protégé's role in negative mentoring experiences. *Journal of Vocational Behavior, 65*(2), 255–275.

Eby, L. T., McManus, S. E., Simon, S. A., & Russell, J. E. A. (2000). The protégé's perspective regarding negative mentoring experiences: The development of a taxonomy. *Journal of Vocational Behavior, 57*(1), 1–21.

Garnett, J. (1981). *The work challenge.* Leicester: Industrial Society.

Harrison, B., & Weiss, M. (1998). *Workforce development networks: Community-based organizations and regional alliances.* Thousand Oaks: Sage.

Herrington, A., Herrington, J., Kervin, L., & Ferry, B. (2006). The design of an online community of practice for beginning teachers. *Contemporary Issues in Technology and Teacher Education, 6*(1). http://www.citejournal.org/vol6/iss1/general/article1.cfm

Klasen, N. (2002). *Implementing mentoring schemes: A practical guide to successful programs.* Oxford: Butterworth-Heinemann.

Koc-Menard, S. (2009). Training strategies for an aging workforce. *Industrial and Commercial Training, 41*(6), 334–338.

Kram, K. E. (1983). Phases of the mentor relationship. *Academy of Management Journal, 26*(4), 608–625.

Kram, K. E., & Isabella, L. A. (1985). Mentoring alternatives: The role of peer relationships in career development. *Academy of Management Journal, 28*(1), 110–132.

Lincoln, Y. S., & Guba, E. G. (1985). *Naturalistic inquiry.* Beverly Hills: Sage.

Lo, M.-C., & Ramayah, T. (2011). Mentoring and job satisfaction in Malaysian SMEs. *Journal of Management Development, 40*(4), 427–440.

Lombardo, M., & Eichinger, R. W. (2000). *The career architect development planner.* Minneapolis: Lominger.

MacGregor, L. (2000). Mentoring: The Australian experience. *Career Development International, 5*(4/5), 244–249.

McDonald, K. S., & Hite, L. M. (2005). Ethical issues in mentoring: The role of HRD. *Advances in Developing Human Resources, 7*(4), 569–582.

McGurk, J. (2010). *Real-world coaching evaluation: A guide for practitioners.* London: Chartered Institute of Personnel and Development.

Mutte, J. L. (2006). Towards a global HR management model. *Worldlink, 16,* 6–7.

Oakland, J. S. (2004). *Oakland on quality management.* Oxford: Elsevier Butterworth-Heinemann.

Piip, J. K. (2013, November 25–28). *Leadership talent: A model of a contemporary rail leader.* Paper presented at the World Congress on Railway Research, Sydney.

Ragins, B. R. (1997). Diversified mentoring relationships in organizations: A power perspective. *Academy of Management Review, 22*(2), 482–521.

Ragins, B. R., & Kram, K. E. (2007). The roots and meaning of mentoring. In B. R. Ragins & K. E. Kram (Eds.), *The handbook of mentoring at work: Theory, research and practice* (pp. 3–15). Thousand Oaks: Sage.

Short, T. W. (2008). *Strategic alignment and learning in human resource development: A hermeneutic exploration.* PhD thesis, University of South Australia, Adelaide.

Short, T. W., Piip, J. K., Stehlik, T., & Becker, K. (2011). *A capability framework for rail leadership and management development.* Research Report P4.104. Brisbane: CRC for Rail Innovation.

Wallace, M., Lings, I., Sheldon, N., & Cameron, R. (2011, December 7–9). *Attracting young engineers to the rail industry in Australia.* Paper presented at ANZAM Conference, Wellington, New Zealand.

Chapter 8
Educational Technologies and the Training Curriculum

Lesley Jolly, Gregory Tibbits, Lydia Kavanagh, and Lisa O'Moore

Abstract Technologies such as online tools, simulations and remote labs are often used in learning and training environments, both academic and vocational, to deliver content in an accessible manner. They promise efficiencies of scale, flexibility of delivery and face validity for a generation brought up on electronic devices. However, learning outcomes are not the same in all circumstances and contextual and cultural factors can lead to the failure of technology that has been successful elsewhere. This chapter draws on the team's studies of the use of simulators and simulations within the vocational environment of the Australian rail industry to consider how the broader context of the training/educational curriculum affects what works for whom under what circumstances.

Introduction

Technologies such as online tools, simulations and remote labs are often used in learning and training environments to deliver content in an accessible and realistic manner. They promise efficiencies of scale, flexibility of delivery and face validity for a generation brought up on electronic devices. There has, however, been debate over whether such technologies allow for specified learning outcomes to be achieved

L. Jolly (✉)
Strategic Partnerships, Brisbane, QLD, Australia
e-mail: lesleyjolly@me.com

G. Tibbits • L. Kavanagh
School of Mechanical Engineering, University of Queensland, Brisbane, QLD, Australia
e-mail: Gregory.tibbits@uqconnect.edu.au; l.kavanagh@uq.edu.au

L. O'Moore
School of Civil Engineering, University of Queensland, Brisbane, QLD, Australia
e-mail: l.omoore@uq.edu.au

T. Short and R. Harris (eds.), *Workforce Development: Strategies and Practices*,
DOI 10.1007/978-981-287-068-1_8, © Springer Science+Business Media Singapore 2014

as successfully and as thoroughly as through conventional delivery techniques (Lindsay 2005; Trevelyan 2004). At least part of this debate has undoubtedly been fuelled by experiences of training organisations adopting the latest technological innovation with enthusiasm only to find that it makes assumptions that may not fit local circumstances, or it is far harder to implement than expected or that it does not perform as expected. In the case that we will be discussing here, the use of simulators in train driver training, there have been concerns that the investment in these training aids has not been justified by levels of usage or learning outcomes (Kavanagh et al. 2008). It is apparent that educators need a clearer understanding of the factors influencing the achievement of learning outcomes by technological means, because the pressure to use learning technologies as part of a blended learning environment is likely to remain.

While established pedagogy can be used to help with implementation, it will not necessarily provide a complete framework for the educator. For example, learning theory recommends that learning experiences be conducted in learning cycles, through a sequence of:

- orienting students to the learning that will take place and contextualising what is to be learned
- exploring and enhancing knowledge and skills through guided practice
- conducting independent practice of knowledge and skills
- synthesising learnings in order to be able to transfer them to other contexts or environments (Killen 2013).

Within this cycle simulators and simulations could be used to create a context for learning that activates prior knowledge, a setting for guided practice, a setting for independent practice, or a tool that allows disparate pieces of knowledge to be synthesised into practical application. However, knowing what might be attained and how simulators could be used does not identify potential problems and thus provides an incomplete picture. Taking a broader view of the context in which innovations such as this are implemented can help inform our understanding of their performance and is essential for success. Our view of what context is has been informed by the evaluation of educational innovations using the realist approach associated with Pawson and Tilley (1997), which seeks to determine what works for whom under what circumstances.

The realist approach is based on the understanding that the context of an implementation may activate different response mechanisms in different subjects, leading to different outcomes. Identifying the relevant aspects of context, subjects and their responses can explain why some interventions are successful in one area but not in another. This approach to evaluation is based on the premise that it is not enough to ask whether an intervention works or not. In order to be able to elicit the kind of understanding that will allow us to examine the use of simulators we must identify what factors in the context make a difference, and the range of possible responses to the intervention. Pawson and Tilley expressed this as a formula: $C + M = O$, where C stands for 'contexts' (understood as the sociocultural conditions that set limits on the efficacy of the intervention), M stands for 'mechanisms' (the decisions to change that are triggered by the intervention) and O stands for 'outcomes' (which may be unintended as well as intended). We will return to this framework later, but before we do we need to think about what constitutes 'context' in this case.

Curriculum as Context

Educationalists' views of what constitutes curriculum vary from the highly specific content of a course to the whole learning environment. Dillon offered one authoritative definition:

> Curriculum is what is successfully conveyed to differing degrees to different students, by committed teachers using appropriate materials and actions, of legitimated bodies of knowledge, skill, taste, and propensity to act and react, which are chosen for instruction after serious reflection and communal decision by representatives of those involved in the teaching of a specified group of students who are known to the decision makers. (Schwab 1983, quoted in Dillon 2009, p. 343)

This definition begins by saying that curriculum is about outcomes; 'what is successfully conveyed to differing degrees'. Curriculum in this definition also includes the more usual elements of materials, actions, knowledge and skills, but the phrase 'chosen for instruction' draws our attention to the fact that the activities that will develop knowledge and skills have to be designed. People with authority and those who 'represent those involved' need to make choices about what and how they teach. In order to make those choices they need knowledge of the prospective students. To recast this statement into a realist form, we could assume that all curricula operate in contexts that begin at the institutional level. Institutions such as schools, training organisations, workplaces and industries set the conditions under which required knowledge and acceptable practice can be defined. As a result of those conditions, people who are designing syllabi and going into classrooms and training settings make certain decisions about how to develop the required knowledge and practice in their students. The result of their decisions and resources is a set of learning environments that are the context in which students decide what they will do with the learning opportunities on offer. The outcome of those decisions constitute 'what is successfully conveyed' and sometimes that can include things that trainers and educators had no intention of conveying.

Table 8.1 (Jolly et al. 2013) is a diagrammatic model of this understanding of curriculum and is intended to convey the process whereby the decision that is a mechanism in one context becomes the context for subsequent stages. We will draw on this framework to describe and explain the use of simulators in training drivers of trains in the Australian rail industry and show how the broader curriculum context is important to the place of educational technologies in the curriculum.

Table 8.1 The flow of context to mechanism to outcome

← Context →		← Mechanism →	Outcomes
Institutional context The institutional factors affecting the way in which training is implemented **Program context** The nature of training within the program Factors affecting status, purpose and perceptions of training within its program context	**Instructor characteristics** The experience, beliefs and attitudes of instructors before responding to this instance of training **Student characteristics** The experiences, beliefs and attitudes of students prior to responding to training **Assessment** The nature of assessment tasks, the nature of criteria, the weightings of criteria **Training design** The nature, amount and sequence of organisation of training, the topic focus, the resources and learning processes it incorporates and the level and nature of prior knowledge it assumes	**Teacher behaviours** How teachers respond to this training, including decisions, attitudes, interactions **Student motivation** The factors affecting the kinds and level of effort/interest, etc., that students put into training **Student behaviours** The nature and amount of student participation in training, including how and how much they focus on topics, processes and products	**Outcomes** What happened or changed as a result of teacher and student behaviour

Table 8.2 Types of simulators and simulations

	Part task	Full task	Role-play
Conditions simulated	Narrow range, not all real world conditions simulated	All or nearly all conditions simulated	Usually manufactured dangerous conditions to address a particular need or skill
Job performance required	Not whole performance, some aspect of job performance required	Whole or near whole job performance required	Performance required is relevant to conditions simulated, usually some aspect of job performance
Delivery mechanism	Simple devices	Complex devices	Manuals or verbal instruction

Based on Rushby and Seabrook (2007, p. 50)

The Broader Context of Simulator Training in Rail

The rail industry uses a number of different types of technologies to train and assess drivers, track controllers and guards. There are full cab simulators which mimic particular train cabs and provide drivers with a computer-generated view of a virtual world outside the cab as well as real cab controls and occasionally motion corresponding to the computer-generated view. This world may be manipulated by trainers to provide different scenarios and driving conditions and it is this kind of simulator we will be concerned with here. Other kinds of simulation include models of parts of the equipment and role plays. Such simulations vary according to the degree of reality presented and the aims of the training, as well as the prominence of role play (see Table 8.2).

The value of using a simulator in training 'primarily stems from its ability to provide practice opportunities in environments that replicate important features of the "real world" environment' (Salas et al. 2009, p. 329). In other words it may not be necessary to reproduce reality in its entirety and in fact there is significant basis for thinking that too much reality can be counterproductive (Dahlstrom et al. 2009).

The full-cab simulators in use in the Australian rail industry have largely been designed to mimic the physical environment of the driver's cab and when new locomotive types are purchased it is common practice for a matching simulator to be purchased. At the time our study began, one of the participating organisations had recently invested $17 million in new simulators and required further information on the impact they produce or how they could best be used. Indeed, most operators we spoke to felt that they were not using the full potential of simulators in developing and monitoring driver performance standards (Kavanagh et al. 2012). The following description of the broader training curriculum focuses on the curriculum context surrounding simulator use and leads on to a discussion of what this tells us about the perceived underperformance of simulators in this setting.

Rail organisation	Classroom (%)	On the job (%)
#1 (2011)	65	45 (from interviews)
#2 (2009)	50–65	35–50
#3 (2009)	20	70

Table 8.3 Time spent in the classroom or on the job (total not 100)

Institutional Context

Tradition is important in the rail industry, not just in Australia but also abroad (Gamst 2001; Rail Safety and Standards Board 2009). Historically, training was performed on the job, in an apprenticeship arrangement. New drivers would learn about driving on the job from experienced drivers and the progression from station worker to guard to fireman to driver could take a decade. This model of training has been changing in the last decade or so in response to accident investigations and resource constraints, but lives on in the culture of the industry as 'the right way to learn'. This has significant impact on the way simulators are employed, resulting in their use almost exclusively to practise train control and paying less attention to higher order communication and network awareness skills.

In Australia most workers are 'life-time' rail workers (Australasian Rail Association 2006, p. 34). This means that some drivers have been working in the same organisation as drivers for decades. They experienced traditional training and they share this history with new drivers. Some managers, tutors and controllers, many of whom are former drivers, similarly value the traditional training path. This creates an industry with a strong organisational memory and a reluctance to change how things are done, including training.

Even today most applicants for driver positions are already working in the industry, usually as guards. Some organisations do not recruit drivers from 'off the street'; however, this policy is changing in some organisations due to driver shortages. When a driver switches organisations they undergo a full training regime, regardless of their experience or competence.

The current training regime in Australia involves formal training in the classroom or simulator and on-the-job training. The proportion of these forms of training in different organisations is shown in Table 8.3.

The proportion of formal training has increased for a number of reasons. One reason concerns resources: traditional training requires the use of working locomotives and track access for on-the-job training and the availability of locomotives and track for training is decreasing due to the increased utilisation of the rail network. Concurrently, the rail industry has a skills shortage, particularly for driver positions with many drivers approaching retirement age (Australasian Rail Association 2006).

The push for simulators and more formal training is also a response to accident investigations in Australia and the UK which recommended better training to increase safety (Cullen 2001; McInerney 2001, 2005).

The investigation of the Glenbrook disaster discussed simulators at length and recommended them for their ability to simulate unusual conditions.

> The use of modern simulators would enable trainee drivers, and drivers whose competency is being assessed, to be exposed to driving at night, driving in rain, driving when there are signal

failures, driving when points are set the wrong way or any of the other many potentially hazardous circumstances to which a driver will be exposed on the track. (McInerney 2001, p. 124)

In addition it was noted that simulators could be used for more than emergency or degraded conditions, but also for route training and for training drivers, guards, signallers and controllers to work together (McInerney 2001). Our study of the use of simulators (Kavanagh et al. 2012) failed to find these latter suggested uses and instead the simulator was treated as a proxy for the train controls, with some, but not great, attention to potential hazards.

Training organisations that use simulators have often acquired simulators with the purchase of new locomotive units. New locomotive units are infrequent events in the rail industry, occurring every decade or so. Simulators are therefore not frequent purchases and over time it becomes harder and harder to keep their software up to date. The workforce has a perception that railway simulators are somehow sub-standard:

> But see the railway simulators are nowhere near as sophisticated as like the simulators for pilots have got for jumbo jets and the like. The simulators for jumbo jets, they can actually, I think they get a better feel and everything, and the controls are exactly the same, they function exactly the same, like a real jumbo jet. They program in emergency situations and everything, whereas the railway simulator, you can't get any of that kind of thing. (trainee driver, Organisation #1, 30 April 2010)

Another important aspect of the institutional context is that educational levels in the rail workforce are low. Less than 50 % of a sample of 252 managers have a diploma or higher level of certification (Short et al. 2011, p. 8). It is assumed that the education levels of the operational workforce would be at best similar but more likely less than that of managers. As a whole, exposure to post-secondary education within the workforce is low and this has implications for how education and training is conducted and perceived by instructors and students.

Program Context

The content of a driver training course is heavily rules-based and procedural. These rules and procedures are delivered in modules which are parcels of content with titles such as 'Course ST0007B Train operation', 'Course ST0009 Shunting', or 'Emergency procedures'. A module is usually covered within a day and certainly within a week and assessment follows immediately after the training session. Content consists of definitions, descriptions of procedures, checklists, suggested activities and practice exercises. An example of the content from the 'Course ST0009 Shunting' is presented in Table 8.4.

Each module is assessed with workbook-style questions, and achieving a pass mark for each and every module is a necessary condition for being a driver. The most common form of class session we observed was 'chalk and talk' style with instructors working through PowerPoint slides and the workbook and trainees expected to remember and repeat highly detailed and technical information.

Table 8.4 Example of content from ST0009 Shunting

Definition	**Shunting instructions**	Shunting instructions are messages that are transmitted from the employee conducting the shunting moves to the locomotive driver
		The locomotive driver must be kept fully informed about shunting operations
		Shunting instructions may contain special **shunting commands**, or they may be messages, which help to clarify shunting activities
Descriptions of procedures	**Entering and leaving terminals**	Before entering or leaving terminals, locomotive drivers make radio contact with the person responsible for shunting to find out about the movement of their train in the terminal. The person shunting tells the driver information about the movement of the train, including details of any other shunting activities in progress
Checklists	**Shunting and driving responsibilities**	During shunting operations, the employee directing the shunting movements must keep the locomotive driver informed of *all shunting moves*
		• The driver must *acknowledge* all movement commands after the person shunting says 'Over'
		• You *must transmit instructions to the driver at intervals not exceeding 10 s* or until the shunting movement is complete
		• If the driver *does not receive a transmission within 10 s,* the movement must be immediately stopped
		• Shunting movements must not recommence until communication has been restored and all employees *clearly understand* the situation
		• Always use Pacific National *standard shunting commands*
		• If there is any doubt about the safety of a shunting movement, *the driver must immediately stop* and check the situation

In contrast to the classroom delivery of information, the on-track training is highly experiential and much higher in status. Simulators have the potential to mimic the experiential dimension of on-track training but the perception of trainees and experienced drivers alike appears to be that they do not.

Initially, trainee drivers who have been recruited off the street have positive attitudes to simulators and can see how they will augment the training.

However, this perception changes after the drivers complete some on-the-job training, when their attitudes shift to be more similar to those of established drivers. This was apparent after two observations of the same driving school 6 weeks apart.

One of the trainees explained 'that as soon as we did one of the empty drives, we realised how useless the simulators were, in terms of the feel of the train' (trainee driver, Organisation #1, 30 April 2010). An experienced driver explained his perception of the simulators as:

> See, the only contact with simulators I've had was – I'd already been driving for well over 10, 15 years – it was only 5 years ago or something that we had a go at the simulators. I didn't find the simulators very helpful, I suppose they are to a degree, but it's just chalk and cheese from simulator to actually being out on a real train. (trainee driver [transferred from freight operation], Organisation #1, 30 April 2010)

While many drivers told us that the simulator was 'nothing like the real train', the way that simulators are used within the formal training program, and the difference between that training program and actual work experience, may be feeding into this perception.

Instructor Characteristics

The classroom and simulator instructors are former drivers who are involved full time in the instruction and assessment of drivers. They have received minimal training to be educators, but have usually completed a 5-day Level IV Certificate of Workplace Instruction. As former drivers, instructors are aware of traditional methods of training and are responsible for some on-the-job training of new drivers. They are responsible for the transferral of much traditional knowledge, norms, attitudes and behaviours of the industry to drivers. Everyone in safety-sensitive roles in the industry goes through regular competence assessment but the instructor's assessment is similar to that for drivers, which is to say it assesses their ability to drive a train. There is no ongoing competence assessment for training skills.

Simulator operation can be complicated. Instructors are taught how to use the simulator by the simulator manager, who in every case we examined was an ex-driver with a passionate interest in simulators and computers, rather than someone with dedicated training in simulator use and development. Once again, it was familiarity with driving and the industry that was the prime criterion for such jobs. As part of the context of simulator use, then, the preponderance of drivers and the high status accorded to driving trains leads people to make choices about how simulators are used that may have negative consequences.

Student Characteristics

As most of the trainee drivers are from within the industry they have some knowledge of driving, for example familiarity with some rules and procedures and routes. Most guards have been in the cab and may have operated the train under guidance from the driver. One trainee explained that drivers like guards to be able to handle the train in case something incapacitates them: 'I actually had to be … drivers have said you are driving [mumbled] – said that I was going to drive and I said no, I'm not, and he said yes, you are' (trainee driver [formerly guard], Organisation #2, 13 July 2009).

The driver workforce has very few members who are not white males and the sociocultural profile is likely to reinforce negative attitudes to classroom training and the 'poor substitute' perception around simulators in comparison to the actual practice of driving trains. While there is increasing computer literacy amongst the workforce, the glamour of the train still trumps electronic technologies like the simulator.

Assessment

For trainee drivers, every module is assessed. Assessment questions were sometimes exactly the same as the workbook practice questions. It was not uncommon for trainees who failed an assessment to be given the opportunity to reconsider their answers orally. Trainers justified this by reference to the fact that their trainees were not comfortable in educational settings but 'really knew, but had problems with the [wording of the] question or panicked due to exam conditions'.

Overall training is assessed as 'competent' or 'not yet competent'; however examples of performances being rated 'not yet competent' were not observed. Management staff were asked about this situation and insisted that trainees could be and sometimes were deemed not yet competent. Further training was required for these students and occasionally, we were told, such students do not complete their training.

Simulators are not regularly used for assessment purposes but one organisation used them to assess drivers' abilities in wet weather when there had been no opportunity to test that on track over an 18 month period due to a prolonged drought. That same organisation also gave drivers the option of completing some of their regular competence assessment in the simulator.

During one such assessment, the examiner and the driver discussed what had occurred in some depth between scenarios. This was not a one-sided communication from the tutor telling the driver what they should have done. In this instance the driver was queried about certain aspects of the performance in a non-judgemental manner. The examiner and driver then discussed, as equals, alternative actions. Using the simulator meant these discussions could happen immediately after the assessment event; on a train in-depth discussions would have to happen at the end of the drive, so as to not distract the driver.

Although the McInerney Royal Commission explicitly recommended the use of simulators for driver assessment, there is strong resistance to this in the industry for the contextual reasons already outlined.

Course Design

In most organisations the first scheduled simulator session in a training course is a 'simulator familiarisation session'. This can occur on the first day of driver training, but is generally performed within the first month of training and typically lasts for about half a day. All students are scheduled to operate the simulator for 15–30 min each and the purpose of this session is to familiarise students with the train cab and controls. In addition students learn the basics of train handling, that is, which lever and buttons to press and in what in order. This information is not replicated for each student, but each student receives assistance from the tutor in the cab in response to what is happening in the simulator.

Other key lessons using simulators are 'non-technical skills', 'faults and failures' and 'train management/handling'. These sessions are usually scheduled for a full day but time spent in the simulator is commonly half of the day preceded by a didactic classroom session, and each student may operate the simulator for 10–15 min. The 'non-technical skills' session practices communication between the driver and other workers on the network, including guards and controllers whose roles are acted in the session by the trainer. The faults and failures session focuses on common things that can go wrong on the locomotive, such as fuse, door and brake failures, and how to correct these failures is also taught on the simulator. For example, the simulator screen can display the fuse box as it appears on the real train and students have to select and manipulate the appropriate fuse on the screen to correct the fault.

'Train management/handling' is about the smooth, efficient operation of the train, including how and when to apply brakes and thrust. Students are coached through the timed application of brakes and acceleration by the trainer who is in the simulator with them. This session can include train management in degraded conditions, such as fog, rain or frost, which are factors that can influence how the train operates. These sessions are usually conducted on simulated real-life routes, meaning that 'general' train management skills may not be learned as much as driving a particular route smoothly.

Other less common lessons on the simulator include emergency procedures, new route familiarisation and new locomotive familiarisation. This training is completed once by the entire workforce. With the acquisition of new locomotives, which is an infrequent event happening once a decade or less in an organisation, a new simulator is sometimes purchased as part of the locomotive deal. This simulator is used to prepare the drivers for the new locomotive and this event only occurred once during this research.

In all simulator sessions tutors avoided creating realistic situational stresses as could be expected in real emergencies. The simulators were not simulating workload and psychological stresses for emergency situations (Rushby 2006). In more routine simulator sessions the effects of boredom, for instance, were not being simulated.

Most simulator sessions are scheduled for a whole training day, from 0830 to 0430, for a whole school of trainee drivers (8–20 students). Table 8.5 collates

Table 8.5 Simulator session frequency (2009)

Organisation	Length of training (weeks)	Simulator sessions (days/school)
#1	46	8
#2a	40	4–5
#2b	13–17	4–5
#3	73	0
#4	20	0

information about training regimes supplied by industry partners and demonstrates that each organisation instructs drivers differently.

The information was obtained in 2009 and changes may have occurred. Nevertheless the general feature of only a few simulator sessions per school is still current. As training is conducted during business hours, each simulator session is no more than 6 h in duration. Each student receives less than 1 h actively using the simulator for the scheduled session. Furthermore not all rail organisations use simulators. Organisations that do not use simulators often recruit drivers from other companies as opposed to training them and therefore conduct less training and in turn have invested less in training facilities and equipment.

Observed simulator sessions were often shorter than the allotted time. This actual use of the simulator, as opposed to the scheduled use, reduced student operation of the simulator to less than 30 minutes per student

Simulator sessions follow classrooms sessions of the same content and are perceived as part of classroom instruction rather than a practical exercise or on-the-job learning. Although the original recommendation to adopt them included reference to their use for team-based training and network awareness, this association with the classroom work leads to an emphasis on procedures and rules rather than situated performance.

This use of the simulators is a conscious choice, driven by the broader contextual factors of institution and industry. In contrast, in other countries such as Norway simulators are used intensively for months before drivers go on to trains and driver training is integrated with that of guards and track controllers through use of the simulators. The whole set of assumptions around training and its delivery leads to quite different uses here.

Instructor Behaviours

Despite an emphasis on the use of simulators for training in degraded conditions, the most persistent and obvious behaviour amongst instructors is their reluctance to treat the dangers as dangers. We were repeatedly told that trainees were nervous and so trainers did not want to put them off. As a result the degraded conditions were reduced in many instances to jokes. For example, when a student was driving in the simulator it was common for the instructor to place obstacles on the simulated track, such as kangaroos or cars. These were placed randomly (sometimes in places where they could not be) and suddenly so that students did not have much chance to respond appropriately. Further when a student did try to respond appropriately, by braking for instance, the instructor on occasion told them to keep driving. These objects were placed to startle the student as a lark, rather than a genuine simulation of an emergency situation.

Catching students out was also observed in other ways. Obscure rulings or signals were used to test or trip up students. Sometimes when an object was placed on the track the student was required to respond correctly when previous objects had not needed that response. A student explained after his first experience driving the simulator: 'Given a bit more time, I think we, you know, would get it pretty right. Apart from all the faults they throw at you at once' (trainee driver [formally guard], Organisation #2a, 13 July 2009).

The decisions instructors make about the learning opportunities they offer trainees are important mechanisms in the process of training and in this case it is clear that they are determined by contextual factors as our curriculum model suggests.

Student Motivation

This is vocational training; trainees are learning to drive trains to perform the job. This is the main motivation for performing the training. Within that motivation there are other motivations, as for instance the fact that some trainees are interested in trains as machines. These trainees remember and can communicate the various statistics of different locomotives including locomotives not used by their organisation. For them performing the job is an opportunity to align their career with their interests. However, most trainees are attracted to train driving by the high salary. Train drivers are paid higher than the Australian average wage of $70,000 p.a. (Australian Bureau of Statistics 2012). In one organisation, drivers earn $93,000 p.a. and guards $85,000 p.a. Ore train drivers working on remote mines can earn between $150–200,000 with fly in/fly out regimes. With overtime and other assorted benefits train drivers are exceptionally well paid, especially when considering the education levels required.

In our research trainees continually expressed a preference for practical learning on the job. This preference is probably due to a mixture of the lack of educational experience of new drivers, and the stories of tradition told by tutors and experienced divers. On-the-job training is considered to be more relevant. A trainee expressed their preference:

> I guess with a lot of us not being in the formal classroom environment for some time and in my case 20 years, that first week of general corporate rot is just as boring as bat shit but as soon as it went from that to the actual drive the train bit it became a lot more relevant, and the more relevant the more enjoyable it was. (trainee driver, Organisation #1, 12 May 2010)

Student Behaviours

We observed that students using the simulator were enthused. They focused on the process of driving. They were diligent in responding to instructions. They did not ask many questions, but the questions they asked were simple yes/no questions regarding rules. Students were not upset when their turn in the simulator had finished but some expressed a desire for more time. While driving the simulator students are concerned with driving in the right way, such as stopping at the correct location and driving to the speed limit. They are not concerned with the reasoning underpinning driving rules and routines, only their correct application. They get little chance to demonstrate their ability to deal with actual workplace demands such as having to drive, communicate with controllers and guards, and observe signals all at the same time.

As described in the course design section students operate the simulator for less than half an hour. This means that most students are not operating the simulator for most of the session. The behaviour of those not operating the simulator was very different. These students passively observed their peers from another room via monitors. Sometimes the instructor drew attention to particular aspects of the drive, particularly for the first few operations of the simulator. As the session continued students became more disengaged and they used their mobile phones, talked amongst themselves or napped. Sometimes trainees who were not actually in the simulator were asked to view safety videos or review course materials in another room but trainees and trainers alike were sensitive to the lack of meaningful activity of this group (the bulk of the class) and this sometimes further contributed to truncated simulator sessions.

Outcomes

The best outcome of simulator training in this industry is where simulations prompt drivers to reflect on actual practice and develop strategies for realistic responses (Kavanagh et al. 2012) and this is exemplified by the session we described above where trainer and driver could use the experience of the simulator drive to discuss best responses. A related one is simulators' ability to provide improved preparation for dealing with stressful workloads and environments. We had no opportunity to observe such situations in our study but the workforce are sceptical of simulators' ability to do this. Instead there is a perception that simulators are second-class substitutes for trains and that time spent on them is largely wasted. It is reasonable to assume that this perception alone will have a considerable negative impact on any learning that does take place in simulators.

Discussion

We have chosen to describe at length the curriculum surrounding the use of simulators in train driver training because it is a good example of the how context (in this case curriculum) influences mechanisms (decisions about what should be conveyed and how and about how to respond to what is offered) leading to particular outcomes.

Context

Indicators of a poor fit between simulators and this industry begin to emerge at the broadest level of context, that of the institution of the rail industry and the kind of training programs that industry approves. The institutional context is the environment that shapes and guides patterns of instructor and student behaviour. The institutional context also limits the possibilities of course design and implementation.

The referral to and connection with the past is perceptible in the rail industry. Obsolete technologies are still used in the industry, outdated signal mechanisms for example. Rules which were necessary in the past have been made redundant by technology and yet, these rules are still taught and used in very rare situations. The method for assigning access to a single-line track is a case in point. Older drivers who have been in the industry for decades experience this tradition and tell new staff about it. These older drivers were themselves told stories by experienced drivers. The end result is a workforce with a formidable memory of their history. As one HR manager told us:

> they still sort of always default to things – I am going to be very sarcastic here – things like shovelling coal into the engine, you know, well, we don't need that anymore. For some reason it is still on the books, you know what I mean? (HR manager, Organisation #1, 7 October 2010)

This innate conservatism leads to mechanisms such as decisions about who gets recruited, and hence what kind of trainees and trainers are using the curriculum.

The educational levels of the workforce influence the decisions about training. Some older drivers have not completed secondary education. This means that train drivers have little exposure to formal classroom-based education and share an attitude that is often dismissive of further education. For instance, a driver was talking about the current hurdles necessary to become a train driver. He complained that one guard he knew of would never become a driver 'because he can barely type his own name' but he 'knows the track' and would be a fine driver. He was dismissive of the recruitment process and claimed those in charge of it were 'educated twits!'

Entwined with this dismissive attitude to formal education is a positive attitude towards on-the-job learning. The workforce generally has had little success with classroom-based education, but learns from experience on the job with relative ease. This is evident in the fact that most drivers learn about driving the train by driving the train. They can go on the job and see and do, without having to 'learn'. Further the tradition of the industry encourages and values apprenticeship-style learning. A tutor explained:

> I'm a little bit old school. I think that you can't teach experience, you know. You can teach out of a book, but you can't teach experience, and train driving is a lot about experiences with different scenarios that you strike out on track and that it's pretty hard to capture on paper, day-to-day things. (trainer, Organisation #2a, 15 March 2010)

The preference for on-the-job practical learning was evident throughout the industry. One trainee explained the difference: 'You can do that because you're seeing exactly what you have to do, on the spot and in reality, whereas from the book or board or whatever it's never going to be as good' (trainee driver, Organisation #1, 30 April 2010).

It is surprising that these attitudes do not lead to a better perception of the simulator, which could be considered experientially based. We have argued elsewhere (Kavanagh et al. 2012) that the reason for this is that the simulator is used for too narrow a range of tasks and it is embedded in and associated with classroom teaching that is the opposite of experiential. It is mainly used as a train-handling substitute and in that capacity it is not perceived to give the feel of the real train. It could be used more extensively in team-based training or for the practice of network awareness and communication skills, but this mechanism is not triggered in this context because the traditions of the institution are too strong.

Mechanisms

The institutions, the broader context, set the conditions under which the training program operates and limits the decisions that can be made about how it will operate. We have already alluded to the fact that in this context an important mechanism is the choice to employ certain kinds of people because that sets the context for subsequent choices about how course will be designed and taught. Many trainers in the rail industry rose through the ranks. Even though they are now trainers, they have experienced train driving, and the associated tradition and history. They implicitly accept the traditional training as they experienced it because it worked for them and they may not be aware of alternative training techniques and technologies. This leads to a mechanism or set of decisions that always privileges on-track experience and denigrates everything else including the simulators. This can be seen in course design decisions such as the unused downtime for those not actually in the simulator, the cursory use of assessment and the emphasis on rules and procedures over integrated knowledge application.

Curriculum design decisions, the characteristics of students and the characteristics of trainers all combine to trigger a set of mechanisms in trainees with respect to the simulator that undermine its ability to contribute to effective training. Trainees, drivers and trainers all told us 'it's nothing like a train' and treated their activities in it accordingly. The curriculum model offered here has drawn our attention to the root cause of the attitudes that impact on simulator effectiveness, but it has also made clear that getting better outcomes is going to be a complex business that will have to take account of the whole range of curriculum factors.

Conclusion

Our original hypothesis (Kavanagh et al. 2012, p. 24) about the use of simulators in train driver training is represented in the realist style in Table 8.6.

The much more complicated reality looked more like Table 8.7 (Kavanagh et al. 2012, p. 34):

Table 8.6 Hypothesis of simulator use

Context	+	Mechanism	=	Outcome
Rail companies are required to pay attention to driver emergency training as a result of fatal accidents in the UK and Australia. At the same time some training organisations are finding it difficult to source trains and track for training purposes These circumstances will make the adoption of a wider range of training options, such as the use of simulators, more attractive than they have previously been (C_A)		The use of full-cab simulators in driver training will 'change the balance of choices' (Pawson and Tilley 1997, p. 122) open to training organisations by allowing more realistic practice of emergency procedures (M_A)		When M_A is introduced into C_A, training organisations will install simulators and/or adopt other simulation techniques, thereby increasing drivers' 'ability to deal with an emergency situation' (Cullen 2001) and to enhance 'public safety and … sound economic management' (McInerney 2001)(O_A)

Table 8.7 Reality of simulator use

Context	+	Mechanism	=	Outcome
'Not a bullshit exercise': training exercises expected to be relevant and helpful	+	Authentic experience, underlying knowledge and generic skills development combined in active learning episodes	=	Simulations prompt drivers to reflect on actual practice and develop strategies for realistic response
'Can't get the trains': rising costs of on-track training	+	Simulators used as substitute for on-track time	=	Rise in perception that simulators are second-class substitutes for trains
Train driver's job understood to include alertness, communication, teamwork, mechanical knowledge as well as train handling, at all times	+	Opportunities provided for safe supported failure in complex performance	=	Improved preparation for dealing with stressful workloads and environments

Understanding why the reality looked like that has forced us to consider the whole training curriculum, and not just the immediate conditions of use of this particular technology. Using Schwab's definition, we have explored what is conveyed to learners, who conveys it to whom and why they all arrive at the decisions they do about its worth and purpose. What emerges clearly is that new technologies cannot just be added in to an existing curriculum. We need to take account of the ways in which the whole curriculum, the whole context, as we have described it here, changes the meaning and operation of any innovation we introduce.

References

Australasian Rail Association. (2006). *The changing face of rail*. http://www.ara.net.au/UserFiles/file/Publications/TheChangingFaceRail%20Final.pdf

Australian Bureau of Statistics. (2012). *6302.0 Average weekly earnings, Australia*. Canberra: Australian Bureau of Statistics. http://www.abs.gov.au/AUSSTATS/abs@.nsf/allprimarymainfeatures/7F76D15354BB25D5 CA2575BC001D5866?opendocument. Accessed 12 Apr 2012.

Cullen, L. (2001). *The Ladbroke Grove Rail Inquiry: Part 1 report*. Norwich: Her Majesty's Stationery Office.

Dahlstrom, N., Dekker, S., et al. (2009). Fidelity and validity of simulator training. *Theoretical Issues in Ergonomics Science, 10*(4), 305–314.

Dillon, J. T. (2009). The questions of curriculum. *Journal of Curriculum Studies, 41*(3), 343–359. doi:10.1080/00220270802433261.

Gamst, F. C. (2001). Craft seniority: The essence of the 'rail' world. *Anthropology of Work Review, 22*(4), 21–24.

Jolly, L., Brodie, L., et al. (2013). Improving teaching with research: The role for theory-driven evaluation. In C. Rust (Ed.), *Improving student learning through research and scholarship: 20 years of ISL* (pp. 52–66). Oxford: Oxford Brookes University.

Kavanagh, L., Jolly, L., et al. (2008). *Driver performance courses: Preliminary project*. Brisbane: Cooperative Research Centre for Rail Innovation.

Kavanagh, L., Jolly, L., et al. (2012). *P4.103 Evaluation of simulators: Final report*. Brisbane: Cooperative Research Centre for Rail Innovation.

Killen, R. (2013). *Effective teaching strategies: Lessons from research and practice* (6th ed.). South Melbourne: Cengage Learning Australia.

Lindsay, E. (2005). *The impact of remote and virtual access to hardware upon the learning outcomes of undergraduate engineering laboratory classes*. Melbourne: Department of Mechanical and Manufacturing Engineering, University of Melbourne.

McInerney, P. A. (2001). *Special commission of inquiry into the Glenbrook rail accident*. Sydney: Government of New South Wales.

McInerney, P. A. (2005). *Special commission of inquiry into the waterfall rail accident: Final report*. Sydney: The Commission.

Pawson, R., & Tilley, N. (1997). *Realistic evaluation*. Thousand Oaks: Sage.

Rail Safety and Standards Board. (2009). *Locomotion No. 1 to simulation: A brief history of train driver training on Britain's railways*. http://www.rssb.co.uk/SiteCollectionDocuments/pdf/reports/Research/T718_trng_rpt.pdf. Accessed 23 July 2012.

Rushby, N. (2006). *How will we know if games and simulations enable learners to learn anything? And as a corollary: How will we know why they've learned anything?* London: Conation Technologies.

Rushby, N., & Seabrook, J. (2007). *Recent advances in simulation training and assessment for the rail industry: Results and case studies*. London: Conation Technologies.

Salas, E., Rosen, M. A., et al. (2009). Performance measurement in simulation-based training: A review and best practices. *Simulation & Gaming, 40*(3), 328–376.

Short, T. W., Piip, J. K., et al. (2011). *A capability framework for rail leadership and management development*. Brisbane: Cooperative Research Centre for Rail Innovation.

Trevelyan, J. (2004, June 27–30). *Lessons learned from 10 years' experience with remote laboratories*. Paper presented at the international conference on engineering education and research, Olomouc and Bouzov Castle, Czech Republic.

Chapter 9
Leading Multiple Generations in the Australian Rail Workplace

Tom Short and Roger Harris

Abstract The emergence of multi-generational organisations and the need for leaders to develop 'generational competence' is a contentious topic in the literature. Academics argue that multi-generation organisations are nothing new and warn us of the dangers of making sweeping generalisations about the behaviours and outlook of people who belong to a particular age classification. Conversely, market surveys and consulting reports, primarily led from the USA, claim the existence of such a growing phenomenon and suggest that organisations must treat different cohorts of employees in a way that capitalises on their age-related values and working preferences. These studies have given rise to popular terms such as Baby Boomers and Generation X and Y.

This chapter draws on research findings to uncover how one industry in Australia is dealing with a workforce of four generations. We comment on how the rapidly ageing industry is facing major challenges in transferring tacit knowledge and skills from one generation to the next and how workforce development activities accommodate the needs of different age groups such as attracting apprentices, up-skilling returning workers and assisting those who are ready to retire. The findings remind us of the need to plan and prepare for career transitions at all generational levels.

Introduction

Employee turnover in traditional industries is starting to hurt organisations as global mobility of people grows and long-serving and experienced Baby Boomers retire to make way for younger generations (PricewaterhouseCoopers 2006; ARA 2008). While the global financial crisis (GFC) in 2008 delayed the onset of these events, many rail organisations are now seriously considering how they can minimise risks

T. Short (✉) • R. Harris
School of Education, University of South Australia, Mawson Lakes, SA, Australia
e-mail: tom.short@unisa.edu.au; roger.harris@unisa.edu.au

T. Short and R. Harris (eds.), *Workforce Development: Strategies and Practices*,
DOI 10.1007/978-981-287-068-1_9, © Springer Science+Business Media Singapore 2014

such as skills shortages and depletion of core capability. Top of this list is how to manage the transfer of highly valued tacit knowledge from departing senior employees to younger and/or less experienced co-workers. Arguably, industries are facing an impending crisis, at both ends of the age spectrum, because disproportional numbers of older employees are expected to leave in the next decade, yet many industries are not attracting sufficient young people to replace them.

While knowledge acquisition and skill depletion across generations is not a new event, the challenge of managing and leading multi-generational groups is complex, not least because of the many variables existent within traditional industry contexts. Research has recognised 'the notion of context as a primary area of focus' (Jepson 2009, p. 37), and that too little attention has been given to how the 'internal context of an organisation affects behaviour' (Porter 1996, p. 264), of which succession and career planning are key components. For leaders, the contextual questions in areas of workforce development are how to maximise these multi-generational exchanges by recognising, engaging and motivating longer-serving, senior employees while developing and inspiring younger generations in an industry that is perceived to be less attractive than it was 40 years ago (Wallace et al. 2011).

In this chapter we explore areas where multi-generational issues lurk within the Australian rail industry and bring together relevant findings from a number of our research projects in workforce development between 2008 and 2013. Workforce development is a relatively new concept used by policy makers and educationalists to differentiate workplace training from, and contribute to, other development activities such as workforce planning, mentoring, coaching, engagement and retention (Harris and Short 2014). The research program was undertaken under the stewardship of the Cooperative Research Centre (CRC) for Rail Innovation, supported by the Australian government. Australia's rail industry is just one of a number of national sectors undergoing major reform as a result of globalisation, technology, workforce mobility and an ageing population. Nowadays, the key challenge is blending rail's strong legacy and traditions with the need to modernise, to re-emerge as the most eco-sustainable option for future mass transportation within and across state borders.

Faced with these strategic goals, we suggest the emerging presence of a multi-generational workforce may become an issue for rail leaders. One rail report has proposed that new strategies are needed to retain knowledge by making the industry an attractive place to work, for example by retaining experienced staff and introducing flexible, innovative work practices (ARA 2008). Another recommended formal workplace mentoring programs to bridge age cohorts and help transfer tacit knowledge (PricewaterhouseCoopers 2006), while yet another found that only a small number of younger people preferred to work with older employees, perceived as less tech-savvy (Sardo and Begley 2008). In this chapter, therefore, we consider how rail organisations are dealing with their multi-generational workforces and how issues within this area could feature in workforce development strategy. We aim to contribute to knowledge by adding insights garnered from the Australian rail context.

Background from the Literature

Awareness of Issues Within a Multi-generational Workplace

The topic of multi-generational workplaces is attracting heightened attention among organisational leaders due to a growing realisation that very soon, if not already, a typical workplace could have up to four generations of employees working under the same roof (Haynes 2011; Proffitt Reese and Sharpley 2013). This situation is not unusual in traditional family units where most people learn how to communicate, relate and co-habit in a harmonious way. However, in the workplace four generations might present leaders with new challenges and a range of issues such as how to accommodate the needs of older workers (Erlich and Bichard 2008), engage a new generation of graduates (Shaw and Fairhurst 2008) and attract sufficient numbers of younger workers to replace thousands of impending retirements (Wallace et al. 2011). From a human resource development (HRD) perspective, understanding generational differences and how they coexist in a workplace may help to define an organisation's future 'generational competence' (Jimenez 2009, p. 50) and underpin competitive success (Glass 2007).

Generational Characteristics

Recently many authors have realised that changes enacted by each generation represent not only a major component in the make-up of society, but how it responds to a wide range of events. Society at large is going through a period of radical change as life expectancy increases and improved healthcare reduces age-related barriers to workforce participation. The sense of wellbeing resulting from these changes brings new challenges to the way people view their worlds. Social researchers have identified five generational groups, all with different characteristics. Although it is not always wise, or accurate, to generalise human behaviour by age group (Johnson and Lopes 2008), it is nevertheless helpful to consider these insights and relate them to our experiences at work. Studies have focused on the unique preferences and behaviours of generational groups, first introduced in 1970 with reference to Baby Boomers. These groups have become popular definitions to classify how different generations share a particular way of experiencing the world. Importantly, these classifications have also grown in the academic disciplines of business, psychology and social sciences to become part of HR language. Theoretical views and reliable evidence are mixed, but some literature, predominantly undertaken by consulting organisations in the USA (Johnson and Lopes 2008, p. 33), suggests that understanding the attitudes and behaviours of each group may help organisational leaders to attract, recruit, lead, engage and retain employees. According to Hammill (2005) and many others, these age groups are broadly described as:

- Veterans, born between 1922 and 1945
- Baby Boomers, born between 1946 and 1964
- Generation X, born between 1965 and 1980
- Generation Y, born between 1981 and 2000
- Generation Z, born after 2000 (not discussed further in this chapter).

Veterans

This generational group, also known as Traditionalists or the silent generation (Kapoor and Solomon 2011, p. 309), grew up and came through the second world war with a strong 'sense of duty ... and see work as an obligation and that authority must be respected' (Haynes 2011, p. 99). Veterans have a clear approach to leadership based on classical management theories, experienced through command and control techniques (Hammill 2005) with a strong work ethic and preference for discipline. They also prefer to receive information in a 'straight-forward and summarised way such as direct mail, memorandums or any other form of written communication' (Dahlroth 2008, p. 32).

Baby Boomers

Baby Boomers, or Boomers, have lived through an accelerated period of civil rights, exploration of space and women's liberation. Glass asserted that Boomers are more 'optimistic, idealistic, driven' (2007, p. 99) and are willing to sacrifice personally and professionally in order to achieve success. Boomers are seen as 'highly competitive micromanagers who disdain laziness', but are willing to 'network and seek consensus with others' (Crumpacker and Crumpacker 2007, p. 353). Gursoy et al. (2008) reported that Boomers were brought up to respect authority, but they dislike change and the thought of having to learn new ways of doing things. Yet they like to be involved in decision-making processes, enjoy working in teams, have embraced technology such as email, yet value person-to-person communications (Hammill 2005).

Generation X

Generation X (or Gen X) values a more egalitarian approach to work, seeing everyone in the workplace as an equal partner and expecting their experience to be respected (Haynes 2011). Gen X tends to be self-reliant, independent and can sometimes be sceptical of authority, having grown up in an era of massive economic upheaval and workplace uncertainty. For these reasons, Gen X places higher value on maintaining a healthy work–life balance and has learned from parents that long service and adhering to company rules will not guarantee job security (Gursoy et al. 2008). The Gen X workforce is a relatively small population estimated at only 60 %

of the Boomers and the following cohort, Gen Y (Pitt-Catsouphes and Smyer 2007). They work alone, multi-task, change jobs more frequently, are technologically literate and value lifelong learning because they believe that career success will depend on continuing education and the development of new skills (Bova and Kroth 2001; Mann 2006).

Generation Y

Generation Y (or Gen Y or Millennials) will enter the workforce in far greater numbers than Gen X and has many similarities with Boomers (Pitt-Catsouphes and Smyer 2007; Kapoor and Solomon 2011). In contrast with Gen X, this generation is less independent and favours teamwork, but prefers to follow 'detail-orientated instructions and value constant feedback' (Glass 2007, p. 101). The overriding characteristic of Gen Y is their natural comfort with technology and ability to deal with change. Gen Y embraces technology of all types and prefers digital media to physical interaction because of their life experiences; however, this preference for electronic communication has led to criticism that Gen Y in the workplace has underdeveloped relationship-building, conflict resolution and problem-solving skills (Artley and Macon 2009). Lesonsky suggested that, while Gen Y understands the need for structure and lines of authority, it is 'not afraid of authority, seek[s] freedom and like[s] to be treated as equals' (2011, p. 1).

Impact of Generational Diversity

The literature on generational diversity is growing and shaped by the context of each setting, leading to an inevitable realisation that multi-generational workgroups in twenty-first century organisations will present concurrent, but not disconnected, opportunities and leadership challenges in the years ahead. In the Australian rail sector, reports (PricewaterhouseCoopers 2006; ARA 2008) acknowledge the ageing workforce and the need to attract younger workers, yet at the same time recognise the high value of Baby Boomer employees who hold tacit knowledge and are delaying retirement. However, Legas and Sims argued that retaining Boomers past retirement may be 'problematic for workplace harmony' (2011, p. 2) and might prevent the much smaller cohort of ambitious Gen X professionals from achieving promotion.

Of all generational groups, Gen X is reported to be the most adaptable, independent and mobile when searching for advancement, but they also value work–life balance and will not become workaholics in the same way as Boomers (Bova and Kroth 2001; Williams and Page 2011). Therefore, when Boomers eventually retire, the comparatively smaller Gen X may become overwhelmed and unable to provide sufficient continuity of leadership. This shortfall could then produce a very steep learning curve for inexperienced Gen Y leaders who may achieve promotion 10

Table 9.1 Generational preferences in eight work areas

Work areas	Veterans	Baby Boomers	Generation X	Generation Y
Employment	Job for life	Longer serving	Multiple employers	Multiple careers
Way of learning	Education	Training	Self-study	Mentoring
Employee behaviour	Company: loyal	Job: dedicated	Career: self-reliant	Family: work–life balance
Organisational structure	Command and control	Top-down hierarchy	Functional matrix	Broad framework
Employee motivation	Directed	Consultative	Self-starting	Team-oriented
Work tenure	Lifelong	Stable	Transitional	Planned
Means of communication	Chain of command	Face-to-face	email	iPhones/tablets
Attitude to authority	Obedient	Deferential	Sceptical	Unfazed

years ahead of their time and have little opportunity to learn vital knowledge and skills from retiring Boomers (Dohm 2000).

A further paradox for organisations is reported in the area of intergenerational communications, and how employees relate together in a harmonious way. Commenting on the changing nature of traditional life in America, Jauregui reflected on how work has become the only venue where people can 'learn about each other, how to work together and exchange political and social views' (2007, p. 347); but importantly, this is where members of different generations communicate en masse, so leadership messages have to be clear. Part of the problem may come from a breaking of tradition in the way people progress through their employment life and how juniors have always filled the shoes of those colleagues who advance in much the same way as people take their place in family roles. However, the postmodern pattern of dismantling organisational hierarchy and the emergence of matrix-style structures have created workspaces less bound by age-related knowledge and progression – best typified by Gen Y employees helping Boomers to cope with the onset of technology and digitisation of work.

The impact of globalisation on Australia has diversified the mix of generations, not only old and young, but eastern versus western cultures and a New World ideology contrasted with the classical traditions of Europe. Multi-generational and multinational workforces have become a topic of great interest, and in particular how organisations cope with the transfer of knowledge and culture from one generation to the next. What makes this challenge complex is the way different generations view work, what engages them in work and how they choose to communicate. While Appelbaum et al. (2005) wrote of organisational myths relating to generational differences, Pitt-Catsouphes and Smyer (2007) have suggested we should think differently about how and why age matters, redefining how chronological age might be separated from career age. As a summary, Table 9.1 highlights a selection of preferences from four generations across eight work areas reported in the literature.

Approach to Research Study

Our methodology for this chapter combined three approaches. Firstly, we conducted a targeted review of relevant literature in the area of multi-generational workplaces; secondly, we examined recent reports developed for policy makers within the rail industry; and thirdly, we synthesised relevant findings from our CRC research studies. The research from three universities embraced, across the eight projects drawn on for this chapter, the topics of leadership and management development, mentoring and coaching, skills recognition, industry attraction and retention, e-learning, skilled migration, competence assurance and simulator evaluation. Each of these projects was conducted over a 1 or 2 year period between 2008 and 2013. The projects were undertaken in seven private and/or public sector rail organisations located in five Australian states.

In relation to employee size, these rail organisations represented half of the rail industry and accounted for the learning and development of almost 20,000 employees at varying levels of generational and occupational seniority. The research was qualitative-interpretive, using case studies, semi-structured interviews and focus groups, and supported with data from surveys. The strengths in using this methodology were that data were industry relevant and that findings were cross-referenced with academic literature as well as industry documents.

We compared characteristics of the three generational groups in the eight work areas (Table 9.1) to suggest a selection of behaviours and preferences across generational groups. In addition, we appropriated five leadership challenges identified by the UK's Leadership Trust – globalisation, sustainability, diversity, technology and change (Damon 2007) – and used them as a conceptual framework to analyse key themes relating to multi-generational workforces in Australian rail. These challenges were supported by Howard and Wellings (2009), who asserted that how we respond to work complexity, technology, speed of change and global competition is a central part of organisational leadership. We particularly focused on how the rail organisations accommodated these challenges in the formulation of their HR strategic architecture (Thompson 1995) and practice.

Findings and Discussion

The findings highlighted in this chapter are a blend of information obtained from the reports on the eight research studies and are therefore indicative of how the Australian rail industry is responding to multi-generational issues. Heeding the observation of Black and Earnest (2009) on the complex web of relationships, motivations and interactions within leadership issues, for the purpose of this analysis we developed a list of characteristics of 'generational competence' against the eight work areas featured in Table 9.1. These characteristics, which can be viewed through the thematic lenses of the five leadership challenges, are summarised in Table 9.2 as a conceptual framework.

Table 9.2 A conceptual framework for analysing multi-generational workplaces

Work areas	Characteristics of organisational 'generational competence'
Employment	Approaches to work and diversity are arranged so as to implement effective knowledge transfer across generational groups
Way of learning	Challenges and approaches to the delivery of learning and employee development are accommodated
Employee behaviour	The focus of diverse employee groups is maximised to ensure effective implementation of work priorities and to positively influence discretionary effort
Organisational structure	Contradictions and confusions between the preferences of generational groups and organisational hierarchy are accommodated
Employee motivation	Employee engagement is maintained in the organisation in terms of diverse preferences for working with others
Work tenure	Succession planning and retention issues are maximised to maintain performance
Means of communication	HR strategies deal with the organisation's need to communicate at enterprise, team and individual levels
Attitude to authority	Leadership and management authority is practised across multi-generational groups

⇧   ⇧   ⇧   ⇧   ⇧

Leadership challenges as thematic lenses	Globalisation	Sustainability	Diversity	Technology	Change

Extracting findings of relevance to multi-generational workforces in our rail research reports, we then used this conceptual framework as a simple barometer to indicate where the rail organisations rate in terms of contextual awareness on these strategic themes. We employed three broad descriptors to assess indicative levels of 'generational competence' in these rail contexts, summarised in Fig. 9.1. While the notion of generational competence is open to conjecture and academic debate, in the following sections we discuss findings from our rail studies that provide examples for each of these leadership challenges.

Globalisation (Higher/Moderate)

Globalisation is now a commonly understood phenomenon and deals with such matters as the impact of a smaller economic world, free market competition, faster travel, labour mobility, diversity and the influence of multinational organisations (PricewaterhouseCoopers 2006; ARA 2008). Although Australian rail organisations do not physically transport people or freight across international borders, globalisation is felt through competition for talented people, the relatively small population, variable exchange rates, the influence of China and the knock-on effect of these issues on operating costs. Australia's relative success in dealing with the GFC, a

Higher level	Moderate level	Lower level
Evident in many policy documents, organisational systems and communication processes. Awareness of the external context flowed through workforce development programs and affected internal practices to build generational competence.	Evident in some policy documents and organisational systems. External context rarely featured in internal communications. Multi-generational issues were inward looking but recognised the external environment as a strategic influence in generational competence.	Less evidence in policy documents or systems relating to the external context. Internal communications and procedures were aligned to the internal needs of the organisation and adopted a limited account of generational competence.

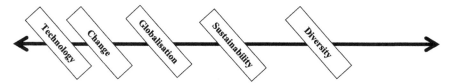

Fig. 9.1 Contextual awareness and a 'generational competence' continuum

minerals boom and arguably less discriminatory practices in hiring older people have attracted skilled migrants from all age groups. In the area of rail leadership capability, the arrival of senior experience, largely from the UK, has averted a potential gap in local leadership talent. This influx follows a report that Australia had the lowest number of talented people available for senior leadership roles (9 %) in comparison with other major economies such as Europe (26 %), yet was investing more in leadership development than many other nations outside of Asia (Infographics 2011). For rail, this situation has created a temporary gap in leadership capacity, which is accentuated by the trend for younger Australians to seek overseas experiences after graduation or before settling into a longer-term career choice – a lifestyle pattern Arnett referred to as 'residential mobility' (2000, p. 268).

Diversity (Lower/Moderate)

We found that rail organisations were attempting to meet the challenges of a maturing and largely male-dominated workforce by adopting policies relating to the diversity agenda such as increasing skilled migration, allowing older employees to transit slowly into retirement and increasing the pool of marginal workers. Here we use the term 'marginal worker' to describe cohorts of non-traditional or mainstream employees that include, but are not limited to, part-time employees, female participation, the return of retired workers and inclusion of people with special needs. In one important area, train driver capacity, our findings indicated that organisations were overcoming skills shortages by focusing attention on attracting and recruiting more women. Once seen as a traditional, male-centric occupation requiring long service and on-job experience, development of virtual reality simulation has added professionalism to the role of train driver and generated wider perceptions of who can become a train driver. In our case studies, female drivers were present in all age groups (Gen X, Y and Boomers) and every respondent had made a lateral career choice to become a train driver.

Our research also found an increase in the use of formal mentoring to capitalise on the presence of a multi-generational workplace, especially in the area of knowledge transfer. In the case of train drivers, trainees were encouraged to take part in driver mentoring programs and draw support from an experienced colleague who was quite often an older colleague and not part of the management structure or assessment process. The literature review confirmed that mentoring was becoming highly valued in mixed-generation groups and was seen by Gen Y employees as more relevant and less hierarchical than formal approaches to learning (see Table 9.1).

Sustainability (Moderate)

Sustainability has become a major concern, especially for rail organisations striving to balance ecological imperatives with commercial goals. In Australia a combination of the GFC and increasing public awareness of climate change has spurred a range of eco-efficient initiatives in the rail sector aimed at maximising the use of technology to create more comfortable and convenient transportation options. Viewpoints differ on how the politics of sustainable development link to generational values, but one report has suggested that Gen X and Boomers have sheltered behind short-term prosperity and failed to act, and that Gen Y might be the first 'sustainable generation' (Guardian Sustainable Business 2011). The Sky Future Leaders Survey (2011) reported that Gen Y graduates knew more about their organisations' visions and values than their record on sustainability; nevertheless they were keen to avoid making the mistakes of their predecessors. One 'guiding step' offered by the National Centre for Sustainability, a collaboration of Australian educational institutions, encourages organisations to '[d]evelop an environment which supports human dignity through gender and racial equality and promotes intergenerational respect and also encourages ethical business practices' (2012).

The need for intergenerational respect was a recurring theme in our research on leadership development and workplace mentoring. Mentoring was seen as a valued one-on-one relationship that offered a safe and confidential learning environment, where individuals could let off steam and take time to focus energy on their own learning needs. Mentoring also included the acquisition of new knowledge, learning how to deal with difficult people, gaining access to new networks or simply thinking through a range of work-related problems and how they could be resolved by the mentee (Short and Cameron 2013). We found that mentoring was most valued by leaders who volunteer to participate, particularly senior or more experienced mentors who gained a sense of personal motivation from passing on tacit knowledge or wisdom to younger colleagues because they had an innate desire to preserve the rail legacy. Likewise, graduates reported a similar level of enthusiasm for formal mentoring opportunities with senior managers as a way of building new networks and developing a career pathway with someone who had 'been there'.

Our research into rail leadership capability revealed that managers desired more self-awareness, inclusivity, caring and authenticity within the industry, including a requirement for leaders at all levels to be more in tune with the external or macro challenges facing rail organisations and then to be able to translate this mindfulness into practical actions that were considered by followers as sensible, consistent and fair. This cohort was mid-career, well within the Gen X or graduate entry level Gen Y age groups, and was more likely to be wary of 'green washing', a term describing a 'company, or organisation, that spends more time and money trying to convince customers that they are green than actually implementing business practices that minimise their environmental impact' (Talbott 2012, p. 8). We found considerable evidence of continuing dialogue on sustainability across the generations at rail conferences and in masters programs, but beyond this broad awareness at the strategic level, little evidence that rail organisations were integrating the topic of sustainability into mainstream management training curricula. Another rail report found that for Gen Y engineers working for an environmentally responsible organisation was less important than finding opportunities for career progression and job security (Wallace et al. 2011). These findings aligned with those of the Sky Future Leaders Survey (2011).

Technology (Higher)

Once at the forefront of technology during the industrial age, rail organisations in the twenty-first century are striving to reclaim their place in the hearts and minds of future employees who are excited about technology and innovation, and are tech-savvy. Our research findings indicated that the leadership culture of rail in Australia continued to uphold a technical mindset and readily embraced new technology (Short and Piip 2012), but the widespread dispersal of diverse technologies across the nation meant that employees in some organisations had different technical challenges from their counterparts in other organisations. However, rail reports concluded that the prevailing culture of valuing technology over people was creating a paradox for rail leaders as they endeavoured to manage multi-generational workers. On one hand, the industry acknowledged the importance of attracting and engaging Gen Y employees who had grown up with new technology and systems, yet on the other, the highest percentage of leaders in our research sample (58 %) was in the Baby Boomer generation and sometimes these employees were regarded as less tech-savvy than other groups. Barriers to the effective use of e-learning included the age of trainees and their lack of IT skills, accessibility of training, a dearth of engaging material, and the lack of interaction as compared with traditional training (Brown et al. 2006).

In rail, computer-based technologies were used to train people in diverse locations, but the success of these techniques depended upon the quality of e-learning materials, the ability/motivation of trainees to use them, and the seniority of trainees undertaking development. While there are inherent dangers in over-generalising issues relating to age, older frontline personnel were generally perceived to be less tech-savvy than younger graduates. At the early career level, e-learning programs and formal mentoring or coaching were used frequently and successfully with younger generations, but Baby Boomers still preferred traditional training courses and on-job experiences. To compensate for this generational diversity, learning groups in rail used a blend of delivery techniques and ensured that learning was not only focused on the organisational context, but also accommodated the learning preferences of different age cohorts via a mix of seminars, online learning, work-place mentoring and on-job coaching.

Change (Higher)

In this final section we consider the broad implications of how these work areas and generational preferences, illustrated in Table 9.1, might assist or obstruct different generations in dealing with change. In our research this focus included, but was not limited to, meeting career development needs, building safe environments and focusing on vested interests.

We suggest the way people approach and build their careers is likely to be a reflection of the work environment, societal culture and opportunities available at the time. We know that all age groups value secure employment in uncertain times (Johnson and Lopes 2008), but our evidence in rail supported the literature and reminded us that Boomers were raised to focus on building single careers, staying in situ to become long-serving employees, and progressing through the ranks of hierarchical structures. These traditions were reinforced by rail Veterans who entered the workplace fully expecting a job for life, income security and rewards for hard work and loyalty. The downstream consequence of these traditions meant that Boomers continued to place high value on acquired tacit knowledge, experience and tenure. Moreover, many Boomers were keen to share this experience through dependency-related processes such as mentoring, coaching, on-job training and tell-ing of historical narratives, but they disliked being forced to compress their wisdom into convenient sound bites for the sake of timeliness. We found that mentors volun-teered to help, but quickly become disheartened when their mentees wanted selec-tive input rather than the full story.

The literature suggests that Gen X employees are more independent, self-reliant and inclined to build careers in several organisations within the same sector. However, our findings indicated that new leaders in the Gen X cohort sometimes overlooked the presence of the Boomers' tacit experience for the sake of bringing about change, and instead relied on safe knowledge from their former position(s). This situation put organisations in a tenuous position we later termed recovery-based leading and learning (Short and Harris 2014), where teams were asked to reinvent or re-work existing processes for the sake of demonstrating change. The comparatively short tenure of Gen X leaders meant that the full impact of such lead-ing was not always apparent until after the agent had moved into another role, leaving Boomers bewildered and sceptical about changes introduced by Gen X. Our research, in fact, found Gen Y more comfortable working alongside Boomers and more accepting of their tacit experience than were Gen X. This finding conflicted with an earlier report (Sardo and Begley 2008) and indicated that Gen Y would commit to an organisation and career choice for a given time, before moving on to one or more diverse careers later in life. We found Gen Y much more accommodating of Boomer experience, willing to learn from senior colleagues, happy to pass on IT skills and more accepting of a semi-structured work environment. In our research, Gen Y mentees placed high value on building new networks across all levels of the organisational hierarchy, were not intimidated by position or power and engaged more comfortably in a consultative team environment. They were happy to engage in face-to-face mentoring, valued by the Boomers, but later used e-mentoring and text messaging after the relationship had been established. As one Gen Y expressed it, 'When you're new to an organisation, you don't have established relationships; mentoring gave me an automatic relationship and that was important at the time' (rail graduate).

In many of our rail projects we found mentoring and coaching to be a growing leadership occurrence and helpful to the development of 'generational competence'. These processes were perceived to be contributing to employee wellbeing by providing safe environments where all age groups could talk about issues openly and refocus their own career planning or development needs. One respondent said, 'Trainers pass on knowledge, workplace coaches help you to improve your performance and mentors help you to cope with emotional challenges within the job – issues that the mentee many not want to discuss with others' (manager).

All age cohorts in rail were continually trying to balance a complex mix of demands, but frequently the unique needs of different employee groups were being overlooked in the pursuit of business improvement. This relentless focus on performance resulted in higher levels of workplace stress, or burnout, and people responded in different ways. For example, particular individuals simply lost control and vented their emotional energy through concentrated periods of anger, and this frustration led to uneasy and unproductive relationships with co-workers and the boss. Others chose to withdraw their discretionary effort, became indifferent, or underperformed through lack of personal motivation. These tensions developed unhealthy levels of anxiety across all age groups which resulted in lapses of concentration, drifting minds, physical absenteeism, or in the worst case situation a total withdrawal of cooperation.

For these reasons, rail organisations were keen to adopt workforce development processes based on the interests and motivations of each age group, thereby tapping into rich sources of engagement. This involved aligning individual needs with project outcomes using consultation and collaboration to decide how knowledge and skills could be utilised. This process was best illustrated in the rail industry's response following a number of unforeseen natural weather events which occurred in Australia during the research period. People of all generations were forced to work together and deal with change in order to keep the rail networks running safely. During these episodic events, situational leadership and the need for goodwill created a high state of generational competence as people of all ages, backgrounds and abilities pulled together in pursuit of the common purpose.

Conclusion

At the time our research program commenced in late 2007, we did not appreciate fully how the existence of a multi-generational workplace would arise in our projects, nor the ways in which the GFC in 2008 would reshape the workplace agenda in Australia and its approach to HRD decisions. After a time we replaced our ideas on education and training themes with a new and more holistic paradigm: workforce development. Then the emergence of 'generational competence' from our individual projects in the post-GFC environment brought into sharp focus the arrival of new approaches to HRD practices that had special relevance to achieving the strategic agendas of rail executives. We found from many of our projects that rail organisations were much better prepared to deal with some generational issues than others (as reflected in Fig. 9.1), due to the technical nature of the industry and its significance to the Australian economy. We also discovered that softer and more flexible approaches to workforce development, such as coaching, mentoring and informal learning, were better suited to multi-generational settings and encouraged improved workplace relations. The findings reminded us of the need to plan and prepare for career transitions at all generational levels, including entry-level employment, mainstream work progression, fractional work and impending retirement.

References

Appelbaum, S. H., Serena, M., & Shapiro, B. T. (2005). Generation 'X' and the boomers: An analysis of realities and myths. *Management Research News, 28*(1), 1–35.

Arnett, J. J. (2000). High hopes in a grim world: Emerging adults' views of their futures and generation X. *Youth and Society, 31*(3), 267–286.

Artley, J. B., & Macon, M. (2009). Can't we all just get along? A review of the challenges and opportunities in a multi-generational workforce. *International Journal of Business Research, 9*(6), 90–94.

Australasian Railway Association (ARA). (2008). *A rail revolution*. Canberra: Australasian Railway Association.

Black, A. M., & Earnest, G. W. (2009). Measuring the outcomes of leadership development programs. *Journal of Leadership and Organisational Studies, 16*(2), 184–196.

Bova, B., & Kroth, M. (2001). Workplace learning and Generation X. *Journal of Workplace Learning, 13*(2), 57–65.

Brown, L., Murphy, E., & Wade, V. (2006). Corporate elearning: Human resource development implications for large and small organizations. *Human Resource Development International, 9*(3), 415–427.

Crumpacker, M., & Crumpacker, J. (2007). Succession planning and generational stereotypes: Should HR consider age-based values and attitudes a relevant factor or a passing fad? *Public Personnel Management, 36*(4), 349–369.

Dahlroth, J. (2008, August). *The generations factor*. Association Meetings, p. 32.

Damon, N. (2007). Leadership challenges facing business today. *Personnel Today*. http://www.personneltoday.com/articles/article.aspx?liarticleid=42275. Accessed 27 Sept 2012.

Dohm, A. (2000). Retiring baby boomers. *Monthly Labor Review, 123*(7), 17–25.

Erlich, A., & Bichard, J. A. (2008). The welcoming workplace: Designing for ageing knowledge workers. *Journal of Corporate Real Estate, 10*(4), 273–285.

Glass, A. (2007). Understanding generational differences for competitive success. *Industrial and Commercial Training, 39*(2), 98–103.

Guardian Sustainable Business. (2011, December 7). Will our future leaders be the first 'sustainable generation'? *Guardian Sustainable Business Blog*. http://www.theguardian.com/sustainable-business/blog/sky-sustainability-future-leaders. Accessed 18 Oct 2013.

Gursoy, D., Maier, T., & Chi, C. (2008). Generational differences: An examination of work values and generational gaps in the hospitality workforce. *International Journal of Hospitality Management, 27*(3), 448–458.

Hammill, G. (2005). Mixing and managing four generations of employees. *MDU Magazine*, Winter/Spring. http://www.fdu.edu/newspubs/magazine/05ws/generations.htm. Accessed 30 June 2009.

Harris, R., & Short, T. (2014). Exploring the notion of workforce development. In R. Harris & T. Short (Eds.), *Workforce development: Perspectives and issues* (pp. 1–16). Singapore: Springer.

Haynes, B. P. (2011). The impact of generational differences on the workplace. *Journal of Corporate Real Estate, 13*(2), 98–108.

Howard, A., & Wellings, R. S. (2009). *Global leaders forecast 2008/2009*. Bridgeville: Development Dimensions International.

Infographics. (2011, October). Leadership at home and abroad. *People Management*, pp. 42–44.

Jauregui, E. A. (2007). The citizenship harms of workplace discrimination. *Columbia Journal of Law and Social Problems, 40*(3), 347–377.

Jepson, D. (2009). Leadership context: The importance of departments. *Leadership and Organisational Development Journal, 30*(1), 36–52.

Jimenez, L. (2009, June). Management implications of the multi-generational workforce. *Profiles in Diversity Journalism*, p. 50.

Johnson, J. A., & Lopes, J. (2008). The intergenerational workforce, revisited. *Organization Development Journal, 26*(1), 31–36.

Kapoor, C., & Solomon, N. (2011). Understanding and managing generational differences in the workplace. *Workplace Hospitality and Tourism Themes, 3*(4), 308–318.

Legas, M., & Sims, C. (2011). Leveraging generational diversity in today's workplace. *Online Journal for Workforce Education and Development, 5*(3). http://opensiuc.lib.siu.edu/ojwed/vol5/iss3/1/

Lesonsky, R. (2011). How to manage employees from every generation. *Business Insider Australia*. http://au.businessinsider.com/managing-different-generations-in-the-workplace-2011-1. Accessed 8 May 2013.

Mann, J. (2006). Generations in the workplace. *The Bulletin, 74*(1). http://www.acui.org/publications/bulletin/article.aspx?issue=398&id=888. Accessed 8 May 2013.

National Centre for Sustainability. (2012). *What is sustainability*. http://www.swinburne.edu.au/ncs/whatissustainability.htm. Accessed 11 Oct 2013.

Pitt-Catsouphes, M., & Smyer, M. A. (2007). *The 21st century multi-generational workplace. Issue Brief 9*. Chestnut Hill: Center on Aging & Work, Boston College.

Porter, L. W. (1996). Forty years of organisational studies: Reflections from a micro perspective. *Administrative Science Quarterly, 41*, 262–269.

PricewaterhouseCoopers. (2006). *The changing face of rail*. Canberra: Australasian Railway Association.

Proffitt Reese, M., & Sharpley, T. A. (2013). Four generations, one workplace – Can we all work together? *Inside Indiana Business*. www.insideindianabusiness.com/contributors.asp?ID=925. Accessed 8 May 2013.

Sardo, S., & Begley, P. (2008). *What's age got to do with it?* Melbourne: Australian Human Resources Institute.

Shaw, S., & Fairhurst, D. (2008). Engaging a new generation of graduates. *Education + Training, 50*(5), 366–378.

Short, T., & Cameron, R. (2013). *Mentoring and coaching in the rail industry*. Research report P4.119. Brisbane: CRC for Rail Innovation.

Short, T., & Harris, R. (2014). The future of workforce development: Old wine in new bottles. In R. Harris & T. Short (Eds.), *Workforce development: Perspectives and issues* (pp. 351–372). Singapore: Springer.

Short, T., & Piip, J. (2012). *Rediscovering rail toolbox safety meetings: Leading innovation and learning towards better customer service*. Paper presented at the engineering leadership conference, Adelaide, 30 May–1 June 2012.

Sky Future Leaders Survey. (2011). *The sustainable generation*. Isleworth: British Sky Broadcasting Group.

Talbott, S. L. (2012). *Generation Y and sustainability*. University of Tennessee honours thesis projects. Knoxville: Tennessee. http://trace.tennessee.edu/utk_chanhonoproj/1498. Accessed 11 Sept 2013.

Thompson, J. L. (1995). *Strategy in action*. London: Chapman & Hall.

Wallace, M., Lings, I., et al. (2011, December 7–9). *Attracting young engineers to the rail industry in Australia*. Paper presented at the 2011 ANZAM Conference, Wellington, New Zealand.

Williams, K. C., & Page, R. A. (2011). Marketing to the generations. *Journal of Behavioral Studies in Business, 3*, 1–17.

Chapter 10
How to Identify and Teach Abstract Skills: A Case Study of Personal Practice

Lisa Davies

Abstract In this chapter I discuss recent research in an Australian industry sector which focused on the development of a skills recognition framework for the Australian rail industry. The research process identified that many people who are technical experts become managers in the industry despite lacking the abstract, tacit, holistic or soft skills that are required to manage and lead people. Skills recognition assessments (which include recognition of prior learning and recognition of current competencies) are a valuable component of training, human resource management and workplace development. They also have a place beyond programs that are designed to formally accredit pre-existing learning. I consider ideas and practices around recognition of learning, skills and capability as the foundations for a wider view of skills recognition; one that is forward looking, focused on learning and is more connected with workplace issues and practices. I draw attention to the tacit skills and soft skills (abstract skills) that are less likely to be recognised in formal competency-based frameworks, or even to be acknowledged as vital components of the suite of skills and experiences needed by people in managerial and senior roles in general. I identify a process for educating managers to accept that abstract skills are a vital function of management. I explain the use of informal skills recognition assessments as a means by which abstract skills – or lack thereof – can be evaluated, and detail how to teach some aspects of these skills.

L. Davies (✉)
School of Education, University of South Australia, Mawson Lakes, SA, Australia
e-mail: lisa.davies@unisa.edu.au

T. Short and R. Harris (eds.), *Workforce Development: Strategies and Practices*,
DOI 10.1007/978-981-287-068-1_10, © Springer Science+Business Media Singapore 2014

Introduction – Skills Recognition

Skills recognition (SR) processes have emerged as valuable components of training, human resource management and workplace development programs and they have a place beyond assessments that are designed to formally accredit pre-existing learning. They can be undertaken informally to assess the skills and knowledge that people do – or do not – have, and hence can be used to identify where gap training would benefit an employee.

There are various views about what skills recognition is and what processes may be involved. In Australia, they have generally been referred to as recognition of prior learning and recognition of current competencies. To make this a little more complex, both here and internationally, additional terms are used to describe aspects of skills recognition. These include, among others: assessment of prior learning, accreditation of prior experiential learning, accreditation/assessment/recognition of prior (experiential) learning, accreditation of prior learning and achievement, prior learning assessment and recognition, recognition of non-formal and informal learning and validation (Maher and Morrison 2010, pp. 7–8). In this chapter I will use the term 'skills recognition' as it encompasses all of the above activities.

Abstract Skills

While undertaking a 3-year research project into workforce development strategies in an Australian industry sector, we were interested in learning whether non-technical skills, also referred to as abstract, soft, holistic, tacit and employability skills, were recognised and valued. We were also looking to ascertain how these abstract skills were currently being assessed in formal and/or informal skills recognition processes, and if these processes could be improved.

The term abstract 'skills' is referred to variously in the literature and in workplace practice and often clusters with soft, tacit, holistic and/or employability skills. The Australian Quality Framework (2013) defines employability skills as communication, teamwork, problem solving, having initiative and enterprise, the ability to plan and organise, self-management, learning and technology. These are currently under review. The Australian Council for Educational Research (2013) measures people's aptitudes in the area of abstract skills by testing their ability to identify abstract patterns and rules and relationships, to generate and evaluate hypotheses and to draw conclusions.

In the relevant literature, abstract skills are also considered to include organisational skills, the ability to engage in positive verbal communication via active listening, to work collaboratively, to use tact and diplomacy in negotiations, to be able to give and receive feedback, to write fluently when producing reports and business cases and so on, to think metaphorically, to have well-developed analytical skills, personal critical insight, situational awareness and to take responsibility for one's decisions (Metz et al. 2012; Sowa 1984; Logsdon n.d.). Metz et al. also underlined the importance of people in technical and engineering roles having well-developed abilities to 'visualise in three dimensions' (2012, p. 1). This proposal is particularly relevant to this chapter as the research in which this chapter is partly centred was undertaken in the Australian rail industry.

In 2012 a final report based on research funded by the Australian Department of Education, Employment and Workplace Relations (DEEWR) found that there were still inconsistent definitions of employability skills, and defined them as 'the non-technical skills and knowledge necessary for effective participation in the work-force, as distinct from those required more broadly in society' (2012, 20). They noted too that the workplace context was a key factor when assessing these skills. In summary, they proposed that there was a need to develop a framework to allow employers to have an enhanced understanding of what these abilities are, to increase consistency of interpretation and assessment of employees and potential employees. This was closely allied to some aspects of our investigations.

In his research in the Australian rail industry, Short (2012, p. 1) found that 'meta-competencies' – allied to abstract skills – which are those abilities that encompass relationship building, interpersonal communication and self-awareness were not skills that all managers had developed, and that their importance was not under-stood. Related to this, he also proposed that well-developed self-awareness and strong levels of self-efficacy were essential psychological attributes for modern managers (Short 2012, p. 2). Short and Piip further proposed that the additional non-technical skills that managers need also include 'situational awareness, work-load management, working with others, decision making, conscientiousness, com-munications and self-management' (2013, p. 2). For clarity in this chapter, the term 'abstract skills' encompasses all of those referred to above.

In this chapter I examine some of the findings from the research in the rail indus-try. I then focus on how abstract skills can be identified through the use of informal skills recognition assessments. I conclude by detailing how some elements of abstract skills –such as the ability to listen actively and to undertake positive negotiations – can be learned by employees in their organisational settings.

The Context

The context of our research emerged as crucial. While skills recognition assess-ments often focus on technical skills, some of the participants in our research, who included learning and development managers, human resource managers, trainers/assessors and some SR recipients, also considered that the possession of what they often referred to as soft or abstract skills was vital for people in their industry. Moreover, they agreed that these skills should be assessed and recognised more readily both within formal and informal skills recognition assessment processes and in workforce development more broadly.

One participant, who was a trainer/assessor from a large state passenger rail company, suggested that abstract skills were vitally important in the safety-critical rail industry. He proposed that learning from aviation in this regard would be useful and explained that: 'I mean good decision making in aviation makes the difference between life and death, and it can be the same here'. In the following discussion, I summarise the findings about abstract skills in the rail-centred research.

Lack of Awareness of the Relevance of Abstract Skills

Some managers and employees showed a lack of awareness about what constituted non-technical or abstract skills, why they were valuable, how to assess their presence, and/or how they could be learned. These findings suggest that there is a need to for managers and employers to understand and acknowledge that abstract skills are essential to safety-critical work such as risk management and decision making and in safety-critical sectors such as transport. As one industry expert put it:

> I mean the whole law is based around risk management, risk assessment, making decisions, but that is as a core skill set is one that, you know, probably dangerous for me to say this, but it's not well developed across the industry.

A trainer/assessor from a passenger rail company stressed that the industry needed to improve training and assessment of what they called soft skills such as situation awareness. Furthermore, they summarised their own experience as being that, while the technical aspects of rail work were not necessarily highly demanding, when things went wrong it was tacit or soft skills that were needed to enable people to make rapid, relevant responses and to take a lead in crucial decision making.

Difficulties with Identifying, Assessing and Training Abstract Skills

Views of trainers and assessors about what and whether abstract skills could be taught or gained through experience varied. While some trainers stressed that employees can be trained to have heightened awareness and decision-making capacities to handle demanding situations, other interviewees suggested 'common sense' – which they colloquially referred to as 'soft skills' –was innate and could not be learned. One learning and development manager from a medium-sized state passenger rail service noted that assessors were not provided with information and guidance on how to assess soft skills:

> OK, they're your employability skills which are built into each unit of competence, right, so there are five employability skills which are assessed holistically, and that's the reason why they were developed that way. So you've got problem solving, you've got team work, you've got being able to use technology in the workplace, you have, what are the other two,

the other two, language, literacy and numeracy, and I forget what the fifth one is. They're what you call your soft ones, but they are a strong part of the assessment guideline, under the assessment criteria of any unit of competence. They must be assessed in accordance with the performance criteria ... How do you measure it though? ... Alright, that's always the problem ... Any training that's involved with designing and developing assessment tools does not cover off on this effectively.

The notion of teaching these skills was also seen as potentially problematic, as teaching them was not well understood across the industry:

I mean we teach them non-technical skills. I don't think people here understand what non-technical skills really are; I don't think they understand ... Non-technical skills is something you can teach across all Australian railways, that is something you can teach across those, I guess you'd call them 'soft' skills.

By contrast, another participant stated that they did not think that abstract skills could be taught:

I look at skills and some skills can be learnt and some cannot. Like you've either, you know, got common sense or you don't. You can't actually train, and I train lots of people, you can't train the common sense into somebody.

The above statement also suggests that the participant did not understand what abstract skills were. Similarly another participant explained:

We've got lots of technical knowledge but we've got no natural leadership, we've got no ... behavioural-based skills that would enable this business to go further, so you need to really look at (1) in the role that you're recruiting for, can the technical side of that be trained? Well the majority of the time it can be a behavioural characteristic such as leadership or drive or motivation. Can that be trained? Well not necessarily because, you know, by the time these guys get to the point where they're at ... it's very hard to mould somebody.

Another industry expert also explained that different roles and areas of rail varied in terms of soft skill requirements. In particular he pointed to how infrastructure working differs from other operational areas of rail; sound team-working skills were required when dealing with the things that could occur suddenly in this sector. From another perspective, a learning and development manager who specialised in leadership and management suggested that among several reasons for the technical focus was that it was relatively cheap and easy to teach and assess technical experience, whereas assessing the presence of abstract skills was difficult. This understanding about an underlying pragmatism in relation to employee development was a very useful insight.

Comments from other participants suggest however that perhaps a different kind of training, one that facilitates the gradual building of responsibility and decision making, might foster the development of behavioural skills that their industry training often did not include. A train driver trainer/assessor who previously worked in aviation compared training and assessment in rail with that of aviation. He noted that in aviation employees are supported to gradually take on greater responsibility for independent decision making, whereas it was his observation that in rail trainees were fully supervised and were then abruptly left to their own devices at the end of their training period.

Including Abstract Skills in Skills Recognition Assessment

As a number of interviewees pointed out, although soft skills such as team work or communication skills may be written into assessment criteria, they are not necessarily used or assessed adequately. One compliance/competency officer suggested that this was due to the industry failing to appreciate the value of abstract skills. She suggested that these had lost their focus by being embedded in narrower range employability skills, rather than being addressed as separate key competencies. This reflected the findings of the research funded by DEEWR referred to above.

Under the Australian Qualification Framework, specific abstract skills that were clustered under the heading 'employability skills' tended to be considered to be a low priority by rail managers and trainer/assessors. Few of the 74 research participants raised the matter of employability skills, and those who did often suggested that such skills were not well identified or well assessed in rail. Moreover, by being placed within the limitations of eight specific employability skills, other important abstract skills could be overlooked. A learning and development manager from a medium-sized passenger rail service explained: 'It's the qualitative abstract part, the employability skills part that you want in the individual that can't be measured out of straight performance criterias [sic]'.

Another interesting perspective explained by a trainer/assessor from a large public state passenger rail company highlighted a 'triangle' of three key area of competence: soft skills, technical skills and 'the rules'. The rules loomed large in this industry! As several interviewees pointed out, a big obstruction to giving skills recognition to *technical* competencies is that technical skills and legal obligations were perceived to vary from company to company, state to state, passenger to freight, and between locations. Non-technical, certified skills were on the other hand seen to be transferable.

Some interviewees did inform us of the ways in which soft skills were being recognised and harnessed to identify employees suited to higher-level roles and responsibilities more readily. A learning and development manager from a multinational freight company outlined how they were using what they referred to as soft skills identification to build a more robust training system among train drivers.

Abstract Skills and Management Positions

Having well-developed abstract skills was highlighted as crucial in management and corporate positions. Some interviewees suggested that one of the problems with management in the rail industry was a lack of focus on soft skills, or more specifically business acumen, among managers. The current culture of seniority was seen to promote rail employees on the basis of longevity and accrued seniority rather than the acquisition of the kinds of abstract skills required to manage at higher levels. A learning and development manager from a large public state passenger rail company commented:

> But you know it's like a lot of places, there are a lot of people that are, say, technically or operationally very, very competent and very clever and very smart but their soft skills, their business acumen, that's like been something that's not, you know, not huge at [our organisation].

A learning and development manager from a medium-sized state passenger rail service also explained that, as the rail industry currently valued on-the-job experience over education, it was difficult to develop leadership programs that focused on needed abstract skills as there was 'quite a strongly held view that training should be done on the job, and that's all you need to know'.

One interviewee, a human resource manager from a large state passenger rail company, pointed to what she referred to as the 'hidden curriculum' – the skills and knowledge that are related to specific organisational expectations as distinct from workplace knowledge that employees bring into their workplaces. Another difficulty that was cited was that a manager needed some degree of personal critical insight and relevant education to understand the importance of abstract skills.

In summary, while there were some differing perspectives, it emerged in general that the participants in this research who were involved in workforce development thought that abstract skills were required in almost all roles in the industry to a greater or lesser degree, and that promoting people on the basis of years of service and highly developed technical skills did not necessarily lead to the right people going into management.

From Research Findings to Professional Practice

In the following section, I describe hands-on methods that identify abstract skills – or the lack thereof – informally, and how some aspects of abstract skills can be taught in the workplace.

Some Informal Techniques That Can Be Used to Identify Soft Skills

A key to assessing abstract skills well is for the assessor to be well versed in what constitutes these attributes, and to apply their knowledge judiciously in informal ways for the benefit and development of employees. It is also essential that employees understand that abstract skills are central to effective management and that they can be learned. Managers also need to understand that having well-developed abstract skills are crucial to being a successful manager or leader.

Table 10.1 Informally identifying your skills and experience

People skills and experience	Financial skills and experience	Software skills and experience	Technical, hardware skills and experience	Project management skills and experience

In a former occupation, I often facilitated workplace interviews in which technical personnel felt that, as experienced and successful software engineers, programmers and technicians, they should be able to move upwards to go straight into management positions. They were motivated not only by an increased sense of personal kudos, but also by the higher salaries that were usually paid to managers and some salespeople, when compared to technical employees. Given the frequency of this request to be promoted into management, I developed the following techniques which have practical utility across a broader range of contexts.

Using Informal Skills Recognition Assessments to Evaluate Abstract Skills

My initial conversation with the aspirational employee was a general discussion in which I asked them to tell me about themselves, their career goals and what they considered their personality to be like. I followed this by asking them why they wanted to go into management and what skills they thought they could bring to a management position.

The following diagram illustrates a grid of skills required for managers that I developed through questioning our successful project managers and senior employees about what they proposed were the necessary skills and attributes of a successful project manager and manager in general. Importantly, the fact that I asked for their input increased the likelihood of their buy-in to the process. At that time I was a member of the board for the University of South Australia's Bachelor of Business Information Systems degree and Master of Business Information Systems, from which I also derived pertinent information. I also undertook a literature search to further develop the components of this table. I used this table (Table 10.1) in meetings with our employees so that we could both – and I use the word 'both' deliberately – begin to understand what skills they had, and what was required in general for a project manager in that industry sector. (Note: I tailored this table slightly for differing roles.) At all times, I explained that this was not a test scenario, but one in which I could then identify areas in which they may need more training or more management experience than they currently had. I also explained that I might also be able to identify people who were ready to go into management roles. Rather than using the (then) very embryonic and at times differing criteria as detailed in early iterations of project management certifications, I used non-educational jargon to detail the attributes that were required of a sound project leader or manager to undertake their roles successfully.

The first step was to obtain their workplace curriculum vitae – which were updated at each performance review – to ensure that they reflected their current skills and experience. I then gave them a copy of this, and asked them to talk me through it, then to transpose the information that was in it into a table as below. They were also asked to add additional columns or rows where necessary.

At the completion of this exercise I verbally prompted them if they had not transposed all of the relevant examples. Following this exercise, I then gave them a copy of the following table (Table 10.2) which detailed the skills and aptitudes that I had identified as being required to be a successful project manager.

I gave a copy of this table to the applicants who were interested in management positions and asked them to rate themselves for each component, with a total score out of 100 %. I also told them to add any skills that they had that were not documented.

Table 10.2 Detailed lists of necessary skills for successful project managers

People skills	/100
Show leadership in the workplace	
Demonstrate the ability to establish and maintain people networks	
Demonstrate highly developed interpersonal skills for customer service, client negotiations, dealing with difficult people in the workplace, relationship management	
Demonstrate the ability to give and receive constructive critical feedback	
Demonstrate the ability to give positive feedback	
Demonstrate the ability to receive negative feedback	
Take ultimate responsibility for decisions	
Manage client escalations	
Undertake performance management or development reviews	
Demonstrate understanding of organisational behaviour and change management strategies	
Undertake management of industrial relations (senior managers only)	
Develop teams and individuals	
Coach and mentor people	
Demonstrate highly developed listening skills	
Demonstrate highly developed critical self-insight	
Demonstrate the ability to delegate interesting technical tasks	
Financial skills	/100
Demonstrate accounting skills	
Demonstrate budgeting skills	
Undertake forecasting	
Software skills	/100
Demonstrate expertise in the use of spreadsheets, e.g. Microsoft Excel	
Demonstrate highly developed writing skills using relevant technology	
PM software, e.g. Microsoft project	
Technical, hardware skills	/100
Have domain knowledge and experience with the client industry	

(continued)

Table 10.2 (continued)

Project management skills	/100

   Apply contract and procurement procedures

   Demonstrate the ability to apply project scope management techniques

   Demonstrate the ability to apply time management techniques

   Demonstrable the ability to apply cost management techniques

   Implement operational plans

   Identify risk and apply risk management processes

   Run status meetings and write and deliver reports

   Manage services and sustainability

   Implement and monitor environmentally sustainable work practices

   Use a project management methodology e.g. PRINCE2 or PRiSM (Projects integrating Sustainable Methods)

   Use and manage any of the following methods:

   Critical chain project management

   Event chain methodology

   Process-based management

   Agile project management

   Lean project management

   Extreme project management

   Benefits realisation management

   Apply quality management techniques: the ISO standards ISO 9000, a family of standards for quality management systems, and the ISO 10006:2003, for quality management systems and guidelines for quality management in projects

   Understand and manage ethics and values, both local and international

   Take ultimate responsibly for failures

   Monitor a safe workplace

Self-rate your ability below in each of the five rows, with 100 % being perfect level of skills and attributes

They invariably rated themselves as having 120 % (or similar) skills and abilities in the column headed technical skills, and often added special skills and experiences that they had, which were often of a technical nature. While they may have over-rated their level of technical competence, this also suggested that they overrated the relevance of their technical skills to project manager positions. Many were unaware of the importance – or even existence – of the highly developed interpersonal skills and critical self-insight that are required to be a successful and engaging manager or leader.

Several different research projects in the Australian rail industry also reported this lack of understanding about the crucial need for people in managerial positions to have well-developed abstract skills and critical self-insight (Short 2012; Short and Piip 2013; Davies and Maher 2013; Davies et al. 2013). I will now describe how informal SR assessments can be used to determine the presence – or lack – of abstract skills, and how to teach and facilitate the learning of abstract skills in a practical manner in any number of organisational contexts.

Informally Assessing Abstract Skills: Probing Questions

Some of the engineers asserted that they had highly developed people skills. In cases where I had not observed these in the workplace I probed with questions such as:

- How would you show your leadership in the workplace?
- How would you deal with someone who is so stressed that they come into your office and start crying?
- How would you explain to a member of your team in a performance review that they are not developing their skills as quickly as the other members of the team?
- How would you respond to a team member who tells you that 'everyone says behind your back that you aren't a good manager'?
- How would you deal with a team member who has pasted very critical comments about you on their Facebook page and in their tweets?

Examples of Difficult Workplace Scenarios

I also asked them to give me examples where and when they had used their people skills. If they were unable to provide many, I used scenario-based exercises and asked them to explain to me how they would manage these situations and why they would do so in their chosen way, as follows:

- You are undertaking a performance review of a team leader. It has been your observation that the team leader is too blunt and inflexible when giving directions to the team and they have complained about this to you. You explain this, but the team leader is defensive and refuses to accept these as being valid observations. What do you do?
- A client phones you and states angrily that the 'expensive, experienced programmer' that you sent out to their site arrived and looked flustered and said 'but I've never programmed in Java at this level before'. How do you react to the client? What do you say to the programmer?
- When a team is left short of people because they are off with illness, a woman who is competent technically, but who is known to be very negative about her job, is sent in to back fill your team. You greet her and say, 'Thanks, we need you here for the next few days.' She replies, in earshot of everyone: 'This isn't what I was hired to do. I'm only here because I have to be.' What is your response?
- You have been asked to prepare a 1-h PowerPoint presentation to show to potential new clients – a team of five people – who have booked to fly in from interstate for 1 day to see your proposed software solution for their problem. You need to detail how you will undertake their proposed project. You will need people, costing and time frame, key gates and importantly the benefits that they will reap by using your solution. This presentation is in 2 days' time. You are

already committed to focusing on two other time-urgent issues that blew up the day before, and you assured those clients that you would resolve their issues very quickly. What would you do?

• You note that one of the members of the team appears to engage in 'presenteeism', that is, they are physically at work, but appear to spend time in non-productive ways. How do you address this?

• You have a graduate programmer who is rapidly outstripping their team colleagues in their programming ability, interpersonal skills and business acumen. How do you acknowledge this without annoying the other members of the team and potentially causing divisiveness and lowered morale?

The responses to these scenarios – which are not unusual for managers to experience in workplaces – often indicated that they would not be able to manage them, and were floundering as to what to do. This exercise readily identified the need for training and/or gap training, which they readily accepted as they now understood why they needed it.

Other participants in the exercise were honest about their lack of knowledge in non-technical areas and often explained variations of the theme that they had not thought about the need for those skills and attributes. Many tended to focus on how difficult it is to take responsibility, give corrective and/or negative feedback, and negotiate with clients. Many identified that they would have a lot of difficulty in delegating interesting technical tasks. Others focused on their lack of knowledge about or experience with accounting and/or project management methodology. Having identified their own gaps, they self-identified that they were not yet ready for management positions without undertaking more education and work shadowing to gain experience.

At times, some people complained that their own managers did not have these skills and attributes either; however I pointed out that this was a conversation for a different time and place, as we were currently focusing on them and their skills today, to assist them to identify areas in which they could develop their potential as managers by undertaking relevant training, work shadowing, having a mentor and so on. This process was an informal process of skills recognition and gap analysis; it worked well and was well received.

Teaching Active Listening Skills

As a result of these activities in which they self-identified a need for some form of gap training, I developed a series of workshops that initially focused on one aspect only of interpersonal skills, so that they had time to practise one element over 3 h, rather than deluging them with highly complex information in one session. It should be noted here that these participants all worked together in the organisation with varying degrees of familiarity with each other, and hence I did not need to engage in as much trust building as I would do when facilitating a session with people who did not know each other. Given that, in general, the employees were rational, pragmatic men (many of the women being employed in sales and education in the organisation) I used personality indictors to determine their personality types. They invariable disclosed as having internal values related to logic, rational thought and basing judgement on hard-nosed evidence, which they termed 'fairness'. It was interesting to quiz them to respond to the following question: 'Which statement can you relate to best?'

- 'If I am fair, everyone will be happy.'
- 'If everyone is happy, then I have been fair.'

This activity gave me some insights into what their drivers were in workplace relationships, and how they might approach people-centred problems in their teams. Those who chose the former emphasised what they perceived as fairness (i.e. everyone gets treated based on merit and rational business decisions in a meritocracy) and that this choice would make the team happy. However they might be unable to understand that, for some people, fairness occurs when everyone is happy with the decision. Those who chose the latter tactic may not have been aware that choosing decisions that make everyone happy is not always the best way to make decisions and can lead to disputes and/or poor business decision making. Perhaps, not surprisingly, the majority of the people who self-described as rational and logical decision makers opted for the former statement. At times, some questioned whether anyone would choose the latter! These conundrums are frequent events in many workplaces and it can require highly developed abstract skills to know when and what kind of decision process to take in any given situation.

With this kind of information and given a propensity for them to use 'unasked-for advice giving' freely in any human interaction, I developed highly interactive sessions that focused on the ability to develop active listening skills (Bolton 1986). These were well attended sessions, in which in the initial half hour I outlined (on PowerPoint and with verbal description), a simple grid of what constituted active listening and what and why some other activities blocked interpersonal communication. Many found this information to be quite a revelation; they now understood why their partner/wife/husband reacted in the ways in which they often did, when they were 'only trying to help by finding a solution'.

I used the following grid (Table 10.3) on a PowerPoint and also as a handout to give a simple visual representation of which responses in human verbal interactions block communication and/or aid communication and, importantly, why this is so. The scenarios were based around a person coming into your office to tell you some news about themselves. The important caveat here was that if the person who came into your office clearly asked for your advice by saying something like 'what do you think I should do?' or 'I need your advice about something', then you were free to give advice. But this is not the case in the scenarios that follow in Table 10.3.

In the following handout (Table 10.4), I gave specific examples.

We then discussed these scenarios. I then broke the participants into groups of three or four people and asked them to develop their own scenarios on the following worksheet (Handout 3). I told them to choose one about a person who felt that they

Table 10.3 Communication blockers and communication enhancers (Handout 1)

Communication blockers			Communication enhancers	
Giving *unasked*-for advice	Talking about your own example (fake empathy) and taking over	Trivialising the situation	Checking that you understand by asking for more information	Mirroring the emotional content of what the speaker is telling you
What I would do is …	Yes, when that happened to me, I did …	That happens to everyone	Am I correct in saying that you just said …?	Nodding, agreeing
Why don't you do …	That happened to a friend of mine, and they did …	So, what's new? I've already been there, done that	So do you mean that …?	Reflecting the same emotions on your own face
If I were you, I would …		It could be worse	Actively listening to the other person	Actively listening to the other person (and not saying much at all!)
The message that is received				
You are too stupid to have worked out what to do, so I'm telling you what to do (because I'm so wise and experienced)	Your example is more important than the teller and you are taking over. You are no longer listening and now it's not about the original teller	You aren't strong enough, you don't know about the real world (whereas I do)	You are interested; you are trying hard to listen well	You are focusing on them and what they are telling you, and you are reflecting what they feel (anger, sorrow, joy, etc.)

had been unjustly treated at work, and one about a person who had some exciting news to tell them. Importantly, I reminded them that they had to refrain from giving advice up to the stage (if it ever occurred) when the teller finally said something like 'so what do you think I should do?' (Table 10.5)

The teams swapped scenarios, and the teams then had to develop communication blockers and, more importantly, active listening responses, that is, those that would enhance communication in these scenarios, and explain how these worked.

They were then divided into teams of two, and had 4 min to develop a different example of one person with some important or exciting or personal news, and how the other could respond to it in a way that demonstrated active listening and hence enabled communication. They then role-played these to the class, each role-play taking 2 min. The participants often engaged in very funny and highly spirited attempts to reflect what the person opposite them in role-plays were feeling, rather than giving unasked-for advice. It took a lot of practise, and after 3 h they were all keen to try their new skills in the workplace and at home. Realising that if,

Table 10.4 Specific examples of communication blockers and communication enhancers (Handout 2)

Communication blockers					Communication enhancers	
Giving unasked-for advice	Talking about your own example (fake empathy) and taking over	Trivialising the situation	Checking that you understand by asking for more information	Mirroring the emotional content of what the speaker is telling you		
Example: Kim comes into your office to tell you that they have just been told to work back through the weekend, despite already having done so for the past 2 weeks						
What I would do is just tell them that I refuse. Why don't you tell them that your child is sick and you can't do that? If I were you, I'd speak to HR	When that happened to me, I was working in another company and we all got asked this on a regular basis and you will never believe what happened …	I've already worked over 3 weekends. I've seen it all before	What! Do you mean that they are expecting you to work yet another weekend? That is crazy!	Look of shock on your face, looking equally aghast, saying 'that's awful!'		
The message that is received						
You are too stupid to have worked out what to do, so I'm telling you what to do (because I'm so wise and experienced)	Your example is more important than the teller and you are taking over, no longer listening and now it's not about the original teller, but is about you	You aren't strong enough, you don't know about the real world (whereas I do)	You are interested; you are trying hard to listen well	You are focusing on them and what they are telling you, and you are reflecting what they feel (anger, sorrow, joy, etc.)		
Example: Kim comes into your office and tells you that that she has just found out that she is going to be an Aunt for the first time						
Trust me; don't let them use you as a free babysitting service	When that happened to me I was over the moon. Here is the latest photo of my nieces and nephews. They are all so bright!	I already have 6 nieces and nephews	Wow, the first one, that's great news!	Look happy and pleased to hear this news, jump up and shake hands		

Table 10.5 Developing a scenario (Handout 3)

Communication blockers			Communication enhancers	
Giving unasked-for advice	Talking about your own example (fake empathy) and taking over	Trivialising the situation	Checking that you understand by asking for more information	Mirroring the emotional content of what the speaker is telling you

Example: feeling unjustly treated at work …

Example: happy, positive news …

for example, they were in stressful situations they may revert to their old habits, I ran top-up sessions 4 weeks apart, adding new information to each session about another aspect of communication, until they felt that they were more fluent in this aspect of interpersonal exchanges.

Is It Possible to Teach Personal Critical Insight?

In performance reviews managers often identified the need for their team workers and support staff to develop personal critical insight so that they could engage with their team members and clients more positively and with increased confidence. This was suggested to overcome what was identified as an often high degree of defensiveness about perceived criticism of their work. Context here was again critical. These intelligent, tertiary-educated engineers and software developers identified themselves as being just that, intelligent and highly skilled, and they focused on their technical skills and intellectual ability as the core of their identity. Any critique, however constructively given, was perceived as an attack on their entire being.

Given the complexity of teaching critical self-reflection and self-insight to people who were not engaged in the kind of occupations that require constant personal reflection such as teachers, health workers and so on proved challenging. After thought and discussion with the education manager, we decided instead to build on their developing active listening skills, and adopt an approach of facilitating sessions centred on learning how to be a skilled negotiator as practical skills such as negotiation skills can be taught relatively easily, and skilled negotiators become more confident in their roles.

Hence we broke down theories about what underpins negotiations to untangle them and make them more comprehensible to our employees. To ensure that the information was clear and easy to follow, we focused on distributed negotiations and integrative negotiations (Brett 2007, pp. 2–3).

In handouts and on PowerPoint (see Tables 10.6 and 10.7) we initially explained that in 'distributed negotiations' one person wants to win as much as possible of the

Table 10.6 Developing a scenario that illustrated a distributive negotiation (Handout 4)

A distributed negotiation		
The players	The bargained-over resources	The tactics used (be specific and relate to your scenario)
e.g. Player 1: salesperson (be specific about context)		
e.g. Player 2; potential client (be specific about context		
Questions for you		
What is Player 1 likely to be feeling during the process?		
What is Player 2 likely to be feeling during the process		
Is this good or bad for your business relationship?		
What is the likely outcome?		

Table 10.7 Developing a scenario that illustrated an integrative negotiation (Handout 5)

An integrative negotiation		
The players	The bargained-over resources	The tactics used (be specific and relate to your scenario)
Questions		
What is Player 1 likely to be feeling during the process?		
What is Player 2 likely to be feeling during the process?		
Is this good or bad for your (business) relationship?		
What is the likely outcome?		

resource about which they are bargaining. This is a win-lose approach. Saner (2000) explained that the kind of tactics that are often employed in distributed negotiations include starting with a very high demand which you realise you will not be likely to achieve, but it sets the bar desirably high on your side. Other tactics include using force or threats to intimidate the opponent (my deliberate use of the word in this context) and prolonging the bargaining process, while making only minor concessions, which you pretend to be major to placate the opponent.

'Integrative approaches' by contrast are negotiations in which a win-win scenario is sought. Problem-solving strategies such as looking at all aspects of the negotiation rationally, without resorting to the kind of tactics described above, are intended to end the negotiation with all parties satisfied with the outcome. They emphasise the use of sharing information and openness (Lewicki et al. 2003; Walton and McKersie 1965). Following the information and discussion, we then broke them into groups of two to do the following exercises. We asked them to develop their own scenarios, as this unpicking of the constituents of a negotiation aided their understanding and ability to relate the contents to their peers later. They were then again broken into groups of two, and were asked to complete the following exercise about an integrative negotiation.

This exercise was repeated three times. In the second two instances, we asked them to develop a scenario of their own, which they then had to swap with other pairs – without their responses to the questions – who then had to put in their responses in the above grid. After some weeks, we quickly went through a shortened version to remind them of these simple approaches to negotiations in the workplace. The essence here was, again, to start with simple methods that they could understand and practice, so that they were learned. This raises the question of how long it takes to learn something. The literature varies, but there is agreement on several factors. Understanding may be difficult, but learning something can be much more difficult as, in summary, it takes, time, rehearsal (practise) and revision, meaningfulness of the information, content relevance and, importantly, motivation. In addition to this, awareness of one's own learning strategies is central to successful learning (McInerney and McInerney 2006, pp. 96–123, 126–132, 144–149). Following the brief revision, the participants were then scaffolded through more complex scenarios, all of which they had to develop as in the previous sessions, until they were more confident in their interactions. These sessions were highly successful.

During performance reviews and later discussions about their potential to enter management positions, they were all much better equipped to discuss their developing skills in the areas of active listening, which is so central to team work and listening to clients, and of negotiations in their own workplace and with clients and customers in other organisations. Even more importantly, they had developed a much greater understanding of the relevance of having well-developed abstract skills when in managerial positions, and that they still needed more development in this area themselves.

Conclusion

It has emerged from the literature, from the findings of a 3-year research project and my own workplace experiences that managers in technically focused organisations often do not understand the importance of having well-developed abstract skills. This is poor role modelling for younger employees, particularly those who are new to the workforce and who aspire to management roles.

Formal skills recognition to assess evidence for the awarding of an accredited certification is obviously important, but informal uses of skill recognition can also identify why, where and how employees need to undertake further training and education to develop those abstract skills. These can be learned. But, as with any new skill, it takes time, effort and practice, the material must be meaningful and relevant, and the rationale for undertaking it must be compelling. At the centre of this process is acceptance by management that this is useful. Also, the skill of the assessor, educator or workforce development person must be high.

Note: All direct quotations from participants in our research are used with permission, granted via signed permission forms approved by the University of South Australia Human Research Ethics Committee and signed by the people who were interviewed during the research.

References

Australian Council for Educational Research. (2013). *Core skills profile for adults: Abstract reasoning.* http://www.acer.edu.au/tests/cspa/abstract-reasoning. Accessed 9 Aug 2013.

Australian Qualifications Framework (AQF). (2013). *Australian qualifications framework.* 2nd edn. http://www.aqf.edu.au/. Accessed 22 Aug 2013.

Bolton, R. (1986). *People skills.* New York: Simon and Schuster.

Brett, J. M. (2007). *Negotiating globally: How to negotiate deals, resolve disputes, and make decisions across cultural boundaries.* San Francisco: Jossey-Bass.

Davies, L., & Maher, K. (2013). *Final major report for the CRC for Rail Innovation. P4.111 Project, A skills recognition framework.* Brisbane: CRC for Rail Innovation.

Davies, L., Maher, K., Stehlik T., Short T., Cameron, R., & Morrison, A. (2013). *Final major report for the CRC for Rail Innovation, August, P4 111 project, a skills recognition framework.* Brisbane: CRC for Rail Innovation.

Department of Education, Employment and Workplace Relations (DEEWR). (2012). *Employability skills framework stage 1: The final report.* Canberra: DEEWR.

Lewicki, R. J., Barry, B., et al. (2003). *Negotiation* (4th ed.). Boston: McGraw-Hill/Irwin.

Logsdon, A. (n.d.). *What is abstract reasoning?* About.com. http://learningdisabilities.about.com/od/glossar1/g/abstractreason.htm. Accessed 6 Aug 2013.

Maher, K., & Morrison, A. (2010). *The literature review: Current and emerging issues in skills recognition as relevant to the Australian rail industry.* Brisbane: CRC for Rail Innovation.

McInerney, D. M., & McInerney, V. (2006). *Educational psychology: Constructing learning* (4th ed.). Sydney: Prentice Hall.

Metz, S. S., Donohue, S., & Moore, C. (2012). Spatial skills: A focus on gender and engineering. In B. Bogue., & E. Cady (Eds.), *Apply research to practice* (ARP) resources. http://www.engr.psu.edu/AWE/ARPResources.aspx. Accessed 6 Aug 2013.

Saner, R. (2000). *The expert negotiator.* The Hague: Kluwer Law International.

Short, T. (2012). Learning how to lead self before leading others: An industry perspective from Australia. *Development and Learning in Organizations, 26*(3), 11–15.

Short, T., & Piip, J. (2013). *Building leadership capability down-under: Hard shell, soft centre.* Paper presented to the 2nd World Congress on Rail Training, St Pölten, 24–26 April.

Sowa, J. F. (1984). *Conceptual structures: Information processing in mind and machine.* Reading: Addison-Wesley.

Walton, R. E., & McKersie, R. B. (1965). *A behavioral theory of labour negotiations: An analysis of a social interaction system.* New York: McGraw-Hill.

Chapter 11
What Makes e-Learning Work?

Kieren Jamieson, Sukanlaya Sawang, and Cameron Newton

Abstract This chapter examines lessons learnt from a study of the use of e-learning within the rail sector in Australia and explores factors that inhibit or advance its organisational effectiveness. We examine the social, organisational and technical influences on the way employees perceive and use e-learning. By examining these issues, we aim to demonstrate that successful organisational adoption of e-learning is influenced by factors beyond the systems themselves and requires a more holistic understanding of the target workforce and the suitability of the e-learning tasks. Without a clear understanding of these relationships, organisations run the real risk of investing heavily in e-learning without receiving benefits or, worse still, impacting negatively on their ability to deliver training.

Introduction

Corporate e-learning has become popular as an alternative method of corporate training. While corporate e-learning is an excellent alternative training approach, adoption of corporate e-learning has been very low (Bonk 2002). As corporate e-learning has potential benefits for organisations, from financial to human capital

K. Jamieson (✉)
Central Queensland University, Rockhampton, Australia
e-mail: k.jamieson@cqu.edu.au

S. Sawang
QUT Business School, Queensland University of Technology in Brisbane,
Brisbane, Australia
e-mail: s.sawang@qut.edu.au

C. Newton
School of Management, Queensland University of Technology in Brisbane,
Brisbane, Australia
e-mail: cj.newton@qut.edu.au

T. Short and R. Harris (eds.), *Workforce Development: Strategies and Practices*,
DOI 10.1007/978-981-287-068-1_11, © Springer Science+Business Media Singapore 2014

perspectives, an important question for HR practitioners is how to introduce e-learning in organisations effectively. In this chapter we take the findings from a study of e-learning use in six Australian rail organisations and investigate factors that employees reported as benefits (or attractors) and inhibitors (or barriers). In analysing qualitative feedback, we identify and group these factors, explaining how they impact on the e-learning experience. We begin by briefly examining the extant literature and discussing some of the factors and learner traits that contribute to successful e-learning. We then describe the study and provide respondent profile data. We begin the findings by explaining some of the key attractors to e-learning that contribute to success. Following this, we reflect on the inhibitors and the issues raised by survey respondents that acted as barriers to e-learning adoption and use. We aim to develop constructive recommendations for corporate e-learning adoption and implementation.

Background

E-learning is broadly defined as distance education that uses computer technologies, information communication technologies (ICT), mobile technology and learning management systems (Sawang et al. 2013). Due to cost effectiveness, many organisations have converted their traditional training delivery methods to an e-learning approach (Strother 2002). However, the trend towards e-learning is not without its challenges. A combination of organisational and individual factors determines the effectiveness of e-learning in meeting corporate and personal objectives and needs.

The literature indicates that for e-learning in organisations to be successful technical and learning support mechanisms must be in place and it must be authentic and appropriate for the content. Tangible institutional support is required to successfully introduce corporate e-learning (Selim 2007). Organisations can increase corporate e-learning adoption through supportive provision such as usage training, equipment and infrastructure. However, the e-learning tasks themselves must engage users and provide real, authentic learning experiences. Authentic learning typically focuses on 'real-world, complex problems and their solutions, using role-playing exercises, problem-based activities, case studies, and participation' (Lombardi 2007, p. 2). Due to advances in technology it is now possible to offer employees authentic learning experiences ranging from simulation to real-work problem solving.

The authenticity that can be created using e-learning allows individuals to gain new knowledge that helps them to solve problems in their professional lives (Huang 2002). When e-learning incorporates authenticity as a part of its modules, employees feel more motivated to use e-learning due to the authentic activities that they can apply in their real work situation (Sawang et al. 2013). This is one key element that drives innovation adoption. Therefore, authentic e-learning can increase the likelihood of employees adopting e-learning for professional development (Sawang et al. 2013). However, as we discuss later in this chapter, e-learning users report many other more basic, though interrelated, organisational factors that benefit and inhibit e-learning.

While a range of possible individual characteristics influence e-learning adoption, the IT adoption literature reports that the most important are self-efficacy and openness to experience (e.g. Hong 2002; Straub 2009). Self-efficacy is confidence in one's ability to complete a task; in an e-learning context, a task represents the use of e-learning (Hong 2002; Sawang et al. 2013). Psychologist Albert Bandura (1997) explained that highly self-confident individuals will believe that they have the ability to cope with a new challenge and will then initiate an action to manage the challenge. Similarly, levels of self-confidence play a critical role in e-learning adoption. For example, employees who have more confidence in their computer skills are more likely to prefer the use of web-based training (Hong 2002). This is reflected in marketing research, as level of self-confidence among consumers is a critical driver of IT-related products/services such as e-banking and e-tax (Wang 2003). This is similar to the information system (IS) literature, where technological self-efficacy, or confidence in one's ability to complete a task using technology, is a key predictor of individuals' IS adoption (e.g. McDonald and Siegall 1992; Compeau and Higgins 1995). In the innovation literature, early adopters are described as having high self-efficacy (Burkhardt and Brass 1990; Pedersen 2005).

American psychologists McCrae and Costa (1997) classified human personality into the 'big five' personality traits: extraversion, agreeableness, conscientiousness, neuroticism, and openness to experience. The trait of openness to experience has been demonstrated to significantly influence adoption behaviour (Sawang et al. 2013). In the e-learning context, individuals who are willing to experience new things are expected to be more likely to adopt new e-learning strategies and systems as a part of their learning and development. While the findings from the study reported on in this chapter support these individual traits, we identify many more factors that affect e-learning. In particular, we discuss the effects of perceptions and user agency (control of learning).

In this chapter we identify and explore practical examples of organisational and individual factors that affect e-learning in rail organisations. While these align with the findings identified in the extant literature, we suggest that e-learning success is complex and relies on a number of interrelated elements and strategies.

The Study

The findings from this chapter are the result of a two-part study as part of project P4.110, 'Collaborative E-learning in Rail', which we conducted in order to identify the different approaches to e-learning both outside and inside the rail industry. The study assessed the applicability of e-learning to a rail context, and identified the major benefits and the barriers to successful implementation. We collected data in an e-learning climate and administered aptitude surveys to employees of six participant organisations between 2011 and 2013. We distributed hard copy surveys as well as a link to web-based questionnaires to all participant organisations. The surveys took approximately 15 min to complete and aimed to gather data from users of e-learning as well as from non-users, employees and managers. The findings in this chapter are drawn from the sections of the surveys that asked respondents to nominate specific benefits and barriers. Qualitative theme analysis was undertaken on data provided in the form of comments in the surveys.

Respondent Profile

In 2011, 1,268 questionnaires were completed and returned, of which 1,149 were completed online and 119 respondents returned a hard-copy survey. In 2013 a total of 1,801 questionnaires were completed and returned, of which 1,671 were completed online and 130 respondents returned a hard-copy survey.

In 2011 the gender profile of respondents was two-thirds (69 %) male and one-third (31 %) female. In 2013 approximately three-quarters of respondents (74.3 %) were male and one-quarter (25.5 %) were female. In 2011 the age profile of respondents was half (52 %) between 36 and 55 years of age. In 2013 two-thirds of all respondents (69 %) were between 36 and 55 years of age. The majority of respondents were older; this reflects the rail industry as a whole with an average age higher than the general population.

In 2011 a quarter (25 %) of respondents who provided position details worked in managerial or supervisory roles. In 2013 close to a quarter (22.9 %) of respondents who provided position details worked in a managerial or supervisory role and another quarter (24.3 %) in professional or technical roles.

In 2011, 28 % of respondents had a certificate/diploma qualification and 36 % had a higher qualification. A quarter of all respondents (25 %) had a high school diploma as their highest qualification. These results could be expected given the large number of management and professional respondents. In 2013 most respondents had a certificate/diploma (29.2 %) qualification or higher (37.4 %). Close to a quarter of all respondents (22 %) had a high school diploma as their highest qualification.

Findings

Comments from the study were predominately more negative towards e-learning than supportive and as a result the findings are skewed towards factors that act as inhibitors. However, many factors that negatively influence e-learning can be 'flipped' in order to become beneficial. For example, poor ICT infrastructure and support, if corrected, becomes a key element in underpinning successful e-learning deployment. Other factors, like the quality of the e-learning content, act as both benefits and barriers to e-learning. Many factors are closely related; for example, inhibiting factors such as time and place. Perhaps the strongest finding from the study is that perceptions are extremely important and difficult to overcome. While the actuality or reality may differ, this finding is critical in understanding why many organisations struggle to successfully implement e-learning in the face of prior failed implementations and poor user perceptions of management objectives and the systems themselves.

Factors that Benefit e-Learning

The majority of respondents reported predominately individual factors that made e-learning attractive, with those from management identifying some organisational issues such as cost and compliance. Findings were best summarised by one respondent who noted that e-learning is 'quick, cost effective, can save potential embarrassment for some by brushing up on weaknesses in private [and] provides an avenue for those who want to engage in discretionary learning'. In this section, we report and expand upon these themes.

Cost

Much is made of the fact that e-learning is cheaper than face-to-face training. From an organisational perspective, this is a key attractor to implementing e-learning. As we will discuss later, this benefit is also one of the key factors that act as an inhibitor of e-learning adoption from a user perspective. The cost factor encompasses a broad range of underlying elements. From an administrative perspective, e-learning creates an inexpensive and integrated way of tracking employee competencies for compliance and promotion purposes. In terms of training large numbers of employees spread over a number of geographical locations, its 'anywhere anytime' feature potentially avoids additional logistical costs. As one respondent noted, 'E-learning is the economical way to train most people in a large, far-flung organisation. No travel, no accommodation, no staff shortages, no venue hire, no staff expenses, etc.'

Convenience

Many respondents favourably reflected on the convenience factors associated with e-learning. E-learning gives its users agency over when and where they undertake training, making convenience an attractor. This convenience was illustrated in a number of ways. For example, being able to make the most of an employee's time was evidenced by one respondent's comment that '[e-learning] allows me to make use of my long commute times, at the moment I am wasting 2 h each day that could be better utilised for eLearning'. Many respondents described how they enjoyed the flexibility of being able to do the training from a location of their choosing, for example: 'I get to create my own schedule to complete the training and set the environment also, such as at home or library'. The convenience of online and on-demand training also linked back to cost in that respondents observed that e-learning was not restricted by class size and was therefore available even if the 'class' was not large enough to justify a trainer. Moreover, shift workers saw the financial benefits of the convenience of undertaking e-learning in their own time. One remarked, 'I don't lose money by having a roster change for training'.

Learning Style

A consistent theme from respondents was the beneficial and attractive nature of the learning style associated with e-learning. Respondents who felt their learning style was not appropriate for face-to-face training or who felt constrained by the pace of traditional approaches identified advantages of e-learning. Being able to have agency over the pace of learning was frequently mentioned. For example, one respondent commented, 'in a classroom situation, the trainer has to teach by the lowest denominator. I am quick and hate wasting time waiting for others to grasp meanings. E-learning is best for people like me.' Similarly, those who found group learning difficult made remarks like 'self-learning is not as intrusive as classroom learning where people "feel like they are back at school"'. Other respondents noted that e-learning has the potential for rapid feedback, something that many learners find important. For example, one respondent stated: '[e-learning gives me] immediate feedback on exercises and an opportunity to redo exercises to correct mistakes'. The learning style provided by e-learning was also a strong inhibitor as we will discuss later.

Learning Resource

Closely related to convenience and learning style is the ability of e-learning systems to act as repositories of training materials and other key resources that can be accessed to refresh an employee's memory of the correct process or action in a given situation. This central storage point for resources, if structured appropriately, provides a one-stop point of reference. As one respondent noted, such learning resources mean 'the information is readily accessible for revision in a structured form – especially when hard copies are lost/misplaced'.

Career Progression

E-learning potentially allows employees to take control of their own career progression by completing additional training so that they qualify for promotion. This was a strong incentive for employees to undertake courses, especially in their own time. One respondent remarked, 'it [enables] me to complete the courses I need to do [in order to act in] jobs … and … already have the qualifications for promotion when the opportunity arises without waiting for others to arrange it'. This form of agency is closely related to the convenience factor.

Quality, Consistency and Equity

Some respondents felt that e-learning was of a higher quality and more consistent than traditional face-to-face learning. It was observed that, by removing trainers, on completion of an e-learning module '[you have had the] same message as everyone else … no poor teachers' and 'the quality of the training is not dependent upon the company engaging a quality and informed trainer'. Others remarked on the issue of equity in that everyone within an organisation had equal access to the same training, no matter where they were, for example, 'regional people can access the same sort of courses and learning opportunities'.

Factors that Inhibit e-Learning

As discussed previously, the majority of respondents nominated more factors that acted as inhibitors to e-learning rather than attractors or benefits. Rather than interpreting this as a prevailing negative perception of e-learning, the challenge for organisations considering this technology is to learn lessons from this valuable feedback. Respondents reported largely practical and often interrelated issues that organisations must address in order to underpin successful e-learning. Perhaps the theme and cautionary warning from these factors was best summed up by one respondent's assessment of their e-learning experience:

> Supposed benefits such as 'when and where you want', when coupled with increasing demands of the workplace, easily translate into drawbacks. Being in your usual environment means you may be drawn away from learning by the usual interruptions, and other people may not give you adequate time to learn. The relatively informal nature of the learning may mean it is merely added on top of your usual workload, instead of having space and time specifically made to accommodate it.

In this section, we report and expand upon these themes.

Lack of Appropriate Learning Space

One key finding from the study was that users of e-learning frequently reported that organisations had failed to consider where the activity was to be undertaken. Respondents frequently made comments like 'the major issue for me would be having to do it at my desk, as it would be impossible to concentrate due to noisy environment and constant interruptions' and 'when we are sent away for training courses, most other commitments cease during that time. If we are working our own way through the course at our desk, interruptions will prove detrimental as our daily commitments will not cease and training [becomes] broken and disturbed'. Many respondents observed that a busy physical work environment was far from suitable for e-learning and requested dedicated quiet training rooms where they could go to complete the activity.

Lack of Dedicated Time

A closely related and equally prevalent theme was a failure of organisations to set aside time in which to undertake e-learning. Perhaps this was best summarised by one respondent who said:

> E-learning requires time to do the learning. When not taken out of the workplace to learn it just becomes all too hard to set aside the time to do it. People come to your work station, the phone keeps ringing and the emails keep arriving. It is impossible to convince people that their problem needs to be put on hold while you 'play' on the PC. Being removed from the workplace solves these issues. Perhaps e-learning at a site removed from your normal location is the best option.

Organisations that treat e-learning as a side task that is expected to be slotted into an employee's normal work make the activity immediately less attractive to employees, potentially leading to resentment. As one respondent noted, 'it is not good enough for my superiors to say "when you get a chance, look at this" and expect training to be done'. Perhaps an underlying issue could be the perception by some managers within organisations that e-learning is not 'real' training, so does not need dedicated time. As one respondent stated, 'some organisations ... do not see e-learning as "training" therefore managers may interrupt training courses or not see them as a priority as the employee is sitting at their desk'.

Negative Lifestyle Impacts

Following on from the lack of time and appropriate learning space, many respondents indicated that they had to undertake e-learning in their own time at home in order to 'get it done'. While some respondents were happy to do this, many made comments about the impact on their home life. For example, '[I] have hideous shift work hours and fatigue is a genuine barrier. Family and social commitments can seriously affect one's ability to undertake e-learning on top of normal working hours'. Others felt it was unfair to have to undertake e-learning in their own time given they would not be paid for it. As one respondent noted, 'doing e-learning in my own time means that I would not be getting paid. I WOULD NOT compromise my family time to do work outside of work time and not get paid for it.'

Unclear Benefits

Perhaps these lifestyle impacts would be mitigated if employees could see the benefits of e-learning. As one respondent stated:

> I'd love to participate in lots of small e-learning modules, as long as they actually meant something. As long as we could then put them on our resume or they went towards higher pay or greater privileges. No-one wants to put the extra effort into learning something unless there is a clearly defined benefit they will obtain by having completed it. We all have lives, families, other external activities we are involved in and VERY few of us have extra time and energy to invest in training as well.

This indicates that just providing e-learning online is not enough if employees are expected to undertake it in their own time.

Learning Style Mismatch

One of the more interesting findings from the study was an almost polarised view of the learning style associated with e-learning. While one group of respondents liked the way in which e-learning gave them control of the pace and learning experience, another group were equally as insistent that they felt online training was incompatible with the way they needed to learn. Most of the feedback centred on the lack of interaction, both with a trainer and with other class members. Respondents commented that they felt less motivated when undertaking e-learning. For example one noted, 'I learn better if someone is helping me throughout the process and guiding me, otherwise I lose motivation'. Another remarked, 'I value highly the ability to network and learn from other students in a group situation – while this can be simulated online, it does not match the spontaneity of a group learning environment'. Others felt the lack of real-time interaction contributed negatively to motivation, stating that 'E-learning is an insulated, mind numbingly boring way to learn'. Finally, the purely virtual approach to training materials was perceived as a barrier, with many remarking that the lack of hard-copy manuals or materials made it more difficult for them to use or apply the training on the job. As one respondent remarked, '[it would] be helpful to have hard copy "textbook" or downloadable pdf files available to supplement online information and refer to in times or places when computer [is] not available'.

Lack of Quality, Design and Appropriateness

Quality, one of the attractors to e-learning, also was frequently mentioned as a barrier. Respondents noted that e-learning often contained 'outdated materials' and that the content quickly became 'stale'. This may reflect a lack of maintenance of online programs but also highlights the difference from the dynamic nature of face-to-face training. Face-to-face training is relatively easy to change on the fly in order to integrate and deliver new materials or changes to processes. The same change in e-learning requires a planned modification to the e-learning content. This goes to the core of e-learning in that, however good the platform is, the content must be accurate and of a high quality. The design associated with delivering effective online training cannot be underestimated because, as one respondent noted, 'poorly designed programs are a turn off, very difficult to persevere and complete the training'. Another respondent described his experiences with e-learning as 'badly designed, poor instructions, no feedback and unimaginative'. It is important that content is pitched at the appropriate level, as one respondent stated:

> The main barriers would be relevance of the content – realistically whoever designs these courses must be former primary school teachers! You read a passage that will say, always look left before crossing the road then you get a multi choice that says what should you do if you cross the road: a) order a pizza, b) call your friend, c) look left.

Feedback also indicated that some respondents felt that e-learning sometimes covered topics that were not appropriate for online training, believing that some organisations took a 'one size fits all' approach. Respondents indicated this affected the competency of the employees, noting that 'they get through the e-learning but can't carry out the requirements later' and that, for some training, 'nothing beats on the job learning', especially for more hands-on competencies.

Poor Technology and Support

A key lesson from this study was the need for reliable technology and support of the e-learning platform. Respondents reported situations where they were expected to undertake e-learning yet 'there are only four computers for over 800 staff'. When computing resources were available, they were sometimes old PCs with slow or unreliable network connections. Many respondents who were positive about e-learning complained that they could not access the e-learning platforms from home; in other words, no access was possible from the internet. Some respondents noted that queries about the content of e-learning systems are not answered in a timely manner, with one stating that 'I find it essential to have someone on hand to give some direction (computers never do that well) and to be able to ask the awkward questions when things don't work as the program thinks they should'. Another aspect of the support issue was an underlying organisational assumption that the employees were computer literate. As one respondent noted, 'I know how to drive a train but just because everyone has ridden on a train at some stage I don't assume that they know how to drive one! Basic computer courses would be the way to go'. Another stated, 'everybody assumes you have a computer and an email address, and you know how to use one'. This indicates that some organisations need to make more effort to skill employees in computer use before deploying e-learning.

Negative Perceptions

Whether negative perceptions are based in fact or not, once formed they are difficult to counter. The respondents' comments included a consistent series of themes surrounding beliefs about e-learning. The predominant theme was that e-learning was the cheap and expedient option that delivered a lower-quality training experience. Typical comments included '[e-learning is] an easy and cheap option for a company to adopt, but the results do not reflect value for money or learned skills' and 'I can see that management would like the cheap and swift deployment of this type of training, at the detriment to quality'. Some respondents linked e-learning to job loss. For example one stated that 'e-learning is purely a cost/job cutting tool by employers who are not interested in staff development, but more in the bottom line i.e. $'. This perception, that organisations deployed e-learning because they did not care about training, was reflected by respondents who thought of e-learning as the 'lazy option' and 'second-best'. Other respondents perceived evidence of this 'second-best' training because of differences in the way management was treated, with one stating, 'e-learning is seen as cheap i.e. They don't care about the course, it is unimportant, the workers aren't worth spending money on so give them an e-course but give the bosses the real thing'. Other respondents believed that e-learning was deployed just for compliance purposes; for example, one stated that 'e-learning is often used as a means of ensuring corporate compliance with various regulations rather than developing staff and the content tends to reflect this'. These perceptions that e-learning is not 'real' and is just window dressing was best summarised by the comment that 'e-learning seems like a cop-out, i.e. a way to make out that an organisation is committed to training, but not actually providing much in the way of resources'. Interestingly, one of the reported attractors to deploying e-learning is its relatively lower cost and ability to track compliance. The challenge appears to be convincing employees that, just because it is cheaper, it is not necessarily inferior.

Recommendations

From the findings of the study, we are able to make a number of practical recommendations that organisations should consider before implementing e-learning. We have grouped these recommendations into four themes: policy and planning, design, technology and education.

Policy and Planning

1. **Set clear goals and expected outcomes.** Before embarking on the process of implementing e-learning, organisations need to clearly identify *why* they are want to use it and what benefits they expect it to deliver. This creates a method of evaluating whether e-learning is successful and instils corporate transparency that will assist the change management process.
2. **Set aside dedicated e-learning spaces.** If employees are expected to undertake e-learning during working hours, then they need to have access to dedicated well-equipped training spaces. This space needs to contain up-to-date technology, high-speed networks and, if possible, be physically separate from employees' normal working environments.
3. **Dedicate time for e-learning.** Policy and management practice should support e-learning by ensuring employees have dedicated, uninterruptible time for e-learning tasks. As is clear from this study, successful e-learning cannot be interleaved between normal working tasks.
4. **Maximise access to e-learning.** Policy and technology should support employees who wish to undertake additional e-learning for career progression. Additionally, consider allowing access to e-learning platforms from outside the organisational intranet by implementing policy and technology for connectivity via the internet.

Design

1. **Place emphasis on training and content design.** By designing high-quality e-learning content that is appropriate to the required competencies, users are presented with a real and useful learning experience. This is critical in fostering positive perceptions of e-learning. Moreover, effective content design maximises the opportunity to equip employees with the desired competencies.
2. **Keep content up to date.** E-learning content should not be treated as static and should be under constant review and maintenance. Stale content leads to mistrust and negative perceptions of e-learning.
3. **Consider blended learning.** It is important to realise that e-learning is not a training panacea. Some training will be more appropriately delivered face-to-face. Consider a mix of training methods and technologies that will deliver the best outcomes. Use the strengths of e-learning where possible, but be mindful of its shortcomings.

Technology

1. **Get the technology right the first time.** Ensure that the e-learning platform is underpinned by scalable and reliable technology. Ensure that users have access to appropriate technology in the form of PCs and mobile devices. By making sure the technology delivers a high-speed, reliable and interactive learning experience, organisations can maximise the chance that users will react positively to e-learning.
2. **Support the technology and e-learning platform.** Users of e-learning need rapid personal support if they encounter problems when undertaking e-learning. An inability to resolve a problem with e-learning can result in poor perceptions of the technology and task abandonment.

Education

1. **Provide computer literacy training.** Do not assume your employees can use computers or have the necessary skills to undertake e-learning. Ensure there are quality computer literacy programs in place before mandating e-learning: note that these may require some face-to-face presentation.
2. **Explain why e-learning is being used.** Employees need to understand why e-learning is being deployed. This is critical in countering the perception that e-learning is 'cheap' and 'inferior' to 'real' face-to-face learning.
3. **Explain the benefits of e-learning.** Identify and communicate the benefits of e-learning to employees. While e-learning might be organisationally mandated, failure to explain the relative advantages of e-learning will almost certainly lead to user resistance.

Conclusion

In this chapter we have examined user-sourced data concerning the factors that benefit and inhibit e-learning in organisations. It is clear that many factors exhibit binary effects, for example, the learning style provided by online training is attractive to some users yet acts as a detractor for others. Design and the quality of the e-learning content are critical in acceptance and use: good design leads to positive experiences; bad design leads to negative. The results from the study indicate that many factors contribute to the overall effectiveness of e-learning and that it is essential to address these in order to avoid negative perceptions.

While past literature focuses on individual differences (such as personality traits) and e-learning adoption, individual effects can be mitigated if organisations consider policy and planning, design, technology and education as part of their e-learning implementation. Simple non-technical issues such as dedicated space and time for e-learning are essential. Treating e-learning like any organisational change and employing effective communication to educate users about the benefits and reasons for the implementation is one strategy to mitigate user dissatisfaction. Organisations can focus on creating a supportive environment towards e-learning adoption. Employees' perception of the relative advantages of e-learning will be a catalyst for wide e-learning adoption. In conclusion, organisations considering e-learning adoption need to be aware that it is a complex task that needs up-front commitment to establishing the best environment for its deployment in order to maximise the likelihood of success.

References

Bandura, A. (1997). *Self-efficacy: The exercise of control*. New York: Freeman.

Bonk, C. J. (2002). *Online training in an online world*. Bloomington: CourseShare.com.

Burkhardt, M. E., & Brass, D. J. (1990). Changing patterns or patterns of change: The effects of a change in technology on social network structure and power. *Administrative Science Quarterly, 35*(1), 104–127.

Compeau, D. R., & Higgins, C. A. (1995). Computer self-efficacy: Development of a measure and initial test. *MIS Quarterly, 19*(2), 189–211.

Hong, K.-S. (2002). Relationships between students' and instructional variables with satisfaction and learning from a web-based course. *The Internet and Higher Education, 5*(3), 267–281.

Huang, H. M. (2002). Toward constructivism for adult learners in online learning environments. *British Journal of Educational Technology, 33*(1), 27–37.

Lombardi, M. M. (2007). Authentic learning for the 21st century: An overview. *Educause Learning Initiative, 1*, 1–12.

McCrae, R. R., & Costa, P. T., Jr. (1997). Personality trait structure as a human universal. *American Psychologist, 52*(5), 509–516.

McDonald, T., & Siegall, M. (1992). The effects of technological self-efficacy and job focus on job performance, attitudes, and withdrawal behaviors. *Journal of Psychology, 126*(5), 465–475.

Pedersen, P. E. (2005). Adoption of mobile internet services: An exploratory study of mobile commerce early adopters. *Journal of Organizational Computing and Electronic Commerce, 15*(3), 203–222.

Sawang, S., Newton, C., & Jamieson, K. (2013). Increasing learners' satisfaction/intention to adopt more e-learning. *Education + Training, 55*(1), 83–105.

Selim, H. M. (2007). Critical success factors for e-learning acceptance: Confirmatory factor models. *Computers & Education, 49*(2), 396–413.

Straub, E. T. (2009). Understanding technology adoption: Theory and future directions for informal learning. *Review of Educational Research, 79*(2), 625–649.

Strother, J. B. (2002). An assessment of the effectiveness of e-learning in corporate training programs. *International Review of Research in Open and Distance Learning, 3*(1), 1–17.

Wang, Y.-S. (2003). The adoption of electronic tax filing systems: An empirical study. *Government Information Quarterly, 20*(4), 333–352.

Part III
Developing Leadership, Talent and Innovation

Chapter 12
Building Leadership Capability: What It Means for Rail Organisations

Tom Short, Tom Stehlik, and Janene Piip

Abstract This chapter draws attention to the pressing need for all organisations to build leadership capability at a time in history when leadership is a recurring and significant theme in popular discourse. According to international experts, leadership is the most pressing issue facing organisations today because of the turbulent and complex environments where endless change and unexpected events have become the norm. In Australia, the pool of leadership talent has decreased at a faster rate than many other parts of the world, while at the same time investments in leadership development activities are higher than many other developed countries. In this chapter we aim to demystify the challenge of building leadership capability and move beyond the rhetoric to explore what can be done as part of a workforce development strategy. This chapter reports on findings taken from a leadership study undertaken between 2009 and 2011 which contributed to the development of a leadership capability framework in the Australian rail industry. The study concluded that many industries such as rail should utilise top-level frameworks of good practice while also making leadership development fit the local context of each unique environment.

Introduction

In Australia, as elsewhere, leadership and the need to build leadership capability in all types of organisations are recurring themes in academic publications and appear as keynote topics at professional conferences. These narratives focus on the pressing need to develop leadership capability (CIPD 2009), or remind us that the pool of talented leaders is decreasing; and arguably to a lower level in Australia than many

T. Short (✉) • T. Stehlik • J. Piip
School of Education, University of South Australia, Mawson Lakes, SA, Australia
e-mail: tom.short@unisa.edu.au; tom.stehlik@unisa.edu.au; janenepiip@gmail.com

T. Short and R. Harris (eds.), *Workforce Development: Strategies and Practices*,
DOI 10.1007/978-981-287-068-1_12, © Springer Science+Business Media Singapore 2014

other parts of the developed world (Infographics 2011). Global organisations such as the World Federation of Personnel Management Associations have reported on at least two occasions that the development of future leadership capability is one of the top three priorities facing organisations, along with the management of change and discovering a reliable way to measure the effectiveness of human resource activities (Gould 2005; Mutte 2006). In Australia, the Karpin Report (Karpin 1995), the most comprehensive insight ever into the way managers and leaders were prepared for work, made 28 recommendations for improving leadership development by the year 2010. In spite of this, 16 years later, a review revealed 'patchy implementation' (IBSA 2011, p. 28), identifying that many of the leadership and management challenges identified in 1995 had not yet been realised. This lack of action to develop leadership talent has spurred a major training investment in Australia, more in fact than many other countries outside of Asia (Infographics 2011).

These reports of increases in leadership development will come as welcome news for those institutions and enterprises that make a living from creating the next generation of leadership theory and practice. In the area of human resource management (HRM), few topics have attracted more interest than leadership development and this fascination has held the attention of business schools and other organisations for decades. Arguably, leadership has 'been studied more extensively than any other aspect of human behaviour' (Higgs 2003, p. 27) and there are almost 'as many definitions of leadership as there are persons who have attempted to define the concept' (Bass 1990, p. 11). In recent years, the debate has been extended, with a recurring focus on leadership as something distinct from management, but some reports now suggest that leadership capability and management practices are inseparable and further analysis is no longer needed (Burgoyne et al. 2004).

Leadership is undoubtedly big business, and estimates vary, but the global market for this component of human resource development (HRD) strategy (recently re-labelled as workforce development) was estimated at US$37 billion per year in 1996 and may be as high as US$70 billion today (Boyatziz et al. 1996). In 1999 over 8,000 publications were produced worldwide on the topic of leadership, including 2,000 books from North America alone, one reason why US firms were perceived in the 1990s as trailblazers in the area of leadership and people management (Day 2001; Green 2009). This ongoing interest is motivated by a solid belief that effective leadership in a globalised economy has a profound influence on an organisation's performance culture, competitive advantage and longer-term survivability; or in the worst case scenario, susceptibility to failure (Buus 2006; Oakland 2004; Thompson 1995).

The rail industry in Australia is just one sector that has reflected on how leadership capability could be improved in the face of these global challenges. Industry reports have highlighted the need for greater levels of inter-organisation cooperation to harmonise the implementation of workforce development strategies and practices; and this includes finding a collaborative way to attract, train, retain and improve the effectiveness of rail leaders (PricewaterhouseCoopers 2006; ARA 2008). This chapter reports on findings taken from a leadership study, undertaken between 2009 and 2011, that explored how collaborative approaches to developing a framework of leadership capability might not only lead to greater economies of scale, but also enable an inter-company transfer of leadership talent within the sector and develop a refreshed, innovative rail leadership culture. We conclude that many industries such as rail should utilise top-level frameworks of good practice while also making leadership development fit the local context of each unique environment. In the remainder of this chapter we describe the key elements of these frameworks and the implications for workforce development strategy and practice.

Background Scenario

Not too long ago, when leadership seemed much more straightforward than it does today, traditional approaches to developing leadership capability came from the classical works of great thinkers such as Peter Drucker, Warren Bennis, Henry Mintzberg, John Adair and latterly Stephen Covey. Theories and practices on leadership and management were extracted principally from Anglo-American studies conducted largely among white males. Within the US literature, leadership findings were most frequently drawn from studies in the business sector and leadership training was based on the notion that leaders achieve tasks through the united capability and willingness of team members, sometimes called followers or subordinates. In these early days, effective leaders performed highly structured and hierarchical activities based on the skills of planning, organising and controlling; but later, in the 1980s, this approach gave way to team-based problem solving where leaders acted more as facilitators and change agents in rationalised and flatter structures (Robbins et al. 1997). At the same time, these early leadership studies focused on the pros and cons of using intuitive leadership qualities, leadership styles and leadership actions for a range of given situations. However, this narrowness of study did not take into account the growing diversity found in other contexts, such as Australasian society or leaders in the Australian workplace. Until recently, very little was known of how leadership actually happened in Australia (Dalglish and Evans 2007; Green 2009).

While the fundamental building blocks of these early paradigms remain relevant today, only a few of the big thinkers foresaw the looming complexity of leadership in a new world order that would become more globalised, mobile, driven by technology, eco-aware and culturally diverse. Nowadays organisations are forewarned that sustainable human resource management and social capital building are the new narratives of leadership, but few know precisely how these issues will develop or what issues will arise next. It is unclear whether the forces of globalisation will enable or constrain the notion of sustainable HRM, and in today's frenetic business climate it is almost impossible to predict how leaders can keep up with the changing demands placed on their organisations. Put simply, we live in turbulent times and leadership strategies that worked yesterday can so easily become inappropriate tomorrow. These challenges are captured in the mainstream media by global problems such as the global financial crisis in 2008, leadership betrayals, political upheavals and natural disasters where leaders are thrust into the spotlight to deal with major incidents and then disappear out of sight once the big event has passed. Australian people are accustomed to dealing with episodic events such as bushfires, flooding, heatwaves and major incidents in the public transport sector. In these dramatic situations leadership capability becomes a high profile concern that is often unchallenged by followers at the time and driven by an instinctive need to overcome the challenge in the best way possible. However, sometime later, evaluation and a critical reflection process takes place to examine how leaders performed, challenge assumptions with the benefit of hindsight and decide how improvements can be made. One example of this post-event evaluative approach to leadership can be found in a publication issued by the Australasian Fire Authorities Council (2007) detailing a leadership capability framework for volunteer fire fighters. The study was driven by a strategic need to increase the capability of volunteer leaders at all levels and help them better prepare for future events.

Development of Capability Frameworks

Over the last 20 years, capability frameworks have grown in popularity and become attractive to employers as a way of structuring HRD processes. To be specific, leadership capability frameworks have expanded to become a major area of interest in parallel with the need to improve organisational performance. Yet despite much effort to standardise leadership capability, only an optimist would attempt to prescribe one best-practice model for all situations. Capability frameworks are defined by industry sectors, professional associations, national development bodies or academic institutions, but they can also be developed to meet the special needs of one organisation (such as the AFAC). In most cases, capability frameworks are based on a contingency approach to HRM (Boxall and Purcell 2003) and heavily contextualised.

The significance of context in leadership development will feature later in this chapter, because reports have suggested that attempts to create harmonised, generic models of leadership capability may struggle when they do not take situational variations into account. It is known that 'organisations tend to emphasise the leadership capabilities that are acceptable, legitimate and feasible within their cultural contexts' (Yeung and Ready 1995, p. 532) and the contingency or situational approach to leadership addresses, in part, the unique context or environment in which leadership operates, such as the follower–leadership relationship (Graen and Uhl-Bien 1995). Therefore, placing leadership and management in the Australian rail context is important for understanding the current practices and future challenges for a national sector such as the rail industry. Against this background, one common capability framework might struggle to incorporate every situational variable, but a comparative study of eight nations (Yeung and Ready 1995, p. 543) has indicated five universally valued outcomes of a leadership capability framework:

1. increasing the leader's capacity to articulate tangible visions, values and strategies
2. encouraging the leader to be a catalyst for cultural change

3. enabling the leader to achieve results
4. enabling the leader to empower others
5. encouraging the leader to exhibit a strong customer (or service) orientation.

Why Defining Leadership Capability Has Become So Problematic for Australian Rail

Using the Australian rail industry as a contextual lens, it is possible to delve further into why developing leadership capability has become so challenging for organisations, and these lenses draw our attention to time and place. Like many other sectors in Australia, the rail industry has found itself caught up in a macro-environmental conundrum. Firstly, many Australian organisations are still linked with Britain, they have offshore ownership and habitually use Anglo-American models of leadership, but at the same time they are located in a rapidly changing South-East Asian economy – an economy that is energised by global competition, high productivity, increasing diversity and less hierarchical traditions.

Secondly, the pioneering mindset of early settlers has influenced what it means to be an Australian leader, but sometimes these inward-looking characteristics such as mateship, egalitarianism, individualism and the 'tall poppy' syndrome are not always congruent with outside perceptions (Ashkanasy and Falkus 1997). Outside of Australia the term 'tall poppy' is used in a disapproving way when people of high merit are cut down or criticised because their achievement is attached to elevated social status; but in Australia the term is not always seen as negative and is tolerated as a way of protecting the underdog. Green (2009) found that Australian managers tended to overrate their performance (against outsiders) because they did not recognise that their own practices were poor. Moreover, these intrinsic and deeply held values clash with overt managerialism, such as command-control styles of leadership.

Thirdly, the onset of leadership capability frameworks and competence-based qualifications in Australia was influenced by neo-liberal training policies and new vocationalism in the workplace. These strong influences from the UK and Europe sparked a series of radical reforms and change management programs in the 1990s and were aimed at counteracting the impact of global competition – mainly by trying to replicate practices in the more productive Asian economies. Changes were operationalised in many organisations through workforce development strategies and the systemised implementation of widespread standards to deal with individual variations in performance and align workplace behaviour with what employers valued (Cacioppe 1998; Bullock et al. 2000).

Fourthly, many Australian rail organisations today are coming to terms with the inherent challenges existent in a three or four generation workplace. Of major concern is how to transfer expertise from departing Baby Boomers to talented Generation Y leaders. In a multi-generational workplace approaches and preferences to leadership capability appear to differ across each age group, and in rail there has been a historical leaning towards hard-edged leadership skills such as planning, organising and controlling, at the expense of softer skills such as caring, engaging and communicating with people.

To conclude this section, leadership capability is now considered a distinct organisational competency that is crucial to business success (Yeung and Ready 1995). There are scores of leadership capability frameworks used around the world, but principally all of these frameworks aim to improve business performance, engage workers and improve competitive advantage across a range of industries. Moreover, when leadership capability frameworks are developed locally they have been found to psychologically align employees with the goals of their organisation and gain much needed buy-in towards a business mission and/or values (Short et al. 2011). Leadership capability frameworks can be developed from any number of competency-based definitions or superior leadership practices; that is to say, they can adopt a function-centred view of leadership, broken down into tasks or themes. Common items in capability frameworks include any number of predefined behaviours such as how leaders are expected to communicate, manage and organise work, motivate individuals, take decisions and show initiative (Burgoyne et al. 2004). Hirsh and Bevan (1988) analysed the content of 100 competence frameworks from forty organisations and found that:

- Leadership capability concerns managers in the context of their organisation and the job role.
- Leadership competencies are associated with superior job performance.
- Leadership competencies are described in terms of behaviour that can be observed on the job.

Organisational Context

The recurrent need to align workforce development projects with organisational context has attracted increased attention in the literature (Black and Earnest 2009) and specialised industries mentioned earlier, such as the AFAC, have developed leadership capability frameworks that attempt to meet the contextual and performance requirements of their own unique environment. Other industries, such as rail, have been mindful of this approach. We found, however, that the significance of context is an underexplored area of leadership and it rarely features on the HR strategy agenda beyond recognition of the need for skills in technical management. However, we believe that rail could learn from the AFAC leadership capability framework because it was created using a well-founded technique and it is transferable to many industrial sectors. The capability framework is divided into four stages:

- using an environmental scan to become familiar with the current situation
- analysing present-day knowledge and research about effective leadership practices
- identifying a range of existing frameworks used to develop leadership capability
- establishing criteria to assess and evaluate leadership programs.

Using a similar process to the AFAC, we will examine these four areas further, but considered them in a rail industry setting.

Environmental Scan

'Environmental scan' is a popular phrase in the repertoire of professional strategists and is used to describe an analytical process that identifies and interprets a range of internal and external influences on organisations. Sometimes expressed by the acronym SWOT, this process involves a detailed evaluation of known or perceived strengths, weaknesses, opportunities and threats – not only pertaining to the present, but also looking forward into the future. In this study the environmental scan involved a blend of activities such as reviewing the national and international literature on leadership development; examining over 170 organisational documents for clues on policy and practice; and talking with key managers located in a selection of rail organisations. Later, we reflected on the implications of this scan and identified at least ten findings that might shape the development of leadership capability in a rail context.

Leadership or Management

The literature on leadership development recognises that the recurring debate about separating leadership from management is relevant, and has been helpful in raising awareness of the different functions, but also concluded that the discussions have become exhausted and superseded by a more holistic and blended viewpoint. This consolidation has occurred because the increasing rate of change experienced in today's organisations is forcing managers, at all levels, to deal with many interwoven or complex leadership and/or management situations on a daily basis. Consequently, leadership capability has become an important variable in enhancing management performance and building organisational capacity. We recalled earlier in this chapter that routine management tasks rarely call for exceptional leadership skill in times of stability and can be achieved with prescriptive solutions drawn from tacit knowledge and experience; but in more complex and fast-changing or episodic situations, managers rely on a range of specific leadership capabilities to deal with new and unknown challenges, not only within their own skill set, but also among those in their work teams.

Commitment from the Top

Our findings revealed that senior executives in successful organisations are highly proactive in developing leadership skills of managers at all levels and this behaviour is the first stage in developing a sustainable leadership culture within the organisation.

The second stage in developing a leadership culture is to create a longer-term strategy that identifies and utilises an inclusive framework of leading practice, and is designed to fit the organisational need. Importantly, we recognised that a rail-specific leadership capability framework should be strategic and broad enough to accommodate the contextual needs of each rail organisation, irrespective of size or composition. We concluded that, when organisations have pre-arranged commitments to workforce development and financial investments tied up in successful leadership programs, they are unlikely to support an over-prescriptive solution for the sake of industry harmonisation.

Strategies to Consider the External and Internal Environments

Our study showed that organisations can no longer afford to operate in self-contained silos and the environmental scan reminded us that successful enterprises engage in complex processes of building 'strategic architecture' (Thompson 1995, p. 36) which align internal capabilities and resources in such a way that they deal effectively with the external challenges. Therefore, a strategy on leadership development should include building internal capabilities, or skill sets, that support the organisation's mission, goals and critical success factors. Furthermore, in successful rail organisations, the business strategy and planning around leadership development should utilise tools such as performance management, coaching, formal mentoring and other HRD learning techniques to identify good leadership practice within the internal environment and then project this capability to build relationships with external stakeholders such as customers.

Developing Leadership Capability at Different Levels and Contexts

Notwithstanding the trend in recent years to downplay traditional organisational hierarchies in favour of flatter and leaner structures, the study reflected a continuing division in the type of management training offered to different levels of manager. The use of MBA programs for executive development, diploma courses for middle managers and frontline management initiatives (FMI) for supervisory training were good examples of this ongoing segmentation. Therefore, creating a workforce development strategy that identifies the distinctive leadership skills and behaviours at each level of the organisation is still considered important. Not surprisingly, in highly stratified organisations such as the larger public sector rail enterprises, a traditional, triangular or hierarchical structure prevails and situates the critical mass of supervisory leaders at the front line (73 %), with fewer managers in middle (19 %) or higher level positions (8 %). More importantly the segmentation of leadership capability is also defined by the functional responsibilities at each level in addition to hierarchical seniority. This is defined as the capability to:

• lead oneself (all individuals)
• lead others (especially front-line managers)

- lead improvement and change (critical among middle managers)
- lead other leaders (essential for senior managers).

Using Emotional Intelligence to Draw Out the Best in Others

Within contemporary management theory emotional intelligence (EQ) has become a widely known and popular discourse. EQ is the ability to identify, assess and control the emotions of self, of others and of groups; but the human aspect of EQ among leaders is concerned with understanding individuals at a psychological level and what motivates them to perform at work. The literature argues that effective leaders are thought to have heightened levels of EQ and this awareness enables them to get the best out of colleagues (Barling et al. 2000; Wolff et al. 2002). However, this attribute need not necessarily be limited to the normal boss–subordinate relationship as EQ can be used in an upward or sideways direction or outside of the normal work setting. Our research concluded that traditional industries could make more use of EQ, especially when professional development activities are aimed at raising self-awareness. Frequently, employees in rail organisations are promoted to supervisory levels at the front line based on superior technical knowledge rather than their people management skills and without consideration of their perceived level of EQ. While these objective or technical attributes are important to achieving the task, having the capability to get this work completed through softer methods, such as consulting with people and considering their input, is increasingly seen as more significant in progressive organisations.

Exposing Leaders to Micro and Macro Contexts

We know from the literature that leadership is an all-embracing and urgent topic that currently affects organisations worldwide (Gould 2005; Mutte 2006), yet many of the challenges facing leaders are comparatively minor and enacted at a local level. Incorporating learning opportunities and experiences that are local as well as drawing on national or international contexts are both important when designing leadership development programs for sustainable outcomes. Furthermore, the ability to contemplate possible scenarios before they arise based on up-to-date knowledge and experience can enable managers to develop a wider range of problem-solving skills. As a result, more cross-fertilisation between like-minded industry organisations, through the widespread uptake of a unified capability framework, could provide an opportunity for better industry-based learning experiences within each organisation. Types of learning activities within a recognised capability framework could include but not be limited to intra-organisational work shadowing, mentoring, workplace exchanges, social and/or professional networking and collaborative leadership projects to provide rail industry experiences inside or outside of the current organisation setting.

Leadership Culture, Employee Motivation and Engagement

Our study found that organisational culture is not only influenced by senior executives, but also developed from a collective effort among local and work group leaders. The value of leadership capability soon permeates into the organisation's culture when the language of leadership is part of the business discourse. The rail organisations we studied used many HRM practices to deliver this discourse such as briefing systems, performance management, coaching projects, professional development tools, suggestion schemes and climate surveys. The influence of senior management cannot be overstated in ensuring the sustained success of leadership development projects. Active participation in leadership development programs by senior managers reinforces top-level engagement and contributes strongly to employee motivation. For leadership development to be sustained as a characteristic of the organisational culture, it must become an integral part of the business strategy and upheld within the personal values of everyone in key positions of influence.

Women in Leadership

The influence of women in modern workplaces has grown as they are increasingly included in leadership roles traditionally held by men as well as through their contribution to flexible working arrangements, part-time roles and parenting leave arrangements. However, the case study organisations in our research program has indicated that rail industry organisations have been slower to react to these changes, especially in technical areas and traditional jobs because of the dominance of men in these roles. Many of the strategies utilised by rail do not purposely discount women in the workplace, but rather the strategies are not designed purposely to rule women into the jobs. Therefore, different strategies and leadership styles will be required to become more inclusive of women, including attraction, retention and leadership development strategies. However, this finding may not apply to all levels. Contrary to the notion of a 'glass ceiling' for female managers, the number of women in leadership roles in six large Australian rail organisations during 2009–2010 showed a distribution inversely proportional to the managerial level. In other words, there were higher percentages of women in senior management roles (22 %) than at middle management (18 %) and the front-line levels (16 %).

The Socially Based Leader and Leadership Development

We know from this study that one exciting new topic in the field of leadership development is the concept of building social capital and sustainability within an organisation. Socially shaped leadership strategies deal with future proofing an organisation and influencing the nature of change management – to the extent that technological strategies are more likely to fail if the social dimensions are neglected. Social capital and sustainability help to facilitate the development of leadership skills in a wider cohort of people, enabling greater strength within the whole organisation. As such, the enterprise does not rely on a small number of key people to lead the organisation and talented juniors become ready to succeed in higher level roles. The success or failure of a successful leadership development program and ensuing culture of leadership is therefore dependent on senior managers both initiating and participating in training initiatives that build social sustainability, thereby role modelling good behaviour for junior managers. However, when senior managers do not participate in building social capital, their subordinates may become disheartened and perceive the indifference as a lack of authenticity in the leader's behaviour.

Evaluation and Continuous Improvement of Development Activities

Finally, we know from respondents in this study that building a successful leadership development program can be costly. At the time of our research (2009–2011), rail organisations were matching the national trend by investing significant amounts of the training budget on leadership development projects; however, industry reports also reflected on the universal lack of reliable and robust evaluation, especially the failure to identify the effectiveness and longer-term outcomes of funds invested. Without robust evaluation tools and continuous improvement processes, organisations are more likely to make poor investment decisions on an ongoing basis, which are expensive and time-consuming. Other studies show that when training investments cannot show a positive return, executives soon lose confidence and the credibility of the program is put at risk (Short 2008).

PESTE Analysis

In addition to the SWOT technique, a complementary analysis helped to illuminate the political, economic, social, technological and environmental issues within the rail setting (sometimes abbreviated as a PESTE analysis). For rail organisations the amalgam of these two interconnected considerations helped to define the meaning of leadership in Australia. Table 12.1 summarises a broad range of considerations presented as four themes. Taken together, these two analytical approaches clarify the rail environment and provide a platform on which the industry might think about leadership capabilities needed in the future.

Thinking About Leadership Practice

Earlier in this chapter we referred to Hirsh and Bevan (1988), who suggested that the main advantage of using leadership competency frameworks is to assist in the alignment of observable and contextually relevant behaviours with superior

Table 12.1 Summary of PESTE Analysis

Learning from the global literature	Accommodating the rail context	Leadership in Australia	Utility of capability frameworks
Understanding the new leadership agenda	An older workforce, soon to retire	Breaking down the interstate mindset	Competency vs. capability debates
The need for better qualified managers	Technical-centric style of management	Transition from British colony to global player	Mixed history of capability frameworks
Learning how to lead and manage change	Multiple levels of hierarchy	Culture and leading in an Australian way	Analysis of capability frameworks
Management vs. leadership skills	Lack of leadership education and training	Employment relations and engagement	Identifying key leadership capabilities
Transferability of leadership skills	Attraction and retention of talented leaders	Public vs. private sector mindsets	Defining relevant capability clusters
The impact of globalisation	Varying standards between organisations	Small business to multinational scope	Spotting emerging capabilities
Becoming a global manager	Dealing with gender inequity and diversity	The meaning of nation building	Letting go of expiring capabilities
Competition and performance improvement	Raising levels of literacy and numeracy	A shortage of leadership talent	Recognising the key meta-competencies

performance. Therefore, and keeping our study true to the rail context, we used a quantitative survey of practising managers to identify leadership behaviours that are not only relevant and current, but observable on the job. Using an online information collection process, we analysed over 680 comments in response to four questions about effective role modelling of leadership behaviours, not only of self, but also of each respondent's line manager. We segmented the results into the six leadership themes as shown in Table 12.2.

A notable characteristic of these six themes is that three capabilities focus on planning, organising and achieving results (some may call these hard management skills) while three capabilities focus on softer, people-related issues and how people should be treated (some may say the essence of leadership). In Australia, a country located in the South-East Asia/Pacific region, these complementary themes could easily become labelled the yin and yang of leadership – perhaps reflecting a single reality that, while leaders always have at least two choices in resolving complex issues, they are merely representing two sides of the coin. In our second stage analysis activity, we developed each of these six leadership practices further into six sub-practices, more accurately portraying observable leadership actions that can be evaluated at the team and individual levels. Taking the theme of 'strategy', Table 12.3 shows one example of how we developed this second-stage process into sub-themes using feedback from the respondents and findings from the literature review. Taken together a new framework of 36 leadership sub-practices provided the building blocks of rail leadership capability.

Table 12.2 Six themes of leadership practice

Theme	Leadership practice
Strategy	How the leader perceives external opportunities and translates this vision into plans where resources can be deployed to surpass the competition and survive
Organisation and planning	How the leader identifies, allocates and manages resources in a systematised and structured way to optimise their use
Results and performance	How leaders enhance operations and build a culture of continuous improvement by making timely decisions and formulating goals or objectives to achieve productive outcomes
Caring and compassion	How leaders recognise, show genuine concern, respect and support people to maintain health and wellbeing in the work environment
Authenticity and truthfulness	How the leader demonstrates honesty, integrity, resilience and professionalism, using internal policies and political awareness to maintain a truthful culture
Inclusivity and engagement	How the leader positively influences others, negotiates, shares information and uses feedback to engender the engagement of individuals and work teams

Table 12.3 Six sub-practices of the strategy theme

Strategy theme	Leadership sub-practice
Clear vision and purpose	Provides direction towards long-term aims and objectives
Takes intelligent risks	Evaluates the upsides and minimises the adverse effects of the downsides
Shows innovation	Develops ideas and fresh thinking on how to create new opportunities
Inspires others	Creates a sense of belief and inner passion towards the purpose
Sees the big picture	Relates shorter-term activities and issues to the broader context
Shows insight	Deduces the inner nature of things and relates it to experience or the situation

Meta-competencies

The use of qualitative questions in case study surveys not only allows respondents to express their deepest beliefs in relation to their lived experiences of the work environment, but also allows researchers to identify recurring patterns of common leadership behaviour, sometimes referred to as meta-competencies. The notion of meta-competency has been in existence for some time and is a term used to distinguish the higher-order abilities that are connected with being able to learn, adapt, anticipate and create (Brown 1993). The meta-competencies come into play when leaders deal with complexity and they represent 'the range of perceptions which exist about an individual manager's performance, as well as focusing on the irrationality and unpredictable personal feelings' (Brown 1993, p. 35). For these reasons, meta-competencies are not easy to define thematically and have blurred edges which allow them to blend easily with adjoining capabilities. This concept is represented by the diagram and hatched lines in Fig. 12.1.

Self-awareness – communication skills – relationship building					
Strategy	Organisation and planning	Results and performance	Caring and support	Authenticity and truthfulness	Inclusive and engaging

Fig. 12.1 Positioning of three meta-competencies

Fleming described the concept of meta-competence as 'that which allows someone to locate a particular competence within a larger framework of understanding' (1993, p. 6). In this study, our analysis of 20 leading leadership capability frameworks revealed three common themes of leadership behaviour that are better classified as meta-competencies, or capabilities: self-awareness, relationship building and communication skills. Taken together, we consider these three meta-competency areas to be over-arching attributes because they permeate through leadership behaviour and have primacy over the other six themes.

Self-Awareness, Relationship Building and Communication Skills

Over the last few decades, a new variation of leadership capability has emerged and been applied widely in professional roles where managers are empowered to create and define their own work roles; but in order to achieve this a much higher level of self-awareness is essential. Self-awareness is fast becoming regarded as a cornerstone of effective leadership and requires a wide range of cognitive processes to be used:

- focusing attention and evaluating current behaviour against intrinsic standards and values
- recognising one's personality characteristics, strengths, weaknesses, likes and dislikes
- having a clear perception of one's personality, emotions and self-esteem
- knowing how you relate to others and what makes you happy.

A heightened self-awareness can allow leaders to understand other people, evaluate how they are perceived as leaders and predict how they would respond in given situations. In this study, feedback received from the online survey allowed managers to engage briefly in a process of self-reflection and evaluate many aspects not only of their own sense of self, but also of their workplace leaders and other role models. Developing self-awareness is a prerequisite to building strong interpersonal relationships and communicating effectively, as well as developing empathy for others. Moreover, self-awareness is one of the attributes of emotional intelligence, together with social awareness, self-management and relationship competence (Goleman 2000). According to a report by Hayman (2010), self-awareness among Australian managers was at an all-time low and this deficiency was having a drastic impact on both individual and organisation performance. The report revealed a significant disconnect between managers' perceived and actual behaviours.

Today, in a network society, relationship-building skills have become a necessity for leaders at all levels and are considered essential to business success. Relationship building establishes and maintains an effective working partnership with a variety of internal and external stakeholders and fosters greater collaboration. Building relationships and reliable networks is essential to business success and overcoming setbacks in human interaction. Leaders can be much more effective when people and situations are fully understood. In an examination of over twenty established capability frameworks used in this study, building relationships was the top facet from a list of 30 leader capabilities and the second was communication skills. The significance of how, why, where and when a leader chooses to communicate has become embedded in leadership training programs. Some claim that it is the dominant competence of any capable leader, using statements like 'leaders communicate and communicators lead' (Rosswurm 2012, p. 1). Communication skills underpin effective leadership. Good leaders are mindful of how and what they communicate to other people in word and deed. Communication skills relate to a range of oral, written and non-verbal techniques leaders use to get their messages across.

Identification of Best Practice Leadership Models

In the study of management and leadership, theorists use concept models and frameworks to interpret and understand how organisational systems function. Later, some of these frameworks become popular operational tools and well-established in the marketplace by practitioners (Hedberg and Mumford 1975). In this study, rail organisations were trying to move to a new place and build a harmonised leadership culture, transitioning from the current uncoordinated practices to a new environment where leadership capacity could be developed for the whole sector. Table 12.4 shows the contrasting nature of these practices.

Earlier reports from the rail industry had indicated a need for harmonised practices and improved standards of leadership capability, and a desire to make the workplace more engaging to employees, at the same time attracting new external stakeholders such as younger workers (PricewaterhouseCoopers 2006; ARA 2008). In order for this change to happen, an acceptable model of best practice was needed to incorporate feedback from the industry, make use of existing resources in the external environment and embrace new learning from the literature. Importantly, the model would need to be straightforward and allow individual organisations room to manoeuvre within broad guidelines.

Figure 12.2 shows the rail leadership development framework and each section is described below. This model assembles the components of leadership capability mentioned previously in this chapter and presents the findings as schematic and memorable representations of each key stage, showing in a holistic way the interdependence between individual parts and the whole. Importantly, the framework assumes a level of organisational commitment, defined earlier as leadership principles, and these are explored further in the final section relating to assessment and evaluation.

Table 12.4 Changing practices

Old way	New way
Fragmented approach	Integrated and systematic approach
Reactive	Proactive and planned
Focus on management issues	Focus on building leadership talent
Short-term operational needs	Longer-term strategic needs
Intermittent levels of support	Top-level support driven by vision and values

Adapted from Svendsen (1998), p. 4

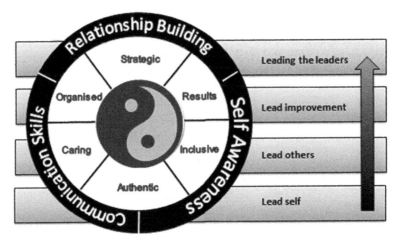

Fig. 12.2 Rail leadership capability framework (Used with permission of the Australian Government CRC for Rail Innovation 2011)

Step 1: Developing Meta-competencies

In practice, Step 1 would involve the leader individually assessing their current level of capability in the three areas of self-awareness, relationship building and communication skills. Later, this assessment of meta-competencies could be compared with a wide range of psychological assessment instruments and used as a learning needs analysis for professional development.

Step 2: Alignment with Six Leadership Capabilities

Earlier in this chapter we described a suite of six capabilities which are the leadership behaviours that are most relevant in the rail context. These six capabilities (strategic, organised, results-driven, caring, authentic and inclusive) represent broad areas of leadership attributes and behaviours as reported by rail managers. Additionally, we segmented each of the six areas further into six sub-descriptors making a total of 36 observable leadership capabilities to aid leadership development. Importantly, this step involves balancing the harder and softer skills needed in a modern workplace where traditional command and control techniques from a bygone era are no longer seen as acceptable.

Step 3: Tiers of Progressive Development in Relation to the Leadership Role

It is clear that leaders exist in all parts of an organisation; some leaders work remotely, some leaders are more senior than others, and other leaders work in teams. We aim to capture these different roles in the rail leadership framework and make provision for professional development in a range of operational contexts.

- Leading self: Considered the responsibility of leaders to maintain a sense of self-control and personal integrity. We suggest that self-development is a five-stage process: (1) assessing self, (2) identifying options for change, (3) planning for change, (4) taking action and (5) evaluating the outcomes.
- Leading others: Learning how to lead others is a complex interpersonal skill and comes more naturally to some managers than others. In Australia, the frontline management initiative (FMI) is the recognised and nationally available management training program, particularly suited to new leaders at supervisory or first-line management levels. In a similar way to other countries, the FMI program was developed in the mid-1990s to meet a national need, following extensive research that criticised the performance and effectiveness of Australian front-line managers (Karpin 1995). Earlier reports had indicated that the FLM program could be used not only as a national benchmark, but also as a personal development opportunity for managers to obtain formal qualifications. Charles Handy (1996), an international guru and author on management, claimed that the shifting power base in a global economy resided at the front line because this cohort was closest to the customers. The FLM program, and similar programs, was developed as a foundation or entry-level qualification, positioned at Level 4 on many national qualification frameworks, and created a pathway for progression to higher qualifications commensurate with increased levels of management and leadership responsibility.
- Leading improvement: In our research study, a detailed examination of management documents in five settings revealed that rail organisations frequently incorporate leadership development programs into their broader human resource strategies that aim to develop a culture of business improvement. Embedded within these policies were documents and systems that communicated the organisation's vision, values, overall mission and statements about critical success factors. Business improvement frameworks have become commonplace in modern organisations because they help to shape the mindset of leaders and systematically align the longer-term strategic aspirations with more immediate planning and operational requirements. Later, simplified versions of these frameworks are cascaded into the wider organisation through a variety of communication channels and used as part of a team and performance development system to manage change.

- Leading leaders: Perhaps the most striking development in leadership practice over the past 30 years has been the change in how leaders monitor and engage with juniors, peers and those in higher positions. Following the demise of rigid hierarchical reporting (and transfer to matrix management processes and multi-disciplinary project teams) today's leaders may no longer be the most senior people present in a situation. Junior or less experienced managers frequently find themselves managing and leading senior or more experienced colleagues. Exchanging power for team responsibility poses ethical challenges not only for senior leaders but also for juniors who lead the seniors and may be required to accomplish a given task without having control of much-needed resources. In these environments, workplace coaching, mentoring and the use of technology have played an important part in developing the three meta-competencies of leadership mentioned earlier because they are non-threatening and focused on improvement. An ultimate extension of this concept can be found in leadership communities of practice where leaders:

  - develop members' capabilities through the collaborative process of building and exchanging knowledge
  - rely on members to volunteer and become involved
  - share a passion and commitment, and identify with the group's expertise
  - remain in place as long as there is an interest in maintaining the group
  - do not focus solely on the accomplishment of a work project, do not have pre-determined milestones and are devoid of management hierarchy.

The term 'community of practice' was first introduced in the early 1990s and used within the framework of situated learning (Lave and Wenger 1991). Situated learning takes place in a specific context and is normally a social process where knowledge is co-constructed and developed by members of the community.

Assessment and Evaluation Considerations

Finally, no study on leadership development would be complete without due consideration to the important areas of assessment and evaluation. The term assessment is used widely in education and training projects to determine the validity and reliability of a learning process and also to consider how the training intervention has reflected current thinking and can be generalised to a wider setting. Assessment broadly includes all activities that educators and learners undertake to get diagnostic information that can be used to modify programs and ensure ongoing relevance (Black and William 1998). Organisations are unlikely to support development frameworks if the methods and application tools used are not fit for purpose, out of date or not transferable to local contexts.

We conclude that the sheer presence of an industry-wide leadership framework and range of application tools would provide a reliable assessment strategy for rail executives and managers to make decisions on developing their current and future leaders. As managers become increasingly mobile in their search for a new challenge, a national framework of leadership capability would enable a uniform assessment of leadership potential, enable meaningful skills recognition processes to occur and reduce the costly risk of failure. So, in very simple terms, the leadership framework could become an instrument of assessment. Day (2001) and Leskiw and Singh (2007) described these processes as leadership insurance and, according to Mabey (2005), capability frameworks provide a number of valuable assessment opportunities:

- informing and clarifying the imperatives of development
- guiding and directing, making sense and providing meaning for stakeholders
- inspiring the participants
- providing what is needed (validity) to the organisation and staff
- defining a framework or syllabus for education and training
- representing the current requirements
- enabling consistency and benchmarking
- providing equality of opportunity.

In this study, we have interpreted the term evaluation as a judgement about the worth of doing something and its positive impact on the stakeholders involved. For example, our research program was essentially a 2-year evaluation activity to ascertain the worth of deploying a harmonised approach to the development of leaders in an industry sector. We conclude that there is merit in adopting a leadership development framework to build leadership culture and industry capacity, and deal with pressing issues such as leadership succession and talent management. However, we also acknowledge the limitations of our research because program evaluation is a significant area of study and cannot be treated fully in one chapter, so we have contained our comments to the most pertinent findings.

In unison with hundreds of similar settings the world over, Australian rail organisations have not always used evaluation instruments effectively to measure the impact of leadership development. Calculating a return on investment, or identifying an acceptable cost benefit or return on expectation are slippery activities at the best of times and finding reliable metrics on the impact of leadership training programs has eluded HR professionals for decades. There are many reasons behind these difficulties, not least the challenge of attributing improvement to one particular program, especially when individuals are involved in multiple development activities at the same time. Adult learning activities fuse together in a holistic way; they have multiple facets and behavioural changes can happen much later, once the information has been processed and internally critiqued. Moreover, leadership development and the associated change in organisational culture takes a long time to work through the internal systems, but often requires a much longer period than the current incumbents are prepared to stay in their organisations. When leadership programs are introduced as part of a recovery-based initiative by a new chief executive officer (CEO) or senior HR manager, the program can soon fall into disarray when a CEO leaves and the next one takes over. In Australia the average tenure of CEOs is currently 4.4 years compared to 7.1 years in Europe (Johnson 2013; Short and Harris 2014).

Significance of Formative Evaluation

Tyler (1947) was an early pioneer in education reform who addressed the subject of program evaluation and suggested that learning should be evaluated in three stages: before, during and sometime after a learning event. 'Formative evaluation' describes an event that takes place before, or during, a learning activity and is distinguished from summative evaluation, which normally takes place at the end. While most commonly employed to monitor ongoing activity, formative evaluation can also be used in a pre-program context. For the purpose of this study we have used the term in the setting where senior executives might use a formative evaluation framework to judge the readiness of their organisation to embark on building a leadership development culture. Ten principles taken from the study could assist as a formative evaluation of the top-level commitment to host a single-industry harmonised leadership development program.

Ten Principles to Build a Rail Leadership Culture

1. Executives should show commitment to harmonising leadership development activities in the rail industry.
2. Improved quality, cost saving and added value underpins a harmonised leadership capability framework.
3. The framework should be used as a strategic guide to training providers, consultants and HR professionals.
4. Leadership development should be segmented to reflect different tiers and leadership contexts within the industry.
5. The framework should allow rail organisations to integrate their own components and preferences.
6. Leadership development should accommodate the context of the Australian rail industry.
7. Leadership development should be aligned and blended with national/academic qualification pathways.
8. There should be recognition of prior learning, experience and skills.
9. Leadership development should accommodate blended learning, utilising mentoring and coaching techniques.
10. Leadership development should be conducted largely on the job with input from education and training.

Earlier in this chapter we commented on the need for top-level commitment in resourcing and sustaining a rail leadership culture. However, we acknowledge that putting these principles into practice may not lead directly or immediately to excellence in leadership, not are these criteria intended to replace other forms of evaluation.

Conclusions

The challenges for organisations in implementing ideas from research such as those presented in this chapter are many, especially when current practices are already well-entrenched. Problems such as time to consider how and what to change and who is going to undertake these tasks are very real considerations. As we outlined at the beginning of this chapter, Australian rail organisations have realised that developing leadership capability frameworks across the industry is one way of addressing the challenges of leading contemporary workforces that operate in fixed yet traditional structures. In reality, while the task of changing current leadership practice may appear monumental, small but incremental changes are possible if some of the sections presented in this chapter are considered as stand-alone ideas in a leadership capability strategy within individual organisations. Therefore we have outlined a range of these key strategies and practices in contemporary leadership capability within the context of Australian rail organisations, based on the findings of a national research study into leadership and management development. However, while suggesting that such strategies and practices need to be contextually relevant and developed in accordance with local needs and resources, we also conclude that they can be applied and adapted across a range of organisations in diverse settings, since leadership and workforce development have been established as fundamental to best practice in promoting effective organisational culture, strategy and performance at a global level. The lesson of best practice from this research in Australian rail industry organisations is the development of the high-level leadership capability framework as a guiding structure that can be used in many settings. The framework goes some way to addressing the perplexing questions of who, what, when, how and why leadership practice can or will be changed at the local level and can be adapted as global conditions change.

References

Ashkanasy, N. M., & Falkus, S. (1997). The Australian enigma. In R. M. House (Ed.), *Cultures, leadership and organizations: GLOBE – country anthologies* (pp. 299–334). Thousand Oaks: Sage.

Australasian Fire Authorities Council. (2007). *Leadership capability framework*. East Melbourne: Australasian Fire Authorities Council.

Australasian Railway Association. (2008). *A rail revolution: Future capability identification and skill development for the Australian rail industry*. Canberra: Australasian Railway Association.

Barling, J., Slater, F., & Kelloway, E. K. (2000). Transformational leadership and emotional intelligence: An exploratory study. *Leadership & Organization Development Journal, 21*(3), 157–161.

Bass, B. M. (1990). *Bass and Stogdill's handbook of leadership: Theory, research and managerial applications*. New York: Free Press.

Black, A. M., & Earnest, G. W. (2009). Measuring the outcomes of leadership development programs. *Journal of Leadership and Organisational Studies, 16*(2), 84–196.

Black, P., & William, D. (1998). Inside the black box: Raising standards through classroom assessment. *Phi Delta Kappan, 80*(2), 139–148.

Boxall, P., & Purcell, J. (2003). *Strategy and human resource management*. Basingstoke: Palgrave Macmillan.

Boyatziz, R. E., Leonard, D., Rhee, K., & Wheeler, J. V. (1996). Competencies can be developed but not the way we thought. *Capability, 2*(2), 25–41.

Brown, R. B. (1993). Meta-competence: A recipe for reframing the competence debate. *Personnel Review, 22*(6), 25–36.

Bullock, A., Stallybrass, O., & Trombley, S. (2000). *The Fontana dictionary of modern thought*. London: Fontana.

Burgoyne, J., Hirsh, W., & Williams, S. (2004). *The development of management and leadership capability and its contribution to performance: The evidence, the prospects and the research needed* (DfES research report 560). London: Department for Education and Skills.

Buus, I. (2006). The evolution of leadership development: Challenges and best practice. *Industry and Commercial Training, 37*(4), 185–188.

Cacioppe, R. (1998). An integrated model and approach for the design of effective leadership development programs. *Leadership and Organizational Development Journal, 19*(1), 44–53.

Chartered Institute of Personnel and Development. (2009). *Building leadership capability for change: An interview with Gary Hamel*. CIPD podcast episode 32. http://www.cipd.co.uk/podcasts/_articles/garyhamel.htm?view=transcript. Accessed 9 July 2009.

Dalglish, C., & Evans, P. (2007). *Leadership in the Australian context: Case studies in leadership*. Prahran: Tilde University Press.

Day, D. V. (2001). Leadership development: A review of context. *Leadership Quarterly, 11*(4), 581–613.

Fleming, D. (1993). The concept of meta-competence. *Competence Assessment, 22*, 6–9.

Goleman, D. (2000). Leadership that gets results. *Harvard Business Review, 78*(2), 78–90.

Gould, C. (2005). Change dominates global HR agenda. *Wordlink, 15*, 1–2.

Graen, G. B., & Uhl-Bien, M. (1995). Relationship-based approach to leadership: Development of leader–member exchange (LMX) theory of leadership over 25 years. Applying a multi-level multi-domain perspective. *Leadership Quarterly, 6*(2), 219–247.

Green, R. (2009). *Management matters in Australia*. Canberra: Department of Innovation, Industry, Science and Research.

Handy, C. (1996). *Beyond certainty: The changing worlds of organizations*. Boston: Harvard Business School Press.

Hayman, P. (2010). Two thirds of Australian managers have low self-awareness. *Dynamic Business*. http://www.dynamicbusiness.com.au/hr-and-staff/manager-self-awareness-1958.html. Accessed 16 Jan 2011.

Hedberg, B., & Mumford, E. (1975). The design of computer systems: Man's visions as an integral part of the system design process. In E. Mumford & H. Sackman (Eds.), *Human choice and computers* (pp. 31–50). Amsterdam: North-Holland.

Higgs, M. (2003). How can we make sense of leadership in the 21st century? *Leadership and Organisational Development Journal, 24*(5), 273–284.

Hirsh, W., & Bevan, S. (1988). *What makes a manager? In search of a language for management skills* (Institute of manpower studies report 144). Brighton: Institute of Manpower Studies.

Infographics. (2011). Leadership at home and abroad. *People Management*, October, 42–44.

Innovation and Business Skills Australia (IBSA). (2011). *Karpin report revisited: Leadership and management challenges in Australia*. East Melbourne: Innovation and Business Skills Australia.

Johnson, J. (2013). Australia's CEO turnover rate surges. *Leaders in Leadership*. http://www.johnson-executive.com/_blog/blog/post/Australias_CEO_turnover_rate_surge. Accessed 23 May 2013.

Karpin, D. (1995). *Enterprising nation: Renewing Australia's managers to meet the challenges of the Asia-Pacific century. Report of the Industry Task Force on Leadership and Management Skills*. Canberra: AGPS.

Lave, J., & Wenger, E. (1991). *Situated learning: Legitimate peripheral participation*. Cambridge: Cambridge University Press.

Leskiw, S.-L., & Singh, P. (2007). Leadership development: Learning from best practices. *Leadership and Organization Development Journal, 28*(5), 444–464.

Mabey, C. (2005). *Management development works: The evidence.* London: Chartered Management Institute.

Mutte, J. L. (2006). Towards a global HR management model. *Worldlink, 16,* 6–7.

Oakland, J. S. (2004). *Oakland on quality management.* Oxford: Elsevier.

PricewaterhouseCoopers. (2006). *The changing face of rail: A journey to the employer of choice.* Canberra: Australasian Railway Association.

Robbins, S., Bergman, R., & Stagg, I. (1997). *Management.* New York: Prentice Hall.

Rosswurm, G. (2012). Leaders communicate and communicators lead. Smartblog on leadership. http://smartblogs.com/leadership/2012/07/27/leaders-communicate-and-communicators-lead/. Accessed 1 Oct 2012.

Short, T.W. (2008). *Strategic alignment and learning in human resource development: A hermeneutic exploration.* Unpublished Ph.D. thesis, University of South Australia, Adelaide.

Short, T., & Harris, R. (2014). The future of workforce development: Old wine in new bottles. In R. Harris & T. Short (Eds.), *Workforce development: Perspectives and issues* (pp. 351–372). Singapore: Springer.

Short, T. W., Piip, J. K., Stehlik, T., & Becker, K. (2011). *A capability framework for rail leadership and management development* (Research report P4.104). Brisbane: CRC for Rail Innovation.

Svendsen, A. (1998). *The stakeholder strategy: Profiting from collaborative business relationships.* San Francisco: Berrett-Koehlert.

Thompson, J. L. (1995). *Strategy in action.* London: Chapman & Hall.

Tyler, R. W. (1947). *Basic principles of curriculum and instruction.* Chicago: University of Chicago Press.

Wolff, S. B., Pescosolido, A. T., & Druskat, V. U. (2002). Emotional intelligence as the basis of leadership emergence in self-managing teams. *Leadership Quarterly, 13*(5), 505–522.

Yeung, A. K., & Ready, D. A. (1995). Developing leadership capabilities of global corporations: A comparative study of eight nations. *Human Resource Management, 34*(4), 529–547.

Chapter 13
Workplace Coaching: Context and Challenge

Roslyn Cameron

Abstract Coaching is an emerging profession and human resource development intervention that draws upon an array of theoretical foundations, approaches and contexts; consequently defining the practical application of coaching techniques is not a straightforward exercise. Attracting, developing and retaining quality employees is a major issue for organisations who are seeking to increase organisational performance and maintain competitiveness. Coaching is one strategy that can assist organisations to retain talented people who play critical roles. This chapter looks at the development and deployment of coaching in one industry sector where the need to facilitate performance, learning and improvement are ever-present in an environment of rapid and constant change. We discover how coaching can benefit individuals and organisations; how organisations can use coaching to develop leaders, stimulate change and align human resource development interventions to strategic organisational goals; how to increase the professionalisation of coaching to safeguard any risk to participants; and approaches to evaluating the effectiveness of coaching.

Introduction

Coaching is an increasingly popular intervention for the development of skilled managers, effective leaders and teams and sustainable organisations. 'Managerial coaching is viewed as a potential way to improve learning processes within organizations, and thus improving competitive advantage' (Hagen and Aguilar 2012, p. 366). A key component of the relentless drive for competitive advantage is the need to be flexible, responsive and adaptable to market forces and the

R. Cameron (✉)
School of Management, Curtin Business School, Curtin University, Bentley, Australia
e-mail: r.cameron@cqu.edu.au

T. Short and R. Harris (eds.), *Workforce Development: Strategies and Practices*,
DOI 10.1007/978-981-287-068-1_13, © Springer Science+Business Media Singapore 2014

changes that need to be undertaken to achieve this. Driving change within organisations requires effective leadership, change champions, and effective change management practices and strategies. Coaching is fast becoming part of the organisational arsenal to achieve the change required for organisational competitiveness and sustainability. Nonetheless, these efforts can be stymied by a 'strong immunity to change' (Berg and Karlsen 2012, p. 177), which has seen traditional forms of management and leadership development producing poor results. According to Berg and Karlsen (2012) these ineffectual outcomes are due to several factors including training founded on simple and basic theoretical approaches and associated models that are incompatible with the complexity of leadership contexts; the gap between theoretical knowledge and the application of this knowledge; and issues with individuals' abilities to enact behavioural change. '[T]he individual's self-efficacy with regard to his or her own capacity to change may be too little, at the same time the temptation to continue as usual (old behavioural patterns) is too big' (Berg and Karlsen 2012, p. 177).

So what can organisations do to counter these tendencies within the more traditional approaches to management and leadership development? Recent large-scale research has shown that coaching is increasingly being seen as an approach that can counter these issues. It goes beyond what Atkinson referred to as 'mass baptism, sheep dips and big training events' (2012, p. 21). A key function of coaching is 'to provide a basis for changing the mindset and the behavior' (Berg and Karlsen 2012, p. 194). As Atkinson asserted, 'Coaching focuses upon moving well beyond the transfer from "simple" to "complex" learning which can lie at the very heart of "attitudinal change"' (2012, p. 20). Berg and Karlsen investigated how coaching can influence management development and the applied use of leadership tools:

> One of the main findings is that coaching is a helpful training process to learn about the manager's toolbox and to develop new management behavior. Furthermore, data revealed that the management training should be based on the specific work challenges that the participants experience at their workplace. Based on a variety of work challenges, the participants highlighted the following tools as most important: emotional intelligence, empowerment, self-management, signature-strengths, and positive emotions. (2012, p. 177)

Tailoring the coaching interventions and associated tools to authentic work challenges that participants can apply through their daily work activities would seem to be one of the most effective approaches.

In this chapter I look at the practical side of planning coaching within organisational contexts before briefly presenting a case study of the development of a coaching framework for the Australian rail industry. I will present the context, benefits and innovative practices before concluding with some of the key challenges for those wishing to implement and develop workplace coaching.

Launching a Coaching Program: Organisational Challenges and Strategies

As the Association for Coaching has noted, 'The primary objective of Coaching from the perspective of the purchaser of coaching is to develop the individual's business performance' (2004, p. 3). So what do organisations need to consider when first deciding upon coaching as an organisational development intervention?

There are several foundational requirements before a coaching program can be contemplated and these include the levels of commitment to coaching required from the organisation and its senior management. In addition to this the purposes and aims of the intended coaching need to align with the overall strategic goals of the organisation. As with many HR interventions strong strategic positioning of the planned intervention is important from the outset, with associated measures for evaluating the effectiveness and return on investment. The support of senior executives who have access to organisational resources and decision-making processes is paramount. Research undertaken by Alagaraja (2013) provided strong evidence for the ability of strategic human resource development (SHRD) to mobilise organisational alignment. She identified some critical factors:

> Internal stakeholder orientation towards SHRD and the role of human resource development (HRD) in facilitating the implementation were also identified as critical factors. Organizational alignment emerged as an implicit consequence, while patterns of misalignment created barriers towards achieving the full benefits of SHRD. Furthermore, HRD displayed a high level of resourcefulness to become a strategic asset in the organization. I argue that the relevance and power of HRD lie in its ability to engage and respond to stakeholder expectations and involvement in organization change efforts. (Alagaraja 2013, p. 74)

Coaching and HRD are therefore said to be key strategies for organisational change and its management. Wilson (2011), p. 410 has designed a very practical framework for developing what she refers to as a coaching culture and part of this framework is a set of questions organisations first need to address in what she has termed the organisational health check:

- What is already in place?
- What needs to be addressed?
- Are focus groups/surveys/meetings required?
- What resources are available?
- What is already looked after through existing programs?
- Which programs should be kept and which could be replaced by a coaching program?
- What types of interventions will suit?

The organisational health check is one of ten key points in Wilson's (2011) 'ten point plan' for developing a coaching culture. Several of these questions in the organisational health check suggest that the proposed coaching intervention could be integrated and embedded into existing programs and/or broader organisational development programs. 'Coaching is not an isolated phenomenon, but a viable, effective management performance improvement technique that can complement and enhance other improvement programs such as career planning and performance feedback' (Zeus and Skiffington 2000, p. 103).

Coaching is typically embedded in leadership identification and development activities and in long-term change management strategies. This makes for a much more effective and organisation-wide use of the intervention where the impacts on cultural change will be best felt. 'Working through learning and development strategies, most organisations can acquire the internal capability to drive change and make learning and coaching the sustainable culture' (Atkinson 2012 p. 22).

Another crucial point in the ten point plan is the identification of key organisational stakeholders. These stakeholders are defined as 'people who are affected by, or have an interest in, the coaching program' (Wilson 2011, p. 410). These stakeholders will of course vary in relation to the type and structure of an organisation; nonetheless the key stakeholders are typified as the influencers, approvers, users and shapers. The influencers are usually members of the governing board of directors, human resource or organisational development managers/directors and heads of various organisational departments. The approvers are typically the chief executive officers, directors of finance and departmental heads. The users are those members of the organisation that are closer to the frontline management of the organisation's operations and include managers, team leaders and account managers. Lastly, the shapers are likely to be the managers of human resource functions related to learning and development, heads of HR functions and departmental heads (Wilson 2011). The logical step following this identification process becomes yet another of the points in the ten point plan: creating buy-in from these key stakeholders. This process is not without its own challenges.

As the process progresses, planning the coaching program becomes crucial and part of that planning involves decisions about what and how to measure the outcomes and benefits of such an intervention, piloting the program and the process of continuous evaluation and improvement begins. Once these key planning milestones have been accomplished it is time to implement the coaching program.

As Bates noted, 'defining, conceptualizing, and measuring performance are complex and problematic tasks' (1999, p. 61). As a result he has developed a set of practical steps to guide those tasked with developing measures to evaluate coaching:

- chart and evaluate how performance has already been used and measured
- examine the use of performance measures at different levels of analysis and their interrelationships
- investigate issues surrounding the multidimensionality of performance and the use of multiple or composite measures
- conduct construct validation of performance measures
- use utility approaches to performance measurement
- finally, develop a situational framework for the analysis and application of appropriate performance measures and measurement processes (Bates 1999, pp. 61–62).

I now turn to a case study of an industry that invested in research into coaching and mentoring as part of a broader workforce development research and development program funded jointly by the Australian government and the Australian rail industry over a 7-year period. The case highlights some of the key issues and challenges organisations and industry sectors face when first deciding upon the large investment coaching programs present.

Coaching in the Australian Rail Industry

The Cooperative Research Centres (CRC) program is an Australian government initiative that supports end-user driven research collaborations to address major challenges facing Australia. The aim of the CRC program is to support 'end user driven research partnerships between publicly funded researchers and end users to address clearly articulated major challenges that require medium to long term collaborative efforts' (Allen Consulting Group 2012, p. 1). The CRC for Rail Innovation was established in 2007 for a 7-year period to coordinate and manage research projects into issues that were present in the Australian rail sector. This has involved the strategic participation of various key companies from within the rail industry in the Australasian region, as well as seven universities across Australia (CRC for Rail Innovation n.d.). The CRC for Rail Innovation research program has invested AUD $100 m in rail research across six research themes, one of these themes being workforce development. The CRC for Rail Innovation funded a workforce development project on mentoring and coaching and the key findings and results from the coaching component of this project form the basis of the case study to be presented here. To this end in this chapter I aim to present industry-funded and applied research on the contexts and challenges of undertaking a coaching program in contemporary organisational settings.

The Context and the Challenges

Alagaraja referred to the importance of the 'operating environment (global market, industry space) and firm-specific factors (e.g. demographics and new leadership)' (2013, p. 74) in the ability of an organisation to accelerate the adoption of strategic human resource development initiatives. The external and internal environment of the Australian rail industry has played a significant role in determining many workforce development initiatives for that industry.

The Australian rail industry, like many other industries in industrialised western nations, has been facing an array of workforce challenges and risks stemming from large demographic challenges, the effects of globalised economies and supply chains, advances in technology and the need to remain competitive and sustainable in an environment characterised by constant change, adaption and renewal. In addition to this major players within the rail industry have in recent times been subjected to a series of restructuring and ownership/governance/funding changes made even more complicated by state and federal political and policy changes and impacts from economic downturns, resource commodity booms and commodity price fluctuations. During this time the Australian government also announced substantial investment in rail infrastructure projects which coincided with private investment in large rail infrastructure projects associated with the resources boom. All in all the environmental factors external to rail organisations, or what Alagaraja referred to as the operating environment, have had a significant impact on the workforce issues within the sector.

Internal factors impacting the sector include key workforce risks as outlined in research commissioned for the sector. The Australian Department of Education, Employment and Workplace Relations (DEEWR) funded research for the Australasian Railway Association (ARA) which resulted in the report, *A Rail Revolution* (ARA 2008). The report analysed the rail workforce and developed a set of six key workforce risks facing the industry. One of these workforce risks specifically focused upon the need for major cultural change. The following two points detail that risk:

- Leadership role in change. Leadership in the industry will be essential to change the industry for the future.
- Employees participating in change. The current culture within rail will restrict the industry's ability to successfully address these workforce risks (ARA 2008, p. 14).

To counter the six identified key workforce risks the report proposed a set of strategies, the first being to position the culture of rail for the future. The report made four recommendations under this strategy:

1. Create an externally focused benchmarking culture around people practices to drive industry performance of objective measures to ensure long-term sustainability of the industry.
2. Establish a high-performance culture, incorporating performance-based rewards as a brand element within the industry and market this brand to the internal and external labour markets to attract and retain high-performing workers and maximise productivity within the current workforce.
3. Investigate strategies to improve employee engagement within the industry, through a range of strategies including employees, via their managers and companies as a whole, to maximise retention and productivity.
4. Create cultural change at company and industry-wide levels (e.g. via communication, involvement, participation) to ensure openness to change (not resistant) to create the long-term sustainability of the industry (ARA 2008, p. 16).

The context and workforce challenges facing the Australian rail industry were and are complex, and innovative strategies were needed to enable the industry to meet these challenges. The *Rail Revolution* report became a foundational piece of research that informed the development of many of the workforce development projects that were funded through the CRC for Rail Innovation from 2009 to 2014. As a result the stated aims of the mentoring and coaching research project were:

- to investigate innovative models and practices in relation to mentoring and coaching so as to best inform the development of a contextualised national mentoring and coaching framework for rail
- to produce rail-relevant mentoring and coaching research deliverables that can be easily implemented and integrated into existing rail HR structures.

The focus of this case study is the coaching component of this research (refer to Chap. 7 for details on workplace mentoring). The coaching component of the project involved a combination of quantitative and qualitative data collection. The first stage of the research involved an online survey of members of the ARA followed by two in-depth case studies of two major rail organisations in two different states. The latter involved a series of semi-structured interviews with rail coachees, internal rail coaches and managers, and external coaches used by the two organisations.

Key findings from the research synthesised the benefits of coaching derived from both the quantitative and qualitative data and the review of existing literature and research. These findings are summarised in Table 13.1 under the subheadings of organisational benefits and benefits to individuals.

In addition to the benefits summarised in Table 13.1 the online survey found that of those respondents to the survey (64 rail organisations) 71 % used coaching in the last 5 years and 79 % intended using coaching in the next 3 years. The top three reasons for using coaching were succession planning, employee retention and increased productivity, and the top three levels targeted for coaching were middle management, first line managers and senior management. A significant finding was the use of internal and external coaches. Four per cent of the rail organisations used only external coaches, 33 % used only internal coaches and 63 % used a combination of both internal and external coaches. The top three reasons for using external coaches were for management development, executive coaching, and coaching for a particular skill or need (Short and Cameron 2013, p. 86).

The semi-structured interviews conducted across the two participating organisations revealed several important themes: the importance of coaching frameworks and models, the importance of the coaching relationship, the strengths and benefits of both external coaches and internal coaching, challenges of calculating return on investment, and the relationship between coaching and leadership. A coachee from one of the organisations provided the following perspective on how they applied what they had learnt from their coaching experience to change their behaviour towards the managers they lead:

> Something I learnt through having a coach was thinking about that in terms of part of your role as a leader, is around coaching your managers, and I guess that point around facilitating rather than directing, facilitating them through issues that they're resolving, trying not to go in and say 'Well this is how you solve it'. It's more like getting them to, again, build their confidence and skill set up. So how do you go about it? I guess in the first place it's starting to put a common language around it, creating expectation.

Table 13.1 Benefits of coaching

Empirical data and findings of this study	Literature and published research
Online survey	
Organisational benefits:	*Organisational benefits:*
Succession planning	Improved performance
Employee retention	Building of employee engagement
Increased productivity	Executive coaching: improved senior leadership
Management development	Fostering collaboration and loyalty
Executive coaching	Leadership development
Coaching for a particular skill or need	Talent retention
More strategic perspective taken	Reduction in turnover
Better integration of employees into new jobs	Increased transfer of learning
	Improved managerial skills and overall managerial capability
	Development of a coaching culture
Individual benefits:	*Individual benefits:*
Performance issues addressed	Increased self-esteem
Raised self-awareness	Reduces stress
Behavioural issues addressed	Improved workplace communication
	Work–life balance
	Increased job satisfaction
	Career development
	Improved leadership skills
	Increased emotional intelligence
	Increased motivation
	Clarity and focus
	Behaviour change
	Increased emotional intelligence
Semi-structured interviews	
Organisational benefits:	
Leadership development	
Benefits through the employment cycle: *attracting, recruiting and selection of new recruits; on-boarding of new recruits; performance management; career development; succession planning/leadership development; management skills development; transition to retirement*	
Increased buy-in for achievement of organisational goals	
Increased accountability	
Increased engagement with organisational objectives	
Better managed projects	
Individual benefits:	
Improved interpersonal skills	
Team-building skills	
Reduced workplace conflicts	
Direction and focus	
Balancing work and life	
Reduced stress	
Better time management	
Increased self-awareness	
Increased managerial competency	

Source: Short and Cameron (2013), p. 61

A manager from the same organisation used coaching to address leadership issues in a particular area:

> I had an assumption that there were leadership issues in a particular area, and that the adverse action claims and the bullying claims, all of those things were driven by leadership issues and I needed someone with a strong coaching background and a strong leadership understanding, and she's been working with that group for 18 months and the success rate is fantastic.

A key HR manager in the other organisation described how influential a couple of senior appointments were in focusing upon organisational change and the subsequent investment in leadership development, which had coaching as a central component:

> We had a couple of senior appointments, first with [name 1] and then with two senior managers after that, [name 2 and name 3], and [name 3] particularly came in with an agenda to change the business that he was taking over to compete with the competitive, with the private sector. That was within the rail construction side and infrastructure maintenance side, but he saw that to do that the first thing you needed was leadership. So he came in and he wanted leadership, so it gave us a big opportunity to start building where we had some ... This gave us our first better chance to look at a development front, and looked at what [name 3] had previously done at [company 1], and worked with him and a provider to identify a development program that would basically help change the behaviours of the people that we already had there, knowing that they'd been selectively bred for decades to look at things without behaviours in there, without leadership in there, and we had to break the old norms.

As a result of the overall research the rail industry was supplied with a set of deliverables and these included the research reports generated from the research as well as more practical deliverables such as coaching guidelines and a website. The coaching guidelines were structured around three key sections, strategy, development and implementation, as displayed in Fig. 13.1.

A key component of the coaching guidelines was an emphasis on adhering to ethical codes of conduct and professional standards. The coaching profession has identified the need to increase the professionalisation of coaching to safeguard any risk to participants and clients. Coaching as a profession has developed significantly in the last decade, with a number of international and national bodies emerging as leading bodies in the profession. Most notable is the International Coaching Federation. Organisations that are contemplating the use of coaching need to safeguard themselves on two levels: in the procurement and quality assurance of external coaches, and in the development of internal codes of conduct for internal coaches. The standards for coaching in organisations developed in Australia (Standards Australia 2011) identify the following key ethical considerations:

- confidentiality
- conflicts of interest
- multiple relationships
- record keeping (confidential and secure)
- contracting (terms and conditions)
- integrity (acting honestly and fairly in practice)

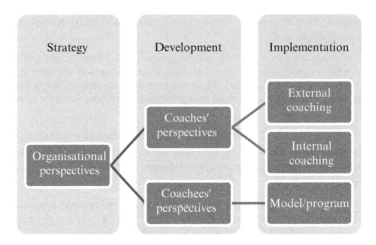

Fig. 13.1 Structure of coaching guidelines (Source: Short and Cameron 2013, p. 5)

- competence of the coach
- supervision and ongoing professional development
- professional responsibility to the coachee
- referrals
- termination
- self-management
- professional indemnity and public liability insurance.

Innovative Strategies and Future Challenges

The Role of Coaching in Strategic HRD

Rock and Donde (2008) presented what they claimed to be a new way of using coaching to drive wide-scale organisational change. Key to this approach is the utility of internal coaches, integrating coaching into the broader organisational systems for people, performance and culture, and aligning models of coaching to organisational strategy. Rock and Donde found that:

> training leaders to be internal coaches is a more scalable, sustainable and robust approach to driving change and improving performance than hiring external coaches. Early indicators are showing significant increases in retention, engagement, productivity and performance, as well as ROI (17X), across organisations that have developed internal coaching. (2008, p. 75)

One of the rail organisations had embedded coaching within several leadership initiatives that were being rolled out across several business units. Not only do organisation-wide strategies enhance talent acquisition, development and retention

(Alagaraja 2013), they also ensure greater levels of shared meaning across the organisation. The development of internal coaching capacity is essential for developing a coaching culture:

> Internal coaching works. It is becoming the initiative of choice in organisations undergoing change, and looking to embed a coaching culture. Of importance is how the internal coaching initiative is designed, packaged and implemented, ensuring alignment with the organisation's vision and longer term strategy. (Rock and Donde 2008, p. 78)

Thinking strategically and embedding coaching within strategic human resource development (SHRD) allows an organisation to implement innovative changes throughout the organisation more quickly and effectively. This allows for a process that devolves the responsibility and implementation throughout the organisation, which can lead to greater movement towards strategic change. Alagaraja's research on the role of SHRD in facilitating strategic alignment pointed to profound transformational change:

> SHRD implementation contributed to the integration of goals for employees, departments and the organization. By developing shared partnerships with other members of the senior leadership team, the HRD function relied on internal stakeholders to deliver and support key SHRD practices. These formative partnerships increased HRD visibility and actively shaped SHRD implementation as an emergent process involving managers outside HRD and HRM. (Alagaraja 2013, p. 92)

Evaluating the Effectiveness and Impact of Coaching

> Billions of dollars are spent annually on programs to develop organizational leaders, yet the effectiveness of these programs is poorly understood. (Goldman et al. 2013, p. 63).

Measuring the impact and effectiveness of coaching remains one of the main challenges facing organisations and human resource practitioners. Results from a survey conducted by the Association of Coaching a decade ago found little evidence of evaluation approaches to coaching effectiveness: 'It appears that there is little genuine measurement of the benefits of coaching currently within organisations. The survey highlights the lack of measurement organisations currently have for measuring the benefits of coaching' (2004, p. 1). This survey found that the dominant evaluation methods were feedback from the coachee followed by feedback from the coachee's manager. Atkinson reflected back and made the interesting point that:

> in the early days, coaching was seen purely as an 'unstructured', 'getting to know you' and 'touchy feely' intervention. Now, with robust coaching methods, that is a relic in the past. Where coaching is tangible and delivers ROI is where it is taken seriously by businesses. Coaches who work on 'hard' as well as 'soft' issues will be more valued in most business communities. (2012, p. 22)

Bates advocated a return on investment approach to evaluating coaching: 'In measuring performance, the criteria are the dependent variables, behaviours, or outcomes used to represent the larger performance domain. Choosing criteria involves answering the question of what performance to measure for a given purpose and also how to measure it' (1999, p. 50). Nonetheless, Bates admitted that this is not an easy task: 'The availability of good measures assumes that particular attributes of interest can be identified and assessed. However, the attributes like performance can sometimes be difficult to quantify because of their complexity and magnitude' (1999, p. 51).

As I mentioned earlier in this chapter, coaching goes beyond the one-off classroom-based training event and involves more experiential approaches. Human resource practitioners are being challenged as to how to evaluate these interventions sufficiently in order to capture the complexity of outcomes (beyond individual and easily measurable learning outcomes) that emerge from contemporary coaching interventions. When peer and team coaching is added to the mix then the task of measuring outcomes and effectiveness becomes even more complex and challenging. Traditional approaches to training evaluation are incompatible with contemporary approaches to coaching and leadership development, as Ely et al. described:

> the more conventional training approach of waiting until the end of coaching to conduct an evaluation fails to reflect the dynamic and organic nature of the coaching intervention which changes over time in response to the client's successes and setbacks. Additionally, coaching interventions tend to be longer than traditional organizational training and span across multiple months. (2010, p. 588)

Ely et al. went on to distinguish between traditional leadership development and coaching in four ways:

> Leadership coaching differs from traditional leadership development in four ways: (a) leadership coaching focuses on the needs of the individual client as well as the client's organization and the unique characteristics each brings, (b) leadership coaching requires coaches to have unique skill sets, (c) leadership coaching places a premium on the client–coach relationship, and (d) leadership coaching demands process flexibility to achieve desired results. These four (client, coach, client–coach relationship, and coaching process) provide a foundation for understanding the unique nature of leadership coaching, the resulting framework, and implications for its evaluation. (2010, p. 586)

Watkins et al. (2011) advocated a theory of change approach to evaluating executive coaching. Key to this approach is the identification of critical incidents of new behaviour and the examination of resulting changes that then occur at both the individual and organisation level. This approach to evaluation 'relies on repositioning management learning in leadership development programs and incorporates theories of action, workplace, and organizational learning' (Watkins et al. 2011, p. 208). This is a deviation from the traditional approaches to evaluating training interventions such as the new forms of experiential leadership development programs:

> As executive leadership development programs become more informal and experiential, traditional evaluation models of learning transfer based on fixed objectives do not capture emerging program outcomes. What is needed is a more robust approach for increasingly complex environments that looks at open objectives and changes that have occurred that affect both the individual and the organization. (Watkins et al. 2011, p. 208)

Ely et al. advocated a systematic and integrated framework for evaluating coaching that 'includes formative evaluations of the client, coach, client–coach relationship, and coaching process, as well as summative evaluations based on coaching outcomes' (2010, p. 585). This two-pronged approach involves summative evaluation to assess the outcomes of the leadership development program. This summative evaluation needs to contain both distal and proximal outcomes. The formative evaluation focuses upon the coaching processes and is undertaken to improve the development and implementation of the leadership program. This evaluation needs to involve multiple stakeholders, sources of data and methods for collecting that data.

Conclusion

In this chapter I have explored the contemporary utility of coaching within organisations along with the challenges and some innovative practices. Contemporary coaching approaches differ from more traditional approaches to the development of leaders. 'Simply stated, coaching can be shaped to achieve very precise changes in behaviour. Coaching addresses behaviour change more effectively than training' (Atkinson 2012, p. 22). In an era when attracting, developing and retaining quality employees is a major issue for organisations in terms of increasing organisational performance and maintaining competitiveness, coaching has become a key strategy. 'Coaching can develop large scale organizational change very quickly if you focus on the right people participating in the coaching process with those people pivotal to the success and wellbeing of the organization' (Atkinson 2012, p. 20). In this chapter I have looked at the development and deployment of coaching in one industry sector where the need to facilitate performance, learning and improvement are ever-present in an environment of rapid and constant change. Coaching presents an array of benefits not only to the individual but to organisations. A key part of this process is to plan and design the coaching as part of wider SHRD, ensure the professionalisation of coaching, and adopt innovative approaches to evaluating the effectiveness of coaching interventions. Organisations are beginning to use coaching to develop leaders, stimulate change and align human resource development interventions to strategic organisational goals in innovative ways. A key challenge remains: how do organisations best evaluate these complex outcomes? In this chapter I have offered some insights into coaching evaluation approaches that attempt to cater for this contextualised complexity; however these challenges will remain due to the very nature of coaching.

References

Alagaraja, M. (2013). Mobilizing organizational alignment through strategic human resource development. *Human Resource Development International, 16*(1), 74–93.

Allen Consulting Group. (2012). *The economic, social and environmental impacts of the Cooperative Research Centres Program.* Canberra: Department of Industry, Innovation, Science, Research and Tertiary Education.

Association for Coaching. (2004). *Summary report: ROI from corporate coaching.* London: Association for Coaching.

Atkinson, P. E. (2012). Return on investment in executive coaching: Effective organisational change. *Management Services, 56*(1), 20–23.

Australasian Railway Association (ARA). (2008). *A rail revolution: Future capability identification and skills development for the Australasian rail industry.* Canberra: Australasian Railway Association.

Bates, R. A. (1999). Measuring performance improvement. *Advances in Developing Human Resources, 1*(1), 47–67.

Berg, M. E., & Karlsen, J. T. (2012). An evaluation of management training and coaching. *Journal of Workplace Learning, 24*(3), 177–199.

Cooperative Research Centre for Rail Innovation. (n.d.). *Welcome to the CRC for Rail Innovation.* http://www.railcrc.net.au/ Accessed 20 Sept 2012.

Ely, K., Boyce, L, A., et al. (2010). Evaluating leadership coaching: A review and integrated framework. *Leadership Quarterly, 21*, 585–599.

Goldman, E., Wesner, M., & Karnchanomai, O. (2013). Reciprocal peer coaching: A critical contributor to implementing individual leadership plans. *Human Resource Development Quarterly, 24*(1), 63–87.

Hagen, M., & Aguilar, M. G. (2012). The impact of managerial coaching on learning outcomes within the team context: An analysis. *Human Resource Development Quarterly, 23*(3), 363–388.

Rock, D., & Donde, R. (2008). Driving organisational change with internal coaching programmes: Part two. *Industrial and Commercial Training, 40*(2), 75–80.

Short, T., & Cameron, R. (2013). *Mentoring and coaching: Final report.* Brisbane: CRC for Rail Innovation.

Standards Australia. (2011). *Handbook: Coaching in organisations.* Sydney: Standards Australia.

Watkins, K. E., Lysø, I. H., & deMarrais, K. (2011). Evaluating executive leadership programs: A theory of change approach. *Advances in Developing Human Resources, 13*(2), 208–239.

Wilson, C. (2011). Developing a coaching culture. *Industrial and Commercial Training, 43*(7), 407–414.

Zeus, P., & Skiffington, S. (2000). *The competence guide to coaching at work.* Sydney: McGraw-Hill.

Chapter 14
Identifying Leadership Talent

Janene Piip and Roger Harris

Abstract Leaving the identification of leadership talent to chance has ongoing consequences for organisations. Those aspiring to navigate new business opportunities in interconnected global economies should know that talented leadership is needed at all levels in joined-up approaches to business, not only at the top. This is evident as traditional organisations shift from a manufacturing base to having a more knowledge-intensive focus as it is intangible, just as much as tangible, skills that contribute to an organisation's success. Consequently, the calibre of leadership talent in an organisation is a direct result of a number of factors relating to what organisations as well as individuals do to identify and develop the potential of both current and aspiring leaders. This chapter discusses the consequences of current organisational practices and then discusses considerations around how to identify the 'talents' required for leaders at the middle and frontline in one case study industry.

Introduction

Two major developments are affecting many Australian businesses, especially in traditional sectors such as manufacturing and transport. The shift from an unskilled worker base producing and manufacturing goods to more knowledge-focused industries is having an intense effect on businesses' ability to enable the performance, productivity and engagement of people with new types of work. Talented leaders are the lynchpin in setting directions, guiding and enabling people in such times of uncertainty and change. Nonetheless, leadership talent issues are a concern for industries both in Australia and across the world (PricewaterhouseCoopers 2012; ManpowerGroup 2011; Hahm and Leisy 2010).

J. Piip (✉) • R. Harris
School of Education, University of South Australia, Mawson Lakes, SA, Australia
e-mail: janenepiip@gmail.com; roger.harris@unisa.edu.au

T. Short and R. Harris (eds.), *Workforce Development: Strategies and Practices*,
DOI 10.1007/978-981-287-068-1_14, © Springer Science+Business Media Singapore 2014

A study conducted by PricewaterhouseCoopers for the Australasian rail industry (Australasian Railway Association 2008) identified cultural change, and the role of leaders and leadership, as the third highest risk to the ongoing viability of the industry. Taking responsibility for new initiatives, the ability to change the way current practices are viewed and enacted, and the ability to conceptualise new ways of solving novel problems are all now considered key roles of talented leaders. In these traditional types of industries, where there is a need to devise innovative products and services and leverage knowledge and intellectual property, there are character-istically dangerous and safety-critical operating environments that result in certain ways of doing things. Moreover, there are many leaders who have made this type of industry their lifelong career. While this rail industry report did not describe which leaders would be instrumental in bringing about change, this challenge was spotted in the statement that it will not only be leaders at the top who drive transformation but 'middle [and frontline] management, employees, unions, employee representa-tives' (2008, p. 14). An industry leader suggested identifying talented leaders and their commitment to the change task will be one of the key factors in shaping the industry of the future: 'A leader's role in changing the organisational culture comes about from their ability to be single-minded and decisive about their direction and 'having the confidence in what they are wanting to undertake' (executive leader, Innovative Rail).

Yet, despite the numerous studies of organisations, leadership, talent and talent management, the reality of identifying leadership talent in organisational practice is not portrayed in any detail in the literature. Many reports take a conceptual, theoretical or high-level approach. While the peak body tasked with improving workplace pro-ductivity and performance in Australia confirmed the importance of leadership talent in organisations in their recent human capital report, like many others, it stopped short of describing how to identify leaders or leadership talent (Australian Workplace Productivity Agency 2013). The perception from the global literature is that identify-ing leadership talent as a stand-alone subject has been given limited precedence since most of the scholarly writing still purports that 'leaders' in organisations are executive or senior leaders. Leaders at other levels such as the middle and frontline are rarely the subject of writing about leadership or being 'talented'. In this chapter, therefore we focus on middle and frontline leaders and how leadership talent is identified in organisations, considering that all leaders contribute to business success in a knowledge economy. We pose questions such as what is leadership talent, who is a talented leader, and how can they be identified to assist others with similar issues.

There are two important purposes of this chapter: to offer insight into current practice in these situations and to highlight the consequences of how some organisa-tions are currently identifying leadership talent practices, identified from recent research. Within the academic literature, it is recognised that contextual studies can offer new knowledge about existing organisational practice when environmental conditions are changing. McGahan (2007, cited in Colquitt 2011) claimed that there are five ways that research studies can influence and develop practice: (1) by offering new insights into old problems, (2) by explicating the effects of new practices, (3) by highlighting the consequences of current organisational practices, (4) by suggesting

Table 14.1 Leadership talent as potential to develop further

	Noun	Adjective
Statement	He/she has potential	He/she is a potential leader
Definition	Something that can be developed	Existing in possibility, capable of development

a specific theory to explain the current situation, and (5) by identifying a phenomenon that opens new areas of inquiry and practice. While we take into account all five ways that research can influence practice, the main thrust of this chapter will follow the line of enquiry proposed by (3) highlighting the consequences of current organisational practices for identifying leadership talent in organisations.

Our discussion in this chapter, therefore, focuses on the importance of identifying leadership talent at the middle and frontline levels, implications and consequences of current practice, and suggestions for practical strategies to identify leadership talent in organisations.

What Is Leadership Talent?

The literature on talent management often gives a broad-brush approach to what is meant by 'talent' without providing any organisationally specific definition. Leadership talent is even less well described and some writers hope that leadership is an innate or natural skill of managers, a component of talent, already possessed by people who are talented (Tarique and Schuler 2010; Stahl et al. 2012). Silzer and Church (2009) also had this conundrum about identifying talent because in organisations there are people who are already in certain roles such as leadership and those who aspire, or have potential, to be in those roles. For those reasons they stated that thinking about talent is better considered as 'potential' to develop 'talent' or to become further 'talented'. This approach is especially important considering that our goal is to describe how to identify leadership talent across the organisational levels rather than just at the top, and no one leader could be expected to know everything about leadership as an experienced, aspiring or beginning leader. In Table 14.1, 'potential' follows the thinking of Silzer and Church (2009), being described in terms of a noun or an adjective to illuminate how an approach to leadership talent might be considered.

A Skills-Based Approach to Leadership Talent

We take up the term 'leadership talent' from a skills-based approach (Northouse 2010) rather than from approaches such as the 'philosopher king' (Plato, 400 BC), 'great man' (Carlyle 1869), 'scientific selection' (Taylor 1911), 'style' (Stogdill 1974), 'trait' (Kirkpatrick and Locke 1991) or 'the differences between a manager and a leader' (Zaleznik 1977).

In the two parts of the term 'leadership talent', leadership is described as an action-oriented process comprising skills that can be developed (Northouse 2010). Leadership talent therefore is related to potential, what might be possible for these different groups of leaders, and to a theory of performance (Boyatzis 2008). Boyatzis further described that increased performance as a leader occurs when the person's talent is aligned with personal motivation, the job demands and the context of the organisational environment. While leadership in the literature has many definitions, our study got to the root of a definition of leadership in the Australian rail industry context fairly quickly, emphasising 'leading people' rather than 'managing projects'. One executive leader described leadership as follows:

> I think that leadership is about leadership rather than managing and it's about building teams; about building relationships with people who lead those teams and setting the appropriate examples. There's a vast difference between managing – situations can be managed, people need to be led – and I think that one needs to recognise that leadership takes precedence over management. (executive leader, Innovative Rail)

While this definition was articulated easily, translating the definition from a statement into organisational practice with strategies to identify leadership talent was found to be not so straightforward. This high-level statement therefore needs further explanation.

Leaders cannot do everything by themselves; instead they enable others to perform (carry out or achieve action). Complexity in the environment means that individual leaders must use their talents to gain the commitment and following of team members towards the pursuit of 'action' to achieve organisational goals (Clarke 2013). In a skills-based approach there are thought to be three domains of 'action' and these skills can be developed (Northouse 2010): (1) domain knowledge of a job role (technical skills such as engineering) underpins how to do the job task, and assists with planning and organising, while (2) human relationship and (3) conceptual or change skills add to this combination. Laker and Powell (2011) explained that technical skills (hard skills) can be readily learnt because they are precise, have certain exact principles and are involved with working more with equipment, data, machines and so on than with people. On the other hand, soft skills are related to human relationships, conceptual ideas, change and critical thinking. Soft skills rely on relationships with other people, openness to try new experiences and ideas, learning ability and motivation, and come from an intrapersonal base or within the person (locus of control, Lefcourt 1991). While technical skills form the underpinning knowledge of leading others, the greatest focus for talented leaders in changing business environments now needs to come from the human relationship and conceptual domains to enlist team members' support, and to lead and guide people through uncertain passageways of change. These intangible soft skills rely on the leader's ability to understand self, accept and reconcile feedback about how one comes across to others as a leader, and develop relationships with and between people (Northouse 2010).

As can be seen from this précis, these skills apply to leaders at the middle and frontline equally as to leaders at the top, and to those in all types of industries, not only for leaders in our rail case study. The only variation might be that the technical skills would vary by industry. Middle-level leaders therefore should have talents or skills to be able to achieve performance through teams of frontline leaders by enacting goals set by executive leaders, and translating those objectives into action. Talented frontline leaders should have skills to liaise with middle-level leaders to coordinate business operations at the frontline or operational level of the organisation by enacting the organisational strategy through the filter of several levels of leadership.

Defining Leadership Talent

Stating an organisationally specific meaning of leadership talent and establishing the capabilities valued by the organisation are important first steps in identifying talent. In our case study rail organisations, leadership talent was not well defined. As one leader said, 'it's all up in people's heads' (HR leader, Innovative Rail). As a result, undescribed definitions meant that organisations focused on senior leaders with certain talents, overlooking the middle and frontline. Executive or senior leaders valued high cognitive skills and technical competence, which led them to focus on looking for leaders only with these capabilities. However, our study identified that technical ability by itself does not necessarily correlate with leadership ability. At the middle level, this leader believed that a definition is necessary to explicate what it is that organisations are looking for in their leaders:

> I mean leadership to you may be totally different to me and depending on what your observations in life about what leadership are. Some people have no leadership, to observe around them. They may not have father figures, mentors or be in a role that they see an active leadership in play to get cues from or they may be seeing leadership that might be utterly horrible and getting all the wrong ideas about what makes effective leadership. (middle leader, Innovative Rail)

Defining leadership talent assists organisations to consider whether their organisation has:

- the values and beliefs to support the philosophy and vision for identifying leadership talent,
- described the leadership capabilities for leaders at each level,
- identified and communicated the leadership talent capabilities throughout the organisation,
- engaged in a joined-up approach to identifying leadership talent by working in partnership with line managers and human resource managers throughout the organisation, and
- taken a sustainable view of leadership talent management that is longer than a yearly timeframe.

The Case Study

We take up the example of the case study from the rail industry to describe the current process of identifying leadership talent. There are two profiles of rail organisations in Australia. In their most simplistic form, one is passenger transport and the other is freight transport. However, within these overarching profiles, there are certain niche areas of rail business such as manufacturing, managing, maintaining and leveraging hard, physical and intellectual property resources owned by rail companies, to name just some of the specialised areas. Historically, these types of industries have been perceived to be a 'man's domain', with little representation of the diversity of the whole population, and a focus on hard skills and 'getting your hands dirty' to be a good leader. The innovation needed in leadership of new types of rail businesses was demonstrated by an executive leader in one company as follows:

> Innovative Rail is undergoing significant growth as a result of the booming mineral industry in this state. Only five years ago we were researching how to transport a million tonne per annum. We are currently around 50 and in two years we are going to 70 million tonne, so it's more than doubling in our business. What that has required is large numbers that need to be delivered in a defined period of time … We've had to make some big changes in our structure. It has meant that certain people have had to take on new roles.

Growth in both sectors of the industry highlights the role and importance of middle and frontline leaders as they are usually close to day-to-day interactions with customers. This means they hear customer feedback and view potential innovations for future service delivery, manage teams in safety-critical situations and deal with diverse groups of people in their teams. These factors were not always recognised by executive leaders as they planned future business developments.

Consequences of Not Describing 'Leadership Talent'

Our study identified a number of organisational consequences of not establishing what 'leadership talent' means, not formulating a definition, promoting the importance of senior leaders over other leadership levels and focusing identification efforts here.

Operational leaders such as middle and frontline leaders comprise more than 82 % of leaders in our study, compared to 8 % at the executive levels (Fig. 14.1). This finding was confirmed in an associated rail industry study by Short et al. (2011) and is probably a typical arrangement in many hierarchically structured organisations.

The study identified that most of the leaders at the middle and frontline did not have formal qualifications in leadership or management, and some had no qualifications at all. Many had been in similar leadership roles for numerous years, and some for between 35 and 42 years. Experienced middle and frontline leaders

Fig. 14.1 Leadership levels
in rail organisations showing
unqualified leaders at middle
and frontline

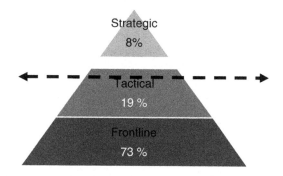

demonstrated industry-specific expertise that enabled them to be successful in operations of particular companies. 'Deep constructivism' and expertise in these roles came as a result of profound understanding of the technical issues of the industry, estimated to require between 10,000 and 20,000 h or more than 5 years of experience (Swanson and Holton 2009). The organisations' reluctance to alter leadership, especially at the middle and frontline, to maintain operations was evident, as many leaders stayed in these roles until retirement: 'I'm a bit disappointed with losing my manager because he's a wealth of knowledge – 42 years in this environment' (frontline leader, Innovative Rail).

How Leadership Talent Is Currently Identified

In contrast to middle and frontline leaders, executive leaders tended to change positions and organisations more frequently as new opportunities arose. All had achieved professional qualifications in engineering, business and finance. Considering that middle and frontline leaders comprise the largest cohort of leaders leading business units to achieve whole-of-organisation productivity in changing economic situations, this finding caused us to consider current practice, how leaders are identified, what processes are in place for leadership renewal and any processes for feedback and appraisal of current performance. The whole-of-business impacts of not describing leadership talent, failing to consider the importance of middle and frontline leadership roles, and placing most emphasis on senior leaders were:

- The largest group of leaders in the organisation lacked formal qualifications in managing and leading others.
- Leadership talents were not defined for middle and frontline leaders.
- Leadership was enacted according to impressionable role models from the individual's life and personal experience.
- Individuals were developing their own definition of leadership talent.
- Leadership skill gaps were diagnosed in 'ad hoc' ways.

Middle-Level Leaders

Middle-level leaders had been promoted to their middle-level roles through a mainly informal process of selection and mentoring that was common within the industry. The processes followed informal unwritten rules where some frontline leaders were given a 'lucky career break' to the middle:

> I started out as a junior locomotive operator ... I got my experience up ... I moved to a team leader role ... went to train control ... learnt the role over a number of years ... then I was given a golden opportunity ... to middle leader. (middle leader, Innovative Rail)

This process was described as 'maintaining the community of rail', where being identified and promoted to the middle was based on the ability to be in charge of others at the frontline (command and control), be organised and keep things 'on track'. These 'golden opportunities' excluded others should the leadership opportunity have been more transparent and widely known about. Arrival at these positions was considered a high achievement considering that many did not have formal qualifications, and as a consequence middle-level leaders sought to maintain strong connections with the frontline. By the nature of their unique roles, middle leaders were the go-betweens, interpreting executive strategy and communicating this operational information at the frontline. Their roles were always under threat from different factors, and in the process of rail restructuring one middle leader without the assurance of a formal management or leadership qualification went 'up and down the ladder a few times through different restructures, changes of management' (middle leader, City Trains). Middle-level leaders had been in their roles for many years as tacit industry knowledge had its own peculiarities and was difficult to replicate or replace if key staff left or retired: 'a lot of the roles are not interchangeable, so consequently we do get a lot of people who are here for the long haul' (middle leader, Innovative Rail).

Frontline Leaders

Where there was no defined approach to identifying leadership talent, leaders developed their own ways of identifying new leaders based on their own image of a 'good' leader at the frontline. This comprised the same informal process of singling out potential leaders as at the middle level, providing workplace opportunities and mentoring over many years, as there were no mandatory qualifications to become a leader at the frontline. Many highlighted the profound influence of the mentoring process by certain leaders on their early careers in providing a positive image of a leader which they followed throughout their careers. The informal approach to selection was described in this example as being inducted into the rail culture:

> I've been in the railways since 1988 ... over the years I have just sort of worked my way through the different areas and opportunities came up and I never actually had to apply for

any of the positions I have been in. I have always been asked 'Do you want to do this? Do you want to do that?' and it's just progressed from there till I have got to this point where I am at now. (frontline leader, City Trains).

Once frontline leaders had been endorsed as leaders, many had stayed within familiar boundaries of the frontline hierarchy for long periods. Coping with change, energy, drive, learning and development, and self-actualisation, all indicators of a desire to learn and grow as a leader, were focused on understanding the compliance needs (hard skills) of the organisation rather than on formally developing leadership skills. When it came to thinking about the future and who might aspire to be a leader within their own team, there was a surprising lack of acknowledgement of the need for leadership renewal, and of the need to nurture other potential leaders. There was limited consideration of identifying and developing new leaders from within teams who may aspire to such roles, as the older age profile of individuals in general at the frontline was viewed as a barrier. These frontline leaders had already developed an image of what a good leader should look like, and also what characteristics and behaviours an ineffective leader would display in their industry, and they had applied this profile to members of their team long ago. Current team members were thought to be waiting out their time until retirement, and any new or younger employees did not have the equality of experience or rights to specialised and historical rail knowledge that was needed by leaders. Personal paradigms and assumptions indicated that some older rail employees from different generations had fixed ideas about what it means to be a leader.

Command and control approaches to leadership were common, which tended to result in a 'default' setting for leading others. These approaches overlooked the need to engage individual team members and to enable the best in others, or their individual potential, to materialise. When middle and frontline leaders were asked about being a 'good leader' of people, passion and enthusiasm for innovation, engaging people and thinking about how old problems could be solved in new ways, their responses seemed to lack energy and excitement about doing things differently. This was typified in this response: 'I mean they know where I am if ever they want some advice' (frontline leader, MTAA).

Longenecker and Yonker claimed that 'without effective leadership practices, at all levels of an enterprise, performance improvement and achieving better results will be difficult or even nonexistent' (2013, p.159). Commercial viability of companies is a key driver as environmental conditions change, especially at the frontline. Identifying and positioning leaders with team engagement skills that can convert joined efforts of teams into business productivity seems mandatory. Organisational responses about how to identify these types of leaders at the frontline seemed to be a combination of letting existing leaders run their leadership course naturally to its endpoint without intervention, and one of not knowing the best strategies to improve current practice. As one leader said:

a lot of staff that just can't be considered now because of their age – regardless of their experience and talents, it's tough to put people through a system when they're just on the verge of retirement … why go through the effort? (middle leader, Innovative Rail)

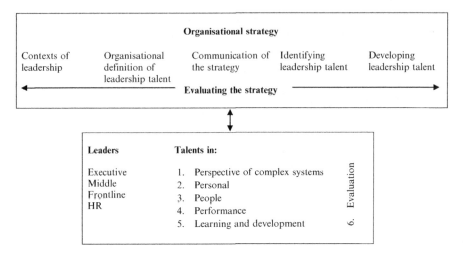

Fig. 14.2 Six components of an organisational framework for managing leadership talent

However, in the main, individual leaders could conceptualise the obvious problems when questioned on an individual level and some provided ideas that focused on four key aspects of identifying leadership talent: perspective, people, personal and performance aspects. From these insights, our study identified that there are two key components to identifying leadership talent. Firstly, there are considerations of what organisations should be doing or need to do to identify leadership talent, and secondly, there are considerations of what individuals should be doing, or need to do, to become talented leaders. We will explore these components further in the next paragraphs.

What Organisations Need to Do to Identify Leadership Talent

A framework to describe what organisations should do to manage leadership talent was drawn up as a result of the study (Fig. 14.2). The framework was found to be useful in focusing organisations on how they could identify both current and aspiring leadership talent. It is ordered in six themes: (1) the contexts of leadership; (2) the organisational definition of leadership talent; (3) communication of the leadership talent strategy; (4) identifying leadership talent; (5) developing leadership talent; and (6) evaluating the strategy and approach. All parts of the framework are provided as an overview as each theme has a number of sub-themes that are interdependent within the framework.

For example, the theme about identifying leadership talent includes four sub-themes that focus organisations to consider the importance of: (1) senior leaders in endorsing, supporting and modelling the desired talent identification behaviour, (2) connected conversations between manager and employee to identify leadership talent, aspirations, motivation and potential, (3) identifying particular technical and business knowledge, and (4) identifying individual performance, motivation and relationships with others.

We compared middle and frontline leaders' ideas with the literature on talent management, and against the six themes of the framework in Fig. 14.2. The approach used in our study provided valuable lessons for practice as it highlighted that a deeper understanding can be gained by seeking the opinions of those who are at the coalface of an issue. We have incorporated the common-sense ideas collected from individuals about what organisations should be doing to identify leadership talent in the following sections, which consider global developments, considerations for organisations in identifying leadership talent, and the talents required for leaders at the middle and frontline.

Contexts of Leadership

The changing contexts of industry, with a greater focus on the global and national rather than only local context, were found to affect operations in the rail case study at the local level in subtle but all-encompassing ways. Changes have included deregulation, the inclusion of multinational companies, ongoing restructuring and the growth in the use of technology as well as monumental societal changes. Leadership practice that sets out to maintain the traditions and history of the industry and contextualised, local knowledge is challenged as a result, and there is a corre-lated impact on the internal environments of organisations. Lyotard (1984) reported that as organisations become part of a global economy that is facilitated by rapid information exchange, local and historical traditions of an organisation or industry can be lost. The key point middle and frontline leaders made was to view this time in history as an opportunity to renew and refresh leadership talent while 'building the community of rail'. As older leaders retire, maintaining the specialised knowl-edge of the industry in a way that can be passed from one generation to the next provides an important connection from earlier times while recognising the future. As one leader stated, 'a proud history ... my brother, father and I have over 65 years in the Australian rail industry, most of the time as leaders' (frontline leader, Innovative Rail). In the absence of any talent identification strategy by organisations, leaders at the middle and frontline maintained their own processes of informally identifying leaders to ensure the longevity of their rail history.

Individual Talents for Complex Systems

The lack of awareness about global, national, business and environmental changes among middle and frontline leaders in some Australian rail companies highlighted that new skills are now required by leaders for more multifaceted environments

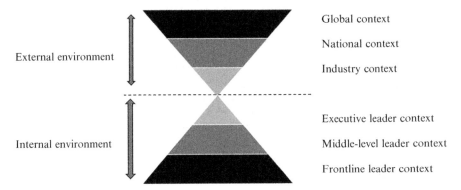

External environment

Global context

National context

Industry context

Executive leader context

Middle-level leader context

Frontline leader context

Internal environment

Fig. 14.3 The contexts of leadership

while considering strongly held rail traditions. This new knowledge comprises an understanding of global systems, global issues and how these systems are interconnected through to the local level. However, the practice of individual selection and mentoring was the only way middle and frontline leaders knew of being able to pass on information and identify the next generation of leaders. This approach unintentionally replicated past practices, identified new leaders in the same image as the current leaders and excluded a diverse sector of the rail population. Strategic interventions in organisations that identify and describe these contexts are necessary to identify talented leaders at the middle and frontline. For these reasons, our framework states that organisations should identify talented leaders who are able to understand the perspectives of complex systems. This includes the three contexts of the external environment – global, national and industry contexts – and the three contexts in the internal environment – the executive leader, middle-level leader and frontline leader contexts. By considering both the middle and frontline as important to the business operations, leadership can be differentiated at these two separate levels. The process of identifying talented leaders therefore has to be one of organisations as well as individuals recognising that this knowledge is needed, and then individuals developing the associated skills and knowledge to assimilate changes from the external environment with internal operations. Figure 14.3 shows the contexts of the external and internal environment of organisations.

Defining Leadership Talent for Organisations and Leaders

Defining what is meant by leadership talent helps both organisations and leaders. For organisations, a clear definition sets up the foundations for a transparent approach to identifying leadership talent as all leaders are clear about what their organisation values at each level of leadership. For individuals, a definition helps both current and aspiring leaders understand what it is that the organisation is looking for in their leaders. We identified that leaders can shape and define themselves

Table 14.2 Capabilities of 'talented leaders' described by middle and frontline leaders

Task and technical skills	Human relationship skills	Change and conceptual skills
The ability to:		
Explain an objective	The ability to communicate with all levels of the workforce	Openness to new ideas
Make quick decisions that are accurate and truthful	People skills, knowledge and experience	Problem-solving skills with innovative solutions
Manage multiple disciplines without specific technical knowledge	Communication and listening skills	Knowledge of the industry
	Someone you can talk to	Motivating team with new ideas
	Honesty	
	Energy, vitality, positive attitude	
	Fairness, straight talker.	

against this organisational definition should it be widely known because everyone understands the organisational purpose of identifying talented leaders and the desired talents, competencies, capabilities and knowledge the organisation is seeking in its leaders.

Our study found that no widespread written definitions of leadership talent were available in any of the organisations. Rail leaders in just three settings were not of the same mind about a talented leader as a result of their wide-ranging individual experiences of leadership and different contextual environments. Some leaders suggested talents necessary for leaders at the middle and frontline but they were not able to offer the entire array of talents now needed by leaders in complex situations. Some of their ideas are presented in Table 14.2 and compared to the skills-based approach described by Northouse (2010).

Defining Oneself as a Leader

As a result of these findings from middle and frontline leaders we considered how a definition would help individual leaders in becoming talented or being able to identify and develop their individual potential. We suggest that a definition has three purposes for leaders seeking to develop their potential and grow in their career: (1) to define oneself as a leader and conceptualise personal change to become a better leader; (2) to seek and consider feedback from others to grow, adapt and change; and (3) to undertake new career experiences to develop and grow.

In the process of defining oneself as a leader, new career opportunities arise and it is a natural progression that the individual changes and moves into different roles. The developing and learning aspect of becoming a talented leader is one key defining factor in identifying talent. It indicates whether the individual leader has the motivation and ability to define themselves according to the competencies required by the organisation and the self-commitment to pursue their goals. In our study, middle and frontline leaders had remained within the confines of their organisational leadership level, constrained by the lack of organisational definition, their lack of qualifications, self-directed learning and motivation to progress higher in the organisation or to different roles. The greatest career growth had been achieved by frontline leaders moving to middle-level roles but further progression to executive roles was not possible for these leaders because they lacked formal professional qualifications. For the time being, defining the talents required for middle and frontline leaders would enable current leaders to identify their leadership skill needs while defining what is required for the next generation of middle and frontline leaders.

Communicating the Approach

Communicating the leadership talent approach goes hand in hand with defining what leadership talent means and why it is important to the organisation. Communication of the strategy, when supported by senior leaders, has the greatest influence in promoting and supporting the leadership talent strategy and message. The approach can then be continually questioned to ensure the message remains transparent and unbiased. We found that middle and frontline leaders believed that communicating the meaning and purpose of the leadership talent management approach should be undertaken by gaining 'real support and commitment by senior leaders for the leadership talent strategy', as one frontline leader described it. He believed that leaders at the frontline could perform more confidently if they were certain they were supported by senior leaders including knowing what was expected of them as leaders.

Identifying Leadership Talent

While our model explicates what organisations and individuals need to do to identify leadership talent, it is the actual processes and actions at the grassroots levels combined with a leadership talent identification 'mindset' that will enable leadership talent to be successfully identified. Given this frame of reference, organisations and leaders should be aware of the importance of leadership talent to the business strategy while being on the lookout for what makes a talented leader. Talented leaders can contribute to productivity gains in the organisation through their ability to:

- develop their own skills for leadership performance, identify others, provide learning opportunities and identify and draw out the latent potential of others,
- use logic and critical thinking to plan, organise and manage hard resources prudently (Yukl 2010),
- motivate teams towards organisational goals and targets using human engagement and people skills (Northouse 2010),
- provide constructive and targeted feedback about performance (Longenecker and Yonker 2013),

- provide new ways of solving problems that save the organisation time and money,
- conceptualise alternative courses of action, and
- be innovative, persuasive and committed to the right course of action (Boedker et al. 2011).

However, our study found that, rather than considering leadership skills in performance appraisal discussions and one-on-one conversations, organisations were more concerned with collecting the 'hard' or quantifiable facts about individuals that related to compliance and training related to legislation, as this example highlights:

> Because of the rail skills set, because of the legislative requirements to justify why so and so was allowed to make that decision or do that type of work, the genuine skill sets like ATQF type stuff we actually track very well ... we're certainly not documenting leadership skills, so who's the best people skills, who can handle the adversarial situations, who's the best person – we don't have that. (HR leader, Innovative Rail)

Where conversations between a leader and team member were held to identify certain skills they focused more on 'how you did in your job' rather than 'career development which should be about how you are doing in your profession ... we don't have the "in your profession" process' (HR leader, Innovative Rail). One middle-level leader had not had any type of discussion with his manager for a considerable length of time: 'probably the first time I've had one for 15 years which is pretty disappointing' (middle leader, City Trains). Identifying talents described for leadership such as who is a 'great people person', who is a team player and looks after their team, who has motivation for learning, who has taken on different workplace assignments and who has conducted surprising acts of leadership were not priorities.

Leaders at the middle and frontline considered that getting to know the people in the organisation (both current and aspiring leaders) should be undertaken by higher level leaders, human resources leaders and line managers to understand individual motivations for leadership careers: 'What are their experiences; what are their skills? Many bring a vast range of experiences when they come to work here' (HR leader, City Trains). Collecting employee information, undertaking talent discussions, performance appraisals and connected conversations was the way one middle-level leader thought this should be achieved: 'so you're looking at people and talking to them, getting to know them, that's the way that you find out how' (middle leader, MTAA). In this way, discussions could identify who has certain skills, specialist expertise and rail knowledge. This employee information should be captured through electronic systems to provide an up-to-date picture of employees' profiles rather than what was happening in this case:

> We have a HR information system but it's very basic ... we're certainly not documenting leadership skills, so who has the best people skills, who can handle the adversarial situations, who's the best person – we don't have that. (HR leader, Innovative Rail)

Since we are discussing middle and frontline leaders who are already employed in the organisation, and those who aspire to move into middle and frontline roles in the future, our goal was to provide strategies of how their future potential or aspirations could be identified and fulfilled. Many of our interviewees had worked in their respective organisations for upwards of 20 years but this does not mean they did not have potential to become better, more skilled leaders. Identifying their base-level skills, providing a base qualification, and developing their leadership skills where there are gaps, may encourage them to develop their own approach to leadership. Our study also acknowledges the widespread need by senior leaders to recognise the importance of middle and frontline leaders in organisations. Further to this theme, middle and frontline leaders provided four main ideas to identify talent:

- undertaking a written skills audit of team members' aspirations and potential for leadership roles and capturing information in an electronic format
- developing written scripts to direct discussions in 'talent conversations' to capture knowledge about current and potential leadership talent. Questions such as 'provide examples of team members who demonstrated leadership in a situation that surprised you' can build on everyday workplace situations where leadership is observed.
- providing opportunities to showcase and develop leadership skills in the workplace
- developing 'joined-up' conversations where line managers are involved in analysing individual performance through conversations and discussions with others.

Developing Leadership Talent

Our model considers that as a result of identifying leadership talent in a more transparent and informed manner, a better focus can be given to developing individual leadership needs where gaps are observed. We found that development approaches for talented leaders are interdependent on successful identification strategies and diagnosis in the first instance. Strategies would involve HR leaders in designing appropriate learning strategies for current and aspiring leaders, 'designing learning between levels and learning with other leaders' and 'identifying leaders who can take the time to mentor future leaders' (frontline leader, City Trains). These development approaches would be more effective than leaving to chance generic leadership development programs for all leaders since: 'you would find out whether a person has a particular trait. Now, some traits aren't conducive to leadership. They are conducive to being an analyst' (middle leader, MTAA).

Evaluating the Leadership Talent Strategy

Middle and frontline leaders did not have suggestions for how the leadership talent strategy should be evaluated. We suggest establishing targets for the identification and development of leaders and then monitoring and evaluating the leadership talent management strategy.

What Talents Are Required by Individual Leaders?

We have described a framework to guide leadership talent identification and decision making in organisations. In this next section, we briefly describe the talents necessary for individual leaders to lead others. Our study acknowledged that underpinning or foundation skills from certain disciplines are necessary for leaders to make sound management decisions. These were previously described as technical or 'hard' or even tangible skills, and provide leaders with the base from which to plan, organise and determine the best courses of action. At each of the leadership levels, these 'hard' or technical skills may be increasingly more involved, difficult or complex. These talents are not included in the framework as they can be learnt through a range of means that are too vast to describe here. The 'soft' leadership skills of human capital are more difficult to diagnose and identify as these skills are related to people, are intangible and are needed to bring new ideas to fruition by engaging and relating with others. They are less well described and are utilised in varying degrees according to the level of leadership but, nevertheless, are required by all leaders. Our framework includes these talents for leaders.

The leadership talents relate to the six key themes of our organisational framework. As a result, we present behavioural statements relating to the underlying theme or construct (Boyatzis 2008) from the organisational framework with the intent of describing an action or what it is that is required for talented leaders. We state the leadership talents in a two-part statement that describes the talent firstly, and the action secondly.

1. *Perspective talents of complex systems.* Talented leaders should be able to scan the perspectives of complex systems to identify and assimilate changes in the environment that influence their role.
2. *Personal talents.* Define themselves as leaders based on understanding themselves, the organisational definition and contexts, and their leadership role and contribution to the organisation's success.
3. *People talents.* Communicate and build relationships with people, stakeholders and teams at the strategic, team and personal, one-on-one levels by speaking, listening and presenting information.
4. *Performance talents.* Identify and enable others, provide the resources for work, and support and monitor performance.
5. *Learning and development talents.* Develop self and others using a range of learning strategies.
6. *Evaluation talents.* Evaluate and improve leadership practice.

Summary and Conclusion

In this chapter we have explained that identifying leadership talent is one of the key challenges for organisations in a global economy. Leaders at all levels are now needed to achieve business outcomes and enable others to perform through the use of contemporary skills that are aligned with the strategy and direction of the organisation. However, the literature provides little direction to organisations facing talent management issues as leadership talent is found to be contextually specific to the industry, organisation and also to the leadership level of companies. By using a case study from the Australian rail industry, we were able to provide an in-depth insight into current practice around identifying leadership talent that may assist organisations in other industries. Our chapter provides points gathered from middle and frontline leaders about important considerations when identifying leadership talent in companies where maintaining historical and traditional knowledge is important yet there is a need to embrace other ways to capitalise on knowledge, intellectual property and other goods and services that were not traditionally supplied. We have considered their ideas in conjunction with the framework that was developed as a result of our study to guide organisations and individuals in identifying leadership talent.

References

Australasian Railway Association. (2008). *A rail revolution: Future capability identification and skills development for the Australasian rail industry.* Canberra: Australasian Railway Association.

Australian Workplace and Productivity Agency. (2013). *Human capital and productivity.* http://www.awpa.gov.au/our-work/Documents/Human%20capital%20and%20productivity%20literature%20review%20M arch%202013.pdf. Accessed 20 Apr 2013.

Boedker, C., Cogin, J., et al. (2011). *Leadership, culture and management practices of high performing workplaces in Australia: Literature review and diagnostic instruments.* Sydney: Society for Knowledge Economics.

Boyatzis, R. E. (2008). Competencies in the 21st century. *Journal of Management Development, 27*(1), 5–12.

Carlyle, T. (1869). *Heroes and hero-worship.* London: Chapman and Hall.

Clarke, N. (2013). Model of complexity leadership development. *Human Resource Development International, 16*(2), 135–150.

Colquitt, J. (2011). From the editors. *Academy of Management Journal, 54*(3), 432–435.

Hahm, E., & Leisy, B. (2010). *Managing today's global workforce: Elevating talent management to improve business.* http://www.ey.com/Publication/vwLUAssets/Managing_Todays_Global_workforce/$FILE/M anaging_Todays_Global_workforce.pdf. Accessed 11 July 2013.

Kirkpatrick, S. A., & Locke, E. A. (1991). Leadership: Do traits matter? *Academy of Management Perspectives, 5*(2), 48–60.

Laker, D. R., & Powell, J. L. (2011). The differences between hard and soft skills and their relative impact on training transfer. *Human Resource Development Quarterly, 22*(1), 111–122.

Lefcourt, H. M. (1991). Locus of control. In J. P. Robinson, P. R. Shaver, & L. S. Wrightsman (Eds.), *Measures of personality and social psychological attitudes* (pp. 413–499). San Diego: Academic.

Longenecker, C. O., & Yonker, R. D. (2013). Leadership deficiencies in rapidly changing organizations: Multisource feedback as a needs assessment tool – Part I. *Industrial and Commercial Training, 45*(3), 159–165.

Lyotard, J.-F. (1984). *Postmodern condition: A report on knowledge* (Vol. 10). Minneapolis: University of Minnesota Press.

ManpowerGroup. (2011). *'Manufacturing' talent for the human age*. https://www.manpower.com.
   au/documents/White-Papers/2011_ManufacturingTalent.pdf. Accessed 23 Jan 2012.
Northouse, P. G. (2010). *Leadership: Theory and practice* (5th ed.). Thousand Oaks: Sage.
PricewaterhouseCoopers. (2012). *Transportation & logistics 2030 volume 5: Winning the talent
   race*. http://www.pwc.com/en_GX/gx/transportation-logistics/pdf/pwc-tl-2030-volume-5.pdf.
   Accessed 28 Sept 2013.
Short, T. W., Piip, J. K., et al. (2011). *A capability framework for rail leadership and management
   development*. Brisbane: CRC for Rail Innovation.
Silzer, R., & Church, A. H. (2009). The pearls and perils of identifying potential. *Industrial and
   Organizational Psychology, 2*(4), 377–412.
Stahl, G. K., Björkman, I., et al. (2012). Six principles of effective global talent management.
   MIT Sloan Management Review, 53(2), 25–32.
Stogdill, R. M. (1974). *Handbook of leadership: A survey of theory and research*. New York:
   Free Press.
Swanson, R. A., & Holton, E. F. (2009). *Foundations of human resource development* (2nd ed.).
   San Francisco: Berrett-Koehler.
Tarique, I., & Schuler, R. S. (2010). Global talent management: Literature review, integrative
   framework and suggestions for further research. *Journal of World Business, 45*(2), 122–133.
Taylor, F. W. (1911). *The principles of scientific management*. New York: Norton.
Yukl, G. A. (2010). *Leadership in organizations* (7th ed.). Upper Saddle River: Pearson.
Zaleznik, A. (1977). Managers and leaders: Are they different? *Harvard Business, 55*(May–June),
   67–78.

Chapter 15
A Moment in Time and Place: Can Highly Contextualised Training Meet National Training Frameworks?

Jill Hadley

Abstract This chapter examines the influence of workplace context on the training and development of senior leaders/managers within an Australian Public Service department. Leadership training in the public sector is of increasing interest to government personnel seeking to improve strategic business outcomes through employing competent, well-trained leaders. In this chapter I investigate the value of a nationally accredited course leading to a qualification delivered within a specific public service context. This chapter is based on an in-depth case study that discusses how leaders/managers applied their learning within their own context and simultaneously met pre-determined national vocational outcomes. I found that learners implementing relevant workplace projects expressed a high level of satisfaction with the training. However, national auditors indicated that attainment of national competency standards may need further attention. The question arises whether providing a nationally accredited leadership course is the best choice for a public service department where context is critical.

Workforce Development

Workforce development involves matching appropriate training provision to the needs of the organisation, individuals and the wider community (AWPA 2012). It takes place within the workplace but assumes various forms, such as formal or informal training, mentoring or coaching. While this study was situated within one large public service department, leadership training in other departments would raise similar issues. Leadership training in the public sector has become a significant topic of analysis as an increasing number of organisations recognise the value

J. Hadley (✉)
School of Education, University of South Australia, Mawson Lakes, SA, Australia
e-mail: jhadley01@chariot.net.au

T. Short and R. Harris (eds.), *Workforce Development: Strategies and Practices*,
DOI 10.1007/978-981-287-068-1_15, © Springer Science+Business Media Singapore 2014

of training for their senior leaders/managers, where 'leadership is not a separate attribute [of leading] but enmeshed with the managerial aspects of their jobs' (Althaus and Wanna 2008, p. 118). In this chapter I focus on how context shaped and influenced leadership training and the robust delivery of learning within a state department when the course was framed within a national set of controls.

Learning may be described as constructing knowledge to increase one's capacity to act effectively (Senge 2006). Learning theorists have moved away from believing that the learner is a passive vessel waiting to be filled with knowledge from an expert source, to the notion of the learner being an active participant who has considerable knowledge and experience that contributes to new knowledge. Research has found that learners in the workplace prefer to learn from holistic experiences that are related to best-practice approaches in their specific industry and from experienced others (Choy et al. 2008). Further research showed that 70 % of all leadership development occurs through on-job experiences, 20 % of learning through relational learning such as coaching and mentoring, and 10 % through formal training (Jennings and Wargnier 2010).

Combining formal training and coaching with on-job experiences would seem to address workforce leadership development in the best possible way. However, the model chosen by this department included another element above and beyond formal training, on-job experiences and coaching – that of national frameworks underpinning the formal training provided. In addition to contextual application of learning, participants were required to demonstrate attainment of national standards leading to a qualification. To understand the characteristics of the public sector context in which this study was situated, I provide a general overview prior to discussing the workforce development model implemented.

The Public Sector Context

Generally, the public sector consists of governments and all publicly controlled or publicly funded agencies, enterprises, and other entities delivering public programs, goods, or services (Institute of Internal Auditors 2011). The Australian Public Service (APS) is a formal organisation that exists to achieve defined outcomes and goals related to the public good. Public sector agencies provide responsive services to the community and government, maintain structures and processes that can adapt to changing public demands, manage all public resources, maintain accountability, develop policies, formulate rules and laws, manage public finances, enforce regulations and implement all government legislative requirements relevant to the agencies (Wyse 2007).

The APS is structured in such a way that its outcomes and goals, identified in relevant strategic plans, are subdivided and cascade down into subdivisions across the organisation. Departments, divisions, sections, units, positions, jobs and tasks make up the structure. Selection, recruitment and subsequent advancement are by merit or seniority. A person employed in a higher position in the hierarchy is presumed to carry expertise in dealing with problems that may arise in work carried out at lower levels of the organisation. This bureaucratic structure forms the basis for the appointment of heads of administrative departments in the organisation and grants status attached to the authority of their position (Australian Public Service Commission n.d.). All public sector personnel are expected to operate in the public interest in a transparent and accountable way. The concept of 'public interest', as opposed to self-interest or commercial interest, is the driver for decision making and the exercise of power and discretion by public administrators. This concept is important in a wide variety of areas, including obligations of ethical leadership and general ethical decision making. As one senior manager interviewed for this study said,

> We have a code of conduct and a commitment to the public. For me there is a genuine love to provide a good quality service to very vulnerable people. The notion of public service is still a good one for government.

The prevailing paradigms of the public service have changed over the last 170 years or so of organised government. 'Tradition public administration' viewed leadership in the public sector as a top-down process as the focus then was on nation building. A central hierarchical structure was based on a division of administrative tasks aligned to several levels of classification, undertaken by a particular office or unit. Leaders were managers who became experts in their technical fields and as such controlled access, information and knowledge within their realms of responsibility through working according to rules and procedures prescribed within written records (Stoker 2006). Although the general climate of public service has evolved, shades of these controls still operate today, as a manager participating in this study described:

> A few years ago we had to set up a disruptive behaviour policy – it was a very political directive. It doesn't matter what we think about it, we just get on and do it. That's what we're told to do; the policy and procedures get developed, we get trained and this is how we operate.

The second era of organised government, 'new public management', arose in the late 1980s as a response to perceived inefficiencies in meeting the demands of public consumers. Government moved progressively towards a more market-driven environment in which competition and productivity were key elements. The purpose was to be more like the private sector in being cost/profit driven and in gaining 'efficiencies' rather than being motivated by values and service. Managers were driven by controls such as performance measures, operational plans, approval processes, staffing decisions over which they had little personal control, as well as by intense media exposure concerning improvements in public sector performance and delivery of services. Key reforms included the purchaser-provider model within organisations in a bid to create lean, flat structures that drove the system rather than bureaucratic oversight. However, prescriptions drawn from the private sector model were often not appropriate for the public sector with its different values base, a plethora of accountabilities and service responsibilities (Stoker 2006; Kelly and Muers 2002).

Today, the focus has moved to generating public value by asking whether the service advances valued social or economic outcomes. Managers are expected to consider whether they can achieve more outcomes with the assets and resources allocated to them. More than ensuring that procedures have been followed, more than asking whether performance targets have been met, managers are expected to act in ways that bring net benefits to society (Althaus and Wanna 2008; Stoker 2006). The following case study provided by a senior manager participating in this study gives an example of societal benefit:

> We run an encounter program that we started four years ago. It involves about $20,000 of current government money – it provides an activity program for 60 people with disabilities for 3 days a week. We have a volunteer coordinator and nearly 30 volunteers. It's very efficient, effective and people work hard to put that program together. Whenever I evaluate our services in the community people always say 'thank goodness for that service.' To me that's government providing a service. NGOs [non-government organisations] could run that but it would be more expensive – it would probably cost about $150,000 based on my experience. People come from all over the state to see how it's working. That's an example of public service working well.

Leadership in the Public Sector

Prominence given to leadership as an organisational management task suggests its importance in today's public sector environment (Althaus and Wanna 2008). Leadership in the public service is defined as

> the capacity at both the individual and institutional levels to identify and define organisational goals and desired outcomes, develop strategies and plans to achieve these goals and deliver outcomes and guide the organisation and motivate its people in reaching goals and outcomes. (Edwards et al. 2003, p. 4)

Management and leadership are not seen as separate functions; in the framework of government and public administration, it is important to see leadership in its managerial and organisational context (2003, p. 5). In the organisational context, new forms of doing business, influenced by globalisation, internet technologies, climate change, market volatility and demographic change, present managers and leaders with new challenges (Innovation and Business Skills Australia 2011). Today's leaders in public sector governance are expected to work in partnership with private and non-government organisations, and to show initiative and take calculated risks to achieve worthy social outcomes (Shergold 2007; Kane 2007). The focus is on a collaborative team approach where the successful leader must gain commitment and cooperation from those for whom they are responsible (Althaus and Wanna 2008).

The Australian Public Service has embraced the concept of institutional leadership development since the inception of the senior executive leadership capability (SELC) framework established in 1999 – now being incrementally reviewed. The capability leadership framework of the APS, of which the SELC forms a part, describes the behaviour expected of public service staff at every level from first grade to Chief Executive. This enables all staff to identify the core capabilities required of them in their current role, and helps them to identify professional development to support career planning, performance development and transition to a new role. Job specifications and criteria for selection are based on the capabilities for the identified classification. The SELC framework identifies five core competencies for senior leaders: shaping strategic thinking, achieving results, cultivating productive working relationships, communicating with influence, and exemplifying personal drive and integrity. Career-oriented public servants must address these criteria in applications for promotion to the Senior Executive Services – a higher level promotional classification. In this way, public sector leadership is distinguished from that of private sector agencies.

> While these five core competencies are regarded as relevant for today's senior leaders, it is clear that APS leaders of the future will face greater economic uncertainty, higher citizen expectations, increasing policy complexity, more rapid technological change and a tight labour market. These challenges will require [leaders] to develop new capabilities and lead their staff in new ways of working – cross-agency, cross-jurisdictional and cross-sector. (Australian Public Service Commission 2009)

Leadership Training

The current investment in training by many departmental organisations is based on the belief that people entering into senior promotional roles can be trained to manifest better leadership skills and develop new capabilities (APSC 2009; Althaus and Wanna 2008). Leadership training programs may be offered in a variety of ways, including outsourcing to or partnering with either a public provider (TAFE) or a private training provider or, alternatively, providing in-house training. In choosing to provide in-house training, organisations also consider whether training will be non-accredited or accredited. In the former, training consists of long or short professional development programs focused on a variety of relevant organisational topics, usually under the guidance of the human resources department.

When accredited training is decided upon, it can lead to nationally accredited vocational, education and training (VET) qualifications offered to internal staff by an organisation's own training arm, known as an enterprise registered training organisation (RTO), which must meet all national standards for vocational education and training (under the *National Vocational Education and Training Regulator Act 2011*). The principal role of an enterprise RTO is to provide comprehensive training programs to internal employees to ensure they perform their jobs well and contribute to the achievement of the enterprise's business objectives. Smith et al. (2009, p. 8) suggested that employers who used nationally accredited training did so because they believed it would enhance their competitiveness by improving quality. Furthermore, the capacity to offer accredited training to large numbers of workers was vital to the organisation's performance and the contribution of nationally recognised training to this outcome should not be underestimated. In addition, organisations that experienced recruitment difficulties because of the specialised nature of their work provided nationally accredited training to foster loyalty, thereby improving retention (Smith et al. 2005). Research investigating the establishment of enterprise RTOs found that 'qualifications play a role in making companies "employers of choice"' (Smith et al. 2005, p. 303). Furthermore, workers with skills and qualifications were increasingly viewed as critical factors in determining effective enterprise performance (Henry et al. 2013).

An organisation choosing to go down the pathway of competency-based training based on nationally accredited standards makes a major commitment not only to training by the organisation but also to this particular type of training. In establishing an enterprise RTO decision makers need to plan carefully for the input of resources to set up and maintain the training organisation balanced against the proposed outcomes that are expected to accrue to benefit the organisation as a whole. Business decision makers expect return on investment in training so they want to see evidence that providing workers with opportunities to gain qualifications in their work time would lead to stronger loyalty and improved retention.

Planning a Leadership Training Course in a Public Service Department

This study was conducted within the specific context of an enterprise RTO recently established in a public service department. Its primary role was defined as 'building capability of the workforce to do their jobs to the best of their ability and to give them a national qualification as the outcome' (archive minutes). In building workforce capability the RTO executive team found themselves confronting three key departmental challenges: not only did they need to demonstrate the value of their contribution to the organisation in order to justify the existence and maintenance of the RTO, but also they needed to plan and oversee a training course designed to meet identified deficits in leadership skills, and they needed the designed training course to align with nationally accredited training qualifications. I discuss each of these demands below.

Value of Contribution

The opportunity to gain a portable national qualification free of charge to the individual was believed to be one viable means to attract more workers and retain staff in the department (Smith et al. 2009). In choosing to put resources and energy into workforce development through the delivery of vocational qualifications, key departmental decision makers in this study made it clear that courses developed should provide return on investment through an up-skilled and informed workforce, thus creating greater efficiencies as well as attracting and retaining personnel.

In this department, workforce analysis trends predicted that at the current rate of turnover 70 % of staff would have left by 2015 due to a number of factors (archive minutes). In the 3 years since beginning to deliver accredited training, staff turnover decreased by 15 % and 88 % of learner respondents believed their workplace performance had improved as a result of their learning (annual report). Ninety three per cent of managers reported that learning had increased the workplace knowledge and skills of their staff since the enterprise was registered as a training organisation (staff survey report). This rapid growth is supported by national research reporting that '94 % of Enterprise RTOs reported an increase in total training undertaken since adopting nationally recognised training' (Smith et al. 2009, p. 295).

Meeting Identified Leadership Skills Deficits

The RTO's approach to training was based on workforce planning that linked job-specific capabilities (based on APS capability frameworks) to career streams, and focused on connecting workforce data with the monitoring of staff capability gaps against service delivery needs. Techniques to collect data included work-group forums, task checklists, work records, meeting minutes and current job descriptions. Workforce data informed job design, learning plans, retention strategies and partnership models.

Human resources personnel had consulted widely across the department with a number of teams regarding their analysis of job roles, resulting in a departmental workforce plan identifying a variety of specific training courses required to meet perceived skills shortfalls. 'Often the first sign that education and training programs are warranted is a specific idea, need, problem or opportunity that surfaces' (Caffarella and Daffron 2013, p. 136). In this case, the 'need' to be addressed resulted from a workforce analysis of the jobs that leaders across the organisation were employed to undertake. Roles were defined as: 'positions with line management responsibility for staff as an essential aspect of their core function' (archives). The desired outcome of the course was developing departmental leaders who understood the variety of factors impinging on choices they made, who understood the philosophy of the department and who understood how all parts of the department went about their operational business (archives).

Workers engaged in building their capabilities were allocated a facilitator from the enterprise RTO to work with them and their line manager in developing an individual learning plan aimed at attaining a qualification aligned to their current job role. The facilitator provided direction, coaching and access to resources, including organising and delivering learning programs and networking opportunities. All training was non-aspirational, that is, it was not directed towards future career prospects, as training and assessment were specific to each participant's current job role. Assessment was conducted in the workplace through demonstrations of job-related tasks or implementation and evaluation of negotiated projects. It had been agreed at departmental executive level that the training must be relevant to the individual participant's agreed performance plan negotiated with their line manager so that it could be seen as an opportunity to develop further leadership skills in their present role.

The performance review process was intended to give participants opportunities to engage in structured work-based experiences, thus contributing to their knowledge and skills that helped not only to achieve organisational objectives but also to build personal capability to facilitate positive change and innovation (Billett et al. 2012, p. 16). It was expected that as managers became more capable and confident they would also become more effective in dealing with the complexities of their job. As a result, it was expected that they would manifest higher levels of job satisfaction and commitment.

Aligning Workforce Development with National Training Standards

Training packages have been developed in response to particular industry training needs and contain nationally endorsed units of competency required by that industry to ensure a person is able to perform a particular job (Tovey and Lawlor 2008, p. 38). In this study, the leadership training course was based on the regulatory requirements of the training package qualifications chosen by the enterprise RTO executive team, that is, two Diplomas of Government from the Public Sector Training Package. Both diplomas had a similar base of study although one had an optional specialisation in management. In making this decision, the executive team had to consider VET training options carefully. The executive team was comprised of education managers, the majority of whom, at inception, had come from other organisations where VET training was their mainstream business.

Understanding the complexities of training packages and the assembling of appropriate units of competency constituting a qualification from the relevant training package also required deep knowledge of VET, as unpacking the meaning and significance of the content contained in the materials warranted careful analysis (Deng 2011). Alongside this knowledge base, course decision makers and subsequent developers had to pay attention to a variety of local divisional requirements that were incorporated into a course structured to meet VET competencies. The two diploma qualifications were framed around clusters of units of competency specified by Public Sector National Training Package rules that also specified the outcomes and assessment requirements for each unit of competency contained in the cluster. Also specified was the evidence to be gathered to determine whether the activity was performed in a competent manner and the conditions in which assessment was to be conducted (National Skills Standards Council 2012).

Developing, Delivering and Evaluating a Leadership Training Course Specific to a Public Service Workplace

Among the components for course development, delivery and evaluation considered here are context, selecting and organising content, and delivering and assessing content (where 'assessment' is the term substituted for 'evaluation') and the role played by facilitators. I discuss each of these components below as facilitators, who were recruited first as developers then as trainers, formulated, delivered and assessed a leadership training course in accordance with instructions from departmental executives.

Context

Context consists of three elements according to Caffarella and Daffron (2013, p. 80), namely human, organisational and environmental facets. In this study, the human element comprised a number of stakeholders such as the learners, their supervisors and line managers, divisional executives, executive directors and facilitators. Those responsible for developing and delivering the course needed to have well-honed communication and social skills in order to negotiate among these relevant stakeholders. The business of negotiating 'activity between and among educators, learners, organisations which have traditions, and other stakeholders all of whom have their own beliefs and contexts' was given close attention (Caffarella and Daffron 2013, p. 30).

Learners identified as having 'line management responsibility for staff' were invited to participate because they were considered to be departmental leaders who could maximise staff contribution to organisational performance through enabling improved use of new and existing skills (archives). Learners' line managers were actively engaged in the training process as they were responsible for nominating participants to the RTO as an outcome of their regular performance review; they were also expected to provide support during the implementation of workplace projects. In constructing and delivering the course, facilitators strove to interpret and translate the frameworks into instructional events and activities with reference to participants' context, while engaging them in the process of constructing their own knowledge and developing desirable abilities and skills. In an enterprise RTO, where training was not core business but addressed business needs, it was essential that participants' workplace contexts were understood and addressed to establish and maintain the credibility of the leadership course.

The second element, learning in the organisational context, went beyond orthodox training systems, and was linked to structures, values and behaviours operating within the workplace (Smith 2001). In so doing it was neither completely formal nor informal learning; rather it supported the claim that an adaptable workforce 'requires sound formal education as well as workforce contexts to ensure acquisition of

Strategic plans $\longrightarrow$ Departmental plans $\longrightarrow$ Operational plans $\longrightarrow$ Business issues$\longrightarrow$
Workforce analysis $\longrightarrow$ Training plans

Fig. 15.1 Foundations for workforce development

knowledge that is transferable to other workplace contexts' (Boud and Garrick 1999, p. 165). As well as organisational processes, attributes considered necessary by the departmental executive included issues and trends impacting on the organisation, policies guiding the work of each of the divisions, and the opportunity to think strategically across the organisation (archives). It was important for facilitators not only to capture knowledge that was integral to the workplace – the policies, procedures, work instructions, organisational structure, terminology and key stakeholders – but also to understand the tacit knowledge that was internalised by departmental staff without them necessarily being aware of its value to others. This type of knowledge was contextually based and was founded on individual experiences, beliefs, viewpoints and 'know-how'. It involved learning and skill but not in a way that was written down. Capturing canonical knowledge was an essential factor in developing and delivering the course as it involved key knowledge that guided staff, such as legislative requirements and codes of conduct. One developer emphasised the latter in an interview: 'the course is embedded in looking at ethical issues and decision making related to the ethical framework and how that applies to each of the workplaces' (Facilitator A).

The third element of context identified by Caffarella and Daffron (2013) is wider environmental factors influencing contemporary public sector leadership capacity. This was addressed in the government edict to achieve horizontal and vertical alignment by connecting policy intent with delivery and to integrate organisational goals with performance (Building capability: A framework for managing learning and development in the APS, 2013). In this case, wider environmental influences on workforce development were considered to be the State Strategic Plan, the Departmental Strategic Plan, and the Government High Performance Framework, with best practice principles, standards of excellence and high performing workplace criteria determining its operating systems, processes and key performance indicators. At the foundation of the leadership course was the State Strategic Plan, on which the Departmental Strategic Plan was formulated and in which the RTO strategic plan was included. The following diagram illustrates the cascading contextual influences on enterprise training (Fig. 15.1).

Selecting and Organising Content

In selecting, arranging and framing content for educational delivery in accordance with executive directives, each of the three developers addressed occupation-specific requirements and the recognition that education and training were associated with ongoing development across working lives through developing individual capacity to achieve workplace objectives (Billett et al. 2012). The course was based on a set of assumptions about learning that embraced several principles of adult education: recognition of the learner's relevant life and work experiences, reflection on experiences to add to deeper understanding and deliberately designed learning events. A critical aspect of the learning model included the involvement of a facilitator who negotiated plans with the learner and their line manager and designed assessment tasks that were congruent with the learner's own experiences, for example reflection journals, peer assessment, group or individual projects, and a range of presentation modes other than writing that manifested context and complexity of learning acquired. To prepare participants for their training, they were sent learner guides/ workbooks encompassing outcomes and structure, prerequisites, relevant qualifications and units of competency, learning method and assessment strategy as directed by the rules of the Public Sector Training Package that determined the leadership qualifications. The course incorporated three sections, the first being compulsory and the other two sections providing an option that each led to a slightly different qualification: Diploma of Government or Diploma of Government (Management).

Delivering and Assessing Content

Underpinning theory with immediate practical application in the workplace was considered to be sound educational practice, as it provides the opportunity to reflect on the skill of managing and the enhancement of capabilities (Blanchard and Thacker 2012). In this situation, learning opportunities were provided in structured workshop sessions delivered at intervals over a period of at least 12 months to address key issues, key concepts, related issues to explore, significance of these issues for participants, and different perspectives where critical thinking and reflection were encouraged. In addition, participation in online follow-up activities and in negotiated projects within individual workplaces was expected where participants were to apply a broader theoretical focus to a specific strategic issue/problem in their own workplaces and to report on outcomes at a final workshop.

Assessment is an essential component of any training plan as it provides facts on the value and worth of the learning acquired by the participant, who must demonstrate the specified level of competency achieved as a result of the training (Tovey and Lawlor 2008, p. 171). In this study, learners were assessed on participation in and contribution to all learning activities provided at each workshop session, personal learning records, online contribution to the group blog, and the presentation and report on the exploration, implementation and evaluation of their work-based learning project. This project was the culmination of all learning acquired and applied over at least the previous 6 months duration. (Two projects were required over the 12-month period.)

In addition, to match criterion-referenced assessment to workplace tasks, facilitators asked learners to present their CV and job description 'so that a cross-check can be made against the competencies aligned to the program' (archives).

The Role of Facilitators

An essential element in the effective delivery and assessment of content and subsequent learning was the expertise of the training facilitators who were considered to be experienced adult educators who helped to manage a process of information exchange (Tovey and Lawlor 2008, p. 217). The facilitator might not be the content expert, but drew out adults' experiences and ideas contributing to the body of knowledge. Contemporary learning theory guiding facilitators in this situation considered learning to be an active and individual process where people developed their own sense of reality from their own unique experiences (Caffarella and Daffron 2013). All eight graduates interviewed for this study commented positively on the role played by facillitators in this course – that of supporting everyone to do their best thinking and practice. Three examples are provided here:

> Facilitator B was a big support and I will be contacting her again for support with my new team. When you go through an education process like that you don't absorb everything and you put things into practice as you need. (Graduate #4)

> I'm really impressed with Facilitator A – she's absolutely five star. She's really knowledgeable and willing to answer your questions. If she doesn't know she follows up and delivers. She's very supportive and very encouraging. She's good value. (Graduate #2)

> You've got a timeline to work on – you've got facilitators bending over backwards to help you – they're all really fabulous. It's really helped me to keep on track. (Graduate #7)

Transfer of Leadership Learning in a Public Sector Workplace

Transfer of learning means how learners apply their learning once they have returned to their workplaces (Caffarella and Daffron 2013, p. 227). In planning for, negotiating and evaluating transfer of learning, facilitators were aware of several factors that helped or hindered the process, among which were learning context, immediate application, workplace environment and eliminating barriers (Daffron and North 2011). An effective context for learning must be used to engage the group in the learning process (Caffarella and Daffron 2013, p. 218). Participants commented several times during researcher workshop observations and in one-on-one interviews that they appreciated and valued the 'safe' group environment in workshops where issues that they were apprehensive about discussing openly in their work environment could be discussed in confidence. One participant reported: 'We all developed continuity and understanding of each other in groups I was in. They were all engaged in each session. We had that openness and honesty that you really need to learn with.'

Providing the opportunity to talk about issues and problems with others was important as it led to an understanding of a piece of knowledge and its application in different contexts through reflection and discussion with others. The learning context also incorporated presentations from key departmental executives on strategic issues, an important facet of workforce development in an enterprise as one graduate commented:

> The talk by the executive leaders was really good because it gave me a broader perspective. It's really helped me to get my head around the bigger picture, how it all fits in together, to develop my political nous – that's a big thing – strategic thinking and political thinking. (Graduate #7)

The transfer of learning was not always easy due, in the majority of cases discussed, to time constraints and lack of team cooperation. One manager whose project aim was to change team negative behaviour found it 'a very painful process', as practices agreed upon by the team were ignored later by half the team. This manager mentioned that the support of the facilitator on this occasion was pivotal in eliminating some of the barriers and in the learning that emerged from this experience. Another manager also mentioned team hindrance: 'In terms of dysfunction we had a lot of people with entrenched negative behaviours. Because of the workshops we've changed the culture of the team.' Generally there was a positive outcome of application of workplace projects. One graduate gave this example:

> I was using my learning as I was doing my work because it was an extended period of time; it was almost six months of applying my learning. What we [manager and team] focused on was how we could align our strengths. We ended up with a series of statements about the team which were appreciative and that became our core of resilience. Now our interactions are richer. We work through our problems in a different way. (Graduate #3)

Workforce Development Outcomes

In investigating one approach taken to workforce development focused on developing the skills and capabilities of leaders within their own context, I will now discuss the perspectives of key stakeholders – learners and their teams, departmental executives, and facilitators – to determine whether, in their view, the training was effective and met their various aims.

Learners, comprising 24 ongoing participants and eight graduates, expressed varying levels of satisfaction – all positive – with the training offered. One ongoing learner summarised this:

> It has reignited my enthusiasm for learning, particularly when you can remind yourself that this is not just learning for learning's sake. You're solving a problem and the integration of your learning into your work means learning is immediately transferrable into your job. So it improves your job performance. (Ongoing learner #2)

One graduate acknowledged that the opportunity afforded staff to enhance their knowledge and upgrade workplace skills through training delivered in their work time and at no cost to them was an organisational bonus:

> I am grateful to the department for providing the enhancement of education because when you're doing outside studies it's hard to fit in with your work schedule and family life. For

us it's great because it's part of learning with applying studies [to the workplace] and we get support from [line] management. (Graduate #7)

On the final evaluation sheets graduates documented that the most significant learning that emerged for them was: helped with strategic thinking (37.5 %); helped with team culture and workplace issues (25 %); and significant personal learning (25 %). Organisational context clearly emerged as an important learning environment, as one graduate expressed:

I understand government more and responsibilities such as accountability to the public. The course gave me a lot of those skills that you only realise you've learned when you're confronted with a situation. I didn't realise I could do this. You learn a better understanding of the government and your responsibilities. (Graduate #8)

The support provided by *key departmental executives* was essential in the ongoing delivery of the course as they expected to see return on their investment through increased retention and loyalty, improved leadership performance, and more highly skilled staff. Support offered to a course was dependent on acquiring a track record though delivering 'well-run, high quality programs that build respect and trust with … regular participants and convey to potential audiences they will get their money's worth' (Caffarella and Daffron 2013, p. 315). One learner discussed this support thus:

The Executive Director of xxx division talks very highly of this course. When he gave his talk to the directors' meeting, he promoted this program and looks very favourably at people who attend these programs. I was involved in heads of department meetings when I was acting [director] and he gave a comprehensive update on speaking about the program – he promoted it very highly to his directors; it promoted a lot of discussion. It's opened up discussion from directors of the value of going to see who's in these programs and speaking directly at them. It's an opportunity to showcase themselves as well. It's a two-way process. Directors enjoy going to speak because they see significant benefits in investing their time in this program. (Ongoing learner #2)

Facilitators were charged with the responsibility of designing, delivering and evaluating a leadership course based on three frameworks: the APS Senior Executive capability framework comprising five core leadership competencies, the workforce plan developed as a result of departmental analysis of leadership skills deficits and the national training frameworks leading to a diploma qualification. While they worked conscientiously and assiduously to meet these three demands, there were shortfalls that emerged in the third framework following a review 2 years after the initial course launch. Registered training organisations are audited regularly by the Australian Skills Quality Authority, as stated on their website: 'ASQA will undertake its role by assessing relevant organisations against the conditions of registration found in the new national legislation, the National Vocational Education and Training Regulator Act 2011 (in Part 2, Division 1, sections 21–30)' (http://www.asqa.gov.au/).

The auditors' task is to ensure RTO compliance with VET quality frameworks and other conditions defined in the act. Among other things, this means that assessment – defined as the process of collecting evidence and making judgements on whether competency has been achieved – 'must meet the requirements of the relevant training package or accredited course and must be conducted in accordance with the principles of assessment and the rules of evidence' (ASQA 2013, p. 1). During an audit of several courses structured in a similar way to the diplomas, the auditors believed the clustering of units of competency and the contextualising of training relevant to specific jobs did not meet all the conditions of assessment. Rather than issuing full registration, auditors granted limited registration with certain conditions requiring immediate rectification. Facilitators returned to their task and with much apprehension examined the course they had been offering over the previous 2 years for robustness and alignment of course assessments with national standards. After critical review and detailed analysis in the following months, one of the facilitators reflected in a focus group interview:

> The content is relevant to organisational needs but the assessments are what are required for audit purposes. I haven't been worried about the assessment of people's skills. I think we have developed those skills we said we would and I mostly know that from feedback. The competencies are being met but it may not be as clearly delineated as it might be. I would like the assessments to be more robust so I feel that the competencies are being covered in all aspects. The big assumption that was erroneously made [at the time of development] was that the competencies are included in their job descriptions which are why assessments don't specifically relate to the content. You can't pull out a job description for the auditor and say, 'this is what they know'. We need to build in information that it meets RTO requirements [for regulation] and it meets what are the organisational needs. (Facilitator A)

It seems from these remarks that training a flexible, adaptable workforce experiencing quality educational events such as work-based projects and activities, and managed by skilled facilitators who focused on processes rather than outcomes (as in competency-based training), presented quite a challenge. Indeed Hodge supported this view, suggesting that, when a complex role such as management incorporating a plethora of contextual practices 'can be encompassed in a statement of a competency standard, then some disconnection between the standards and practice in at least some parts of the field would be expected' (2011, p. 510). Disconnection there was indeed! A statement of disillusionment uttered by a facilitator in a focus group interview summed up the challenge of aligning contextualised training within a public sector environment with a nationally accredited course: 'If you were learning and development [a non-registered unit offering non-accredited training] you'd be doing learning around the organisational needs. When we have the qualifications [accredited training] we don't always have the flexibility' (Facilitator B).

Meanwhile, all await the auditors' next report to determine whether providing a nationally accredited leadership course will continue to be the best choice for this public service department where context is critical. At this moment in time and place, where it seems auditors made the final decision regarding an accredited training option, it was not the best choice. Perhaps the broader question, aired by Guthrie, needs further consideration at a national level: 'If their auditing practices are not in harmony with the intent of the system ... the audit process can potentially stifle the flexibility, innovation and responsiveness that industry says it wants of VET' (2009, p. 27).

References

Althaus, C., & Wanna, J. (2008). The institutionalisation of leadership in the Australian Public Service. In P. Hart & J. Uhr (Eds.), *Public leadership: Perspectives and practices* (pp. 117–132). Canberra: ANU Press.

Australian Public Service Commission. (2009). *Senior executive service report*. Canberra: Australian Public Service Commission. http://www.apsc.gov.au/publications-and-media-current- publications/senior-executive. Accessed 16 Oct 2013.

Australian Public Service Commission. (2013). *Building capability: A framework for managing learning and development in the APS*. Canberra: Australian Public Service Commission. http:// www.apsc.gov.au/publications-and-media-current-publications/building-capability. Accessed 16 Oct 2013.

Australian Public Service Commission. (n.d.). *Publications and media*. http://www.apsc.gov.au/ publications-and-media. Accessed 23–30 Sept 2013.

Australian Skills Quality Authority. (ASQA). http://www.asqa.gov.au/about/consultation/consultation.html. Accessed 22 Oct 2013.

Australian Workforce and Productivity Agency. (2012). *Future focus: Australia's skills and workforce development needs*. Discussion paper. Canberra: Australian Workforce and Productivity Agency. http://www.awpa.gov.au/publications/Documents/Future-Focus-Australias-skills- and-workforce-development-needs-Discussion-Paper.pdf. Accessed 23 Sept 2013.

Billett, S., Henderson, A., Choy, S., Dymock, D., Beven, F., Kelly, A., James, I., Lewis, J., & Smith, R. (2012). *Change, work and learning: Aligning continuing education and training*. Adelaide: National Centre for Vocational Education Research.

Blanchard, N., & Thacker, J. (2012). *Effective training* (5th ed.). Englewood Cliffs: Prentice Hall.

Boud, D., & Garrick, J. (1999). *Understanding learning at work*. London: Routledge.

Caffarella, R., & Daffron, S. (2013). *Planning programs for adult learners* (3rd ed.). San Francisco: Jossey-Bass.

Choy, S., Bowman, K., Billett, S., Wignall, L., & Haukka, S. (2008). *Effective models of employment-based training*. Adelaide: National Centre for Vocational Education Research.

Daffron, S., & North, M. (2011). *Successful transfer of learning*. Malibar: Kreiger.

Deng, Z. (2011). Revisiting curriculum potential. *Curriculum Inquiry, 41*, 538–559.

Edwards, M., Ayres, R., & Howard, C. (2003). *Public service leadership: Emerging issues*. Canberra: Australian Public Service Commission.

Guthrie, H. (2009). *Competence and competency based training: What the literature says*. Adelaide: National Centre for Vocational Education Research.

Henry, M., Lingard, B., Rizvi, F., & Taylor, S. (2013). *Educational policy and the politics of change*. London: Routledge.

Hodge, S. (2011). Learning to manage: Transformative outcomes of competency-based training. *Australian Journal of Adult Learning, 51*(3), 499–516.

Innovation and Business Skills Australia. (2011). *Karpin report revisited: Leadership and management challenges in Australia*. Melbourne: Innovation and Business Skills Australia.

Institute of Internal Auditors. (2011). *Public sector definition, supplemental guidance*. http://www. iia.org.au/. Accessed 23 Sept 2013.

Jennings, C., & Wargnier, J. (2010). Experiential learning: A way to develop agile minds in the knowledge economy? *Development and Learning in Organisations, 24*(5), 14–16.

Kane, J. (2007). The problem of politics: Public governance and leadership. In R. Koch & J. Dixon (Eds.), *Public governance and leadership: Political and managerial problems in making public governance changes the driver for re-constituting leadership* (pp. 131–149). Wiesbaden: Deutscher Universitats-Verlag.

Kelly, G., & Muers, S. (2002). *Creating public value: An analytical framework for public service reform*. London: Cabinet Office Strategy Unit.

National Skills Standards Council. (2012). *Standards for training packages*. www.training.gov.au. Accessed 15 Oct 2013.

Senge, P. (2006). *The fifth discipline: The art and practice of the learning organisation*. London: Random House.

Shergold, P. (2007). What really happens in the Australian Public Service: An alternative view. *Australian Journal of Public Administration, 66*(3), 367–370.

Smith, P. (2001). Learners and their workplaces: Towards a strategic model of flexible delivery of training in the workplace. *Journal of Vocational Education and Training, 53*(4), 609–628.

Smith, E., Pickergill, R., Smith, A., & Rushbrook, P. (2005). *Employers' commitment to nationally recognised training*. Adelaide: National Centre for Vocational Education Research.

Smith, A., Ocskowski, E., & Hill, M. (2009). *Reasons for training: Why Australian employers train their workers*. Adelaide: National Centre for Vocational Education Research.

Stoker, G. (2006). *Why politics matter: Making democracy work*. London: McMillan.

Tovey, M., & Lawlor, D. (2008). *Training in Australia*. Frenchs Forest: Pearson Education.

Wyse, A. (2007). *Executive leadership roles and associated skills: An Australian Public Sector perspective*. Ph.D. thesis, University of South Australia.

Chapter 16
Innovation, Change and the Intrapreneurial Mindset

John Thompson, Jarna Heinonen, and Jonathan M. Scott

Abstract Creativity underpins innovation which, in turn, underpins both entrepreneurship and change. Businesses – not ideas or products on their own – generate revenue; and in today's uncertain world there is a need to commit to ongoing change in these businesses. Much attention has been given to new product development and to process innovation in the 'corporate world', but arguably less to the *mindset* of the intrapreneurial people who are required to drive the change agenda. It is debatable just how seriously organisations seek to identify those people with intrapreneurial attributes and encourage them to identify and seize new opportunities. This chapter examines the role of people in innovation and change, reflects upon relevant aspects of thinking and doing, and offers insight into the 'intrapreneurial mindset', which we conceptualise and distinguish from the small firm–oriented entrepreneurial mindset. The chapter offers a framework – based on talent and temperament attributes – for identifying potential intrapreneurs, and it describes how this framework has been used in a small number of large corporate organisations in the United Kingdom. These findings are put into the context of the manager and leader attributes that are more generally sought by many organisations.

J. Thompson (✉)
Huddersfield University Business School, Huddersfield, UK
e-mail: j.l.thompson@hud.ac.uk

J. Heinonen
TSE Entre, School of Economics, University of Turku, Turku, Finland
e-mail: jarna.heinonen@utu.fi

J.M. Scott
Centre for Strategy & Leadership, Teesside University Business School, Middlesbrough, UK
e-mail: j.scott@tees.ac.uk

T. Short and R. Harris (eds.), *Workforce Development: Strategies and Practices*,
DOI 10.1007/978-981-287-068-1_16, © Springer Science+Business Media Singapore 2014

Introduction

The purpose of this chapter is to examine the role of people in innovation and change, to reflect upon relevant aspects of their thinking and doing and to offer insight into the 'intrapreneurial mindset'. There are a number of reasons why plans for new ideas or products do not always 'work to plan', one of which is a failure to have appreciated that some key assumption – whether it was made explicitly or implicitly – should not have been made. For example, initiatives to increase the number and quality of growth-oriented small businesses fail to produce the projected results if they do not discriminate between the enterprising person (who, with some carefully targeted support, is capable of setting up a micro business with limited growth potential) and the person with the potential to grow something of perceived value. Simply, not everyone who starts a business has the capability to be another Richard Branson or the right temperament and motivation. Nor is anyone with some knowledge of business techniques necessarily a suitable person to advise these start-up businesses: effective entrepreneur enablers relate to the people they work with because they possess a number of the entrepreneur qualities themselves, and can 'think inside the same box'.

In the world of corporate entrepreneurship (CE), where innovation and intrapreneurship are seen as important, there is a similar danger in assuming that techniques based on logical and sequential steps can *always* provide the definitive answer. While these techniques are valuable, they may become so sophisticated that they draw our attention away from other things, especially the 'softer' people aspects. In this chapter we use the terms 'corporate entrepreneurship' and 'intrapreneurship' interchangeably given that intrapreneurship (Pinchot and Pinchot 1978)[1] is, after all, the establishment and fostering of entrepreneurial activity within large organisations and Parker (2011) ultimately found few differences. CE is 'the process whereby an individual or a group of individuals, in association with an existing organisation, create a new organisation or instigate renewal or innovation within that organisation' (Sharma and Chrisman 1999, p. 18).

The underlying premise of this chapter is that if companies are to compete in today's global markets, as well as cope with uncertainty and change pressures, they will need to take both innovation and intrapreneurship seriously. Radiou et al. (2013) contended that 'jugaad innovation', resourcefully improvising solutions using simple means in the most adverse circumstances, has been replaced in developed countries by more institutionalised and structured innovation – and that a new (actually old) mindset is required. *Structured business processes and methods are unfit to deliver the agility and differentiation that enterprises need in a fast-paced and volatile world* (Radiou et al. 2013).

---

[1]Antoncic and Hisrich (2003) referred to the concept of intrapreneurship, not corporate entrepreneurship *per se*. We acknowledge that (depending on the studies) corporate entrepreneurship and intrapreneurship may not be understood as exact synonyms but represent slightly different phenomena of organisational renewal or change (see e.g. Sharma and Chrisman 1999).

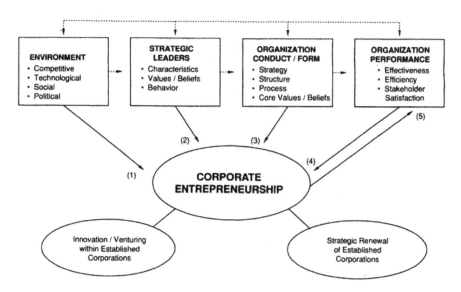

Fig. 16.1   Fitting CE into strategic management (Source: Guth and Ginsberg 1990)

Guth and Ginsberg's (1990) framework (see Fig. 16.1) divided CE into two routes – innovation and corporate venturing on the one hand, and strategic renewal on the other – relating CE to strategic management. In turn, innovation and intrapreneurship need people to think differently and be prepared to get on and do things that drive the change agenda, both reactively and proactively. However, we are not convinced that organisations always factor in the people dimension to the extent we believe is required and, instead, most of the emphasis is on process and sometimes techniques.

The importance of people (employees) has been downplayed in research into CE, which overstates the middle manager's role (Heinonen and Toivonen 2008). Burgelman (1983b) conceptualised middle managers almost as moderators in this process and top managers' role as 'strategic recognition rather than planning' (1983b, p. 1349). To some extent, Burgelman's seminal research seems to have been lost in subsequent literature with a 'middle manager focus'. Evidence indicates that there is a direct link between employee satisfaction, on the one hand, and intrapreneurship and thus the organisation's performance (proxied by its growth), on the other (Antoncic and Antoncic 2011), while Antoncic and Hisrich highlighted 'departures from the customary ways of doing business in existing organisations' (2003, p. 20). Indeed, in terms of intrapreneurial strategy, Ireland et al.'s (2009) model theorised its 'antecedents', 'elements' and 'outcomes', such as competitiveness and 'strategic repositioning'. Bolton and Thompson (2003, 2013) have emphasised the importance of talent and temperament alongside technique in successful entrepreneurs, regardless of the context. Techniques strengthen our conscious thought processes; but we cannot ignore unconscious thoughts, which affect the (often instinctive) behaviour that we frequently attribute to entrepreneurs and intrapreneurs.

To summarise, our objective in this chapter is to reflect a little upon how people think and behave. It is based on our belief that we need more intrapreneurs and we need to find more effective ways of identifying and supporting those people with the greatest potential to be successful intrapreneurs in the general world of business, in established corporations and in the public sector. Many do succeed, despite the challenges and obstacles to their progress – but their route could be less challenging and their progress swifter. Some fail because they do not receive the type of support that they need. Others remain 'hidden in the woodwork' as we fail to discover their true potential.

Innovation and Intrapreneurship

Innovation and business intrapreneurship have a number of constituent elements: ideas (spin-off points), infrastructure (premises, incubators, suppliers, venture capital, corporate resources, etc.), networks (support structures and effective enablers), educated and capable people (to help with the growth of the initiative or business) and intrapreneurs themselves (Bolton and Thompson 2013). While innovators endeavour to produce research and development and innovations in-house, it is clear that they are dependent for their success upon utilising alliance organisations' research through the open innovation paradigm (Chesbrough 2003), locally, nationally, and internationally (Bhidé 2008). Many global companies have significant R&D facilities in China and many other international locations in addition to their country of origin and, therefore, their innovative successes can be linked to the diversity of such innovation triggers.

Ideas come to people 'from anywhere' at any time: when people are deliberately working on a problem or issue, either on their own or in conversation, or anywhere. Although we can train ourselves to think about problems in particular ways, we cannot control unconscious thought processes; and yet people who read and network widely across a wide spectrum put themselves in a position to see and make connections that more specialised people would not be able to make – and thus 'think differently'. They have the potential to transpose ideas from one application area to another. James Dyson's development of the bagless vacuum cleaner borrowed heavily from his knowledge of centrifugal forces learnt when he was spray-painting plastic (Dyson and Coren 1997). Ideas are a critical foundation for innovation – but they have to be acted on. *Simply, viable innovation needs both ideas and people.*

Notably, many of the best ideas for intrapreneurial ventures come from the bottom up as, in the corporate setting, autonomy provides an organisation's members with the freedom and independence needed to pursue intrapreneurial actions (Lumpkin et al. 2009). Different actors have different, mutually interdependent, roles in CE processes and hence CE emerges as 'an outcome of mutually reinforcing pairs or bundles of factors' (Heinonen and Toivonen 2007, p. 179) and is more likely in organisations where all individuals' intrapreneurial potential is identified and nurtured and where organisational knowledge is widely shared (Ireland et al. 2006). On the other hand, employees actively influence upwards (Olufowote et al. 2005; Farmer and Maslyn 1999), in order to get their ideas through in their attempts to develop their workplace. When the ideas meet within this conversational space, individuals construct new meanings and transform the collective experience into knowledge (Baker et al. 2005). Consequently they may find opportunities for learning (i.e. knowledge exchange), which is an essential component of the intrapreneurial activities that enable the organisation to respond to changes in its environment (Dess et al. 2003). This dialogue, defined as reflective conversations enabling inquiry into existing mental models and shaping their emergence, has a key role in CE activities.

While the outcomes of many efforts and initiatives have been disappointing (e.g. an emphasis is on infrastructure at the expense of other areas), at the same time established businesses will always have new ideas and spin-off points; the challenge is to spot those with potential that will not distract attention away from existing core activities and also to encourage, support and reward those people with intrapreneurial potential who might champion the resulting initiative. Some organisations establish effective systems to support intrapreneurs; others 'talk a good story' but little materialises. 3M, as Drucker (2006) and others highlighted, discovered post-it notes by encouraging people to network and offering employees the opportunity to spend 15 % of their work time developing fresh ideas. One inventor had produced a glue whose sticking properties were inadequate for a normal glue, while a colleague who sang in a choir saw the potential value of the new substance because he could mark his score with detachable notelets. 3M encouraged people to network, good ideas were resourced and developed, and would-be innovators were provided with mentors (intrapreneur enablers) as well as financial and physical resources. Success brought rewards for some intrapreneurs.

While universities all too easily focus on science and engineering–driven ideas and infrastructure in the form of science parks and the like, Chesbrough (2003) highlighted how the established model that most key inventions and innovations come from large corporate laboratories has become history as scientists and engineers switch between organisations more freely than in the past. The need for networks that encompass large organisations, universities and new start-up businesses – to share ideas and knowledge and to spread the risk – demands a willingness to establish partnerships and alliances and to share, which requires trust, a people issue. Businesses, therefore, need people as well as ideas. These things are related because, after all, ideas do not make money; products do not make money; it is businesses that make money. Creativity leads to ideas; innovation develops new products from these ideas. We are searching for the right idea, the right product, the right market opportunity and the right timing. Ideas have little real value until something is done with them, until they are put into action. The important chain of events is: see it, seize it, start it and sustain it. Put simply, we might be awash with new ideas but how many of them are going to amount to something valuable? Creativity, then, underpins innovation, which in turn underpins intrapreneurship. Business is a process that starts with ideas, with thoughts, but something innovative has to be done with these thoughts. We can all too easily focus a great deal of attention on the process aspects of innovation and business and sometimes take creativity a little too much for granted, as typically we are dealing with creative people. We teach people creative techniques, but we need to drill deeper. Why and how are people naturally creative? Creativity starts in the mind, with conscious and unconscious thoughts. Do innovators think much about how they think, or do they spend most of their time processing ideas that they come across?

Supporting Innovation

Although technical systems may define optimum or maximum performance, in human activity systems people typically disagree on desired outcomes. Here the working definition of a problem situation is a disparity between what people feel should be happening and what can be observed to be happening. But the nature and extent of the gap is different for different people, depending upon their role, their background, and their personal values and beliefs. The search is for a better way of doing something that can be accommodated by all interested parties, not a search for an ideal. However, there is invariably recognition that fresh, creative ideas – especially ones that can reframe a problem and allow new insights – have a key role to play. There is also an appreciation that progress often involves trade-offs. To improve the performance of something one might have to sacrifice the performance of something else. For example, cost savings may require something to be sacrificed and ideally this must not be something of value for the customer. Alternatively, quality cannot be improved without the possibility of increasing costs – which is acceptable if customers are willing to pay. But sometimes these contradictions can be circumvented. Sometimes quality can be improved with lower costs. There can be increased output from reduced resource inputs.

Underpinning techniques designed to support innovation is the notion that constant innovation is inevitable and with any product or technology there will be continuous and incremental improvement. Innovation and progress is based on knowledge and how it is used. New product and process ideas can be based on new ideas from people who understand the existing products and processes; from new technologies or developments in other industries or fields; or from fashion trends that force a reaction. Christensen (1997) made an important distinction between 'sustaining technologies', which improve the performance of existing products for customers, and 'disruptive technologies', which transform markets and industries, sometimes with, on the face of it, lower performance. Smaller, cheaper motorcycles, for instance, transformed expectations in the market, which grew in size as a consequence, and benefited a number of relatively new competitors. All companies should constantly seek improvements, but it is all too easy to focus on 'sustaining' and ignore 'disruptive' technologies. Organisations may need to disrupt before they themselves are disrupted. But is it conceivable that these disruptive breakthrough ideas do not come from managed techniques but from inspired, visionary insights that individuals have in some uncontrolled way? Their unconscious thought processes bring together different strands in a new pattern.

Simply, we have to manage innovation, do innovation and think innovation. There is a top-down managed approach utilising techniques. There is also a bottom-up approach that attempts to identify and harness ideas from various people and various sources. They are both important.

In their description of the development of low-cost airline Go, Cassani and Kemp (2003) explained how Go's managers used a list of 'features to avoid' in crafting their business model. The following are examples:

- Don't let a frustrated pilot run the business.
- Don't (simply) choose routes that fly to places you enjoy visiting.
- Don't invest in an expensive home cost base.
- Don't use travel agents if it means expensive commissions.
- Don't buy a fleet of different airplanes.
- Don't confuse customers with complex pricing structures.
- Don't feed passengers with tasteless food they don't like.

Whilst there is a clear logic in using this approach to clarify the opportunity, there is also some benefit of hindsight. Ryanair and EasyJet had already built successful low-cost airlines, in turn 'borrowing ideas' from the hugely successful Southwest Airlines in America. When Southwest was started in America in the early 1970s, the approach might well have been different, less systematic and more intuitive. The idea for Southwest came from a perceived excess of demand over supply for regular, convenient and affordable flights between the three main cities in Texas. The very fact that the route structure was based on three cities meant the main airlines' model of hub and spoke routing was never adopted. Protracted negotiations delayed the start-up and cost money. When the flights began everything had to be on a shoe-string; there were no other options. This low-cost no-frills model was, in part, built on necessity, inspirational though it was. Ryanair in particular built on the Southwest model with a series of modest innovations, 'tweaks' really, that reduced costs and thus strengthened margins in a price-competitive industry. Thinking low cost was encouraged as natural behaviour.

Thinking and Acting

In understanding the link between ideas and actions, how we see the world is impor-tant. Some of us see threats where others see opportunities; for some the cup is always half empty and for others it is half full. Why? Intrapreneurs have two linked perceptions of the world. Firstly, they see it as a world full of opportunities and secondly as a world of actions in which they can make things happen. It is as if intrapreneurs have two eyes seeing *opportunities to grasp* and *actions to take*. The brain links these perceptions to give a single view of the world. If the opportunity side is not linked with focused action then in the worst case we have a butterfly that hops from one opportunity to another, never settling for very long. If the action side is not linked with the right opportunity then we have a beaver that builds a perfect dam but in the wrong place.

The link between these two perceptions, then, is important. The mature intrapreneur moves from opportunity to action without difficulty, but for the potential intrapreneur the link may not be so straightforward. The first sign of intrapreneurial talent is generally the ability to spot opportunities but the circumstances may be such that the potential intrapreneur does not have the confidence to go forward and take action. Lack of confidence in the early days is not a sign of a lack of talent. This is seen in other areas when a talent is discovered. Gifted public speakers often admit that they found it extremely difficult when they first addressed an audience. After a while they discover that public speaking comes naturally to them and they begin to enjoy it as their talent blossoms. It is the same with intrapreneurs when they discover that they are able to spot an opportunity and take it to fruition. Once they find they can do this they gain confidence and very soon it becomes something that they do naturally, even habitually – they have discovered that they are intrapreneurs. So, if we want to truly understand our – or someone else's – propensity to innovate and to influence change in the world around us, we need to penetrate the mind (or consciousness) of the innovator/intrapreneur in question.

Many innovators and intrapreneurs bring together ideas and thoughts from all over the place. This could appear to happen somewhat randomly, but it could happen because they are people who are specifically questioning why things are as they are. They are perpetually looking for improvement possibilities. Hargadon (2003) contended that Henry Ford did just that with the assembly line for the Model T. He blended interchangeable parts (taken from the sewing machine industry) with continuous flow production techniques he had seen in soup canning and the assembly layout pioneered in slaughterhouses.

These intrapreneurs and inventors are no smarter, no more courageous, tenacious or rebellious than the rest of us. They are simply better connected. Hargadon may be over-stating the point here, but his argument that there are more intrapreneurs than we yet recognise is well made and they *see opportunity where others see chaos, contradiction and confusion* (Timmons 1989). In addition, of course, they act. It is, of course, interesting that when intrapreneurs and others constantly question and challenge they make others feel uncomfortable and sometimes threatened. They may not always be the most popular people!

Some people also read and study across a wide range of disciplines, looking for things that might be transferable. The transfer process in the end can be either conscious or unconscious. In this context, we perhaps have to accept that there may never be an adequate explanation for the creative inspiration that some people have. Who can explain how Beethoven, Handel and Mozart found their ideas and compositions? If we can find the answer to this then maybe computer composition software will produce music that has the same impact as Mozart.

Moreover, the impacts are not always predictable. The invention of the clock gave us the ability to measure time accurately. This transferable ability for precision measurement has proved invaluable in many other related and unrelated areas. Developments in computing move the computer industry along the track, with both incremental and sea-change improvements. But computer technology has also impacted upon many other industries and made possible what once seemed impossible. In the context of intrapreneurs it is important we understand something of this for, as Hargadon (2003) argued, there are more intrapreneurs 'out there' than we yet recognise. It is important that we find them and nurture them. We need to recognise them and their potential, and believe in them and their potential. They in turn have to believe in themselves and their abilities and in the value of their ideas. It is necessary to understand the extent to which the person 'dares to be different' and has the courage to act.

For this to be the case, the person must be willing to accept failure and the consequences of failure – which is not saying they necessarily expect to fail and certainly not saying they want to fail. Quite the contrary, they want desperately to succeed, often for reasons best known to them.

The Power of Solving Problems Together

It has been commented that 'the way we see the problem is the problem'. We can take this to mean that however we define a problem that is the issue we are going to deal with. We know our problem! The other interpretation could be that it is problematical that our perception of the problem could well be different from the views of others. The problem lies in our attribution of meaning, our personal way of seeing something. The same principles apply to potential opportunities. Some people see a particular situation as an opportunity that they are minded to act on. Others see the same situation and dismiss it as having no consequential significance. Christensen (1997) reminded us that technology advances can sometimes offer more than customers want – 'scientists can over-shoot'. Yet customers do not have all the answers, either!

Innovation literature emphasises the role of intra- [endogenous] and inter- [exogenous] organisational processes relying on extensive communication and knowledge exchange. The recent CE literature – and seminal older studies (e.g. Burgelman 1983a, b) – also recognises the role of both top-down and bottom-up influences in the emergence of CE. Given the crucial importance of the channels transferring the influences within the organisation and the idea of extensive boundary spanning communication, CE can be considered to have emerged particularly when top-down and bottom-up influences meet and negotiate in conversational space and create positive complementarities. Consequently, some researchers have suggested further study into whether there are complementarities among the managerial (top-down) and individual (bottom-up) influences (Heinonen and Toivonen 2008), both anticipated to have their role in CE. Based on complementary theory, both causal directions are worth investigating (see Bresnahan et al. 2002). Due to the role of knowledge exchange and boundary-spanning communication for innovation activities, the focus is on modalities, that is, channels that transfer the influences within the organisation. It is acknowledged that both internal and external knowledge and boundary spanning might be important for CE activities. We consider that an innovation, namely the creation of something new and different (Kuratko and Audretsch 2009), is one outcome of such intrapreneurial activity (Heinonen and Scott 2010). Although innovation is an outcome of CE, on the other hand CE can also be a vehicle to bring innovation to market. In this sense, then, intrapreneurial innovation could be conceptualised not just as a two-way interchange between intrapreneurs and innovations, but as a circular, cyclic process in which one phenomenon contributes to the other, and vice versa. By doing so, they are under the control of their leaders, but the leaders are similarly affected by the employees' behaviour (Heinonen and Toivonen 2007). Straightforward communication is vital for this bottom-up influence to be channelled upwards to the managerial level (Heinonen and Toivonen 2008).

The differential levels of top-down and bottom-up influences, namely intrapreneurial innovative triggers, generate varying synergies between senior managers and employees, which are then either converted into strategic actions or not. Key to successful innovation is the notion of employee involvement or 'high-involvement innovation' (Schroeder and Robinson 1991), a concept that has not yet penetrated the boundaries of the CE discipline and concept.

The FACE of the Intrapreneur

Bolton and Thompson (2003, 2013) have identified certain attributes that define the intrapreneur. The acronym they propose is FACE: focus, advantage, creativity and ego. These are natural and instinctive behaviours that define intrapreneurs' style and approach. The strength of each attribute, and the relationship between them, allows us to understand a person's intrapreneurial potential.

The order in which they work is a mirror image of FACE. Our inner ego determines whether we act at all. This is our inner drive, our motivation to do something. Creativity and advantage work together, to identify and prioritise good opportunities. Creativity generates ideas and spots opportunities; advantage selects ones worth pursuing. Ideas, after all, are not necessarily opportunities. Intrapreneurs do this naturally and instinctively; at the same time, some techniques do provide valuable frameworks for making the assessment. Focus (time, target and action focus) works with our outer ego to make things happen. Our outer ego comprises our courage (our behaviour in the face of setbacks), our responsibility and our accountability. Thus we can see a thinking-seeing-doing chain.

Personalising this process, *creativity* thus affects the type and quality of ideas you have. You enjoy problems and problem solving. You naturally look for new opportunities to be different. *Advantage* helps you select those ideas that are worth pursuing. You understand customers. You have a clear vision for what you are trying to achieve. You appreciate what resources you need and are willing to set off without necessarily having all the resources you know you are going to need. And you are minded to set milestones and review your progress. *Focus* is the third essential requirement. *Action focus* means you are minded to get on and do something. *Target focus* means you know what you are trying to achieve and you will not get distracted. *Time focus* is linked to a sense of urgency.

These three attributes are talents. In one sense, we are either naturally like this or we are not. We can hone our skills and we can be offered certain helpful techniques – such as courses in creativity, problem solving, time management and project management – which will help us improve our performance. But if these are not natural behaviours it is unlikely that we will ever achieve excellence and outstanding performance, although clearly we can improve.

Systematic innovation processes are designed to help people manage creativity and secure advantage. They are, therefore, valuable. But arguably they will always be more effective with people who are already strong in creativity and advantage – and yet many of these people come up with good ideas without the need for designed frameworks. Paradoxically, then, it is tempting to think of techniques as a substitute for talent. Some people need techniques to counter relatively low strengths in creativity and advantage.

Even if we have the talents, we also have to want to do something with them that exploits their true potential. Our temperament must underpin and lead our talents. The most important descriptor of our intrapreneurial temperament is our *ego*, which has both inner and outer layers. Our inner ego is built around our motivation. What is it we want to do and achieve? This needs supporting with self-assurance (we have to believe in ourselves and our talents) and dedication to make what is possible happen. Much of this is known only to ourselves, and to those who are very close to us and live with our dreams and self-doubts, whatever image we might wish to project to the outside world, to other people. The outside world sees more of our outer ego than our inner ego. Here we are talking about our ability and willingness to accept responsibility for our actions and to be accountable. It also embraces our courage: our willingness to take certain risks and our willingness to fail; our willingness to confront situations and not walk away at the slightest hint of difficulty; our willingness to stand up and be counted.

There is a fifth characteristic, *team*. T completes the acronym and makes the word FACET. Team qualities are required to act as a multiplier effect and enable greater output. Intrapreneurs cannot build something of value on their own. They have to harness the skills and support of other key people, whom they have to select and persuade. Part of this comes from effective networking. We all know of teams that work well: they are creative, supportive of each other and they make things happen. Others seem to get bogged down. People argue. There is little trust.

It is not unusual for us to think of management teams as task-based teams, ones that can cover all the important functions such as sales, finance and operations. Utilising the ideas of Belbin (1981) it has also become increasingly normal to look at the natural roles that individuals contribute in team situations, attempting to iron out potential conflicts and engender harmony. Some people are good with ideas, some at group dynamics, some at finding information and others at translating ideas into actions. Intrapreneur teams (teams led by an intrapreneur) and intrapreneurial teams (teams that behave intrapreneurially) ensure that there is creativity (ideas), advantage (clear routes forward) and focus (targets and action plans that get followed through) as well as a real determination to make things happen and achieve results (ego). Chesbrough (2003) reminded us that ideas and information are shared in the most effective networks, and that it was such networks that helped spawn many of the technology advances and new spin-offs that created the Silicon Valley phenomenon.

FACETS and the Corporate World

Thompson (unpublished work) used the online FACETS indicator of intrapreneurial potential that he developed with Bolton (http://www.efacets.co.uk) with a number of large corporate organisations, largely in services rather than manufacturing and exclusively in the UK. All of these organisations had expressed an interest in identifying managers with intrapreneur attributes who might be expected to be important contributors in driving change in their organisation. The indicator had also been used with successful and would-be intrapreneurs around the world and considerable data had been accumulated and analysed, so comparisons and benchmarking were possible. Managers with strong intrapreneur attributes were clearly evident: in a number of instances some very high advantage scores were found, although the spectrum was wide and there were other managers whose advantage scores were relatively low. Perhaps expectedly from managers perceived by their employers to be strong performers in their existing role, their team scores were relatively strong. A number of useful observations have been made.

The organisation needs to be clear about how it will use the data and the insight the data offers. There should be an obvious benefit in being able to identify those managers who possess intrapreneur attributes, especially if change is high on the corporate agenda. But how will the organisation and its senior managers use this insight? The emphasis might be on encouraging these potentially intrapreneurial managers to use their attributes and to be more innovative in the posts they hold. There is also a possibility they might be seconded to special change projects.

How do the individual managers themselves respond? Some of those who were identified as naturally intrapreneurial commented that it helped explain why they sometimes felt they were out of alignment with certain colleagues when they sought to drive change. Others were more reflective about organisational expectations and promotion criteria. If they believed that being at the forefront of change initiatives might work against them, because of an expectation of compliance and risk avoidance amongst certain key colleagues, then they would hold back – but express frustration about the organisation's culture. Only a limited number were in a position where they were already at the forefront of change and saw their behaviour as natural.

Every manager received personal feedback which put the findings in a wider context. Possessing intrapreneur attributes does not mean people will choose to use these attributes in their work environment. They might use them in other aspects of their life, for example. They might also possess strong leader or manager attributes and feel these are more important for progressing up the organisational hierarchy. There was a different issue with some managers whose intrapreneur attributes were low. For them it is important to put these particular FACETS attributes in the context of the different attributes that characterise 'natural' leaders and managers. Where people are instinctively competitive, as many managers are, there is a desire to score strongly in every assessment of this nature. Scoring relatively low as an intrapreneur may well mean that an individual is not naturally a change leader but that for other circumstances they possess exactly the attributes that will be valuable. But this is not automatically the conclusion the managers themselves reach or accept.

In summary, organisations and certain senior managers can use this data to inform how they deploy people in the context of change initiatives, as well as how they might provide appropriate support to help these managers both to develop personally and deliver innovation, and how they might reward them appropriately.

Conclusions

The objective of this chapter has been to reflect upon aspects of both thinking and behaviour by people in organisations in the context of innovation and intrapreneurship. We stated at the outset that it is our belief that we need more intrapreneurs and we need to find more effective ways of identifying and supporting those people with the greatest potential to be successful intrapreneurs. This, we contend, is relevant for the general world of business, for established service organisations and for the public sector. Many individuals in established organisations of all types are successful innovators and intrapreneurs, despite sometimes having to deal with challenges and obstacles that might restrict their progress. Despite this, their route could be less challenging and their progress swifter. However, others either try or fail because they do not receive the type of support that they need or remain 'hidden in the woodwork' as we fail to discover their true potential.

Intrapreneurship, like entrepreneurship, is a process driven by opportunity and a willingness to act on opportunities that have been spotted. It is driven by action. We recognise this but also believe it is important not to believe that techniques that support the innovation process provide all the answers to the innovation challenge for organisations. Techniques have a value, but it is important not to ignore the person. In this chapter we have examined the intrapreneurial mindset and identified key intrapreneur attributes and explored them in the context of both managerial and employee actions, with both top-down and bottom-up forces at work.

We conclude that it is important that both employers and individuals recognise and develop their intrapreneurial attributes and mindset as these may lie behind intrapreneurial behaviour. However, innovation and intrapreneurship, while affected by attributes and mindsets, have an underlying process element which is about making things happen and change, such that action needs to be taken. An intrapreneurial mindset needs to be exploited. The cited research with established corporations confirms that they employ managers with intrapreneurial attributes but it does not follow that they always exploit this potential, or that managers and employees are in a position where they are encouraged to behave intrapreneurially.

References

Antoncic, J. A., & Antoncic, B. (2011). Employee satisfaction, intrapreneurship and firm growth: A model. *Industrial Management & Data Systems, 111*(4), 589–607.

Antoncic, B., & Hisrich, R. D. (2003). Clarifying the intrapreneurship concept. *Journal of Small Business and Enterprise Development, 10*(1), 7–24.

Baker, A. C., Jensen, P. J., & Kolb, D. A. (2005). Conversation as experiential learning. *Management Learning, 36*(4), 411–427.

Belbin, R. M. (1981). *Management teams: Why they succeed or fail.* Oxford: Heinemann.

Bhidé, A. (2008). *The venturesome economy: How innovation sustains prosperity in a more connected world.* Woodstock: Princeton University Press.

Bolton, B., & Thompson, J. (2003). *The entrepreneur in focus: Achieve your potential.* London: Thomson Learning.

Bolton, B., & Thompson, J. (2013). *Entrepreneurs: Talent, temperament, opportunity* (3rd ed.). London: Routledge.

Bresnahan, T. F., Brynjolfsson, E., & Hitt, L. M. (2002). Information technology, workplace, organisation, and the demand for skilled labor: Firm level evidence. *Quarterly Journal of Economics, 117*(1), 339–376.

Burgelman, R. A. (1983a). A process model of internal corporate venturing in the diversified major firm. *Administrative Science Quarterly, 28*(2), 223–244.

Burgelman, R. A. (1983b). Corporate entrepreneurship and strategic management: Insights from a process study. *Management Science, 29*(12), 1349–1363.

Cassani, B., & Kemp, K. (2003). *Go: An airline adventure.* London: TimeWarner.

Chesbrough, H. (2003). *Open innovation: The new imperative for creating and profiting from technology.* Boston: Harvard Business Publishing.

Christensen, C. (1997). *The innovator's dilemma: When new technologies cause great firms to fail.* New York: Harper Collins.

Dess, G. G., Ireland, R. D., et al. (2003). Emerging issues in corporate entrepreneurship. *Journal of Management, 29*(3), 351–378.

Drucker, P. F. (2006). *Innovation and Entrepreneurship*, revised edition, Harper Collins. The original work was published by Heinemann in 1985; the first Harper Collins edition, 1993.

Dyson, J., & Coren, G. (1997). *Against the odds: An autobiography.* London: Orion.

Farmer, S. M., & Maslyn, J. M. (1999). Why are styles of upward influence neglected? Making the case for a configurational approach to influences. *Journal of Management, 25*(5), 653–682.

Guth, W. D., & Ginsberg, A. (1990). Guest editors' introduction: Corporate entrepreneurship. *Strategic Management Journal, 11*(4), 5–15.

Hargadon, A. (2003). *How breakthroughs happen: The surprising truth about how companies innovate.* Boston: Harvard Business Publishing.

Heinonen, J., & Scott, J. M. (2010, September). Organising corporate entrepreneurial innovative activities for the future: Integrating the lessons learnt from the innovation and corporate entrepreneurship literatures. In *Proceedings of the British Academy of Management (BAM) Conference*, Sheffield, UK.

Heinonen, J., & Toivonen, J. (2007). Approaching a deeper understanding of corporate entrepreneurship: Focusing on co-evolutionary processes. *Journal of Enterprising Culture, 15*(2), 165–186.

Heinonen, J., & Toivonen, J. (2008). Corporate entrepreneurs or silent followers? *Leadership & Organization Development Journal, 29*(7), 583–591.

Ireland, R. D., Kuratko, D. F., & Morris, M. H. (2006). A health audit for corporate entrepreneurship: Innovation at all levels: Part I. *Journal of Business Strategy, 27*(1), 10–17.

Ireland, R. D., Covin, J. G., & Kuratko, D. F. (2009). Conceptualizing corporate entrepreneurship strategy. *Entrepreneurship: Theory and Practice, 33*, 19–46.

Kuratko, D. F., & Audretsch, D. B. (2009). Strategic entrepreneurship: Exploring different perspectives of an emerging concept. *Entrepreneurship: Theory and Practice, 33*(1), 1–17.

Lumpkin, G. T., Cogliser, C. C., & Schneider, D. R. (2009). Understanding and measuring autonomy: An entrepreneurial orientation perspective. *Entrepreneurship: Theory and Practice, 33*(1), 47–69.

Olufowote, J. O., Miller, V. D., & Wilson, S. R. (2005). The interactive effects of role change goals and relational exchanges on employee upward influence tactic. *Management Communication Quarterly, 18*(3), 385–403.

Parker, S. C. (2011). Intrapreneurship or entrepreneurship? *Journal of Business Venturing, 26*(1), 19–34.

Pinchot, G., & Pinchot, E. (1978). *Intra-corporate entrepreneurship*. New York: Tarrytown School for Entrepreneurs in New York.

Radiou, N., Prabhu, J., & Ahuja, S. (2013). *Jugaad innovation: Think frugal, be flexible, generate breathtaking growth*. San Francisco: Jossey Bass.

Schroeder, D., & Robinson, A. (1991). America's most successful export to Japan: continuous improvement programs. *Sloan Management Review, 32*(3), 67–81.

Sharma, P., & Chrisman, J. J. (1999). Toward a reconciliation of the definitional issues in the field of corporate entrepreneurship. *Entrepreneurship: Theory and Practice, 23*(3), 11–27.

Timmons, J. A. (1989). *The entrepreneurial mind*. Andover: Brick House Publishing.

Part IV
Harmonising Across Boundaries and Borders: Case Studies

Chapter 17
Recruitment of Skilled Employees and Workforce Development in Germany: Practices, Challenges and Strategies for the Future

Thomas Deissinger and Kathrin Breuing

Abstract This chapter focuses on workforce development in the German context. Two issues are relevant: the first one deals with the links between the standard form of initial VET, that is, the dual apprenticeship system, and formalised further training, which in its various facets has a major function in the German context when it comes to career building, but also to establishing a craft business. Second, companies in Germany, as in other countries, use internal schemes of personnel development and further training to maintain their workforces both in quantitative and qualitative terms. A crucial challenge currently seems to be demographic change, and the way companies try to cope with his challenge has led to new forms of in-company personnel development that were unknown in the past. Both aspects are discussed in this chapter.

Introduction

Workforce development in Germany is partly associated with formal initial and continuing training, but also depends on what companies consider functional with respect to their employees. Besides these formal pathways companies have developed individualised patterns of workforce development, partly as 'branch' typical further training, partly as job-specific ways of competence adaptation in the workplace. Therefore, personnel development, in which training activities play a major role, has no real 'system character' as it is rather heterogeneous building on organisational and economic patterns – quite in contrast to the pedagogical dimension which is a core element of most formal training. Hereby, the so-called dual system has the function of imparting skills for occupations in relevant technical

T. Deissinger (✉) • K. Breuing
Department of Business and Economics Education, The University of Konstanz,
Konstanz, Germany
e-mail: thomas.deissinger@uni-konstanz.de

and commercial sectors of the economy. Against the background of a 'mental pattern' according to which companies and public stakeholders in common feel responsible for the training and recruitment of skilled workers and commercial experts with qualifications below degree level, the system also offers opportunities for the workforce to use their qualifications for further training, be it formal or informal. One of the typical examples for this is the 'master worker/craftsman qualification'. Although workforce development within companies appears to be a rather heterogeneous concept, the German frame of mind holds that an initial vocational qualification normally should be a prerequisite for a career in a company. In recent years, besides the 'non-academic' apprenticeship track, higher education degrees have grown in importance in the German context. This means that new patterns of 'tertiarisation' of VET begin to change the architecture of the German education system. With it, the social composition of the workforce in companies, especially in industrial enterprises, is changing, although this cannot be said of the craft sector which still recruits its workforce in a more or less traditional way.

The following sections focus on two aspects we consider to be relevant for this discussion on workforce development, that is, the links of continuing training and personnel development in and for company workplaces with initial training, especially the apprenticeship system, and the issue of how companies try to cope with changes in their environment – with demographic change at the forefront – to maintain the quality of their workforce in the future.

The Standard Pathway for Skilled Workers: The Dual System of Apprenticeship Training

Germany may be characterised as a country with a 'mass apprenticeship system' based on a strong occupational identity of those holding the corresponding qualifications (Ryan 2003, p. 150). Also in quantitative terms, apprenticeships represent the dominant pattern of initial skill formation below degree level as well as of socio-economic integration into the labour market (Steedman 2010; Deissinger 2010, Deissinger et al. 2012). Since companies normally recruit their apprentices from the lower stratum of the education system, the links between school education and VET are comparatively strong. Although some 15 % of apprentices hold some kind of higher education entrance qualification (*Abitur* or *Fachhochschulreife*), the majority of school leavers are students who have either no aspiration or the possibility to take up studies at a university or other higher education institutions. The specific 'apprenticeship culture' typical for non-academic initial vocational training in Germany has a long-standing cultural dimension (Deissinger 1994), and, despite its medieval origins and 'old-fashioned' terminology, still is one of the pivotal topics of national VET policy. The general significance given to apprenticeship as an institutional solution for the problem of skill formation normally depends on the political focus and the economic relevance of the interaction or interdependence between VET on the one hand and general and higher education on the other. Besides the apprenticeship system, school-based forms of vocational learning, such as 'vocational colleges', also represent more or less traditional courses and qualifications, which are normally institution-based, shaped by state influence and more or less clearly didactically-steered, pedagogical arrangements. There are, however, differences when it comes to formally linking up these traditional structures with other forms of vocational learning. The reason for this is the overall importance which companies dedicate to the dual system when it comes to recruiting skilled workers, artisans or commercial experts below the academic (Master or Diploma) level.

The cultural imprints for this kind of initial vocational training as the first cornerstone of workforce development become obvious once one compares the 'Germanic' model (also strong in Austria and the German-speaking cantons of Switzerland) with 'Anglo-Saxon' solutions for the problem of skill formation. Here, beyond the institutional peculiarity of both general and technical education in a vocational school besides learning in the workplace, the understanding of vocational pathways (Harris and Deissinger 2003) and the value given to VET in general appear to be unique in the international context. These traits of German VET become manifest when we look at the challenges imposed by the European Union with its Lifelong Learning policy and one of its derivates, the European Qualifications Framework. It seems that countries that differ in terms of their VET systems and traditions, especially with respect to the relationship between full-time VET and company-based training, such as apprenticeships, also differ in terms of their adaptability to the overarching European VET policy ideas. One of these ideas is the conceptualisation of National Qualifications Frameworks (NQF) (Young 2003). Work on Germany's NQF had to pick up the issues of re-defining borders, pathways, levels and transition options between VET and other educational sub-systems, and the same for sub-systems within the VET system such as full-time VET, vocational preparation, vocational introductory courses and further training. The result, being rather an incomplete answer to Europeanisation, has been a re-confirmation of the overall significance of apprenticeships and also of continuing training in its wake (master craftsmen, technicians etc.) to which the NQF pays special tribute by, for example, placing the master craftsman qualification (Meister) on the same level as a bachelor degree. This positioning once again underlines the social and economic importance of the apprenticeship system. In a recent press release, the president of the German Chamber Association (DIHK) 'warns' that 'uncontrolled academisation' could be a wrong way for Germany to solve its qualification and recruitment problems in the future (Schweitzer 2014, n.pag.). The background of this warning is the unquestioned outlook that the German economy will run into serious skill shortages in the future due to a demographic curve that is sliding.

Both institutionalisation and didactical standardisation form the basis of the kind of training typical for the German 'learning culture' in the apprenticeship system (Harris and Deissinger 2003). In this system, with its 350 recognised training occupations, the commitment and interest of chambers, trade unions and companies are crucial and therefore the needs of companies and workplace developments as well as organisational or technological changes normally stand at the beginning of establishing or modernising a training scheme. Training schemes, quite in contrast with England or Australia, are comprehensively regulated patterns of vocational qualifications that require a fixed training time, curricular regulation on the side of the vocational school, compulsory general and technical education in school as well as a final examination before the chamber. A specific pedagogical component comes in with the compulsory subjects provided through school attendance in the part-time vocational school, which stands both for theoretical vocational learning as well as general education during the apprenticeship. Ryan puts this in contrast with the British approach to VET: 'A striking difference from Germany is the absence of minimum training periods, such as a 3-year program for bakers. Similarly, apprentices need not take part-time technical education' (Ryan 2001, p. 136) The Vocational Training Act provides for all these regulatory aspects with respect to company-based training (Deissinger 1996). It places vocational training in the hands of firms and chambers and thus emphasises the principle of self-government (Zabeck 1975). At the same time, the Act takes account of traditional features of guild apprenticeships while simultaneously submitting in-company training to homogeneous, supervisable and examinable standards. The 'competent authorities' function not just as examining bodies but also as monitoring agencies for in-company training.

Modernisation within the dual system currently seems to happen mainly on the curricular level. It has materialised in the creation or revision of training schemes within the system of 'skilled training occupations' which now even allow for modest features of modularisation. Implanting modules within training schemes as didactical units with a mandatory but optional character (like in the IT occupations created in 1997) no longer seems to be incompatible with a holistic notion of competence (Euler 1998, p. 96ff.). At the same time, curricular provisions which take account of new technological developments and/or needs of companies to react quickly to these changes, including more flexibility for training, are now much more relevant than some 20 or 30 years ago, when major modernisation activities began to 'cleanse' the existing system of training occupations. Today, using modules in a more open manner means that companies can adapt their workforce development at the state of initial training to their specific organisation and technologies, although there is a general conviction in the research community that the system has to become even more flexible (Euler and Severing 2006; Baethge et al. 2007). On the other hand, interest groups, such as trade unions and chambers, are eager to underline their belief in the efficiency of the dual system as the 'royal road' into skilled employment.

Table 17.1 shows the relevance of apprenticeship training for the two major sectors of the German economy, namely, industry and trade (including commercial occupations) and the craft sector. It also illustrates the fact that the dual system is basically a pathway outside higher education for graduates from lower and intermediate secondary schools (*Haupt- und Realschulen*), but also that branches differ when it comes to predominantly recruiting school leavers from these secondary schools.

Table 17.1 Training sectors in the German economy and dominant qualifications of apprentices

	Number of entrants into an apprenticeship (2012)	Most prominent school qualification of apprentices (2011)
Industry and trade	332,622	Intermediate secondary = 43.6 %
Crafts	147,327	Lower secondary = 52.0 %
Public service	12,102	Intermediate secondary = 49.0 %
Agriculture	13,260	Lower secondary = 45.7 %
Professions	43,014	Intermediate secondary = 56.4 %
Home economics	2,763	Lower secondary = 58.3 %
Maritime	183	No information available
Total no. of entrants	**551,271**	

Source: Bundesinstitut für Berufsbildung (2013, p. 170)

This also means that continuing training and personnel development of the German workforce are closely intertwined with the school system.

The Architecture of Formalised Continuing Training Against the Background of the German Apprenticeship System

There are five major types of further training qualifications at sub-degree level which, in the German context, are relevant for either self-employment or for in-company careers. All these qualifications require completion of an apprenticeship or an equivalent skills level, and they lead individuals to a qualification level which is located above the level of a normal apprenticeship qualification:

- Master craftsmen or master workers (*Meister*)
- Industrial or commercial specialists (*Fachwirte*)
- Technicians (*Techniker*)
- Business specialists (*Betriebswirte*)
- In-company trainers (*Ausbilder*)

Whereas the qualifications of master craftsmen, industrial specialists and trainers (engaged in training apprentices in the dual system) require a chamber examination, technicians and business specialists receive their further training in a vocational school and have to take examinations which are defined and held by the respective federal state's school administration. Vocational schools in Germany are complex institutional entities (Deissinger et al. 2006), with the part-time vocational school normally being the largest segment, but they also comprise, besides the various full-time vocational courses, further training classes with technical or commercial specialisation, among which those for technicians belong to the most relevant ones. These classes, called *Fachschulen*, can only be attended after having completed an apprenticeship, and can also be combined with a *Fachhochschulreife* (entrance qualification for universities of applied sciences). A crucial prerequisite, however, is

Table 17.2 Formal further training qualifications in Germany

Number of passed examinations	2002	2010	2011	2012
Master workers (*Industriemeister*), industry or commerce	9,368	9,678	11,325	9,966
Master craftsmen (*Handwerksmeister*), crafts	26,674	19,659	22,236	22,674
Industrial or commercial specialists (*Fachwirte*)	–	15,084	16,887	17,298
Technicians (*Techniker*)	–	15,978	18,897	–
Business specialists (*Betriebswirte*)	–	3,105	3,552	3,624
In-company trainers (*Ausbilder*)	59,913	67,182	80,280	85,269

Sources: Bundesinstitut für Berufsbildung (2013, pp. 226f., 373, 380), id. (2012, p. 310), id. (2009, p. 283f.), Statistisches Bundesamt (2013, pp. 115, 375ff.)

occupational practice after the initial training in the apprenticeship system (normally 3–5 years). Therefore, an industrial technical worker (e.g. *Industriemechaniker*) would be able to climb up the qualification ladder either by attending a *Fachschule* (technician) or a master worker course in a vocational school, a chamber or with a private training provider.

Most formal continuing training qualifications (Bundesinstitut für Berufsbildung 2013, p. 368ff.) are based on the Vocational Training Act (VTA) or the Craft Regulation Act (CRA). The VTA characterises formal further training, besides re-training and initial training, as an instrument to enable individuals to maintain and extend their vocational competences, to gear them to technical change or to climb up the vocational ladder (*Aufstiegsfortbildung*). In institutional terms, this kind of formal further training is laid down in further training regulations, which have to incorporate, besides examination standards, a clear denomination of the further training occupation, the objectives pursued by the training measure and admission prerequisites for entering the course (sections 53 VTA/42 CRA). Altogether, on the federal level, there are 223 further training regulations. Besides, the chambers also can define legal provisions for the regulation of courses: all in all, these institutions have implemented a total of some 2,500 covering some 750 further training occupations.

Table 17.2 provides statistical information on the various types of institutionalised further training in Germany.

Among these qualifications and underlying VET courses, the *Meister* is a qualification which has its roots in the craft sector, but now also exists in the industrial sector (*Industriemeister*). It is interesting that, from a language point of view, the denomination '*Meister*' has a number of different meanings (e.g. also indicating the status of conductor or composer in a cultural meaning of this term), but when it comes to vocational training it is a 'protected' term: the occupational status is strictly associated with the respective chamber examination (*Meisterprüfung*). The same applies to the 'Industrial Meister' (*Industriemeister*), but not to people who possess a special organisational status in a company and are normally called *Werkmeister* – which does not require a special continuing training qualification at all but can be achieved via the organisational ladder in a company. This, however, also implies that *Werkmeister* can be relevant people when it comes to training apprentices since they have a lot of professional experience. In the German context, we also find expressions using the word *Meister* with respect to a special area of competence where people work, such as *Baumeister* (a person designing churches) or *Bademeister* (a person working in a public swimming pool as a supervisor). These denominations, however, are not the result of formal continuing training, but are mostly based on normal training qualifications or simply depict occupational responsibilities in a special area of employment. Even in the public sector we find the term *Meister* – for example, a mayor is called *Bürgermeister*. Last but not least, Goethe's novel *Wilhelm Meister* puts emphasis on a young man's personal and occupational development by emphasising the status of the *Meister* beyond the qualification dimension of this term. Here it becomes clear that the human being is directed to 'walk' on a vocational pathway which is deeply educational, since it focuses on the notion of 'craft' which stands for the human existence maturing through experience and practical work (Zabeck 2013, pp. 235ff.; Wilhelm 1957, p. 48).

Both in the present and in a historical reflection, the most interesting qualification in the context of further training in Germany certainly is the master craftsman qualification, which has a history reaching back to the rise of the guilds in the Middle Ages (Zabeck 2013, pp. 46ff.). The importance of this type of occupational status is the fact that the craft sector is a strong supplier of training places in the apprenticeship system which is due to the interesting legal regulation that a master qualification (both in industry and in the craft sector) includes the trainer qualification according to the Vocational Training Act (Bundesministerium für Bildung und Forschung 2005).

This Act not only stipulates the rights and duties of trainees and training companies but also prescribes the personal and technical skills of training personnel, which may be characterised as a special group of employees who have undergone formal continuing training as part of workforce development. Hereby, the Act distinguishes between the trainer and the person or firm taking on apprentices (sections 27ff.). The 'personal aptitude' (*persönliche Eignung*) means that a person must not have disobeyed the Vocational Training Act and has to be eligible to employ young people. These preconditions are sufficient for hiring an apprentice. However, a person engaging in apprenticeships also has to prove the competence for instructing the apprentice at the training site, called the 'technical aptitude' (*fachliche Eignung*) unless there is a training officer having the necessary personal and technical qualifications to provide the training (sections 28ff.). Therefore the trainers themselves, besides their 'personal aptitude', must avail of technical (i.e. occupational) and pedagogical abilities and knowledge, which means that they not only have to be expert in their occupation but also have educational and psychological skills, including the application of appropriate teaching and instruction methods. In 1972, the trainer qualification became formalised and was decreed as the *Ausbildereignungsverordnung* (AEVO), which outlines the curriculum for trainer courses normally offered by the 'competent authorities', mostly the chambers (Weber 1985, pp. 60–64).

By stressing the trainer qualification as one of the most important formal, continuing qualifications in the German VET system, the Vocational Training Act has paid tribute to the different historical developments in the craft sector and the branches of industry and commerce. Its stipulations have led to an adaptation and revision of already existing regulations such as the master qualification. In 1972, the *Allgemeine Meisterprüfungs-Verordnung* (General Ordinance for the Master Examination) adopted the AEVO as Part IV of the syllabus governing master training courses (Schwichtenberg 1991, p. 27). The master undoubtedly still represents the major career aspiration of craftsmen and industrial workers, but training as an organisational and educational function has now been opened to a broader range of qualified people including university graduates and, above all, skilled workers, clerks or journeymen. As an innovative measure, the implementation of the 'technical aptitude' in its more extensive meaning including the occupational and the pedagogical aspect has certainly contributed to the 'upgrading' of training as an educational activity and not merely as a part of a company's personnel management (Arnold and Hülshoff 1981).

Against this background, the Vocational Training Act represents the first comprehensive set of legal regulations for in-company initial training as well as continuing training and retraining (section 1) – which may be seen as a continuum of skills formation under the common auspices of companies and the state:

> (1) For the purposes of this Act the expression 'vocational training' means initial training, further training and retraining. (2) The object of *initial training* shall be to provide, through a systematic training programme, a broadly conceived basic preparation for an occupation and the necessary technical abilities and knowledge to engage in a skilled form of occupational activity. Initial training shall also enable a trainee to acquire the necessary occupational experience. (3) *Further training* shall be designed to enable a trainee to maintain or extend his vocational knowledge and abilities, adapt himself to technical developments or obtain promotion in his chosen occupation. (4) *Retraining* shall be designed to qualify a trainee for another form of occupational activity.

The history of vocational training legislation reflects the fact that, both in theory and in practice, the notion of the workshop and the idea that an apprentice should learn his trade under an experienced master worker form the roots of German 'training culture'. The historical differentiation of *Meister*, *Geselle* (journeyman) and *Lehrling* (apprentice) or *Auszubildender* (trainee) is still prominent in the craft sector, which represents some 100 training occupations in the dual system, and is based on special regulations laid down in the *Handwerksordnung* (Craft Regulation Act). Up to the present day, apprenticeships in Germany are based on two legal foundations, namely the above-mentioned Craft Regulation Act (1953) and the Vocational Training Act (1969/2005). Both stand for the vocational/occupational orientation of training within a reliable legal and institutional framework (Deissinger 2009). The notion of training quality standards within each trade, in fact reaching back to the medieval guilds, was re-strengthened in the nineteenth century when industrialisation had begun to change the modes of production and technologies in a number of sectors of the economy. Hence the craft tradition never disappeared completely, since it became the focus of government economic and social policy – and with it the master craftsman qualification that became a crucial part of this 'renaissance':

- In 1845, a Prussian Trade Act (Stratmann and Schlüter 1982, pp. 122ff.), though not repealing freedom of work as a whole, re-imposed restrictions on free craftsmanship by confining the privilege to take apprentices to masters who belonged to a guild in as many as 43 trades. The Act made a precise distinction between small workshops and industrial premises by linking the right to take and train apprentices in handicraft occupations to examined journeymen (Stratmann and Pätzold 1984, pp. 117–119).
- In 1897 a trade act (*Handwerkerschutzgesetz*) re-introduced the requirement of formal vocational skills to train apprentices in the craft sector. Although it did not yet set up the master certificate as a training prerequisite (Knörr 1996, pp. 142ff.), it revived some important stipulations included in the ancient apprenticeship mode. Thus chambers and guilds were assigned to organise examinations for journeymen or masters. Also, indentures as well as a 3-year training period at the end of which the apprentice took his examination (Stratmann and Pätzold 1984, pp. 123f.) became a general and virtually mandatory practice in the craft sector.
- In 1908, the right to train apprentices was confined by law to examined handicraft masters (Winkler 1976, p. 2), and finally, in 1935, the trade law was changed again in favour of the old-established occupations, with the re-introduction of the master qualification as a prerequisite to establish a craft business, still prescribed in current German trade law (Knörr 1996, pp. 169ff.).

Against this historical background, the German model of workforce recruitment and workforce development is, at least partly, a highly formalised one. The reason for this is that the traditional features of vocational orientation and self-government are not only rooted in the medieval notion of occupation-specific craftsmanship. The social, technical and economic relevance of the master craftsman qualification, as it is seen today, is underlined by the fact that this type of a higher vocational certificate is represented in the German Qualifications Framework (DQR) on level 6, which is based on a decision taken in February 2012 by the federal government, the federal states and the social partners. This allocation of a non-academic qualification – the same applies to the above-mentioned 'technician' – on the same level as a bachelor degree clearly mirrors the crucial political attention which VET in Germany is being given even in times of a creeping 'tertiarisation' of its vocational and educational pathways. Hereby, 'equivalence', not 'uniformity' is seen as a justification for this positioning of continuing VET (Bundesministerium für Bildung und Forschung 2011).

The formal dimension of the German Qualifications Framework, however, collides with a consistent policy of 'opening up barriers' in order to enable individuals to proceed from one sector of the education system to another. The fact that master craftsmen now can apply for permission to university studies stands for a stronger political focus on 'parity of esteem' in the wake of the EU's Lisbon-Bologna strategy, incorporating the notion of lifelong learning as a crucial overarching topic (Hake 1999). There is still awareness, though, that vocational qualifications have another function than academic ones. Positively speaking, this means that VET is still predominantly seen as a specific sub-system with its own 'self-reference' (Luhmann 1984) and functionality, especially once one sees the master craftsman qualification as a logical upgrading of an apprenticeship.

Research shows that, in Germany, at least for the time being, vocational qualifications have not yet entered serious competition with academic ones (Hippach-Schneider and Weigel 2012). Companies demand different levels of qualifications, depending on the various functions in the organisation. However, it may be claimed that access to university or other higher education institutions is now more articulated as a social aspiration by many young people. In some way, the so-called 'vocational academies' have satisfied these aspirations. Starting in the 1980s, in the federal state of Baden-Württemberg (Deissinger 2000), the 'dual universities', as they are called today, are a kind of 'academic dual system', and stand for one type of 'tertiarisation' of VET, which is likely to have long-term implications for the apprenticeship system, but also for in-company workforce development. It is likely that, in Germany, pathways that resemble the dual system will remain attractive to employers. In contrast, from a European comparative perspective, it may also be stated that in Germany 'hybrid qualifications', combining vocational with academic entitlements (e.g. the university entrance qualification), are less interesting and relevant in the VET policy context (Deissinger et al. 2013). This once again underlines the importance of certificates that are portable in the labour market and therefore meet the demand of industry in the first place. It has been outlined in this part of the paper that the respect for VET in general and the strong focus on apprenticeship qualifications (Harris and Deissinger 2003; Deissinger 2010) have a number of major implications not only for continuing training but also for in-company workforce development practices.

Workforce Development in the Face of Demographic Change – Knowledge Transfer Strategies of German Companies

In the following, our focus shifts to the organisational level, that is, the corporate level. The notion of workforce development is discussed in the context of demographic change and the corresponding ageing and shrinking of the German working population. What measures and strategies do German firms adopt in order to tackle the demographic development on the labour market? While addressing this question, special attention is given to the aspect of intergenerational transfer of knowledge.

Demographic change has already been a prominent issue in German society, politics and economy for years. The prospect of an increasingly ageing workforce accompanied by a shortage of skilled workers not only alarms employers but also the federal government and the federal states, social security institutions, industry associations and trade unions (Eck and Bossmann 2013, pp. 15f.). Before focusing on the corporate level and the measures taken there to cope with demographic challenges, the phenomenon of demographic change shall be depicted with respect to the German population and its impact on the German job market.

Demographic Change and Its Impact on the German Labour Market

Demographic change is mainly influenced by two factors: population decline and the changing age structure of the population (Statistisches Bundesamt 2009, pp. 5, 12ff.; Statistische Ämter des Bundes und der Länder 2011: n.pag.). Given the continuation of the current demographic development, the Federal Statistical Office predicts a decline of the German population from about 81 million people in 2013 to 65–70 million in 2060 (Statistisches Bundesamt 2009, pp. 5, 46). At the same time, a serious shift of the age structure can be expected. Significant changes will already take place over the next few years, particularly the age groups of 50–65 years (+24 %) and 80+ years (+48 %) will grow until 2020. The number of people under the age of 50, however, will decline (−16 %). By 2060, every third person – 34 % of the whole population – will be 65 years and older and the number of 70-year-olds will be twice the number of new-born children (ibid., pp. 5, 16).

Demographic change is reflected most significantly in the working population: it is this population (age range from 20 to 65 years) that is particularly affected from shrinking and ageing (ibid.: 17). According to the prognosis of the Federal Statistical Office, the German economy will already have to deal with a radical change of its age structure from the year 2017 to 2024. In between, 40 % of the potential working-age population will be 50–65 years old (ibid., pp. 6, 18). Until 2060, the potential working-age population will decrease by 27–34 % (depending on immigration) compared with the 2008 baseline (ibid., p. 17).

Ten years ago, the human resource policy of many German companies was based on the so-called 'deficit model' of ageing – assuming a negative relation of age and achievement – and was characterised by early retirement and youth-oriented recruitment strategies. Today, shortage of labour supply has become reality for many industries and has fostered a change in mentality away from the deficit model towards a potential-oriented perspective on age. Older employees are increasingly valued as an indispensable resource (Bundesinstitut für Berufsbildung 2005, p. 2; Bossmann et al. 2013, pp. 47f.; Cihlar et al. 2014, p. 13; Eck and Bossmann 2013, p. 22; Lesser et al. 2005, p. 3; Seitz and Wagner 2009, p. 170; Wegge et al. 2011, p. 433). The impending shortage of skilled workers arising from demographic change has also forced politicians to react. On the one hand, in order to prolong working life, the early retirement policy of recent years was cut back and the legal age of retirement was raised to 67 years. On the other hand, periods of schooling and training were shortened, aiming at an earlier entry into the labour market for young people (Wegge et al. 2011, p. 434; Eck and Bossmann 2013, p. 22).

As a result of these developments and measures, companies are now facing a fundamental change in the age structure of their workforce – namely, an extension of the age range (Walter et al. 2013, p. 64; Wegge et al. 2011, pp. 434, 441). Different age groups with different strengths and weaknesses meet in the workplace (Bossmann et al. 2013, pp. 45ff.; Cihlar et al. 2014, pp. 14f.; Walter et al. 2013, p. 58; Wegge et al. 2011, pp. 433, 439; Zimmermann 2005, pp. 26f.; Zwack and Schweitzer 2013, pp. 105ff.). Even more importantly, different generations with different values, needs and ways of thinking and working are having to get along with each other (Klaffke and Schwarzenbart 2013, pp. 45f.; Meyers 2009, pp. 202ff.; Schenck 2013, p. 130; Walter et al. 2013, pp. 61f., 64; Wegge et al. 2011, p. 434). The main challenge for companies is to embrace this diversity and to convert the tensions between generations into innovative and creative forces (Seitz and Wagner 2009, p. 159; Klaffke and Schwarzenbart 2013, p. 45). However, cooperation of employees of different age groups and generations, as it has increasingly become indispensable for companies in order to remain competitive, can only work if:

- the post-war generation (1946–1955),
- Baby Boomers (1956–1965),
- Generation X (1966–1980),
- Generation Y (1981–1995) – also known as Millennials – as well as
- Generation Internet (1996-today)

become involved with each other and adopt mutual tolerance, respect and understanding (Klaffke and Schwarzenbart 2013, p. 45; Meyers 2009, pp. 210ff.; Oertel 2007, pp. 289ff.; Schenck 2013, p. 130; Walter et al. 2013, pp. 61f., 64; Wegge et al. 2011, p. 434).

Intergenerational Transfer of Knowledge as a Key Factor for Corporate Success

Besides demographic change, companies have to cope with other megatrends such as intensified competition due to globalisation, shorter reaction times, rapid technical progress as well as the transition towards a knowledge and innovation society (Eck et al. 2013, pp. 36, 41f.; Piorr et al. 2006, p. 83; Schenck 2013, p. 125; Seitz and Wagner 2009, pp. 157, 170; Walter et al. 2013, pp. 25f.). As demographic change has coincided with the emergence of knowledge as a key resource, cooperation of young and old employees becomes increasingly important with regard to in-company transfer of (experience-based) knowledge. Thus, the uncoordinated loss of know-how due to age-related retirements of experts can cause massive problems for companies under current market conditions (Piorr et al. 2006, p. 83; Seitz and Wagener 2009, p. 157). Therefore, enterprises should implement an age-based personnel policy combined with a demography-robust management of knowledge to counter the loss of valuable know-how at an early stage and to keep the innovation potential of an ageing workforce alive at the same time (Schenk 2013, pp. 125f.; Walter et al. 2013, p. 48; Wegge et al. 2011, p. 435).

A survey of human resource managers in the chemical industry in 2006 showed that many companies are aware of the consequences of the demographic trend and respond to these challenges by fostering a preventative conservation of internal knowledge. However, there is still a considerable share of firms that do not take any measures at all in order to avoid the loss of know-how (Bader et al. 2009, p. 38). Overall, 52.3 % of the 198 human resources managers surveyed (gross sample size: 1,311) think that the demographic development will have negative impact on their companies (90.9 % of which are big companies) in the nearer future. Some of the companies have already implemented concrete measures to promote knowledge transfer: 75.4 % work with mixed-age teams and 31.8 % have introduced tandem models. However, 10.8 % of the companies state that they do not foster the exchange of experience and knowledge at all (ibid., p. 38).

Similar data result from a nationwide survey of 537 firms (gross sample size: 1,582) conducted by the Federal Institute for Vocational Education and Training in 2004. Although merely one third (31.3 %) of the respondents felt affected (by the time of the interview) by demographic change (Bundesinstitut für Berufsbildung 2005, p. 1), 81.1 % of the companies said that they promoted knowledge transfer between the older and the younger employees. The most frequently mentioned model is mixed-age teams (72.2 %), followed by support of newcomers by older employees (mentoring, sponsorship, coaching or tandem programs) with 59 %. A large proportion of companies also offer further training on this subject (42 %). Additionally, meetings and workshops, internal seminars, knowledge databases as well as in-company training were mentioned. Considering the firm size, it is the larger companies in particular that actively boost the exchange of knowledge and know-how (ibid., p. 4; Zimmermann 2005, p. 27).

While knowledge transfer was originally regarded and applied as transmission of (specific) experience-based knowledge from older employees to younger colleagues, the idea of mutual learning, with both old and young colleagues acting as knowledge-providers and -recipients, has become increasingly popular. Approaches that are specifically directed to the needs of older employees bear the risk of focusing too strongly on this age group and excluding the younger colleagues. Therefore, human resource development strategies should be enhanced by the aspect of intergenerationality – which means that motivation and working ability of all age groups have to be strengthened. 'The new' should get its chance and 'the old' its recognition (Seitz and Wagner 2009, pp. 159f.). By working together cooperatively, both sides learn from each other – the combination of the up-to-date knowledge of young recruits and the expertise of older colleagues generates added value for companies (ibid., pp. 157, 170; Klaffke and Schwarzenbart 2013, p. 45; Zimmermann 2005, p. 27).

Mixed-Age Teams and Mentoring Programs – Examples from the German Economy

In this part of the chapter, two forms of knowledge transfer are highlighted that play a crucial role not only in literature but also in practice (as the data above show): mixed-age teams – providing for a balanced mix of employees in different phases of working life – and mentoring or tandem programs, allowing older employees to look after their younger colleagues or share a common project with them. First, selected examples from the German economy are presented. Then, possible problems connected with the implementation of the two approaches are described.

The implementation of mixed age teams is an essential step in boosting knowledge transfer at AUDI AG, one of the biggest German car manufacturers. The following quotations show that the company has developed an intergenerational, that is mutual, understanding of knowledge transfer and learning:

> Our employees work in a dynamic environment shaped by constant change and innovation. Therefore we embrace the concept of 'lifelong learning' – for example, by setting up mixed-age teams, in which all the members learn from each other and pass on their know-how, both to young talents and to experienced colleagues. For us, experience is not a matter of age but of commitment. (AUDI AG 2014, n.pag.)

> The advantage of mixed-age teams lies in different characteristics, values, work routines and pieces of experience contributed by different generations. The broader the variation in a team, the more versatile are the solutions offered – and the better is the result in the end. And that is exactly what we need, as cars are very complex products. (Frassek, Project Manager and Demography Expert of AUDI AG, Frassek 2014, n.pag.)

For SICK AG, a German company and world leader in sensor technology for industrial application, the cooperation within mixed-age teams also is a crucial measure in order to cope with demographic change. With the aim 'to link the experience, dedication to quality, process know-how and social integrity of our older employees with the curiosity, up-to-date technical know-how, new methods and often higher speed of the new generation' (Kast, CEO Human Resources of SICK AG, qtd. in SICK AG 2010, p. 2), the company relies on the cooperation of generations and expects the following advantages, among others:

> We are offered different perspectives. Thus, the quality of decision and troubleshooting processes improves. New insights and ideas are possible.
>   The wider span of age in the teams enhances the personal networks. The number of contacts rises, as younger and older colleagues often have different contact persons.
>   The daily exchange at work facilitates mutual competence enhancement – the members of mixed-age teams train each other. (SICK AG 2010, pp. 8f.)

Knowledge transfer is possible even after senior employees have left the company, as the following two examples show. The German Bosch Group, a leading global supplier of technology and services, uses the experience of so-called 'senior experts'. The Bosch Management Support GmbH (BMS), founded in 1999 with the aim to offer counselling by Bosch-retirees and to keep their specific skills and knowledge in the company, builds the foundation for this endeavour (Robert Bosch

GmbH 2009, p. 1f.). Senior experts are contacted whenever quick, short-term and professional advice is needed. By supporting their younger colleagues, senior experts create 'an intergenerational exchange in terms of mutual learning. While our junior managers can introduce their senior colleagues to new software for example, BMS-experts are able to fall back on decades of experience in leadership, motivation and technical know-how' (ibid., p. 2).

Daimler AG, one of the biggest car manufacturers in the world, has established generation management as a strategic initiative in their corporate strategy. The company started a program similar to BMS at the Bosch Group: the initiative 'Space Cowboys – Daimler Senior Experts'. With the objective to strengthen knowledge transfer between experience bearers and newcomers in the company, Daimler-retirees temporarily get back to work in their former departments at Daimler (Daimler AG 2013, n.pag.):

> For our success both factors are important: innovative capacity and comprehensive experience. By means of our initiative 'Space Cowboys – Daimler Senior Experts' we aim at the cooperation of different generations with their very own, specific qualifications. The multitude of their know-how and perspectives contributes vastly to the realization of our growth strategy. (Porth, Member of the Board of Management of Daimler AG, Human Resources and Director of Labour Relations, qtd. in Daimler AG 2013, n.pag.)

A special and innovative approach, awarded by the German Federal Ministry of Education and Research, was developed and implemented at the Mercedes-Benz plant in Bremen (Germany). Here, experienced employees receive training for new occupational profiles alongside young apprentices. The concept is called 'Intergenerational Qualification (IQ)' and aims at generating synergy from the individual qualifications of different age groups (Daimler AG 2014, n.pag.). In the training programs for tool mechanics and cutting machine operators, older employees who were looking for further training have been working side by side with young apprentices since 2011. Two senior employees who take part in this program give an account of the project:

> We applied for the programme because we wanted to learn something new. To go back to school after more than 20 years might have been the greatest hurdle. We had to learn how to learn again.
>
> The interaction of young and old colleagues is what I like most about the programme. It is a special experience to work with the other apprentices that could have been our own children. They sometimes support us at school, because they are still used to this learning environment. When it comes to mechanical skills, it is just the other way round: the experienced colleagues can help the younger ones. (Daimler AG 2014, n.pag.)

The finding that older employees are motivated by the cooperation with junior colleagues is also backed by a recent study published by the ZEW (Centre for European Economic Research). On the basis of data collected from German enterprises, researchers were able to show that mixed-age teams make older employees stay in the company for a longer period of time – contrary to partial retirement programs or further training offers that have less impact or no impact at all (in the case of partial retirement programs) on the duration of employment (Bockmann et al. 2013; Cihlar et al. 2014, p. 15; Walter et al. 2013, p. 60).

Obstacles and Challenges for Intergenerational Knowledge Transfer

Empirical studies show that mixed-age teams and mentoring programs may not only have positive effects, but also negative ones – in terms of ineffective cooperation (e.g. Joshi and Roh 2009; Ries et al. 2010; Wegge et al. 2008). Wegge et al. warn about viewing mixed-age teams as the 'cheap solution' to demographic problems in companies. The authors point out that co-working in mixed-age teams needs to be well-prepared and continuously observed and accompanied for intergenerational cooperation to work (Wegge et al. 2011, pp. 434ff.). Based on the findings of the ADIGU-project (Age Heterogeneity of Work Groups as a Determinant of Innovation, Group Performance, and Health), funded by the German Research Foundation (DFG), Wegge et al. derive five recommendations for business practice – mixed-age teams may be (especially) successful if:

1. the perception of age differences is marginal,
2. there is a positive climate in the team, free of age discrimination and prejudice,
3. the appreciation of age differences is high,
4. the group work includes complex tasks, and
5. the corporate and leadership culture in the company accepts and values age, experience and individual potentials of employees (Wegge et al. 2011, pp. 437ff. see also Klaffke and Schwarzenbart 2013, pp. 44, 47; Oertel 2007, pp. 251ff., 282ff.; Seitz and Wagner 2009, pp. 163f.; Tomenendal 2013).

Zimmermann (2005) and Bader et al. (2009) point out that there are a number of preconditions for successful knowledge transfer in mentoring and tandem programs. Zimmermann mentions trust, mutual appreciation and a common aim as promising conditions for knowledge transfer. In terms of a reciprocal learning process both sides have to benefit from their cooperation – knowledge transfer must not be perceived as a one-way street. As knowledge transfer normally includes the transformation of implicit (practical) knowledge into explicit (verbalised) knowledge, mentoring and tandem partners need to have access to training offers supporting the reflection of their very own knowledge and work experience. Another important factor is the employment contract of each cooperation partner: The fear of senior employees losing their job after having successfully transferred their knowledge has to be softened by a long-term contract. Young employees, on the other hand, also need a secure and interesting prospect in the company: short-term contracts and low salaries (compared with their older colleagues) are likely to lead to a decline in motivation for effective team work (Zimmermann 2005, pp. 29f.; Dworschak 2010, n.pag.; Klaffke and Schwarzenbart 2013, p. 47; Seitz and Wagner 2009, pp. 165ff.).

Bader et al. (2009) suggest that measures for knowledge preservation in enterprises may open up chances and opportunities for mutual exchange and learning, but are often unstructured and will not provide for an efficient transfer of relevant know-how. Outside the framework of systematised learning and teaching processes, knowledge transfer happens only spontaneously. The challenge to transfer knowledge (that refers predominantly to situation-related routines) without a systematic elaboration and structured preparation often puts knowledge bearers under strain. The success of knowledge transfer then depends on the knowledge receivers, who have to identify transfer impulses and integrate them in their own field of action and experience. The authors emphasise that the main task in this context is to identify transfer-relevant experience – not every piece of knowledge offered by senior employees is important for their younger colleagues. Executive managers should get involved to analyse and identify relevant types of knowledge (technical knowledge, project know-how, network contacts etc.). In order to systematise knowledge transfer in companies, Bader, Riese & Piorr propose an intergenerational knowledge management model in seven steps – the so-called Nova. PE transfer cycle that was developed for small and medium-sized companies (Bader et al. 2009, pp. 38ff.; see also Piorr et al. 2006; Seitz and Wagner 2009, p. 167).

Short-Sighted Strategies and the Dominance of Monetary Key Figures

The quotations and practical examples above show that German enterprises are becoming increasingly aware of the impact of demographical change and the necessity for intergenerational knowledge transfer. Nevertheless, the implementation of adequate measures happens too slowly and only sporadically. A holistic intergenerational personnel strategy is still the exception. The economic focus is narrowed to monetary key figures, even more so in uncertain economic times. Demography, age and generation have become topics that are discussed in companies, but only as second-rate categories (Seitz and Wagner 2009, p. 171). In the perspective of many firms, the threat of demographic change still seems to be lurking only in the distant future – compared to many other, seemingly more acute problems (Eck et al. 2013, pp. 36ff.; Berblinger et al. 2013, pp. 394ff.). However, in the face of demographic change – happening also in times of recession and financial crisis – companies should no longer be reluctant to anticipate its consequences (even if these might not yet have surfaced) and to react adequately by establishing a 'holistic' intergenerational personnel strategy (Eck et al. 2013, pp. 41f.; Seitz and Wagner 2009, p. 171).

Conclusion

The German case shows that workforce development has various facets. Besides formalised pathways, especially in the craft sector, companies rely on their own strategies. One crucial challenge seems to be demographic change as companies have to be aware that they need instruments to keep their workforce skilled but also to secure the qualifications and competences of the younger generation. Nobody can anticipate at the moment whether the German economy, with its comparatively strong industrial sector, will recruit more skilled personnel from higher education in the future. At the moment, the traditional pathways, above all the dual apprenticeship system, seem to be relevant and attractive and also remain the focus of national VET policy.

References

Arnold, R., & Hülshoff, T. (1981). *Rekrutierung und qualifikation des betrieblichen Bildungspersonals.* Heidelberg: Esprint-Verlag.

AUDI AG. (2014). *Diversity Individualität und Persönlichkeit.* URL: http://www.audi.de/de/brand/de/unternehmen/karriere_bei_audi/arbeiten_bei_audi/diversity.html. 24 Feb 2014.

Bader, K., Riese, C., & Piorr, R. (2009). Wissen und Erfahrungen älterer Beschäftigter vererben. Ein Modell zum intergenerativen Wissenstransfer in Unternehmen. *Berufsbildung in Wissenschaft und Praxis, 2009*(1), 38–41.

Baethge, M., Solga, H., & Wieck, M. (2007). *Berufsbildung im Umbruch. Signale eines überfälligen Aufbruchs.* Berlin: Friedrich-Ebert-Stiftung.

Berblinger, S., Ďuranová, L., & Knörzer, M. (2013). Demografiemanagement in deutschen Unternehmen. In M. Göke & T. Heupel (Eds.), *Wirtschaftliche Implikationen des demografischen Wandels. Herausforderungen und Lösungsansätze* (pp. 383–397). Wiesbaden: Springer Gabler.

Boockmann, B., Fries, J., & Göbel, C. (2013). *Specific measures for older employees and late career employment* (ZEW Discussion Paper No. 12–059). URL: http://ftp.zew.de/pub/zew-docs/dp/dp12059.pdf. 25 Feb 2014.

Bossmann, U., Schweitzer, J., & Schenck, K. (2013). Können und Dürfen: Zur Leistungsfähigkeit jüngerer und älterer Mitarbeiter. In J. Schweitzer & U. Bossmann (Eds.), *Systemisches Demografiemanagement. Wie kommt Neues zum Älterwerden in Unternehmen?* (pp. 45–62). Wiesbaden: Springer VS.

Bundesinstitut für Berufsbildung. (2005). *Referenz-Betriebs-System (RBS). Information No. 28. Betriebliche Weiterbildung älterer Beschäftigter.* URL: http://www.bibb.de/de/12366.htm. 16 Feb 2014.

Bundesinstitut für Berufsbildung. (2009). *Datenreport zum Berufsbildungsbericht 2009.* Bonn: Bundesinstitut für Berufsbildung.

Bundesinstitut für Berufsbildung. (2012). *Datenreport zum Berufsbildungsbericht 2012.* Bonn: Bundesinstitut für Berufsbildung.

Bundesinstitut für Berufsbildung. (2013). *Datenreport zum Berufsbildungsbericht 2013.* Bonn: Bundesinstitut für Berufsbildung.

Bundesministerium für Bildung und Forschung. (2005). *Die Reform der beruflichen Bildung – Berufsbildungsgesetz 2005.* Bonn: BMBF.

Bundesministerium für Bildung und Forschung. (2011). *Deutscher Qualifikationsrahmen für Lebenslanges Lernen.* Berlin: BMBF.

Cihlar, V., Mergenthaler, A., & Micheel, F. (2014). *Erwerbsarbeit & Informelle Tätigkeiten der 55- bis 70-Jährigen in Deutschland.* Wiesbaden: Bundesinstitut für Bevölkerungsforschung.

Daimler, A. G. (2013). *'Space cowboys – Daimler Senior Experts' starten mit Projekteinsätzen.* URL:http://media.daimler.com/dcmedia/0-921-1281854-49-1594591-1-0-1-0-0-1-0-614232-0-1-0-0-0-0-0.html. 22 Feb 2014.

Daimler, A. G. (2014). *Erfahren in die Zukunft – das Generationenmanagement bei Daimler.* URL:http://blog.daimler.de/2014/01/07/erfahren-in-die-zukunft-das-generationenmanagement-bei-daimler/. 22 Feb 2014.

Deissinger, T. (1994). The evolution of the modern vocational training systems in England and Germany: A comparative view. *Compare, 24*, 17–36.

Deissinger, T. (1996). Germany's Vocational Training Act: Its function as an instrument of quality control within a tradition-based vocational training system. *Oxford Review of Education, 22*(3), 317–336.

Deissinger, T. (2000). The German 'philosophy' of linking academic and work-based learning in higher education – The case of the 'Vocational Academies'. *Journal of Vocational Education and Training, 52*(4), 609–630.

Deissinger, T. (2009). Curriculare Vorgaben für Lehr-Lernprozesse in der beruflichen Bildung. In B. Bonz (Ed.), *Didaktik und Methodik der Berufsbildung* (Berufsbildung konkret, Bd. 10, pp. 60–88). Hohengehren: Schneider.

Deissinger, T. (2010). Dual system. In P. Peterson, E. Baker, & B. McGaw (Eds.), *International encyclopedia of education* (3rd ed., Vol. 8, pp. 448–454). Oxford: Elsevier.

Deissinger, T., Smith, E., & Pickersgill, R. (2006). Models of full-time and part-time vocational training for school-leavers: A comparison between Germany and Australia. *International Journal of Training Research, 4*(1), 30–50.

Deissinger, T., Heine, R., & Ott, M. (2012). The dominance of apprenticeships in the German VET system and its implications for Europeanisation – A comparative view in the context of the EQF and the European LLL strategy. In A. Fuller & L. Unwin (Eds.), *Contemporary apprenticeship: International perspectives on an evolving model of learning* (pp. 160–179). London: Routledge.

Deissinger, T., Aff, J., Fuller, A., & Jorgensen, C. H. (Eds.). (2013). *Hybrid qualifications: Structures and problems in the context of European VET policy*. Bern: Peter Lang.

Dworschak, B. (Fraunhofer-Institut für Arbeitswirtschaft und Organisation IAO). (2010). *Quoted in Frankfurter Allgemeine Zeitung (FAZ.NET), Beruf & Chance vom 26.08.2010*. URL: http://www.faz.net/aktuell/beruf-chance/arbeitswelt/demographie-alte-hasen-junge-huepfer-11028122.html. 22 Feb 2014.

Eck, A., & Bossmann, U. (2013). Demografischer Wandel: Eine kurze Einführung in eine populäre Prognose. In J. Schweitzer & U. Bossmann (Eds.), *Systemisches Demografiemanagement. Wie kommt Neues zum Älterwerden in Unternehmen?* (pp. 15–24). Wiesbaden: Springer VS.

Eck, A., Zwack, M., & Bossmann, U. (2013). Wen muss das interessieren? Die Relevanz des demografischen Wandels für Mitarbeiter, Führungskräfte und Organisationen. In J. Schweitzer & U. Bossmann (Eds.), *Systemisches Demografiemanagement. Wie kommt Neues zum Älterwerden in Unternehmen?* (pp. 25–44). Wiesbaden: Springer VS.

Euler, D. (1998). *Modernisierung des dualen Systems – Problembereiche, Reformvorschläge, Konsens- und Dissenslinien* (Materialien zur Bildungsplanung und zur Forschungsförderung, 62). Bonn: Bund-Länder-Kommission für Bildungsplanung und Forschungsförderung.

Euler, D., & Severing, E. (2006). *Flexible Ausbildungswege in der Berufsbildung*. Nürnberg: Typoskript.

Frassek, D. (2014). *Eine Chance und Bereicherung. Im Gespräch mit Dietmar Frassek. Wissenschaftsjahr 2013 – Die demografische Chance. Eine Initiative des Bundesministeriums für Bildung und Forschung*. URL: http://www.demografische-chance.de/die-themen/stimmen-aus-der-gesellschaft/eine-chance-und-bereicherung.html. 24 Feb 2014.

Hake, B. J. (1999). Lifelong learning policies in the European Union: Developments and issues. *Compare, 29*(1), 53–70.

Harris, R., & Deissinger, T. (2003). Learning cultures for apprenticeships: A comparison of Germany and Australia. In J. Searle, I. Yashin-Shaw, & D. Roebuck (Eds.), *Enriching learning cultures* (Vol. 2, pp. 23–33). Brisbane: Australian Academic Press.

Hippach-Schneider, U., & Weigel, T. (2012). VET qualifications versus bachelor degrees? Recruitment at the intermediate qualification level – Case studies from Germany, England and Switzerland. In M. Pilz (Ed.), *The future of vocational education and training in a changing world* (pp. 259–272). Wiesbaden: Springer VS.

Joshi, A., & Roh, H. (2009). The role of context in work team diversity research: A meta-analytic review. *Academy of Management Journal, 52*(3), 599–627.

Klaffke, M., & Schwarzenbart, U. (2013). Demografie als Chance. *Personalmagazin, 13*(3), 44–47.

Knörr, M. (1996). *Die Berufszulassung zum Handwerk seit dem Ende des Alten Reiches.* Dissertation. Nürnberg.

Lesser, E., Hausmann, C., & Feuerpeil, S. (2005). *Die Herausforderungen des demografischen Wandels: Strategische Handlungsfelder für Unternehmen in Europa.* Stuttgart/Wien/Zürich: IBM.

Luhmann, N. (1984). *Soziale Systeme – Grundriss einer allgemeinen Theorie.* Frankfurt a.M.: Suhrkamp.

Meyers, R. A. (2009). Mitarbeiter im neuen Millennium – Kommunikation zwischen den Generationen. In G. Richter (Ed.), *Generationen gemeinsam im Betrieb. Individuelle Flexibilität durch anspruchsvolle Regulierungen* (pp. 202–220). Bielefeld: Bertelsmann.

Oertel, J. (2007). *Generationenmanagement in Unternehmen. Schriften aus dem Centrum für Management.* Wiesbaden: Deutscher Universitäts-Verlag.

Piorr, R., Reckermann, A., & Riese, C. (2006). Damit Know-how und Erfahrung nicht in Rente gehen! Konzepte für den systematischen Wissenstransfer zwischen Generationen. *SPECIAL Personalführung, 7,* 82–89.

Ries, B. C., Diestel, S., Wegge, J., & Schmidt, K.-H. (2010). Die Rolle von Alterssalienz und Konflikten in Teams als Mediatoren in der Beziehung zwischen Altersheterogenität und Gruppeneffektivität. *Zeitschrift für Arbeits- und Organisationspsychologie, 54*(3), 117–130.

Robert Bosch GmbH. (2009). *Seit zehn Jahren: Karriere nach der Karriere. Bosch Management Support verfügt über 26 000 Jahre Erfahrung. Presse-Information.* URL: http://www.bosch-presse.de/presseforum/details.htm?txtID=4269&tk_id=191. 22 Feb 2014.

Ryan, P. (2001). Apprenticeship in Britain – Tradition and innovation. In T. Deissinger (Ed.), *Berufliche Bildung zwischen nationaler Tradition und globaler Entwicklung* (pp. 133–157). Baden-Baden: Nomos Verlag.

Ryan, P. (2003). Evaluating vocationalism. *European Journal of Education, 38*(2), 147–162.

Schenck, K. (2013). Qualifizierung und Wissensmanagement: Wie Know-how im Unternehmen bleibt. In J. Schweitzer & U. Bossmann (Eds.), *Systemisches Demografiemanagement. Wie kommt Neues zum Älterwerden in Unternehmen?* (pp. 125–146). Wiesbaden: Springer VS.

Schweitzer, E. (Deutscher Industrie- und Handelskammertag). (2014). *Quoted in Spiegel Online, Azubi-Mangel: Wirtschaftsboss wettert gegen Akademisierung vom 03.02.2014.* URL: http://www.spiegel.de/wirtschaft/dihk-praesident-schweitzer-akademisierung-schadet-wirtschaftsstandort-a-950708.html. 1 Mar 2014.

Schwichtenberg, U. (1991). Qualifizierung für die Ausbildertätigkeit. Eine kritische Betrachtung der Vorbereitungskurse für die Prüfung nach der Ausbildereignungsverordnung. In M. Frackmann (Ed.), *Qualifizierungsbedarf und Weiterbildungsangebote für betriebliches Ausbildungspersonal* (pp. 25–40). Alsbach: Leuchtturm.

Seitz, C., & Wagner, M. H. (2009). Wissen intergenerativ erzeugen und transferieren – die Chancen intergenerativer Zusammenarbeit. In G. Richter (Ed.), *Generationen gemeinsam im Betrieb. Individuelle Flexibilität durch anspruchsvolle Regulierungen* (pp. 157–172). Bielefeld: Bertelsmann.

SICK AG. (2010). *Altersgemischte Teams in der SICK AG.* URL: http://www.inqa.de/SharedDocs/PDFs/DE/Gute-Praxis/Sick-Altersgemischte-Teams-in-der-Sick-AG.pdf?__blob=publicationFile. 22 Feb 2014.

Statistische Ämter des Bundes und der Länder. (2011). *Demografischer Wandel in Deutschland. Bevölkerungs- und Haushaltsentwicklung im Bund und in den Ländern.* Wiesbaden: Statistisches Bundesamt.

Statistisches Bundesamt. (2009). *Bevölkerung Deutschlands bis 2060. 12. Koordinierte Bevölkerungsvorausberechnung.* Wiesbaden: Statistisches Bundesamt.

Statistisches Bundesamt. (2013). *Bildung und Kultur. Berufliche Bildung 2012. Fachserie 11 Reihe 3*. Wiesbaden: Statistisches Bundesamt.

Steedman, H. (2010). *The state of apprenticeship in 2010: International comparisons*. London: London School of Economics.

Stratmann, K., & Pätzold, G. (1984). Institutionalisierung der Berufsbildung. In M. Baethge & K. Nevermann (Eds.), *Enzyklopädie Erziehungswissenschaft, Vol. 5: Organisation, Recht und Ökonomie des Bildungswesens* (pp. 114–134). Stuttgart: Klett-Cotta.

Stratmann, K., & Schlüter, A. (Eds.). (1982). *Quellen und Dokumente zur Berufsbildung, 1794–1869*. Köln: Böhlau.

Tomenendal, M. (2013). Zur Effektivität altersgemischter Teams – die Fallstudie eines mittelständischen Dienstleistungsunternehmens. In M. Göke & T. Heupel (Eds.), *Wirtschaftliche Implikationen des demografischen Wandels. Herausforderungen und Lösungsansätze* (pp. 433–443). Wiesbaden: Springer Gabler.

Walter, N., Fischer, H., Hausmann, P., Klös, H.-P., Lobinger, T., Raffelhüschen, B., Rump, J., Seeber, S., & Vassiliadis, M. (2013). *Die Zukunft der Arbeitswelt. Auf dem Weg ins Jahr 2030*. Stuttgart: Robert Bosch Stiftung GmbH.

Weber, R. (1985). *Berufsbildungsgesetz und Berufsbildungsförderungsgesetz*. Bergisch-Gladbach: Heider.

Wegge, J., Roth, C., & Schmidt, K.-H. (2008). Eine aktuelle Bilanz der Vor- und Nachteile altersgemischter Teamarbeit. *Wirtschaftspsychologie, 10*(3), 30–43.

Wegge, J., Jungmann, F., Liebermann, S., Schmidt, K.-H., & Ries, B. C. (2011). Altersgemischte Teamarbeit kann erfolgreich sein. Empfehlungen für eine ausgewogene betriebliche Altersstruktur. *Sozialrecht + Praxis, 21*(7), 433–442.

Wilhelm, T. (1957). *Die Pädagogik Kerschensteiners*. Stuttgart: Metzler.

Winkler, H. A. (1976). From social protectionism to national socialism: The German small-business movement in comparative perspective. *Journal of Modern History, 48*, 1–18.

Young, M. (2003). National qualifications frameworks as a global phenomenon: A comparative perspective. *Journal of Education and Work, 16*(3), 223–237.

Zabeck, J. (1975). *Die Bedeutung des Selbstverwaltungsprinzips für die Effizienz der betrieblichen Ausbildung. Untersuchung im Auftrage des Ministers für Wirtschaft, Mittelstand und Verkehr des Landes Nordrhein-Westfalen*. Mannheim.

Zabeck, J. (2013). *Geschichte der Berufserziehung und ihrer Theorie, 2. Aufl.* Paderborn: Eusl.

Zimmermann, H. (2005). Kompetenzentwicklung durch Erfahrungstransfer. Betriebliche Ansätze zum Erfahrungstransfer zwischen älteren und jüngeren Beschäftigten. *Berufsbildung in Wissenschaft und Praxis, 5*, 26–30.

Zwack, M., & Schweitzer, J. (2013). Unterschiede, die keine Unterschiede machen dürfen: Entstehung und Umgang mit Leistungsunterschieden in Arbeitsteams. In J. Schweitzer & U. Bossmann (Eds.), *Systemisches Demografiemanagement. Wie kommt Neues zum Älterwerden in Unterne*. Dordrecht: Springer.

Chapter 18
To Engage or Not to Engage: What Can the National VET System Offer Enterprises?

Michele Simons and Roger Harris

Abstract One of the challenges facing industry in Australia is finding the best way to harness the opportunities offered by the national vocational education and training (VET) system. The VET system with its network of registered training organisations, and infrastructure of Training Packages and the VET Quality Framework, has the potential to assist organisations to develop approaches to training that are truly national in scope and focus. However, there are significant barriers to realising this goal. This chapter outlines the architecture of the VET system, and then analyses the issues and challenges that industry faces in its efforts to work with the national training system, and the strategies and practices industry uses in addressing them to meet workforce development needs.

Introduction

The capacity of organisations to meet their needs for skilled labour lies at the heart of workforce development strategies. Development of human capital and the skills it engenders in a workforce can be a sustainable source of competitive advantage and growth for organisations (Smith et al. 2012, p. 12). This development can take many forms but in all cases requires some form of learning system to bring about the changes in skills required by an organisation. While many organisations have their own learning and development systems, they also often turn to the national vocational education and training (VET) system as a driver of skill development for

M. Simons (✉)
The University of Western Sydney, Penrith, Australia
e-mail: michele.simons@uws.edu.au

R. Harris
School of Education, University of South Australia, Adelaide, SA, Australia
e-mail: roger.harris@unisa.edu.au

T. Short and R. Harris (eds.), *Workforce Development: Strategies and Practices,*
DOI 10.1007/978-981-287-068-1_18, © Springer Science+Business Media Singapore 2014

industries and organisations and a means of supporting internal learning and development of their workforces (Smith et al. 2012, p. 12; Australian Workforce and Productivity Agency 2013). In order for these aspirations to be realised, industries need to be able to engage with the VET sector.

From the earliest days of training reform in Australia until the present, engagement between industries and the VET sector has presented challenges. The complexity of the sector and its capacity to be genuinely responsive to the needs of industries have often been criticised (see, for example, Senate Committee 2000). A series of reforms has sought to raise employer confidence in the VET sector. The rapidity and frequency of these changes arguably have made the sector more flexible and responsive, but no amount of reform can ever remove the differences that exist between what a large training edifice like the VET system can provide and what an industry or enterprise might need in terms of their specific human capital development needs (Smith et al. 2005, p. 17). Allen Consulting Group (2004, p. 8) argued that organisations prefer training that is enterprise-specific, work-based and directed by the enterprise. In some respects this is at odds with the remit of a national VET system, which emphasises development of more generic human capital that is portable and can facilitate worker mobility. This basic tension, and the ways in which organisations can work with VET providers in order to optimise outcomes for their workforces, is the focus of this chapter.

The chapter commences with an overview of the key structures of the Australian VET system, which organisations need to understand and utilise if they are to engage with it successfully as part of their overall workforce development strategy. We then turn our attention to exploring some of the benefits to be gained and the challenges to be faced in engaging with the VET sector. We conclude with two case studies that illustrate ways in which enterprises have engaged with the VET sector to meet workforce development needs.

An Overview of the VET System Architecture

The Australian VET system is based on an array of institutional arrangements. The OECD reports that it is 'characterised by its flexibility' (Hoeckel et al. 2008, p. 9) in allowing people of all ages to participate yet, on the other hand, there are cries for 'greater simplicity [in governance] to enable responsiveness and flexibility' (Skills Australia 2009, p. 68). Both federal and state/territory governments are involved in policy development and delivery, with providers regulated through the VET Quality Framework. The training market includes public and private providers which compete for clients and training dollars. VET has been labelled 'the technicolour coat of Australia's education system', a patchwork of colours, fabrics, textures and patterns that represents various aspects of VET and the numerous people who consume training (Buddelmeyer, in Atkinson 2011, p. 2). The 'key pillars' of the national training system are nationally recognised qualifications, Training Packages and the

VET Quality Framework, a system that is 'well-developed' (Knight and Mlotkowski 2009, p. 41) and for which 'Australia is much admired' (Skills Australia 2009, p. 42). And yet the National Skills Standards Council (National Skills Standards Council NSSC 2013) has recently advocated for a new regulatory system, as vocational education and training has continued to diversify, evolve and react to a changing economy and market, leading to the need to reduce unnecessary regulation and to provide a framework for the changing market.

The VET system provides individuals with skills and knowledge they need to enter the workforce for the first time, re-enter the workforce after absences, train or retrain for a different job, upgrade their skills, or move into further study in VET or university. It offers a range of nationally recognised qualifications from certificates to advanced diplomas, and in some cases degrees and (vocational) graduate certificates and diplomas. VET is largely funded by the Australian government and state and territory governments, though companies and individuals can also contribute to the costs of training. Companies contribute by purchasing training for their employees; individuals contribute through the payment of course and administrative fees.

VET is provided by registered training organisations (RTOs), which register with the government to teach accredited courses. The bulk of the training is provided by public VET providers; in 2009 more than 76 % of students undertaking training in a publicly funded provider were enrolled in a Technical and Further Education (TAFE) institute or other government providers such as schools, universities, and agricultural and technical colleges (NCVER 2011, p. 2). In addition there are over 4,500 private RTOs, including enterprises training their own employees, private training and business colleges, specialist bodies providing training within their own industry, and adult and community organisations. In total, around 1.7 million individuals are enrolled in the publicly funded VET system (compared with over 1.1 million in universities), representing over 11 % of Australia's population between 15 and 64 years. The VET learner is typically more likely to be an adult, already employed and upgrading their skills, rather than a school leaver (NCVER 2011, p. 3).

Quality of training is monitored under the VET Quality Framework. This framework comprises the national set of standards that assures nationally consistent, high-quality training and assessment services for the clients of VET system. These standards cover RTOs, VET regulators, Training Packages and accredited courses (NSSC 2013).

Training Packages form the linchpin of the national training arrangements. They specify the skills and knowledge that VET learners are required to demonstrate – the approach known as competency-based training. A Training Package is a nationally endorsed, integrated set of competency standards, assessment requirements, Australian Qualifications Framework (AQF) qualifications and credit arrangements for a specific industry, industry sector or enterprise. These materials provide key information for RTOs which ensures that training and assessment are delivered in accordance with industry standards, as AQF qualifications represent 'a key currency in Australia's labour market' (NSSC 2013, p. 2). Training Packages are developed by industry through the relevant industry skills council, and are updated annually by an Industry Skills Council as a rolling, three-year Continuous Improvement Plan to maintain currency. They consist of a number of components that are endorsed by the National Skills Standards Council and, as such, are mandated materials that must be used to develop learning and assessment resources for training that leads to a nationally recognised VET qualification. These mandatory components include:

- *Units of competency* identifying discrete workplace functions and specifying the standards of performance required in the workplace.
- *Assessment requirements* outlining what an industry specifies to ensure that all assessment reflects accepted industry standards and quality assurance standards.
- *Qualifications* indicating how units of competency can be 'packaged' into qualifications under the AQF.
- *Credit arrangements* specifying existing credit arrangements between Training Package qualifications and higher education qualifications in accordance with the AQF.
- *Companion volume implementation guide* providing the information required to implement the Training Package.

In addition to qualifications, Training Packages also allow for the recognition of skill sets. These clusters of units of competency are linked to a defined industry need, or to a licensing or regulatory requirement. They are not a qualification, but can be used as a means of designing learning and assessment resources that directly match the training needs for a specific workplace role.

Apart from general qualifications and skill sets, apprenticeships and traineeships are a notable component of the VET system. They combine training and employment under a legal contract between the apprentices/trainees, training providers and employers. The learners receive a training wage. In some cases, group training organisations employ a group of apprentices and trainees and place them with appropriate employers. A feature of the Australian VET system is that adults can take up apprenticeships, and in 2009, 14 % of commencing apprenticeships and traineeships were aged 45 years or over (NCVER 2011, p. 6). An important factor is that employers are entitled to financial incentives when taking on an apprentice, and these incentives also apply to employers who train or retrain their *existing* employees. It is here that the VET system can have considerable appeal to employers, or not, depending on their perceptions of many other factors which we discuss below.

Enterprises Engaging with the VET System

A National Centre for Vocational Education Research (NCVER) forum in Melbourne in 2011, 'Is VET worthwhile?', concluded that it depends on who you are and why you use it. For enterprises, one of the key challenges is finding the best way to harness the opportunities offered by the national VET system. The biennial Survey of Employer Use and Views of the VET System 2013, conducted by telephone interview with more than 9,000 employers, revealed decreasing proportions of employers using the VET system (Australian Government 2013, p. 8). While in 2005, 29.2 % used it for apprentices and trainees and 24.2 % for nationally recognised training (training not part of an apprenticeship/traineeship), by 2013 these percentages had slipped to 26.9 % and 20.0 % respectively. This reduction in the use of training could be attributed to slower economic growth and lower business confidence in 2013.

The national VET system, however, offers the potential to assist enterprises to develop approaches to training that are truly national in scope and focus. The alternative is for enterprises to design and development their own in-house training that is neither nationally endorsed nor leads to national qualifications that are portable. So what is this potential and what are the barriers?

Arguments for Engagement

Some of the key arguments for enterprises engaging with the national VET system include the following.

Harmonisation

Within any one particular industry, there is the potential for greater consistency in training across the nation in contrast to each enterprise developing, delivering and assessing its own in-house training.

Savings

A significant incentive for enterprises to engage is that they have the opportunity to take advantage of nationally developed and endorsed programs and do not have to re-invent the wheel in developing their own training courses and materials.

External Validation

National courses have the tick of both industry via the relevant industry skills council and government through endorsement under national arrangements (formerly the National Skills Standards Council) which provide a higher degree of credibility and recognition than local, enterprise-based courses can muster, as well as a structured approach to training and career progression. It can also provide a competitive edge in attracting and retaining staff, and an ability to reward and motivate employees and validate their work experiences (Smith et al. 2005, p. 11).

Employer Satisfaction

Regular surveys by the NCVER of employer views on the national VET system are generally very favourable. Levels of satisfaction reported in the Survey of Employer Use and Views of the VET System 2013 (83 %) are comparable with those in 2005 (81 %), (Australian Government 2013).

Qualification Portability

Possession of nationally endorsed qualifications increases opportunities for employees to be more mobile and marketable, not just within their own state but also across the nation and even internationally.

Arguments Against Engagement

On the other hand, various barriers to employers engaging with the VET system persist. Some of the arguments against engaging with the VET system are as follows.

Complexity

The Australian VET system is often perceived as overly complicated. The complexity arises from both its architecture and its activity (as outlined above). It is compounded by the convergence of various factors, such as the sector being governed and funded by multiple jurisdictions, intersections with school, community and higher education sectors, two main sets of clients – industry and individuals – often with different objectives, and significant diversity among its learners and in its products and stakeholders.

Commentators have for some time highlighted this complexity (e.g. Hall et al. 2000; Schofield and McDonald 2004; Mawer and Jackson 2005). Recently, Simons termed the VET system 'a kaleidoscope of institutions' (2013, p. 36), while Beddie et al. even pondered whether these structures are 'a kaleidoscope' or 'merely fragments' (2013, p. 1). Moreover, Skills Australia in *Skills for prosperity: a roadmap for vocational education and training* identified, as one of its nine themes for the evolution of the sector, the creation of 'a simpler system', recognising that the VET sector 'is generally considered both complex and not readily comprehensible to clients' (2011, p. 8). Finally, through the international eyes of the OECD (Hoeckel et al. 2008, pp. 12–13), Australian VET has been seen to lack clarity, suffer potential duplication through the respective roles of the Commonwealth and state and territory governments in planning the VET system and delivering services, and focus on Training Packages that are large and cumbersome, making them difficult to use.

Increased Opportunities to Leave

The argument of some employers is that supporting employees to gain (further) qualifications can be counterproductive, in that this merely increases the chances of these employees – often the more capable ones – moving to other employment or being poached by rival enterprises.

Political Strings and Paperwork

Many complain that there are so many 'political strings' and so much paperwork in becoming involved with the national training system that they prefer to go it alone. Smith et al. (2005, p. 8) referred to the number of regulatory procedures causing concern among enterprises, especially those seeking to become RTOs themselves, while Tyrrel and Churchill found from their survey of enterprise RTOs that the main concerns related to 'external, non-business focused issues', with the major outstanding issue being the implementation of the AQTF Quality Indicator collection surveys within their business environment (2009, pp. 10–11).

Lack of Relevance

This is a commonly expressed reason for not becoming involved in national courses. There is a basic tension in the VET system: the issue of generic courses versus local courses. Training Packages are developed to embrace a whole industry over the entire country, and qualifications specified with them dictate what combinations of units of competency are to be incorporated into training courses. While proponents state that there can be considerable flexibility within these Training Packages, many employers protest that their experience is that there is more likelihood of generality outweighing specificity, and that therefore they prefer to deliver their own locally developed, context-specific training courses that they judge more relevant to their needs. Hall et al. (2000, pp. 27–28) found that employers in the metals and engineering industry believed training under the Training Packages would not be comprehensive or coherent, while those in the information technology industry were sceptical of the applicability of competencies in IT training and were concerned that they were too vague. Smith et al. (2005) and Mawer and Jackson (2005) also found lack of engagement on the part of some employers was due to their dissatisfaction with the relevance of training or with the training providers, and this was reinforced by Rittie and Awodeyi (2009), who concluded that the three consistent messages from employers were concerns over relevance of skills training, training that is too general, and the lack of focus on practical skills. The most recent figures come from the Survey of Employer Use and Views of the VET System (Australian Government 2013), which found that of the 7.3 % employers dissatisfied with nationally recognised training, 35.9 % consider training to be of poor quality or low standard, 26.0 % that relevant skills are not taught, 25.7 % that training is too general and not specific enough, and 15.5 % that there is insufficient focus on practical skills. In addition, 12 % perceived that VET instructors do not have enough industry experience.

Mindsets

Two mindsets are particularly prevalent. The first is the fundamental attitude of some employers in not believing in the benefits of training *per se* – whether local or national – perceiving it not as an investment but an expense. Stanwick (2009) reported that the Australian Industry Group found 52 % of chief executive officers surveyed saw cost as the major barrier to upskilling workers, with 36 % also lamenting the lack of government incentives. The second is the attitude to national training *vis-à-vis* in-house training – enterprises have had a long history of delivering their own training, and accordingly have ingrained ideas about what works best, and how, for them. For example, Allen Consulting Group (2006) in their study of 500 employers found that a key barrier was perceived to be the difficulty of accommodating VET training around their work demands, and Tyrrel and Churchill (2009, p. 3) reported the key business drivers identified by enterprise RTOs were the ability to customise training and assessment needs and to provide control and flexibility over their delivery. Smith and Smith (2009, pp. 300, 304) also reported this belief in enterprise RTOs that better quality could be attained 'by doing it themselves', yet concluded that this may not necessarily be the case, largely because of the twin risks of over-contextualising training delivery and insufficient rigour in assessment processes. Mindsets can be very hard to shift!

Strategies for Furthering Employer Engagement

Many of these barriers could be minimised or even overcome provided certain safeguards are put in place. Some strategies would include the following.

Return on Investment Analysis

The key aspect is whether the lure of economics outweighs most of these arguments against employer engagement. Post–global financial crisis, there is certainly a renewed open-mindedness about the savings that might be obtained from adopting national training courses. This requires a cost–benefit analysis, and the pull of economic savings would need to be sufficiently strong to overcome con arguments.

Close Collaboration Between Partners

If external training is to be sought, close collaboration between a company and a registered training organisation, and careful monitoring of processes and outcomes are required to diminish the likelihood of a lack of trust between the partners as well as to help to maximise the quality and relevance of this external training to the company's actual developmental needs.

Use of a Company 'Evangelist'

If the enterprise is a registered provider in its own right, there needs to be in-house a sufficient familiarity with and expertise in the national training framework to 'translate' the rules and regulations of the VET system for the benefit of the enterprise. Smith et al. (2005, p. 8) referred to the need for a company 'evangelist' (distinct from the general 'training champion'), who should have previous knowledge and experience of nationally recognised training and whose job would be to persuade management to accept this form of training.

Attractive Workforce Development Policies and Practices

Other workforce development policies and practices in the enterprise need to be sufficiently attractive so that they provide a conducive learning climate and culture to retain employees and thereby dilute or gazump any thoughts on their part of acquiescing to poaching overtures.

National Promotion and Marketing

Changing mindsets is the difficult hurdle! What is needed is evidence that (a) training *per se*, and (b) engaging in *national* training are to the benefit of the enterprise. Cost–benefit analyses, robust research evidence, and favourable data on employer and learner satisfaction all would positively contribute. So, too, would national assessments, under the umbrella of the National Agreement for Skills and Workforce Development, which all Australian governments signed in 2009, on such questions as whether training delivers the skills and capabilities needed for improved economic participation (COAG Reform Council 2013). Smith et al. (2005, p. 11) recommended increased national promotion of nationally recognised training. They found that, not only were some non-users in their study completely unaware of appropriate Training Packages and qualifications, but even those who were engaged were sometimes unfamiliar with many of the subtleties involved in using the packages. Thus, these authors concluded that employer complaints about the VET system seemed more related to a lack of understanding of, rather than deficiencies in, Training Packages (2005, p. 54). If that is so, then there is hope that further promotion would help to breakdown inaccurate perceptions and negative attitudes.

Several lessons for the marketing of training can be drawn from the study of Figgis et al. (2001) on training/learning cultures in small and medium enterprises. Real and detailed exemplars are needed in any efforts to convince enterprises to rethink their approach to training; rosy, good news stories, they conclude, are patronising and ultimately unconvincing. Second, there is a need for new, more qualitative indicators that enterprises can use in calculating their return on investment made on training, not merely costs in dollars. Third, a key message is that the kind of culture in an enterprise shapes the value of investment in training and learning.

Recognising the Importance of Informal Learning

The importance of informal learning should not be underestimated. Informality refers to both the specificity of outcomes expected and the formality of guidance given to the learner. Figgis et al. found that the majority of the enterprises they studied considered that informal strategies for developing skills and knowledge in their enterprises were 'more important and effective than the Australian VET sector acknowledges' (2001, p. 5), and that information provided to enterprises by authorities in the sector tends to ignore informal processes. The Survey of Employers 2013 supports the greater recognition of informal learning: 77.6 % of employers reported using informal learning, by far the most common form of training choice, defined as 'training that usually occurs on the job through interactions with co-workers as part of the day-to-day work' (Australian Government 2013, pp. 8, 17).

We now draw on two of our projects as case studies, one at a broader level to illustrate the advantages and challenges through the eyes of various industry leaders in engaging with the national training system, and the second at a more micro level to show how one industry furthered its engagement with that system.

Case Study 1: Evidence on the Pros and Cons of Engagement with the National Training System

The first case study explored leadership in different types of training providers (Harris and Simons 2012). Here we focus only on that part of the research involving 26 interviews held with leaders at various levels from two types of RTO across three Australian states and a range of industries. The RTO types were: enterprise-based organisations (n = 6) – training centres within enterprises whose prime business focus is an industry other than education and training – and industry organisations (n = 5) – industry-sponsored training centres, such as industry associations, professional associations and group training companies, that provide services to an industry sector.

From these interviews relevant information can be gleaned from an *industry* perspective about their views on engaging with the national training system. Specifically, many of their comments (brackets indicate gender and number of interviewee) shed light on why there is not a closer relationship.

Challenges in Engaging as Reported by Interviewees

Prominent among the reasons given for not engaging with the national training system was its complexity. Some organisations felt disinclined to spend the time required to understand it. One leader labelled it 'the compliance maze of the VET framework' (male, #20). Another in an organisation with responsibilities across a particular industry isolated the problem to be

> getting the right information to the right people to make the decisions that they feel comfortable to enrol their staff in VET. So it's about breaking down some of the barriers … it's about letting them know … so they can actually utilise the VET system to their best advantage … no matter how much the government thinks that it gets information out to employers, they still feel very lost about how to actually work within the VET system. (female, #14)

Similarly in another industry, an interviewee critiqued the VET system for its predominant focus on quality assurance and its unwieldiness:

> if I was to specifically talk about the VET sector and nationally accredited training, … the concern is that it's very focused on … quality assurance, but I actually think as a consequence it misses some of those key aspects of delivery, [and] by doing that, it creates an unwieldy system. (male, #24)

Another issue was the perception that TAFE, the public provider, was out of date: 'one of the key concerns of our members was TAFE teachers that had been in the role for 20+ years, [and] had no relationship to industry' (female, #14). Consequently, industry organisations tend to revert to appointing their own trainers

> straight out of industry, which means they're technical experts in their field, very, very capable technicians, who have naturally begun to take a leadership or a training role within their previous employment and seen an interest in moving into delivery of training. (female, #14)

An additional concern with TAFE was its perceived different culture, as expressed in financial terms by another interviewee:

> if they come in from TAFE, … of course they've got to work to a budget, but if they overspend, the business isn't going to fall down; and the different culture in a TAFE institute compared to the private world of running a business, paying for your equipment, your resources, is very different. (female, #29)

A third issue, particularly for enterprise RTOs, was the 'two-way press' to manage change. Embedding RTO functions inside an enterprise presented a unique challenge for these leaders, in having to 'sell' the value of the RTO and 'ensure that senior management, executive management, recognise that we do provide a service, that we do add value to the company' (male, #6). They were subject to change from two directions, having to manage pressures both from the VET sector and regulatory environment, and from the 'evidence-based, organisational side' (male, #28). They therefore had to 'marry those two ... so we're providing them with the best outcomes in terms of the learners' (female, #27).

A fourth issue was the compliance and auditing regime. Some were clearly frustrated with the nature of the process *per se*, perceiving it as merely 'ticking boxes':

> He was ticking boxes, which means I, as the main RTO manager, had to make sure we're in a position to tick the boxes and make sure we're presenting our operations in a way that makes sense to the VET system. (male, #28)

and sometimes conducted by people with little understanding of local context:

> the last time we had an audit we had a guy who was running his own little enterprise, in a private context, trying to come up here and audit the systems for a large government enterprise. He did not understand the nature of our business and our relationship to the VET system, and how compliance would be achieved. (male, #28)

One interviewee was 'cynical about the audit process' (female, #21), while another labelled the audit 'a total farce' (male, #22), principally because they did not believe that the auditor possessed the appropriate skills and that their recent experience had been of a process focused more on quantity of compliance information rather than on quality of training. They therefore had found the experience 'emotionally draining' and 'very stressful' (female, #23).

Yet another highlighted the multiplicity of rules in the regulatory framework, especially for those companies operating across state borders:

> VET is the second most regulated industry in Australia ... every time you have an issue with VET, it seems you've got more rules, and if you're a provider that operates in more than one state ... even though in theory we have a new national regulator, ... there's a fair bit of cynicism around as to what that will do to actually streamline compliance costs because you have different sets of rules required for different governments ... more and more of the money is tied up in compliance costs. Good RTOs are not looking to access government funding. (male, #30)

Others were irritated that it appeared to be only for bringing poor performers up to standard and weeding out 'mavericks', thereby wasting time for those functioning appropriately:

> as much as everybody bangs on about quality systems in the VET sector, every time I see something change it's about trying to capture the maverick providers who are not very good, and we get further and further compliance and regulations, which puts the ones who are operating appropriately under intense pressure, and you end up spending a lot of your time just trying to maintain compliance rather than producing good education. (male, #28)

This was a significant issue for staff in enterprise RTOs, who felt penalised providing training to their very own employees, as this interviewee succinctly summarised:

> I think the enterprise RTO context where we do not offer education to people who are buying education – our function is to deliver education to the people who are employed by us to do a job. I think that represents a unique set of complexities, and I do not think the VET regulatory system understands it. I think they understand private RTOs who provide a service of education delivery; I think they understand TAFE systems; I think they understand community colleges. But I do not think they understand this, and they try to apply the same rules to this situation and the fit is not good. (male, #28)

Overall, some interviewees retained doubts over the quality of external provision of training, and therefore preferred to maintain their in-house training. For these leaders, notions of compliance and quality education were not necessarily the same: 'given my limited exposure to nationally accredited training, I'm not convinced that the structures that are in place are necessarily a commitment to stronger educational outcomes' (male, #24).

A fifth challenge in working with the national training system, especially for enterprise RTOs, related to managing the different cultures within the whole enterprise and the requirements that the RTO demanded. The following quotation illustrates how required training and assessment practices often clash with what is perceived as the 'hands on' culture of the workplace:

> The most common is the written part of the training, the [assessment]. Sometimes they see that as irrelevant, it's what happens out in the crane or what happens in the forklift that's important, but they tend to not think the written side of it is important, so we're always stressing that. (male, #10)

This challenge related not only to the way training and assessment were delivered, but also to issues such as what was 'deemed' to be correct work practices and who held the valued knowledge within the enterprise. In the latter case, experienced workers could see RTO staff as a challenge to their perceived place in the workforce as an 'expert', which at times led to resistance to the work of the trainers. This was particularly the case when dealing with 'very strong personalities' who had been in the industry for a long time, were 'passionate about what they do' and could 'become quite confrontational' (female, #27).

Positive Perspectives as Reported by Interviewees

While these issues were often a challenge, they were not always perceived unfavourably, nor did they necessarily block engagement with the national training system. In many organisations, for example, compliance was considered an integral and necessary part of their operating environment that brought benefits to their organisations. This is best exemplified in the following reflections of a senior leader:

> In a small organisation, things like that always put pressure on people like myself in leadership roles ... On the other side of it, though, I always see something like that as being really important to give you a place to reflect on what you're doing, so while you have to make sure you are compliant, because otherwise you won't be in business, ... we took it as a time to really reflect and ensure that, while we were meeting compliance, we had the processes in place to say 'Okay, look, we could actually do this better'. (female, #19)

Furthermore, the dominant perspective on becoming engaged with the national training system was that there was often a demand for training that was nationally accredited and qualifications that would be portable. One industry interviewee with national responsibilities articulated this view in this way, judging such involvement as an 'additional string to [the] bow' for that organisation:

> [It is] really about trying to spread the opportunities available for our state branches, so effectively there seems to be a demand for the sort of training that we do, and one of the things that appears to be an influence in people taking up that training is being able to access nationally accredited training, and that was the key influence, that it's an additional string to our bow. (male, #24)

Strategies and Practices

Strategies and practices for dealing with these issues were embedded in the interviews. One way of coping with complexity in the VET system and the auditing environment was to equip employees on a regular basis through monthly meetings related to the organisation's own internal auditing requirements and continuous improvement strategies. Each meeting was aligned to a key focus for internal auditing or continuous improvement. In this way, on a yearly rotation, the organisation moved through the VET Quality Framework requirements and the broader VET requirements of an RTO's functions, while also allowing the trainers to have internal professional development. When a re-registration audit became imminent, in the 6 months prior a considerable amount of work was undertaken to ensure trainers would say the right things. As one interviewee confided, 'RTOs have their own language, and it's sometimes different to the auditor's language, so it was about actually aligning this function that we do to a particular audit item, so that everybody was fully aware when they were asked' (female, #14).

A variant of this approach, one with similar purpose though different strategy, was the placing of 'responsibility for quality, delivery and compliance under the VET regulatory system and RTO responsibilities in the hands of the whole team in appropriate ways' (male, #28). It was recognised that this could not be constricted only to managers making all the decisions and doing everything, but that the goal was to build 'a robust, resilient team, achieving the quality that is required'. This could come through opportunities to act in other roles, formal sessions explaining how it all needed to work and bringing in external people to speak. At other times, the organisation retained a consultant to help employees understand VET, make sure that they were addressing all the issues and engage them in professional development.

Another suggestion for coping with complexity in the system was the need for support in understanding more of the opportunities that are available through the VET system. One interviewee recognised that he 'at times finds it very difficult to grasp, so a better understanding of the system and the opportunities that are available would be a support to me' (male, #24). In similar vein, another interviewee pleaded for a rethinking of the auditing processes, especially in the case of auditors handling the differences between the various types of RTO. He acknowledged the need for quality and the need to hold managers accountable for it, but considered that 'the naïve application of a lot of the compliance principles was creating unnecessary burden' (male, #28), and creating tension when there was no need.

Interviewees also referred to their work as advocates for change in external environments – for example, with VET regulators in arguing for changes to support their businesses or 'selling' changes to training requirements inside the enterprise or to businesses within the industry. These quotations from enterprise and industry interviewees illustrate the multiple levels of change and competing interests that need to be balanced:

> I think to convince the workforce ... to change their minds that this is not a joke, this [training] is a serious thing you are about to participate in. (male, #8)

> We have an ability to talk to our members and employers on a regular basis ... we hold meetings where we ... present what we do ... A lot of employers didn't understand how we deliver versus the way other RTOs deliver ... you've got to change the mentality of the employers ... they've got this mindset saying, 'That's the way apprentices should be trained', ... and they're still getting their heads around that. (male, #17)

Specific attributes required to meet many of these workforce development challenges, especially cultural differences in the workplace and dealing with strong personalities, included: having 'a passion for learning, development and training', being 'an effective communicator', being 'very good at imparting knowledge to other employees', and strategic thinking in the sense of having strategies in place 'that try and cut them off at the pass' (male, #6). Power to persuade and convince transitory bosses was also seen as a critical skill. A key notion in the handling of these challenges, particularly managing change, was perceived as 'presence': 'presence. That's a key word for me ... I think you have to be present with your team. You have to be talking, and ... you have to get around to continually tell the story of change' (male, #28).

In considering relations with external providers, many skills were perceived to be in common, but what was not transferable was specific knowledge of the organisation's and industry's work. Therefore, it was important to be able to negotiate with providers and tailor their offerings. As one interviewee said, 'we've contextualised [their program] and added case studies and project work and all that type of thing that is aligned specifically to our industry' (male, #6).

A critical success factor was the ability to integrate learning systems provided by an RTO into the work structures and processes in a way that did not hamper productivity. This required the capacity to identify key people working in a variety of roles where training was required and then to engage them successfully in the work of providing training to other workers. It was also critical that leaders were flexible in their approaches to how training could be constituted from within and alongside the work of the enterprise. This required a continual connection with the work of the enterprise and a level of 'current competence' in trainers that went beyond what was expressed in units of competency to encompass an understanding of the culture, values and norms of the enterprise.

Case Study 2: How One Industry Furthered Its Engagement with the National Training System

The second case study (Simons and Harris 2014) was undertaken as part of the Workforce Development Program of the Collaborative Research Centre (CRC) for Rail Innovation. The research focused on the development of learning and assessment materials for the training of rail infrastructure workers.

Context for the Project

Historically, rail organisations in each state and territory have relied on their own in-house training, delivered either through internal training departments or through relationships with external consultants. In some cases, rail organisations had become registered training organisations in their own right in order to access some of the benefits noted earlier in this chapter that engagement with the VET can provide. This 'patchwork' of approaches, however, had led to considerable fragmentation in the training effort across the industry. Coupled with significant restructuring and reform in the industry, there was a growing awareness of the value in collaboration among rail organisations with regard to approaches to training for their workforces. In these circumstances the VET sector, with its national scope and reach, offered a mechanism by which this collaboration could be achieved.

Three factors acted as catalysts to drive this collaborative approach to training. First, while rail organisations had been well served by these approaches to workforce development, research undertaken for the CRC (McKenzie and Simons 2010) had illustrated how the use of a purpose-built evaluation framework could support decision making and access to industry-endorsed approaches to competence development and maintenance that had national currency. Second, a review of rail qualifications by the Transport and Logistics Industry Skills Council (TLISC) in 2010 led to the development of a Training Package that contains a new training and qualifications framework for occupational groups such as infrastructure workers and rail operations. The development of this new Training Package provided an industry-endorsed national framework of qualifications for a range of occupational groups within the industry, which then had flow-on consequences for existing training systems within rail enterprises. These systems needed to be revised to align with nationally endorsed qualification requirements. Third, the CRC for Rail Innovation provided the ideal vehicle for the development of a *national* set of resources based on the newly endorsed Training Package for Rail Infrastructure Workers.

Developing the Learning and Assessment Resources

The project involved a three-stage process negotiated with the participating rail organisations. The first stage focused on planning and negotiating what learning and assessment resources would be developed. Key goals in this phase included:

- developing a common understanding of the occupational areas that would form the focus for the resources to be developed;
- establishing a development team that had both credibility with the rail industry and a solid grounding in the operation of the VET sector; and
- finalising the skill sets and units of competency that would best match the development needs of the rail organisations.

The development of a shared understanding of the occupational areas that would form the focus of the project was facilitated by the use of a purpose-built evaluation methodology (McKenzie and Simons 2010). Initial negotiations with CRC participants in the project had determined that four occupational areas were to be targeted in the project: track maintenance/inspection, structures, mechanical signalling and ganger/team leader. In order to establish what currently existed in terms of the training for these four areas, a brief mapping exercise was undertaken. This mapping was seen as an effective way of developing a shared understanding of the organisations' training needs. This was important because:

- needs in these areas varied across the participant organisations – some organisations already had training available; others were moving to build on skill sets (e.g. induction, specific skill sets from the newly endorsed Training Package); and in other cases pressing needs arising from the existing workforce profile were being addressed (e.g. ganger/team leader); and
- mapping was seen as a means of capturing lists of training materials already in existence for the four areas, what materials/training were under development and how access to these materials could be made available to the research team to support the development of the new national materials.

A template for the mapping was developed and circulated to the six participating rail organisations. Data from this exercise were then analysed and reported back to a Project Steering Committee which had been formed to oversee the project on behalf of the CRC.

Parallel with this activity, the research team liaised with the TLISC, the developers of the recently endorsed Training Package, and together decisions were made on engagement of an instructional designer to develop the training resources and the processes that would be used to develop them. As a result of these discussions, the TLISC was invited to submit a proposal for the development. This decision was made for a number of reasons, including the following:

- as the developers of the Training Package, TLISC had in-depth knowledge of the package and its contents;
- in developing the Training Package, TLISC had identified a network of subject-matter experts who could be called upon to assist with the development; and
- as the national industry skills council with in-depth knowledge of the rail industry, TLISC had the credibility with industry that was crucial in ensuring their engagement.

The proposal from TLISC was put to the Project Steering Committee and endorsed. TLISC then put forward a submission to undertake the work which, with some further modification, was subsequently accepted by both the Project Steering Committee and the CRC. A dedicated project manager was then allocated to the project, responsible for all aspects of the project, including facilitating engagement with key industry stakeholders through the CRC and managing the design and content of the training resources. This person worked collaboratively with the Project Steering Committee to secure the services of an instructional designer. The choice of the designer was facilitated by rail organisations offering recommendations based on their experiences of working with particular individuals. Again, the individual selected for this process had prior knowledge and experience of working with rail organisations and with the TLISC, as well as knowledge of the VET sector.

When the analysis of the mapping exercise was completed, the Project Steering Committee met to make a final decision about the units of competency from the most recently endorsed Training Package that would be used to form the basis for the development of the training resources. Drawing on the outcomes of the mapping and the current Training Package, the Project Steering Committee determined that learning and assessment resources would be developed for a total of 11 units of competency consisting of a selected number of core units and three skill sets from the TLI10 (Version 1) Training Package that formed the Certificate III in Rail Infrastructure. This decision represented a compromise position among the participants in the project. It reflected the areas of need that were shared across organisations, and where development of training resources was not planned to be undertaken by those organisations but where the CRC project could complement the training priorities within their respective organisations. Interestingly, while this project was underway, the Training Package was subject to further amendments. These were incorporated into a new version of the Training Package released in 2011. Consultation with the Project Steering Committee resulted in some changes being made to the resources that would be developed. Some resources were not to be developed further as the units of competency were no longer components of the skill sets. Again, these negotiations represented a compromise position but one that was clearly framed by the Training Package, which was taken as the industry 'benchmark' for the training of rail infrastructure workers.

The second stage of the project saw the development of the learning and assessment resources. The process used to guide this stage consisted of a number of steps:

- consulting with key industry stakeholders and the project manager to determine the overall plan for the development of the resources
- identifying subject-matter experts to develop the content
- developing and reviewing the first draft of the resources
- undertaking further review and incorporating feedback into a second draft of the resources
- seeking an audit of the draft materials by an independent Australian Quality Training Framework auditor
- seeking further feedback on a second draft of the materials from the Project Steering Committee and key stakeholders
- incorporating this feedback into a final draft of the resources
- conducting a validation exercise using a sample of the resources with selected rail organisations
- editing and formatting the final draft resources
- signing off and releasing the completed materials.

The project manager worked closely with the Project Steering Committee, project leader and the two instructional designers who were employed over the life of the project.

For each unit of competency, a participant guide, a participant assessment workbook and an RTO/facilitator guide were developed. Collectively, this suite of resources formed the basis for the delivery and assessment strategy for the units which individual rail organisations could then adapt to their particular context as required by the VET Quality Framework.

The participant guides specify the learning tasks to be completed by each learner/employee prior to undertaking the assessment tasks set out in the assessment workbooks. Each guide consists of three parts:

- an introduction giving information about the unit of competency, the learning and assessment process, how evidence of competency is to be collected and what the learner/employee needs to do in order to demonstrate competence;
- the learning tasks that assist the learner/employee to develop the knowledge and skills needed to demonstrate competence; and
- a glossary of terms used in the learning resource.

These guides are intended to be used by the learner/employee in conjunction with the support of a trainer or facilitator.

The participant assessment workbooks stipulate the assessment tasks to be completed by the learner/employee in order to demonstrate their competence. Each workbook contains:

- details of the scope of the assessment strategy, with the assessment tasks mapped against the relevant elements from the unit of competency;

- a series of assessment tasks which includes those that must be demonstrated in the workplace and questions that allow the learner/employee to demonstrate their knowledge that underpins their performance; and
- a form for assessor details and feedback to be recorded for the learner/employee.

The RTO/facilitator guides were written to meet the needs of industry stakeholders, assessors, RTOs and auditors. Each guide contains information to facilitate the implementation of the learning and assessment processes for learners/employees for the specified unit of competency. It offers advice on matters such as contextualisation, the issuing of statements of attainment, the roles and responsibilities of facilitators and assessors, and an overview of the potential learners. Each guide includes:

- details of the learning tasks (purpose, instructions for the facilitator, resources and an outline of the knowledge and skills to be covered in the learning process);
- assessment tools and marking guidelines;
- resources to assist with mapping learning and to record evidence;
- information on the use of third party reports; and
- information on recording final results.

The third stage of the project involved the validation of the learning and assessment resources to ensure they met both the needs of the enterprises and the standards expected in the VET sector. The process of validation involved checking the learning resources to ensure they were fit-for-purpose and comprehensive in terms of their coverage of the requirements in the units of competency. It was also concerned with testing that the resources took into account the diversity of learners/employees and rail organisations in which they were to be used; and that the assessment tools and processes would facilitate the collection of valid, reliable, sufficient, current and authentic evidence in order that reasonable judgements could be made about the competence of learners/employees. A sample of the learning and assessment resources was selected for the validation exercises, which included both internal validation by TLISC staff using established TLISC procedures, and external validation by an VET Quality Framework auditor. The resources were also reviewed and in some cases used as part of a pilot in five of the participating rail organisations. The final materials were then prepared for publication and distribution.

Strategies and Practices

This case study illustrates how the architecture of the VET sector provided the scaffolding within which rail organisations could collaboratively develop the resources they needed to build their respective workforces. The outcomes achieved in the project were the result of a number of key strategies. Firstly, the VET sector alone cannot provide resources for enterprises to use without first developing a sound knowledge base to guide decision making. The processes adopted in the project demonstrated how information from a variety of organisations offering training on the same topic can be synthesised to give a clear indication of the extent to which national training resources for an occupational group can be conceptualised. This information formed the basis for their engagement with the VET sector.

Secondly, this work shows how nationally accredited Training Packages can be used as a basis for developing these training resources but this development needs to be facilitated by VET sector experts and industry 'champions' – in this case, the Project Steering Committee. As the developer of the Training Package, TLISC was well positioned to understand the Training Package and the VET Quality Framework requirements that the resources needed to meet, and to translate this information in ways that were accessible for the project participants. Their networks and credibility within the rail industry facilitated the support necessary for the development processes. The Project Steering Committee provided access to equally important resources including the industry subject-matter experts. While a significant amount of the information in the learning and assessment resources was obtained from earlier versions of the materials, input from those most familiar and experienced with actual work functions that are the focus of the training was vital. Through the input from these experts the tacit curriculum became apparent, thus allowing a narrowing of the gap between the enterprise-specific, work-based learning desired by the organisations and the more generic skills development that the VET sector offers.

The process, however, was not without its challenges. The cost in terms of time to establish a shared platform to develop this national approach to training was considerable. One could argue that this initial 'up-front cost' was more than offset by later savings through avoiding duplication of effort in scoping out and developing training programs inside individual organisations. The length of this process was not always commensurate with the perceived immediacy and urgency of some training needs in some of the participant organisations.

The injection of resources that the CRC facilitated should also not be underestimated. Operating within the VET sector to achieve high quality outcomes requires an investment in people (in this case, a project manager and two instructional designers). The sector in and of itself does ameliorate the need for highly skilled VET practitioners who under normal circumstances would have been individually sourced by each rail organisation.

Conclusion

The VET sector has much to offer industries and enterprises interested in enhancing the skills of their workforces in order to drive innovation and respond to changes in external operating environments. The national scale and scope of the sector brings together resources, which can enhance harmonisation of training effort across an industry, offer savings in terms of shared resources and set national benchmarks to assure the quality of training. On the other hand, engagement with the VET sector can be a challenge. Its national scale and scope can also bring challenges for enterprises who are seeking bespoke responses to their training needs. However, as the case studies in this chapter have illustrated, it is possible to bring enterprises and the sector into partnerships that can achieve productive outcomes for both parties. This engagement relies on combining the knowledge, capacities and resources of both the VET sector and the enterprise with the goal of achieving some common aim. These processes require individuals from the VET sector to come to a common understanding of the scope and nature of the needs of industry, while industry/ enterprise representatives need to provide information about their workforce development needs in a manner that allows clear and robust working relationships to develop. Most of all, these partnerships between industry and the VET sector require a shared commitment to the value of monitoring their partnership and workforce development goals they are trying to achieve in order to reflect and learn about how each can work to the mutual benefit of workers, enterprises and industries.

References

Allen Consulting Group. (2004). *The vocational education and training system: Key issues for large enterprises*. Melbourne: Business Council of Australia.

Allen Consulting Group. (2006). *World class skills for world class industries: Employers' perspectives on skilling in Australia*. Sydney: Australian Industry Group.

Atkinson, G. (2011). *Research overview. Vocational education and training: The technicolour coat of Australia's education system*. Adelaide: National Centre for Vocational Education Research.

Australian Government. (2013). *Australian vocational education and training statistics: Employers' use and views of the VET system*. Adelaide: National Centre for Vocational Education Research.

Australian Workforce and Productivity Agency. (2013). Future focus: 2013 national workforce development strategy. Canberra: Australian Workforce and Productivity Agency. http://www.awpa.gov.au/our-work/national-workforce-development-strategy/2013-workforce-development-strategy/Documents/FutureFocus2013NWDS.pdf. Accessed 21 Feb 2014.

Beddie, F., O'Connor, L., & Curtin, P. (Eds.). (2013). *Structures in tertiary education and training: A kaleidoscope or merely fragments? Research readings*. Adelaide: National Centre for Vocational Education Research.

Council of Australian Governments Reform Council. (2013). *Skills in Australia 2012: Five years of performance*. Sydney: COAG Reform Council.

Figgis, J., Alderson, A., et al. (2001). *What convinces enterprises to value training and learning and what does not?* Adelaide: National Centre for Vocational Education Research.

Hall, R., Buchanan, J., et al. (2000). *Making the grade? Globalisation and the training market in Australia* (Vol. 1). Adelaide: National Centre for Vocational Education Research.

Harris, R., & Simons, M. (2012). *'Two sides of the same coin': Leaders in private providers juggling educational and business imperatives*. Adelaide: National Centre for Vocational Education Research.

Hoeckel, K., Field, S., et al. (2008). *Learning for jobs – OECD reviews of VET: Australia*. Paris: Organisation for Economic Cooperation and Development.

Knight, B., & Mlotkowski, P. (2009). *An overview of vocational education and training in Australia and its links to the labour market*. Adelaide: National Centre for Vocational Education Research.

Mawer, G., & Jackson, E. (2005). *Training of existing workers: Issues, incentives and models*. Adelaide: National Centre for Vocational Education Research.

McKenzie, S., & Simons, M. (2010). *Evaluation framework and national curriculum for track safety awareness training: Final report for project P4.105*. Brisbane: Cooperative Research Centre for Rail Innovation.

National Centre for Vocational Education Research (NCVER). (2011). *Did you know? A guide to vocational education and training in Australia*. Adelaide: National Centre for Vocational Education Research.

National Skills Standards Council (NSSC). (2013). *VET standards*. http://www.nssc.natese.gov.au/vet_standards. Accessed 9 Feb 2014.

Rittie, T., & Awodeyi, T. (2009). *Employers' views on improving the vocational education and training system. Occasional Paper*. Adelaide: National Centre for Vocational Education Research.

Schofield, K., & McDonald, R. (2004). *Moving on: Report of the high level review of Training Packages*. Brisbane: Australian National Training Authority.

Senate Employment Workplace Relations Small Business Education References Committee. (2000). *Aspiring to excellence: Report into the quality of vocational education and training in Australia*. Canberra: Senate Printing Unit, Parliament House.

Simons, M. (2013). The future of the tertiary sector workforce: A kaleidoscope of possibilities? In F. Beddie, L. O'Connor, & P. Curtin (Eds.), *Structures in tertiary education and training: A kaleidoscope or merely fragments? Research readings* (pp. 36–47). Adelaide: National Centre for Vocational Education Research.

Simons, M., & Harris, R. (2014). *Training for rail infrastructure workers: Final report for project P4.114*. Brisbane: Cooperative Research Centre for Rail Innovation.

Skills Australia. (2009). *Foundations for the future: Final position paper*. Canberra: Commonwealth of Australia.

Skills Australia. (2011). *Skills for prosperity: A roadmap for vocational education and training*. Canberra: Commonwealth of Australia.

Smith, E., & Smith, A. (2009). Making training core business: Enterprise registered training organisations in Australia. *Journal of Vocational Education and Training, 61*(3), 287–306.

Smith, E., Pickersgill, R., et al. (2005). *Enterprises' commitment to nationally recognised training for existing workers*. Adelaide: National Centre for Vocational Education Research.

Smith, A., Courvisanos, J., et al. (2012). *Building the capacity to innovate: The role of human capital*. Adelaide: National Centre for Vocational Education Research.

Stanwick, J. (2009). *Employer engagement with the vocational education and training system in Australia*. Adelaide: National Centre for Vocational Education Research.

Tyrrel, A., & Churchill, J. (2009). *Profiling the Australian enterprise RTO: Summary report*. Griffith: Enterprise Registered Training Organisation Association.

Chapter 19
Creating a Common Approach to Safety Management Through Structured Training Development

Tamara D. Banks, Herbert C. Biggs, and Nathan Dovan

Abstract The successful management of workplace safety has many benefits for employees, employers and the community. Similar to other areas of job performance, safety performance can be enhanced through appropriate and well-designed training. The foundation of the development of effective training is a thorough training needs analysis (TNA). Currently, the application of psychometrically valid TNA practices for the management of workplace safety is an under-researched topic and limited guidance is available for implementing appropriate strategies. To address this gap in the literature, this chapter will provide an overview of TNA practices, including the purpose and benefits associated with implementing the systematic procedure. A case study will then be presented to illustrate how the TNA process was successfully applied to investigate the training needs of Australasian rail incident investigators to achieve an industry-approved national training package. Recommendations will be made to assist practitioners with implementing TNA practices with the goal of enhancing workplace safety management through targeted workforce development.

Current Approaches to Safety Management

The integration of workplace risk management with organisational operations has gained increased prominence over recent years. In both research and organisational practice, efforts to increase the safety of high-risk production systems have had a greater focus on not only technical and individual-centred measures, but also on safety management, improving the relationship between technology, organisation and human resources (Grote and Künzler 2000). This shift in focus identified

T.D. Banks (✉) • H.C. Biggs • N. Dovan
Centre for Accident Research and Road Safety Queensland (CARRS-Q), Queensland University of Technology, Carseldine, Australia
e-mail: t.banks@qut.edu.au; h.biggs@qut.edu.au; n.dovan@qut.edu.au

T. Short and R. Harris (eds.), *Workforce Development: Strategies and Practices*,
DOI 10.1007/978-981-287-068-1_19, © Springer Science+Business Media Singapore 2014

opportunities not only to reduce accident or incident rates, but also to improve the productivity and economic and financial results of the organisation (Fernández-Muñiz et al. 2009). Safety management systems are mechanisms integrated in organisations, designed to control the risks that can affect the health and safety of workers, and at the same time ensuring compliance with relevant legislation. Safety management refers to the actual practices, roles and functions associated with remaining safe in the workplace (Mearns et al. 2003). Therefore, safety management is more than a 'paper system' of policies and procedures. The most effective safety management systems should be completely integrated into the organisation, and be cohesive systems, incorporating policies, strategies and procedures that provide internal consistency and harmonisation (Fernández-Muñiz et al. 2009). The successful organisational integration of safety management systems is strongly dependent on the advocacy, support and widespread acceptance of the system by all stakeholders. The dominant narrative to describe this process is organisational safety culture.

There is little consensus on the required number of indicators to accurately reflect an organisation's safety culture. However, Wiegmann and colleagues (2004) identified at least five global indicators. The first, organisational commitment, is the extent to which upper-level management identifies safety as a core value or guiding principle in the organisation. Their commitment to safety is reflected by their efforts to ensure that every aspect of their operations is routinely evaluated and modified to improve safety, if necessary.

The second indicator, management involvement, refers to how personally involved upper and middle-level managers are in critical safety activities. This includes maintaining good communication about safety issues both up and down the organisational hierarchy (Wiegmann et al. 2004). Employee empowerment is the third indicator. Organisations with a 'good' safety culture empower their employees and provide clear understanding of the critical role they play in promoting safety. Within the safety culture, this indicator is characterised by employees having a substantial voice in safety decisions, having the ability to achieve safety improvements, holding themselves and others accountable for their actions and taking pride in their organisation's safety record (Wiegmann et al. 2004).

One of the key components of an organisation's safety culture is how safe and unsafe behaviours are evaluated and the consistency with which rewards or penalties are handed out. This is the fourth indicator (Reason 1990). An organisation's safety culture is not only identified by the existence of reward systems, but also whether these systems are formally documented, applied consistently, and explained and understood by all employees (Wiegmann et al. 2004). The final indicator is the reporting systems used in the organisation. An effective and systematic reporting system assists the organisation to identify the weaknesses and vulnerabilities of the safety management systems before an incident occurs. Organisations with a good safety culture should utilise formal reporting systems that are used comfortably by employees. These systems should allow and encourage employees to report any safety occurrences and provide timely and valuable feedback to all employees within the organisation (Wiegmann et al. 2004).

The improvement of working conditions and safety provides many benefits, both direct and indirect. The workers themselves are the direct beneficiaries of safety management systems, since they are often the most affected by any accidents. In addition, organisations also benefit by avoiding potential losses and by improvements in profitability and performance (Fernández-Muñiz et al. 2009). Alternatively, organisations with unsafe working conditions harm the industrial climate and undermine the morale and motivation of employees. Therefore, workplace health and safety benefits the organisation because it keeps employees healthy and productive, decreasing down time and employee absenteeism, while improving workers' job satisfaction and motivation.

Workplace health and safety is an important topic. Preliminary data by Safe Work Australia (2013) identified that in 2010–2011 there were 127,330 serious workers' compensation claims, equating to 12.2 serious claims per 1,000 employees. Work-related injuries and illnesses were estimated to cost $60.6 billion in the 2008/2009 financial year, representing 4.8 % of the GDP. Based on these statistics, it comes as no surprise that many organisations have a continued focus on the antecedents to workplace safety. Attempts to reduce the frequency of accidents or incidents occurring in the workplace require greater collective effort in working towards reducing human error, or making the systems within the organisation more error tolerant (Baysari et al. 2008). There is little doubt that within complex systems human error contributes to a majority of documented incidents.

Justification for the Use of Safety Training to Enhance Safety Performance

Similar to other areas of job performance, safety performance encompasses an employee's behaviour including both their physical actions such as photographing a crime scene and their mental processes such as problem solving. Based on research with army personnel, Campbell et al. (1993) proposed a model of job performance indicating three direct determinants of job performance. They suggested that declarative knowledge (knowing job-relevant information), procedural knowledge and skill (knowing how to perform job-relevant tasks) and motivation were direct determinants of job performance. They further suggested that other factors, such as training, could have an indirect effect on performance through increasing one or more of the direct determinants. Building upon Campbell et al.'s model of job performance, Neal and Griffin (1997) developed a safety performance framework. Similar to Campbell et al.'s model, Neal and Griffin's framework postulated that knowledge, skill and motivation were direct determinants of safety performance and that effective safety training could potentially increase safety performance through increased safety knowledge and skill.

In addition to the above theoretical models that conceptually link how safety training can have an indirect influence on safety performance through increased safety knowledge and skill, empirical research has demonstrated a link between participation in safety training and improvements in safety performance. Burke et al. (2006) identified, reviewed and conducted a meta-analysis on 95 studies from 1971 to 2003 that examined worker safety and health training and reported outcomes on safety performance. They coded training methods and content from least engaging (e.g. lectures), moderately engaging (e.g. computer-based instruction with feedback) and most engaging (e.g. behavioural modelling and simulation). The results indicated that, as the level of engagement in training increases, training will have greater effects in terms of reductions in negative safety and health outcomes. Additionally, irrespective of the engagement level of training, all approaches produced meaningful behavioural performance improvements. Burke et al. (2011) extended this meta-analysis to include additional published studies from 2003 to 2008. Noting that the findings apply to workers in over 16 countries, the same general outcomes as the 2006 study were reported. Additional useful findings incorporated the 'dread factor', which notes, inter alia, that the effectiveness of highly engaging training methods, relative to moderate or least engaging, on enhanced safety performance is more pronounced under conditions of high hazards than under low-hazard conditions. This is an important finding for training design and delivery across multiple industrial settings.

Industry perceptions of the relationship between safety training and safety outcomes appear to be aligned with Neal and Griffin's safety performance framework and the research literature. For example, support for training as an appropriate workplace safety management strategy has been strongly demonstrated in a study with a sample of 231 senior financial executives or managers of corporations in the United States (Huang et al. 2007). When asked what their number one modification would be to improve workplace safety in their company, the strategy that was by far the most frequently reported by corporate financial decision makers was to have more or better safety-focused training and programs. Additionally a survey conducted by a training magazine identified that 77 % of respondents provided safety training for their employees (Machles 2002). This belief by industry decision makers in the potential of training to achieve safety performance improvements has translated into a growing demand for safety training.

Unfortunately training is often undertaken without thorough consideration of training needs. Indeed it was identified through a meta-analysis of 397 studies that only six percent of the researched training programs reported that a TNA was conducted prior to undertaking the training program (Arthur et al. 2003). Although traditional TNA can be considered time consuming and costly, a thorough systematic TNA can be efficiently achieved and is essential to providing a foundation to inform the later stages of training design, delivery and evaluation. Currently limited guidance is available in the literature to assist in the application of psychometrically valid TNA practices for the management of workplace safety. To address this gap, we will now discuss the purpose and benefits of conducting a TNA. We will then provide an overview of TNA strategies and practical guidance on how the strategies can be implemented.

Training Needs Analysis Background

A TNA can be defined as a process of gathering and analysing information to measure discrepancies between current and desired work performance standards and to determine whether any identified performance deficiencies can be appropriately remedied through training. The process has two distinct phases. Firstly in the diagnostic phase the analyst considers inconsistencies in performance standards, current competency levels and future competency requirements and prioritises the needs to address identified deficiencies. In the remedial phase, the analyst devises a strategy to address the identified priority areas of need. Although historically TNA were typically only conducted as a precursor to developing training programs, TNA are now more broadly used as a proactive tool to identify gaps and potential strategies to enhance workforce development. This modern approach to the use of TNA recognises that training will not necessarily be the most appropriate strategy for remedying identified deficiencies in work performance. For example it is unlikely that training will improve performance deficiencies associated with understaffing or poor structural designs. TNA can be considered an essential first step in a workforce development process. Findings from a TNA should inform the subsequent stages of design, delivery and evaluation.

It is commonly acknowledged that there are many benefits associated with the implementation of an effective TNA. It is recognised that TNA findings can inform the development of appropriate training programs to achieve professional growth in employees and to meet organisational objectives through raising the productivity and quality of employee performance (Kai Ming Au et al. 2008). The TNA process can aid in identifying aspects within an organisation that are operating well and aspects that need improvement. Therefore TNA is also a powerful tool for informing organisational improvement (Kaufman 1994). Furthermore research has demonstrated the utility of the TNA process in developing training to increase productivity. For example, a case study (Denby 2010) in an insurance company in the United Kingdom identified a 56 percent increase in productivity when training was implemented that was developed based on their TNA findings.

With regards to safety management, the implementation of a systematic TNA process can provide a framework for incorporating data from varied sources to inform recommendations for safety management strategies. Furthermore the structured process can yield evidence-based justifications for providing specific areas of safety training that are aligned with organisational safety performance objectives. The TNA process can also clarify differences between safety training needs and safety training wants. Focusing on the utility of a training program in achieving performance objectives can assist decision makers in investing resources towards meeting formal safety training needs rather than purely satisfying training wants which may offer limited returns on investment.

Training Needs Analysis Process

To determine the most appropriate TNA process, practitioners should be guided by their purpose and the objectives they seek to achieve through implementing training. Three levels of needs analysis have been proposed, comprising organisational analysis, task analysis and person analysis (Goldstein and Ford 2002). At the organisational level, analysis aims to identify the organisation's objectives and the extent to which training can assist in achieving these goals. The organisation's available resources including finances and employee availability are also examined along with the organisational environment to determine attitudes towards training. Strategies often utilised at this level of analysis include surveys, for example of employee readiness for training, and interviews to obtain data including the organisation's goals and ability to conduct training.

At the task level, analysis aims to identify the tasks performed by employees in the position of interest and the knowledge, skills and abilities that underpin the competencies that are required to be performed under the conditions relevant to the position of interest. A task analysis also seeks to identify how employees obtain each competency and learn to perform job tasks. This step is necessary to determine which competencies can be expected to have been obtained through previous training or experience and which competencies may require additional formal training to assist employees in developing job performance. Strategies often utilised at this level of analysis draw upon traditional job analysis methods and may include interviews, surveys, observations, task analysis inventories and reviewing existing job descriptions or performance appraisal documents.

At the person level, analysis aims to identify the employees who require training. Furthermore, it operates on the assumption that competence will vary between employees and it seeks to identify which competency areas need to be developed within individual employees. Strategies often utilised at this level of analysis to determine individual training needs may include interviews, surveys, job task proficiency tests, and reviewing existing documents such as performance appraisal reports or critical incident reports.

When considering whether training is an appropriate strategy to enhance work performance, practitioners can achieve a thorough needs assessment within an organisation through implementing these three levels of TNA. However in situations where a broader needs assessment is required, for example to determine the training needs for a profession, an additional level of analysis is required. The authors propose that Goldstein and Ford's three-step TNA process needs to be expanded to include an industry-level analysis of training needs. At the industry level, analysis would aim to identify the industry's objectives with regards to the profession of interest and the extent to which training can assist in achieving these goals. Analysis at this level would also seek to identify the training needs and availability of resources across the different organisations that employ personnel from the profession of interest. Strategies suitable for gathering data at this level of analysis include surveys, interviews and reviewing existing documents such as professional competency standards reports.

In addition to considering the most appropriate levels at which to conduct the TNA, practitioners should also consider the steps involved in implementing a TNA. McClelland (1993) presented an open-systems model that can be applied by practitioners to systematically assess training needs. The model is an 11-step approach that conceptually comprises three phases. Phase one is the design phase. It involves defining assessment goals; determining the assessment group; determining the availability of qualified analysts to conduct the assessment; gaining management commitment to the assessment process; and reviewing and selecting assessment methods. Phase two is the implementation phase. It involves determining critical time frames; scheduling and implementing the assessment; and gathering feedback. Phase three is the analysis and reporting phase. It involves analysing feedback; drawing conclusions; and presenting findings and recommendations. To assist practitioners in conducting a TNA, we will now present a case study to provide practical guidance on how TNA strategies can be implemented to investigate industry training needs.

Training Needs Analysis Case Study

We will now present an overview of the implementation of a TNA process to determine the training needs of Australasian rail incident investigators as an example of how industry training needs can be systematically assessed.

Design Phase

The first step in conducting a TNA should be to identify the objectives of the assessment. The objective of the TNA in the case study was to facilitate a collaborative approach to the development of a national competency framework for rail incident investigations. This objective arose in response to challenges being experienced as a result of the absence of a consistently accepted standard of minimal training necessary to perform rail incident investigations in Australasia. With the goal of enhancing human performance regarding incident investigations, the Australian CRC for Rail Innovation commissioned an in-depth training needs analysis. To achieve this objective, the analysts needed to conduct a TNA across varying levels including industry, organisation and task.

Once a clear TNA objective has been determined, appropriately qualified analysts must be selected to conduct the assessment. Analysts can be sourced from within the organisation that is commissioning the TNA or external consultants or researchers can be contracted to conduct the TNA. It is essential that the appointed analysts are qualified to administer an objective assessment. In the case study, external consultants were appointed to conduct the TNA for rail incident investigators. The external consultants had substantial research and consulting experience and qualifications in organisational psychology. Additionally they had specialised experience in conducting TNAs and also conducting workplace safety incident investigations. The use of experienced external consultants with a background in incident investigation allowed for a thorough, objective and efficient TNA to be conducted and avoided any conflict of interest biases that can occur when internal analysts are appointed.

The appointed analysts can then identify the assessment group and work towards gaining management commitment to the TNA process. When selecting the assessment group, analysts should strive to recruit a representative sample with regards to employee age, gender, organisational tenure, experience level and roles. Employee characteristics may have a large influence on the quality and quantity of tasks being performed by employees. In the TNA case study, the analysts sought the assistance of organisational contacts to ensure a representative sample of employees was invited to participate in the data collection process. This allowed the analysts to obtain an understanding of the types of tasks an inexperienced rail incident investigator would perform as compared to a senior rail incident investigator. The sample group should be carefully constructed to include members from all stakeholder groups. This is critical to gaining insights into the potentially differing needs of different organisations. For example the analysts in the case study invited subject matter experts from 19 stakeholder organisations operating in either Australia or New Zealand to participate in the TNA. The stakeholder organisations comprised rail transport service providers, transport investigators, statutory bodies, safety boards, regulators, transport authorities, and private companies that operate trains to transport their stock. Furthermore, to generate commitment from management across the key stakeholder groups, the analysts clearly communicated the goals of the TNA and invited representatives from each of the key stakeholder groups to participate in the process.

The final process in the design phase involves reviewing and selecting assessment methods. The selection of methods should be guided by the objectives of the assessment and the corresponding level of analysis required to be conducted to achieve those objectives. Typical methods comprise face-to-face interactions with subject matter experts through interviews or focus groups, hard copy or electronic surveys, on-site observations of work performance and reviews of existing documents such as job descriptions where available. In the case study, the methods utilised to assess rail incident investigator training needs included focus groups, interviews and surveys with subject matter experts; observations of current training delivery and rail worksites; and document reviews of job descriptions, existing training materials, published research literature, and regulatory and legislative material.

Implementation Phase

Ideally a combination of data collection methods should be implemented during this phase so that data can be triangulated. Using a multi-method approach will allow the data obtained thorough exploratory methods such as reviewing job descriptions to be challenged or validated through a confirmatory method such as interviews. The TNA implementation process will vary depending on the objective of the assessment and the particular combination of methods selected. Regardless of the TNA method selected, we will make some global recommendations to assist in the implementation phase. Firstly, the purpose of the TNA should be clearly communicated to participants. When conducting a TNA for workforce development purposes, participants need to be informed and assured that the information they provide will be treated confidentially. Participants should be asked to provide honest feedback and be assured that their information will not be used for administrative purposes. If participants fear that their responses may influence future promotional or remuneration decisions they may be less likely to reveal information such as knowledge and skill deficiencies.

Data collection tools and procedures should be pilot tested before they are implemented with TNA participants. A pilot test is a useful strategy to gather feedback. It has the potential to identify specific questions or words that are open to misinterpretation and also to determine the time required to administer the method. Based on the pilot test feedback, revisions can be made to enhance the tools or procedures before they are administered to participants.

To increase the accuracy of data collection, careful consideration should be given to the collection environment and the recording process. Data should be collected in an environment designed to minimise distractions and provide participants with privacy, for example a work office. To achieve an accurate record of the data obtained, analysts should either make notes during the data collection process or digitally record the information. For ethical reasons and to maintain participant trust, it is essential that analysts first request consent from participants to take notes or digitally record the session. It is also good practice for the analyst to provide participants with the opportunity to review the notes after the data collection session.

When communicating with participants neutral language should be utilised to avoid leading participants to respond in a particular manner. The body language of analysts should also remain neutral to avoid conveying any judgements of participant responses. Furthermore, Dingle (1995) recommended that analysts should avoid using potentially fear-evoking expressions such as 'training needs analysis'. Preferably, according to Dingle, analysts should focus on expressions of personal qualities required for outstanding performance and describe the assessment process to participants as a 'competence requirements enhancement analysis'.

Data collection questions should be concise and focused on identifying what training is needed rather than just wanted. Open-ended questions that start with 'who', 'what', 'when', where', 'why' and 'how' are suited to an interview format. Comparatively closed-ended questions with forced-choice responses, such as Likert-scales, are most appropriate in surveys. The combination of questions utilised should yield data pertaining to: how important certain tasks are to successfully performing jobs; what knowledge, skills and competencies are required to perform these tasks now and in the future; how well personnel currently perform these tasks; and the likelihood that training or organisational change will improve the performance of these tasks now and in the future.

From a project management point of view, it is important to determine TNA project milestones and time frames. When forecasting project time frames it is necessary to allow sufficient lead-in periods to develop materials such as letters of management support for the TNA process that should be provided to all employees who are invited to participate in the TNA process. Scheduling of data collection can be a challenging process. When scheduling, analysts need to consider many factors such as matching the availability of participants with analysts; providing invited participants with sufficient notice to allow them to be available for participation; and allowing for potential delays from participants in returning data that may need to be analysed before a follow-up round of data collection can commence.

To demonstrate how the above recommendations can be applied in practice, we will now discuss the strategies utilised to successfully implement a TNA of Australasian rail incident investigators. In the case study, the analysts gathered exploratory data through reviewing job descriptions and training documents. Job descriptions were reviewed to identify work tasks, and skill and knowledge requirements. Training documents were reviewed to identify competency areas currently demanded and supplied to the transport industry with regards to incident investigators. A modified-Delphi method involving qualitative and quantitative techniques was also implemented as a confirmatory approach to achieve a robust data collection methodology. The modified-Delphi methodology provided a structured technique to gain consensus from a panel of rail incident investigator experts via interviews and surveys. Three rounds of data gathering and analysis were conducted. In each round of data collection, the findings from the previous round were presented back to the rail incident investigator experts. These experts were provided with the opportunity to confirm, add, delete or amend their responses in light of the group data. An advantage of this technique was that it allowed the experts to remain anonymous to one another, thereby reducing the potential for influence or bias throughout the rounds.

To enhance the accuracy of the data collected, analysts informed all participants that the purpose of the analysis was to investigate the training needs of Australasian rail incident investigators and that the information they provided would only be used to inform the development of an industry-approved national training package. Data was collected in accordance with ethical research standards. Therefore all participants provided voluntary consent before commencing a survey or interview session. Participants were informed that only aggregate data would be reported and that their identity would remain confidential. Interview and survey questions and protocols were pilot tested in another workforce with a comparable reading and comprehension level to the intended target participant sample. Based on the feedback received in the pilot study minor modifications were made to several questions to enhance measurement reliability. Interviews and surveys were conducted in private work spaces at times that were convenient to the participants. At the start of interviews analysts always requested permission to take notes for the purposes of increasing accuracy of data records. This was granted by all participants in the case study. Analysts exhibited neutral verbal and nonverbal communication during data collection sessions to avoid influencing participant responses. Questions were carefully constructed to yield data that would identify the current and future training needs of rail incident investigators in Australasia. Based on previous experience in conducting industry TNA, the analysts set realistic time frames to ensure milestones were met on time. A valuable strategy employed by the analysts in the case study was to maintain regular and open communication with the stakeholders and to work collaboratively with the stakeholder representatives to jointly manage the implementation process.

Analysis and Reporting Phase

For the training needs analysis to be effective, it needs to be driven by a clear purpose, identifying the training needs that currently exist within the organisation, or have the potential to exist at a future time. This information is vital, as it can be used in the design and further development of techniques better addressing and satisfying the needs of the organisation in the most cost-effective and efficient manner possible. An important consideration in this phase is the timing in which analyses are conducted. To minimise unintentional biases creeping into analysis interpretations, all exploratory data should be collected and analysed, then preliminary conclusions drawn. Where possible, qualitative data should be tabulated before quantitative data is analysed to ensure results identified in the quantitative analysis do not prejudice the thematic interpretations of the qualitative data. After preliminary conclusions have been formed, additional rounds of confirmatory data collection and analysis should be used to challenge analysts' assumptions and to build consensus from all stakeholders and relevant parties regarding the final training needs conclusions.

The importance of communicating project findings clearly and convincingly must not be underestimated. A well-written report is often critical to increasing the likelihood of TNA recommendations being implemented. When writing a report, it is of vital importance to consider the needs of the target audience, ensuring that the purpose of the analysis and the recommendations provided meet the needs of all stakeholder groups. In some cases, several versions of the same report may be required to ensure that the report content and style meet the varying needs and requirements of the different stakeholder groups. Further, these reports should remain objective, and be written using neutral, rather than emotive language. It is also highly recommended that reports provided to stakeholders adhere to a traditional business report format. Such formats include: an executive summary; background information on the training needs analysis, including the objective and aims of the analysis; methodology, where the process used is clearly identified to validate the findings and if future replication is required; discussion of the findings and recommendations; and any supplementary materials pertinent to the analysis and report.

Undertaking these recommendations, the analysts in the case study conducted an industry-wide training needs analysis with Australian and New Zealand rail companies in developing a standard training framework for rail incident investigators.

Initial consultations were conducted with key stakeholders, in an exploratory round of data collection, to better identify the background and context of the highly specialised area. Further analysis of job descriptions and training documents identified work tasks and the knowledge and skill requirements for the investigator role. The training documents were also reviewed to further identify the competency areas that currently exist. Thematic analysis of this initial information identified key preliminary conclusions. Using a modified Delphi-methodology, this collated information was articulated back to a sample of 52 subject matter experts for additional feedback. Undertaking this method allowed the analysts' preliminary conclusions to be challenged and validated. Further analysis was then conducted to incorporate the additional data. The revised training needs conclusions were again presented to the subject matter experts for review before a final round of confirmatory data analysis was carried out, identifying ten core competencies pertinent for the training of rail incident investigators. By using this process, the core competencies identified in the final report were validated as an accurate reflection of the training needs of the Australian and New Zealand rail industry. Further, in addition to the production of a final report, regular formal progress reports were distributed among key stakeholder members and stakeholders were provided with regular informal updates to maintain their engagement and support for the project.

Conclusion

Workplace safety can be managed through workforce development strategies including training. For training strategies to be effective, they must appropriately address a deficiency in workforce knowledge or skills. Implementation of the assessment process recommended in this chapter will assist practitioners in conducting an efficient yet thorough TNA. Guided by the purpose in the case study of developing an industry-approved national training package, we have provided examples to demonstrate how the industrial, organisational and task levels of analysis can be applied to investigate industry training needs. Additionally practitioners should implement the recommended person-level analysis of the TNA to identify the training needs of individual employees. The major contributions of the current chapter are expanding the literature to define a new higher-order level of analysis needed to assess industry training needs and presenting a structured and theoretically sound TNA protocol for incident investigators that may be applied internationally to guide workforce development with the goal of enhancing safety.

References

Arthur, W., Bennett, W., et al. (2003). Effectiveness of training in organisations: A meta-analysis of design and evaluation features. *Journal of Applied Psychology, 88*, 234–245.

Baysari, M. T., McIntosh, A. S., & Wilson, J. R. (2008). Understanding the human factors contribution to railway accidents and incidents in Australia. *Accident Analysis and Prevention, 40*, 1750–1757.

Burke, M. J., Sarpy, S. A., et al. (2006). Relative effectiveness of worker safety and health training methods. *American Journal of Public Health, 96*(2), 315–324.

Burke, M. J., Salvador, R. O., et al. (2011). The dread factor: How hazards and safety training influence learning and performance. *Journal of Applied Psychology, 96*(1), 46–70.

Campbell, J. P., McCloy, R. A., et al. (1993). A theory of performance. In N. Schmitt & W. C. Borman (Eds.), *Personnel selection in organisations* (pp. 35–70). San Francisco: Jossey-Bass.

Denby, S. (2010). The importance of training needs analysis. *Industrial and Commercial Training, 42*(3), 147–150.

Dingle, J. (1995). Analyzing the competence requirements of managers. *Management Development Review, 8*(2), 30–36.

Fernández-Muñiz, B., Montes-Peón, J. M., & Vázquez-Ordás, C. J. (2009). Relation between occupational safety management and firm performance. *Safety Science, 47*(7), 980–991. doi: http://dx.doi.org/10.1016/j.ssci.2008.10.022

Goldstein, I. L., & Ford, J. K. (2002). *Training in organisations: Needs assessment, development and evaluation* (4th ed.). Belmont: Wadsworth.

Grote, G., & Künzler, C. (2000). Diagnosis of safety culture in safety management audits. *Safety Science, 34*(1–3), 131–150. doi: http://dx.doi.org/10.1016/S0925-7535(00)00010-2.

Huang, Y. H., Leamon, T. B., et al. (2007). Corporate financial decision-makers' perceptions of workplace safety. *Accident Analysis and Prevention, 39*, 767–775.

Kai Ming Au, A., Altman, Y., & Roussel, J. (2008). Employee training needs and perceived value of training in the Pearl River Delta of China: A human capital development approach. *Journal of European Industrial Training, 32*(1), 19–31.

Kaufman, R. (1994). A needs assessment audit. *Performance & Instruction, 33*(2), 14–16.

Machles, D. (2002). Training transfer strategies for the safety professional. *Professional Safety, 47*(2), 32–34.

McClelland, S. (1993). Training needs assessment: An 'open systems' application. *Journal of European Industrial Training, 17*(1), 12–17.

Mearns, K., Whitaker, S. M., & Flin, R. (2003). Safety climate, safety management practice and safety performance in offshore environments. *Safety Science, 41*(8), 641–680. doi: http://dx.doi.org/10.1016/S0925-7535(02)00011-5.

Neal, A., & Griffin, M. A. (1997, April 11–13). *Perceptions of safety at work: Developing a model to link organisational safety climate and individual behaviour.* Paper presented at the 12th annual conference of the Society for Industrial and Organizational Psychology, St Louis, MO.

Reason, J. (1990). *Human error.* New York: Cambridge University Press.

Safe Work Australia. (2013). *Key work health and safety statistics, Australia.* Canberra: Safe Work Australia.

Wiegmann, D. A., Zhang, H., et al. (2004). Safety culture: An integrative review. *International Journal of Aviation Psychology, 14*(2), 117–134. doi:10.1207/s15327108ijap1402_1.

Chapter 20
Conclusion: Workforce Development – More Than the Sum of Its Parts?

Roger Harris and Tom Short

Abstract Workforce development is an emerging field of practice, one that is increasingly gaining its place in the sun in government policies and organisational practices. However, what Skills Australia has identified as hampering endeavours to build on successful experiences and learn from one another is the diversity of views and understandings. The book therefore serves as a contribution to the demystifying of the notion. This final chapter distils five key messages that emerge from the previous chapters, and summarises the main strategies and practices that have been suggested by the chapter writers. Eight challenges in implementing workforce development are then discussed. The chapter concludes that, while it is indeed important to identify and define its components, workforce development is 'more than the sum of its parts' as the critical aspect is conceptualising how these components need to be configured and aligned in particular organisational contexts.

Introduction

This book is a companion volume to the first book, *Workforce development: Perspectives and issues*. In that first book, we posed the question in the introductory chapter whether the whole is equal to or more than the sum of the parts, and left the reader to ruminate over this conundrum as they read the book (Harris and Short 2014, p. 2). Now, having reached the end of this second book, are we – writers and readers alike – any closer to fathoming an answer?

R. Harris (✉) • T. Short
School of Education, University of South Australia, Adelaide, SA, Australia
e-mail: roger.harris@unisa.edu.au; tom.short@unisa.edu.au

T. Short and R. Harris (eds.), *Workforce Development: Strategies and Practices*,
DOI 10.1007/978-981-287-068-1_20, © Springer Science+Business Media Singapore 2014

That initial chapter cited John Godfrey Saxe's poem, *The blind men and the elephant*, but only the first stanza which left us in suspense – the sight-impaired characters were heading off to discover the whole (the elephant) through 'observation' (in their case, by feel) of the parts. That is where we all (writers and readers) were when commencing the book, anticipating that by observation (in our case, by reading) of each chapter, we would progressively learn what this relatively unknown beast labelled 'workforce development' was like. The bulk of Saxe's poem focuses on what each of the characters experienced, a separate part of the elephant's body, and then from that part, inferring what the whole beast was like. So perhaps we have been inferring what the notion of workforce development is like, as we have moved through each chapter in these two books. By the end, having completed their observations,

> … these men of Indostan
> Disputed loud and long,
> Each in his own opinion
> Exceeding stiff and strong,
> Though each was partly in the right,
> And all were in the wrong!

The writer then leaves us with the moral of this story:

> So oft in theologic wars,
> The disputants, I ween,
> Rail on in utter ignorance
> Of what each other mean,
> *And prate about an Elephant*
> *Not one of them has seen!* (Saxe, in Linton 1878, pp. 150–151)

What about us? Having read nearly 40 chapters, to what extent are we remaining steadfast to our own opinion, however limited that may be, and jumping to conclusions about what workforce development means? Perhaps we can be excused, for while the basic structure of an elephant does not change, we might well observe workforce development taking on different forms in different contexts and in different eras, rather more like a chameleon. And, like the sight-impaired characters, each of us can observe only a limited aspect at a time from our particular standpoint, and each chapter writer can develop their view of the whole (workforce development) only from their own topic perspective.

Yet we, as editors, would hope that you, the reader, would have been able by now to have begun to pull the parts together and to view the notion of workforce development more in its entirety. By now, perhaps you have begun to sense that some elements have been left out. Perhaps you can see that some are included that in your opinion should not have been. Perhaps you believe that some have been overweighted, while others have been under-played. That is highly likely in books of this nature. But we the editors intend for you to have now begun to view this notion of workforce development as a complex entity, as one that can be observed through its component parts and finally seen as a complete whole, where the latter is more than merely the sum of the former.

Key Messages in This Book

In this section, we draw five key messages from the chapters in this book (and its companion volume).

Workforce Development Is a Technicolour Dreamcoat of Many Colours

The first key message through these chapters is that workforce development is a technicolour dreamcoat of many colours, comprising many and various components (the wefts) as well as many and various implementation strategies and practices (the warps). We have clustered these many and various components of workforce development into four main groups. Each of these sections has covered components that we believe are critical for organisations to embrace in their workforce development programs.

The first cluster – those components relating to sustainability, growth and diversity – ranges from attracting and retaining employees through skilled migration activities, promotion to potential young workers via schools and tertiary, building readily accessible and user-friendly career pathways, to catering for the working conditions and learning of older workers, and achieving equity and diversity in the workplace through recognising the knowledge and skills of culturally diverse groups.

The second cluster – those components that contribute to the building of capability and capacity – embraces formal workplace mentoring, the use of technologies in training such as online tools, simulations and remote labs, the leading of multigenerations in the workplace, the identification, development and recognition of abstract (tacit, holistic, soft) skills, and e-learning and what makes it work.

The third cluster – those components that develop leadership, talent and innovation – includes the building of leadership capability, workplace coaching as an intervention for increasing organisational performance and maintaining competitiveness, the identification and development of leadership talent, how highly contextualised leadership training can intersect with national training frameworks, and identification of the 'intrapreneurial' mindset required to drive innovation and change in organisations.

The final cluster – those components that promote harmonisation across boundaries and borders – presents three case studies of workforce development; the recruitment of skilled employees in Germany, the application of national vocational curricula in the development of a unified industry standard, and the creation of a common approach to safety management through structured training.

Each chapter has proffered ideas for facilitating whatever component of workforce development the chapter has covered. These strategies and practices for implementing the workforce development components are also many and varied.

There are too many to reiterate here in the conclusion, but as a form of summary, some of the main actions are outlined in Table 20.1 to provide a composite flavour of what chapter writers have suggested and recommended through this book.

Workforce Development Is a Web of Human Resource Policies, Processes and Practices

The second key message through these chapters is that workforce development needs ideally to be interpreted as a web of human resource policies, processes and practices that are woven together and aligned to the business directions of a particular organisation. An analogous situation is the emphasis on the whole-of-government (or joined-up government) approach to solving societal problems. This approach seeks to apply a more holistic strategy using insights from other social sciences than just economics, and using coordination and integration strategies (Christensen and Lægreid 2007; Mulgan 2005). It is viewed as the opposite of 'departmentalism', tunnel vision and 'vertical silos', and seeks to achieve horizontally and vertically coordinated thinking and action in order to eliminate situations in which different policies and practices undermine each other, so as to make better use of scarce resources, create synergies by bringing together different stakeholders in a particular field, and offer seamless rather than fragmented access to services (Pollitt 2003; Davies 2009; Hodges 2012). Applying this thinking to the workplace, workforce development may then be perceived as a *whole-of-organisation* approach to its workforce in viewing it in intersection with many other strands of organisational policy and practice.

Seen in this way, this concept is 'an umbrella term' covering different dimensions (Ling 2002, p. 624), in that it describes, in the words of Christensen and Lægreid (2007, p. 1060) referring to whole-of-government activity, 'a group of responses to the problem of increased fragmentation ... and a wish to increase integration, coordination, and capacity'. A study of the academic literature is able to provide us with insight into the factors that may comprise organisational capability. But knowledge of such factors is one thing – conceptualising *how* they should be configured and aligned in any particular context is quite a different matter. Not only do organisations differ markedly in the nature and quantum of their resources, they also vary considerably in such significant areas as histories, geographies, environments, psyches, structures and cultures. Thus, just as the effectiveness of sporting teams depends on more than the individuals within them, or recipes on more than the list of ingredients, so too does that of organisations on more than their resources. The key characteristic in all of these is how the component parts are welded together in particular configurations to suit particular environments. And that is problematic, especially in times of continual change! Rapid responses to changing circumstances can make all the difference for sporting teams, recipes *and* organisations.

Table 20.1 Summary of strategies and practices recommended through this book

Chapter	Workforce development focus	Organisations need to …
2	Skilled migration	Seek specialist advice on skilled migration
		Possess high levels of skill in interpreting and implementing national policies in this field
		Engage in closer relationships with higher education providers
3	Attracting young talent	Reach out to school students and tertiary students, through such means as student/parent forums, and quality online resources
		Work with careers advisors and recruitment consultants
		Attend to benefits offered in employment propositions, emphasising not only remuneration but also job security, development opportunities, diversity of experiences and flexible work conditions that young workers report are important to them
4	Career pathways	Develop clear and explicit career pathways information
		Enhance the image of the industry or organisation
5	Older workers	Recognise and acknowledge their learning needs
		Demonstrate equality of treatment of older workers in comparison with younger
		Be aware of the longer-term goals of workers, flexibility of working/learning patterns, rewards systems that appeal to older workers, challenging tasks, job-sharing and opportunities to enlarge job projects
6	Equity and diversity	Recognise and deal with assumptions and myths inherent in the organisation and its practices, giving due attention to the history and structure of power relations
		Value, and develop, the knowledge and skills of culturally diverse groups in their workplace
		Ensure jobs are open to individuals from these groups, including leadership positions, management and skilled roles
7	Workplace mentoring	Follow a common framework, such as the nine-step mentoring framework (in Chap. 7)
		Adhere to a code of practice such as the Rail Mentoring Code of Practice (in Chap. 7)
		Avoid dysfunctional arrangements that may lead to negative experiences, such as inappropriate matching, distancing behaviour, manipulating behaviour and politicking, and lack of mentor expertise
8	Educational technologies	Recognise that cultural and contextual factors influence learning outcomes, that technologies cannot simply be bolted on to existing curriculum, and that serious consideration needs to be given to the ways in which the whole curriculum changes the meaning and operation of any innovation.

(continued)

Table 20.1 (continued)

Chapter	Workforce development focus	Organisations need to …
9	Multiple generations	Develop leaders with 'generational competence'
		Treat different cohorts of employees in ways that capitalise on their age-related values and working preferences
		Plan and prepare for career transitions at all generational levels, including entry-level employment, mainstream work progression, fractional working arrangements and impending retirements
10	Abstract (tacit, soft, holistic) skills	Use formal skills recognition to assess evidence for accredited certification
		Recognise that abstract skills are a vital function in leadership and management
		Use informal skills recognition processes to identify why, where and how employees need further training to develop abstract skills
11	E-learning	Recognise that successful adoption of e-learning is influenced by factors beyond the systems themselves, and requires holistic understanding of the target workforce and the suitability of e-learning tasks
		Be aware that there may be benefits, but there are also inhibiting factors – all must be addressed to avoid negative perceptions
		Consider a number of practical aspects before implementation, relating to policy and planning, design, technology and education
12	Leadership culture	Build leadership capability by: using an environmental scan to become familiar with the current situation, analysing current knowledge and research about effective leadership practices, identifying a range of existing frameworks of good practice used to develop leadership capability, and establishing criteria to assess and evaluate leadership programs
13	Workplace coaching	Determine levels of commitment to coaching from both the organisation and its senior management
		Align the purposes and aims of the intended coaching with overall strategic goals of the organisation, and embed it (typically) in leadership identification and development activities
		Determine measures for evaluating the effectiveness and return on investment, adopting innovative approaches
		Follow a reputable organisational charter for developing a coaching culture, such as the ten-point plan of Wilson (in Chap. 13)

(continued)

Table 20.1 (continued)

Chapter	Workforce development focus	Organisations need to …
14	Identification of leadership talent	Establish an organisation-specific definition of leadership talent and the capabilities valued by the organisation
		Communicate the leadership talent strategy and why it is important to the organisation
		Be on the lookout for what makes a talented leader and identify the talent in a transparent and informed manner
		Develop individual leadership needs where gaps are observed
		Establish targets, and evaluate the talent management strategy and approach
15	Organisationally contextualised training vis-à-vis national training frameworks	Weigh the pros and cons of becoming an enterprise registered training organisation
		Determine how to demonstrate the value of its contribution to the organisation to justify its existence and maintenance
		Determine how best to address identified deficits in leadership knowledge and skills
		Decide how to marry organisation-specific, contextualised training meeting local needs with nationally accredited training qualifications
16	'Intrapreneurial' mindset for innovation/change	Understand and acknowledge what is meant by the 'intrapreneurial' mindset and identify its attributes
		Identify and support those with the greatest potential to be successful 'intrapreneurs'
		Recognise that the key to successful innovation is the notion of employee involvement or 'high-involvement innovation'
17	Recruiting skilled employees	Provide opportunities for employees to link their initial training with continuing training and personnel development, whether formal or informal
		Acknowledge the impact of demographic change, and promote cooperation between the different generations of employees
		Promote intergenerational transfer of knowledge and learning to counter loss of valuable know-how and foster innovation through interactions between the young and the more experienced – e.g. mixed-age teams, mentoring or tandem programs

(continued)

Table 20.1 (continued)

Chapter	Workforce development focus	Organisations need to …
18	Promoting harmonisation through engagement with the national training system	Weigh arguments for engaging with the national training system (e.g. consistency, savings, external validation, employer satisfaction)
		Analyse real and perceived barriers (e.g. complexity in the system, poaching, political strings, lack of relevance, mindsets)
		Use strategies for mitigating such barriers (e.g. ROI analysis, collaboration, company 'evangelist', attractive practices, marketing)
		Decide whether to engage with the national training system
19	Creating common approaches through structured training	Design a training needs assessment – identifying the objectives, choosing qualified analysts, selecting assessment methods
		Systematically assess training needs at the industrial, organisational and task levels to determine industry training needs, as well as at the person level to determine training needs of individual employees
		Analyse, report and validate the findings
		Use the findings in further development of a national training program

Two metaphors in the literature we have found helpful in understanding more about this process of configuring relate to weaving and water tanks. The first metaphor of weaving depicts the building of organisational capability as the synthesis and integration of its constituent elements:

> Just as in weaving, each intersection of warp and weft threads makes an individual knot and, eventually, a completed fabric, in 'organizational weaving', each intersection of human actors and the skills they possess creates a tie carrying with it the opportunity for new knowledge creation and application and, eventually, the social fabric … within which a capability 'dwells' (Spanos and Prastacos 2004, p. 36).

This metaphor stems from accepted notions in the literature that the construction of capabilities is dependent on the organisation's ability to integrate, combine and reconfigure existing knowledge, skills and resources so as to reach higher order capabilities that will accommodate rapidly changing contexts. So what this implies is basically 'the creation and application of new knowledge out of the already existing stocks of prior knowledge held by organizational members' (Spanos and Prastacos 2004, p. 37). This is the challenge for organisations in implementing effective workforce development strategies. Thus, the notion of organisational capability raises the critical issue of whether an organisation contains a group of actors with the requisite resources (essentially the knowledge and skills of its managers and employees) and socio-cultural configuration to perform value-adding activities (Spanos and Prastacos 2004, p. 32).

The other metaphor depicts a tank storing water for irrigation (Williams 2001). The capacity for irrigating land is stored in the tank – the fuller it is, the more capacity it has for providing sustenance. But the ability to irrigate successfully depends on more than the storage of water – for example, climatic conditions, rainfall, quality of tap and water distribution networks. What Williams claims he witnesses is capacity building (building large storage containers) without much capability building (the complex and strategic business of distributing enough water at the appropriate time). This observation could also be made with respect to many organisations. The difficulty in such metaphors, however, is that any potential answer to this complex issue of configuration depends on a range of factors (for example, timing, history and environment) and is unique to each organisation.

Workforce Development Extends Beyond Training and Development, and Human Resource Development

The third key message in this book is that workforce development extends beyond training and development, and human resource development (HRD), even though we commonly see this as the popular or initial interpretation of the concept, or at least the default position for many organisations in tight times. The policy and funding climate that emerged around the late 1980s privileged the development of training. The National Training Reform Agenda commencing around that time was more fundamental and significant than at any other period in history, 'where the needs of the learner came to be subsumed by industrial and economic priorities' (Comyn 2005, p. 24). Key components of this change included the rise of economic rationalism and the new vocationalism (Chappell 2002) emphasising the needs of industry and economic growth, increasing choice and raising standards by market competition, development of an open training market, changes to youth labour markets and the operation of federalism within Australia's education system. The ensuing refocus on micro-economic reform was seen to be the way to promote competitiveness and increase productivity, with one of the key planks being the mandate for competency-based training, which, though embodied in the discourse of Training Packages after 1996, has continued as the imperative for all accredited training.

Inherent in this reform agenda was a renewed focus on skill enhancement. Major changes were made to the national training system to increase competitiveness and responsiveness to the needs of business and industry, and to stimulate employers to invest in human resource development. Hutchings and Holland (2007, p. 243) characterise Australian training and development as having been historically "fragmented and narrowly focused around occupational skills supported by waves of immigration and poaching of staff", where the nation, under such a focus on external labour markets, has stumbled from one skill shortage to the next. These reforms from the late 1980s, and the increasing pressures of globalisation since, have led to the urgent need for organisations to concentrate more on the development and utilisation of *internal* labour resources.

Moreover, while debate continues to rage over the key features of this training reform, one prime effect of this reform has been a shift in political power away from training institutions (the 'supply side') towards industry (the 'demand side'). The reform has been labelled 'industry-driven' and, although few seem to know exactly what that phrase means and agonise over who exactly this 'industry' is and which 'industry' is doing the 'driving', nevertheless the lasting consequence has been the swing in power. Though the training reform agenda had been initially driven by changes in industrial relations, the emphasis changed from 1990 to the need for training reform for general economic and inherent education and training reasons (see Harris 2009).

Important consequences of these twin pressures for the organisational focus to be on internal labour resources and for the training system to be demand-driven have been a stronger stress on enterprises to deliver training and development, and a re-claiming of the workplace as an authentic site for learning. In this process of learning, in effect, being increasingly de-institutionalised, the reform agenda has placed great emphasis on workplaces and the personnel in them to provide relevant, contextualized, job-specific learning opportunities in a manner that will contribute to the growing pool of qualified workers in a cost effective manner. Many workers in a wide cross-section of enterprises are increasingly being asked to take responsibility for facilitating the learning of their colleagues. HR professionals also are assuming an increasingly critical position in the provision of learning and development opportunities. Trends suggest that this shift will become enshrined as a central element in skill formation policies in the near future, as more initiatives seek to achieve the twin goals of making learning and development an attractive undertaking for employers and of ensuring that it is relevant and useful for workers. With increasing responsibility for learning being expected of organisations, and higher value being placed upon workplace learning *vis-a-vis* institutional learning, organisations are experiencing and will increasingly experience the press for more learning and development – a vital plank in any workforce development strategy as reflected through this book, especially in Chaps. 7 (on mentoring), 13 (on coaching) and 15, 18 and 19 (on training).

However, Holland et al. (2007, p. 244) have recently claimed that HRD is still not sufficiently recognised as a source of competitive advantage in Australian organisations. Moreover, evidence from the study of 793 Australian-based organisations by Peretz and McGraw (2009) also showed "an inconsistent pattern in the developmental trend of HRD in Australian organisations". In particular, they found two contrasting developments over the period 1996–2009 – a significant increase in the use of practices concerned with career development and performance appraisal, and a decreasing use of practices relating to evaluation of training effectiveness. They conclude that the pattern of HRD practice is "at best fragmented and at worst internally inconsistent" (p. 7). The term HRD thus does not go far enough to explain what the writers in these two books are interpreting as workforce development. Moreover, Elsey (1997, p. 120), too, has asserted that human resource development has a long history of marginality in its evolution from the first limited notions of industrial training. He has claimed a term like HRD inevitably "has a rather elastic meaning, which allows for some stretching without destroying the general sense of what it is intended to convey". His view of HRD was that it is "not only functionally related to the other operations of HRM [human resource management], but is also an integral part of wider labour market management policies and the microeconomic reform agenda" (p. 136). This interpretation brings us closer to what we are now claiming as workforce development, and similarly Hawke (2008) has claimed that, in embracing staff selection, issues about retention and comprehensive approaches addressing workforce composition and balance, workforce development and HRM 'overlap in almost all of their activities' (p. 11). Yet Tebbel (1999) had questioned whether the HR function was dead in Australia or on the way to becoming obsolete, while still by 2006, Kramer was stating that HRM was 'at the crossroads' in his editorial for a special issue of the *Asia Pacific Journal of Human Resources*. In his view, HR professionals faced many challenges, and their role remained one fraught with tensions because of the need to serve a number of mistresses and masters (Kramer 2006, pp. 130–131). Their role is also 'well acknowledged [to be] potentially ambiguous and complex, given the inherent tensions associated with the reconciliation of organisational and individual interests' (Lowry 2006, p. 135).

Furthermore, Dainty (2011) has recently raised the crucial question of whether HR professionals have the range of skills needed to be effective in a strategic role. Using 360° feedback from 1,005 colleagues of 197 senior Australian HR managers, he investigated the qualities needed to operate strategically, his research casting doubt on whether HR professionals in general can yet claim to be full strategic contributors. While the HR managers were strong in terms of strategic deployment of human resources and were aware of the external environment, the research suggested that they were still not central to the strategy formulation process. Similarly, Smith et al. (2012) concluded from their research involving 134 Australian enterprises that while most had established human resource management and learning and development policies and practices, these tended not to be aligned with strategic organisational goals and there was little evidence that they were designed to develop innovative capacity within the organisations. It was still an area that in general HR professionals had yet to fully embrace. This was supported by Andersen et al. (2007, p. 176) who found only a moderate level of strategic HRM practised within Australian organisations and that the limited training offered to line managers greatly undermines their capacity to perform HR activities effectively and renders them more 'fire-fighters' than strategic partners. Given this ambiguity over both HRD and HRM, it has been both appropriate and timely to be exploring the notion of workforce development and its various components in these two books.

Workforce Development Is an Integrative Response Within Organisations and Across Organisations

The fourth key message from these chapters is that workforce development is to be viewed as an integrative response not only *within* an organisation in order to maximise connections between functions and enhance alignment with organisational directions (an intra-organisational perspective), but also *across* organisations to raise the level of harmonisation in an industry (an inter-organisational perspective). This can have multiple advantages, such as attraction and retention of staff with an industry rather than losing valuable skills to other sectors, sharing of common resources that can still be customised with local and organisational flavours, considerable cost savings that can be made from the development and pooling of such resources, and improvements in service delivery through minimising redundancies and duplication. At a more general level, other advantages can be enhanced capacity to handle increasing globalisation pressures and competition, and the potential to break-down silo mentalities thereby fostering more helpful bigger-picture thinking and innovation. The benefit in boundary crossing is that it can lead to cutting edges where innovation and discovery are more likely to reside.

> Boundaries are like fault lines: they are the locus of volcanic activity. They allow move
> ment, they release tension; they create new mountains; they shake existing structures ...
> they are the likely locus of the production of radically new knowledge. They are where the
> unexpected can be expected, where innovative or unorthodox solutions are found, where
> serendipity is likely, and where old ideas find new life and new ideas propagate (Wenger
> 1998, pp. 254–5).

The potential danger, however, in such crossing is that it can lead to culture/role conflict, tension and confusion. Boundaries can be problematic, with their connotations of marginality and peripherality (Harris and Ramos 2012, pp. 390–392). They are places where we can anticipate problems of coordination, experience issues of miscommunication and expect transformations as people and objects travel across the social landscape (Wenger 1998).

Implementing Workforce Development Is Not Without Its Challenges

The final key message from these chapters is that implementing workforce development, either within organisations or across organisations, is not without its challenges. In the next section we draw attention to eight fundamental issues with which we need to grapple if initiatives for more integrated workforce development are to be effectively deployed.

Implementation Challenges

Feasibility

One issue is feasibility – to what extent is it really possible to share and integrate workforce development strategies and practices in the face of such trends as specialisation, outsourcing, competition from registered training organisations fiercely vying for business, privatisation, and commercialisation where intellectual property becomes a huge concern. The literature suggests that unless cross-sectional or cross-organisational targets are able to receive equal recognition and status as organisation-specific targets, efforts at integration may well be very difficult to initiate and sustain. There will thus be difficulties in obtaining cooperation between organisational sections and between organisations.

Silo Mentalities

Second, silo mentalities are well entrenched, whether state-induced (as in the case of Australia as a federated nation) or organisationally-derived. Sometimes these come into existence for good reasons, and the division of labour and specialisation are inevitable features of modern organisations (Christensen and Lægreid 2007, p. 1063). However, many chapters in this book attest to the fact that, when an organisation undertakes to share, support moves towards integration or engage in collaborative research, implementation is not always possible because the organisation is often locked into existing programmes or strategies, it may be too expensive to change or their strong preference is for what they have traditionally always done. Davies (2009, p. 90) found that consensus that is built on an ethos of partnership is often shallow, and this enables stakeholders to proceed as if they shared norms, meanings and goals, though in reality silo practices remain unchallenged. Thus workforce development policies and activities may be severely curtailed unless first there are fundamental changes in dominant cultures and structural arrangements, and such changes are not going to happen quickly, if at all.

Accountability

Third is the issue of *accountability* – how problematic is it to entertain collaborative actions, common approaches and shared systems on the one hand, and accountability for sectional or organisational performance on the other? Over the years, organisations, or sections of organisations, have become increasingly focused on key performance indicators and targets, spurred on by the global financial crisis and the diminishing availability and accessibility of resources. Most organisations today, necessarily, are becoming extremely conscious of risk management, and when activities are seen to move further away from direct and immediate oversight, concerns about power, control and trust almost inevitably come strongly into play. Moreover, lines of responsibility can become so fuzzy, or stretched, that accountability becomes, or can be perceived to become, a vexatious issue that has the potential to sap the motivation for, and strangle the life from, any efforts to implement workforce development initiatives. Such blurring of responsibilities can then also lead to the concern over who will serve as the watchdog – the inspector – that will be required to adjudicate irregularities, uneven contributions, grievances and the like.

Evaluation

A related fourth issue is that of evaluation – how will levels of effectiveness of integration efforts be judged? Pollitt (2003, p. 43) envisages three alternative though complementary approaches that could be employed. One is to focus on best practice – are the right things being put in place (as gauged from wisdom and experience)? The second is to survey those involved, the key stakeholders – do they believe that these attempts at integration are good or poor? The third is to seek to identify the outcomes – what evidence is there of improvements in policies, programs and practices? However, the problems he sees are that the first tends to be highly context-dependent, and focused on inputs or processes; the second is unlikely to provide sufficient depth, and there is the issue of when to survey as opinions can vary markedly over time; and the third, while being the most reliable, is likely to be complex, expensive and time-consuming, such that 'the study of outcomes is often hard to do at all, and very hard to do well' (p. 46). Hodges (2012, p. 38) concludes that there is little analysis of the success or otherwise of joined-up collaboration in improving service delivery, where much of the research has focused heavily on process issues. Moreover, the existence of multiple collaborators makes more difficult the task of gaining agreement on objectives and outcomes.

Mobility of Personnel in Industry

Fifth, organisational restructuring and shifting contractual arrangements are occurring frequently, and with such mobility of personnel in industry it is difficult to build trust and credibility with personnel in and across organisations and to gain traction in attempting to bring about change. This accentuates the difficulties for HR professionals in effecting worthwhile and long-lasting changes in workforce development practice.

Politics

This is related to the sixth issue of lower versus higher level politics. There is a fine line in effecting change between top-down actions, where the approval of senior executives is necessary, and activities lower down the pecking order.

Efforts at greater harmonisation necessarily involve genuine cooperation, and this is generally achieved more effectively from the bottom up rather than being imposed from the top down; Burnes (2005, p. 85) states that most change efforts fail because they seek to impose top-down, transformational change instead of adopting 'the self-organising approach necessary to keep complex systems operating at the edge of chaos'. In analysing the enablers and inhibitors of line manager involvement, McGuire et al. (2008) highlight that HR strategic partners can play an important role as change agents, internal consultants and facilitators who disseminate learning across an organisation or industry. However, the evidence in many of the chapters suggests that this is very difficult to achieve when personnel are continually shifting positions, companies or industries. Moreover, Davies (2009) has recently drawn attention to the ways in which a partnership ethos can encourage shallow consensus and deflect political conflict at the expense of integration.

Maintaining Consistency

Another connected, seventh issue is how to maintain consistency within a whole organisation, or across a number of organisations. This is particularly an issue for larger organisations, where extended lines of communication mean that the implementation of workforce development visions and strategies is often limited in effectiveness and applied to varying extents and at a variable pace. Hawke (2008, p. 28) found in his small-scale study of six registered training organisations in Australia that they differed widely in their approaches to workforce development and, in the worst case, implementation could be badly distorted and have negative effects on the culture and morale of an organisation. On the other hand, in smaller organisations, with higher levels of informality and personal interaction among management and employees, workforce development can more readily become an inherent part of the way they do business.

Change Takes Time

The eighth issue is that change, in this case towards greater integration of workforce development policies and practices whether within organisations or between them, takes time to implement. We cannot expect instant adoption – new skills, changes in workforce development policies and practices, and the building of mutual trust need considerable patience. In fact, March and Olsen (1983) have suggested that the role of a change agent is more like a gardener than an engineer. It certainly takes time to cultivate and bear fruit.

Conclusion

And so we have reached the conclusion that workforce development is more than the sum of the parts. The components are indeed important to identify and define, but there is also the critical need for configuration and alignment within particular organisational contexts. We need to keep asking ourselves such questions as:

• What kind of people are we trying to develop in our organisations?
• What sorts of mindsets should we be valuing when recruiting employees, building teams, thinking about talent management and implementing workforce development initiatives?
• What are the most effective methods for developing our workforce in our context?
• Are we doing these things right, or should we be considering new ideas and ways of doing?

Reflecting on such questions will assist us in coming to an understanding that workforce development is certainly more than the sum of its parts; and in employing strategies and practices as illustrated through these chapters to address identified challenges, we will come to see workforce development 'as an emerging field of practice' (Skills Australia 2010, p. 70) that is increasingly gaining its place in the sun in government policies and organisational practices. We acknowledge, just as Ling (2002, p. 639) recognises that 'sex was probably going on before it was invented in the 1960s [and] joined-up government [was] being practiced before it was so named', so too has workforce development been in existence for some time before it was so labelled.

However, we hope that this book, together with its companion volume, has helped to demystify and clarify the notion, identify its constituent parts (or at least, some of them) and analyse the issues and strategies that organisations need to address in its implementation. For while there are other partners with a role to play in furthering workforce development, such as government(s) and tertiary education institutions, at the centre of workforce development are the organisations themselves. In Skills Australia's (2010) consultations regarding a National Workforce Development Strategy, the encouraging finding was that despite many considering industry's role to be 'at times token' (p. 69), the consultation process had 'tapped an enthusiasm and growing consensus for urgent change to progress workforce development across Australia' (p. 67). While Australia is gaining a reputation 'as a leader in the field of workforce development' and the OECD recognises Australia as 'an innovator in workforce development and skills utilisation', what constrains efforts to build on successful experiences and learn from one another is 'the diversity of views and understandings' (Skills Australia 2010, pp. 70–71). May these two books be a valuable contribution in helping us not to 'rail on in utter ignorance of what each other mean and prate about an Elephant not one of [us] has seen', as in the case of Saxe's sight-impaired men from Indostan, but instead, engage in helpful unravelling of the notion of workforce development.

References

Andersen, K. K., Cooper, B. K., & Zhu, C. J. (2007). The effect of SHRM practices on perceived firm financial performance: Some initial evidence from Australia. *Asia Pacific Journal of Human Resources, 45*(2), 168–179.

Burnes, B. (2005). Complexity theories and organizational change. *International Journal of Management Reviews, 7*(2), 73–90.

Chappell, C. (2002). Researching the pedagogies of the new vocationalism. In J. Searle & R. Roebuck (Eds.), *Envisioning practice – Implementing change* (pp. 193–199). Brisbane: Australian Academic Press.

Christensen, T., & Lægreid, P. (2007). The whole-of-government approach to public sector reform. *Public Administration Review, 67*(6), 1059–1066.

Comyn, P. (2005). *The rise and fall of the key competencies.* Unpublished PhD thesis, University of Technology Sydney, Sydney.

Dainty, P. (2011). The strategic HR role: Do Australian HR professionals have the required skills? *Asia Pacific Journal of Human Resources, 49*(1), 55–70.

Davies, J. S. (2009). The limits of joined-up government: Towards a political analysis. *Public Administration, 87*(1), 80–96.

Elsey, B. (1997). *Australian graduate human resource studies: The people factor in workplace change management.* Findon: Techpress.

Harris, R. (2009). The historical contribution of adult and vocational education to social sustainability in Australia. In P. Willis, S. McKenzie, & R. Harris (Eds.), *Re-thinking work and learning: Adult and vocational education for social sustainability* (pp. 45–61). Dordrecht: Springer.

Harris, R., & Ramos, C. (2012). 'The one less travelled': Adult learners moving from the academic sector to the vocational sector in Singapore and Australia. *Journal of Vocational Education and Training, 64*(4), 387–402.

Harris, R., & Short, T. (2014). Exploring the notion of workforce development. In R. Harris & T. Short (Eds.), *Workforce development: Perspectives and issues* (pp. 1–16). Singapore: Springer.

Hawke, G. (2008). *Making decisions about workforce development in registered training organisations.* Adelaide: National Centre for Vocational Education Research.

Hodges, R. (2012). Joined-up government and challenges to accounting and accountability researchers. *Financial Accountability & Management, 28*(1), 26–51.

Holland, P., Sheehan, C., & De Cieri, H. (2007). Attracting and retaining talent: Exploring human resources development trends in Australia. *Human Resource Development International, 10*(3), 247–262.

Hutchings, K., & Holland, P. (2007). Recent advances in HRD in Australia: Application and implications for international HRD. *Human Resource Development International, 10*(3), 243–246.

Kramar, R. (2006). HRM at the crossroads: Recent developments and ethics. *Asia Pacific Journal of Human Resources, 44*(2), 130–131.

Ling, T. (2002). Delivering joined-up government in the UK: Dimensions, issues and problems. *Public Administration, 80*(4), 615–642.

Linton, W. J. (1878). *Poetry of America: Selections from one hundred American poets from 1776 to 1876.* http://www.noogenesis.com/pineapple/blind_men_elephant.html. Accessed 30 July 2013.

Lowry, D. (2006). HR managers as ethical decision-makers: Mapping the terrain. *Asia Pacific Journal of Human Resources, 44*(2), 171–183.

March, J. G., & Olsen, J. P. (1983). Organizing political life: What administrative reorganization tells us about governance. *American Political Science Review, 77*(2), 281–296.

McGuire, D., Stoner, L., & Mylona, S. (2008). The role of line managers as human resource agents in fostering organisational change in public services. *Journal of Change Management, 8*(1), 73–84.

Mulgan, G. (2005). Chapter 8: Joined-up government: Past, present, and future. In V. Bogdanor (Ed.), *Joined-up government.* Oxford: Oxford University Press.

Peretz, M., & McGraw, P. (2009). The evolution of HRD in Australia: Rhetoric or reality? *International Employment Relations Review, 15*(2), 1–13.

Pollitt, C. (2003). Joined-up government: A survey. *Political Studies Review, 1*(1), 34–49.

Skills Australia. (2010). *Australian workforce futures: A national workforce development strategy.* Canberra: Commonwealth of Australia.

Smith, A., Courvisanos, J., Tuck, J., & McEachern, S. (2012). *Building the capacity to innovate: The role of human capital.* Adelaide: National Centre for Vocational Education Research.

Spanos, Y., & Prastacos, G. (2004). Understanding organizational capabilities: Towards a conceptual framework. *Journal of Knowledge Management, 8*(3), 31–43.

Tebbel, C. (1999). Selling the concept of strategic HR. *HR Monthly*, July, 17–19.

Wenger, E. (1998). *Communities of practice: Learning, meaning, and identity.* Cambridge: Cambridge University Press.

Williams, B. (2001). *Building evaluation capability.* http://users.actrix.co.nz/bobwill. Accessed 16 Jan 2007.

Index

T. Short and R. Harris (eds.), *Workforce Development: Strategies and Practices*,
DOI 10.1007/978-981-287-068-1, © Springer Science+Business Media Singapore 2014

61499295R00216